A

Short History

of

FREETHOUGHT

A

Short History

of

FREETHOUGHT

ANCIENT AND MODERN

BY

J. M. ROBERTSON

NEW YORK

RUSSELL & RUSSELL

TO

SYDNEY ANSELL GIMSON.

CONTENTS.

viii   CONTENTS.

PREFACE.

SHORT histories are perhaps not among the best of disciplines; and the History of Freethought is at least as hard to write justly or master intelligently in short compass as any other. At the same time, the concise history, which is a different thing from the epitomes denounced by Bacon, has its advantages; and I have striven in this case to guard somewhat against the disadvantages by habitual citation of authorities, and by the frequent brief discussion, in paragraphs in smaller type, of disputed and theoretical matters. These discussions can be skipped by the unleisured reader, and weighed by the student, at pleasure, the general narrative in larger type going on continuously.

Such a book could not be written without much use of the works of specialists in the history of religion and philosophy, or without debt to many other culture-historians. These debts, I think, are pretty fully indicated in the notes; from which it will also appear, I hope, that I have striven to check my authorities throughout, and to make the reader aware of most occasions for doubt on matters of historic fact. The generalisation of the subject matter is for the most part my own affair. I must acknowledge, however, one debt which would not otherwise appear on the face of the book—that, namely, which I owe to my dead friend, J. M. Wheeler, for the many modern clues yielded by his *Biographical Dictionary of Freethinkers*, a work which stands for an amount of nomadic research that only those who have worked over the ground can well appreciate.

Among the many difficulties which press on the writer of such a work as the present, is that of setting up a standard of inclusion and exclusion. Looking back, I am conscious of some anomalies. It would on some counts have been not inappropriate, for instance, to name as a practical freethinker LEONARDO DA VINCI, who struck out new paths on so many lines of science. On the other hand, one might be accused of straining the evidence in claiming as a freethinker a man not known to have avowed any objection to the teaching of the Church. Difficulties arise, again, in the case of such a writer as CARDAN, who figured for orthodox apologists as a freethinker, but who seems to make more for credulity than for rational doubt ; and in the case of such a writer as the pro-ecclesiastical CAMPANELLA, who, while writing against atheism, and figuring only in politics as a disturber, reasons on various issues in a rationalistic sense. I can but press the difficulty of drawing the line, and admit ground for criticism. It has been remarked by Reuss that Paulus, a professed rationalist, fought for the Pauline authorship of the Epistle to the Hebrews in the very year in which Tholuck, a reconverted evangelical, gave up the Pauline authorship as hopeless ; that when Schleiermacher, a believer in inspiration, denied the authenticity of the Epistle to Timothy, the rationalist Wegscheider opposed him ; and that the rationalist (of a sort) Eichhorn maintained the Mosaic authorship of the Pentateuch long after the supernaturalist Vater had disproved it.[1] Analogous anomalies will be found noted in our text ; but it cannot be pretended that all even of the prominent cases of incidental freethinking on the part of the nominally orthodox are recorded ; and I cannot pretend

---

[1] Reuss, *History of the Canon*, Eng. tr. 1890, p. 387.

to be able to detect all the cases of undue conservatism among the professed freethinkers. It must suffice to try to note the general movement.

Another anomaly to be apologised for is the inconsistency in the spellings of some Greek and other proper names. My first intention was to spell all courageously after the originals; but, like so many others, I found myself constrained to compromise. Mr. John Owen, I find, had the courage for PYRRHON and ZENON, but not for PLATON. It is easy to write SOKRATES; but if we speak of LOUKIANOS we are apt to miss, with many readers, the first purpose of history. It had perhaps been better, in such a work as the present, to abide by all the old conventions, grievous as they often are.

The relative brevity with which the manifold freethought of the nineteenth century is treated in the concluding chapter has been a disquietude to me, and may be to some readers a grievance. It was however quite impossible for me to exceed a summary account without entirely over-balancing the volume; and on all accounts the history of rationalism in the modern scientific period seems to need a volume to itself. Despite much labor spent on scrutiny, there doubtless remain in the following chapters only too many errors and oversights. Any specifications of these will be gratefully received.

JOHN M. ROBERTSON.

CHAPTER I.

INTRODUCTORY.

§ 1. *Origin and Meaning of the Word.*

THE words Freethinking and Freethinker first appear in English literature about the end of the seventeenth century, and seem to have originated there and then, as we do not find them earlier in French or in Italian,[1] the only other modern literatures wherein the phenomena for which the words stand had previously arisen.

Apart from *Déiste*, which had begun to come into use about the middle of the sixteenth century,[2] and *Naturaliste*, of which Lechler traces back the Latin form as far as a manuscript of Bodin, dated 1588, the earlier French terms were *esprit fort* and *libertin*, the latter being used in the sense of a religious doubter by Corneille, Molière, and Bayle. It seems to have first come into use as one of the hostile names for the "Brethren of the Free Spirit", a pantheistic and generally heretical sect which became prominent in the thirteenth century, and flourished widely, despite destructive persecution, till the fifteenth. Their doctrine being antinomian, and their practice often extravagant, they were accused by Churchmen of licentiousness, so that in their case the name *Libertini* had its full latitude of application. In the sixteenth century the name of Libertines is found borne, voluntarily or otherwise, by a similar sect, probably springing from some remnant of the first, but calling themselves *Spirituales*, who came into

---

[1] Cp. Lechler, *Geschichte des englischen Deismus*, 1841, S. 458; Farrar, *Critical History of Freethought*, 1862, p. 588; Larousse's *Dictionnaire, s.v. libre pensée.*

[2] Bayle, *Dictionnaire*, art. VIRET, Note D.

notice in Flanders, were favored in France by Marguerite of Navarre, sister of Francis I, and became to some extent associated with sections of the Reformed Church. They were attacked by Calvin in the *Instructio adversus fanaticam et furiosam Sectam Libertinorum qui se Spirituales vocant*, in his *Tractatus Theologici*.[1] The same name of *Libertini* was either fastened on or adopted by the main body of Calvin's opponents in Geneva. They were accused by him of general depravity, a judgment not at all to be acquiesced in, in view of the controversial habits of the age; but they probably included antinomian Christians and orderly non-Christians as well as orthodox lovers of freedom and libertines in the modern sense. As the first Brethren of the Free Spirit, so-called, seem to have appeared in Italy (where they are supposed to have derived, like the Waldenses, from the immigrant Paulicians of the Eastern Church), the name *Libertini* presumably originated there. But in Renaissance Italy an unbeliever seems usually to have been called simply *ateo*, or *infedele*, or *pagano*. "The standing phrase was *non aver fede*."[2] In England, as late as Elizabeth's reign, "infidel" seems to have commonly signified only a Jew or heathen or Mohammedan, being used only in that sense by Shakspere, as by Milton in his verse. Milton, however, had used it in the modern sense in his prose; and it was at times so used even by early Elizabethans.[3]

In England, as in the rest of Europe, however, the phenomenon of Freethought had existed, in specific form, long before it found any generic name save those of Atheism and Infidelity; and the process of naming was as fortuitous as it generally is in matters of intellectual evolution. In 1667 we find Sprat, the historian of the Royal Society, describing the activity of that body as having arisen or taken its special direction through the conviction that in science as in warfare better results had been obtained by a "free way" than by methods not so describable.[4] As Sprat is careful to insist, the members

---

[1] Mosheim, *Eccles. Hist.*, Cent. XIII, Part ii, ch. v, §§ 9-12, and notes; Cent. XIV, Part ii, ch. v, §§ 3-5; Cent. XVI, Sect. 3, Part ii, ch. ii, §§ 38-42.

[2] Burckhardt, *Renaissance in Italy*, Eng. tr. ed. 1892, p. 542, *note*.

[3] If Mr. Froude's transcript of a manuscript can here be relied on. *History*, ed. 1872, xi, 199.

[4] *History of the Royal Society*, 1667, p. 73. Describing the beginnings of the Society, Sprat remarks that Oxford had at that time many members "who had begun a free way of reasoning" (p. 53).

of the Royal Society, though looked at askance by most of the clergy[1] and other pietists, were not as such to be classed as unbelievers, the leading members being strictly orthodox ; but a certain number seem to have shown scant concern for religion ;[2] and while it was one of the Society's first rules not to debate any theological question whatever,[3] the intellectual atmosphere of the time was such that some among those who followed the "free way" in ·matters of natural science would be more than likely to apply it to more familiar problems.[4] It was probably, then, a result of this express assertion of the need and value of freedom in the mental life that the name Free-thinker came into use in the last quarter of the century. When the orthodox Boyle pushed criticism in physical science under such a title as *The Sceptical Chemist*, the principle could not well be withheld from application to religion ; and it lay in the nature of the case that the name "Freethinker", like that of "Sceptic", should come to attach itself specially to those who doubted where doubt was most resented and most resisted. At length the former term became specific.

Before "Deism" came into English vogue, the names for unbelief, even deistic, were simply "infidelity" and "atheism" : *e.g.*, Bishop Fotherby's *Atheomastix* (1622) ; Baxter's *Unreasonableness of Infidelity* (1655), and *Reasons of the Christian Religion* (1667) passim. Stillingfleet's *Letter to a Deist* (1677) appears to be the first published attack on Deism by name. Cudworth, in his *True Intellectual System of the Universe* (written 1671, published 1678), does not speak of Deism, attacking only Atheism, and was himself suspected of Socinianism. W. Sherlock, in his *Practical Discourse of Religious Assemblies* (2nd ed., 1682), attacks "Atheists and Infidels", but says nothing of "Deists". The term Atheist was often applied at random at this period ; but Atheism did exist.

[1] Buckle, *Introd. to Hist. of Civ. in Eng.*, 3-vol. ed., i, 371.
[2] Sprat, p. 375 (printed as 367).
[3] *Id.*, p. 83. The French Academy had the same rule.
[4] Some of Sprat's uses of the term have a very general sense, as when he writes (p. 87) that "Amsterdam is a place of Trade without the mixture of men of freer thoughts". The latter is an old application, as in "the free sciences" or "the liberal arts".

The first certain instance thus far noted of the use of the term " Freethinker " is in a letter of Molyneux to Locke, dated April 6, 1697 (*Some Familiar Letters between Mr. Locke and several of his Friends*, 1708, p. 190), where Toland is spoken of as a " candid free thinker ". In an earlier letter, dated Dec. 24, 1695, Molyneux speaks of a certain book on religion as somewhat lacking in " freedom of thought " (*Id.* p. 133). In the *New Dictionary*, a citation is given from the title-page of S. Smith's brochure, *The Religious Impostor . . . . dedicated to Doctor S-l-m-n and the rest of the new Religious Fraternity of Freethinkers, near Leather-Sellers Hall. Printed . . . . in the first year of Grace and Freethinking*, conjecturally dated 1692. It is thought to refer to the sect of " Freeseekers " mentioned in Luttrell's *Brief Historical Relation* (iii, 56) under date 1693. In that case it is not unbelievers that are in question. In Swift's *Sentiments of a Church of England Man* (1708) the word is found definitely and abusively connoting religious unbelief : " The atheists, libertines, despisers of religion, that is to say, all those who usually pass under the name of Free-thinkers " ; Steele and Addison so use it in the *Tatler* in 1709 (Nos. 12, 111, 135) and Leslie so uses the term in his *Truth of Christianity Demonstrated* (1711).

It was not till 1713, however, that Anthony Collins' *Discourse of Free-Thinking, occasion'd by the Rise and Growth of a Sect called Free-Thinkers*, gave the word a universal notoriety, and brought it into established currency in controversy, with the normal significance of ʻ Deist ", Collins having entirely repudiated Atheism. Even after this date, and indeed in full conformity with the definition in Collins' opening sentence, Ambrose Philips took *The Freethinker* as the title of a weekly journal (begun in 1718) on the lines of the *Spectator*, with no heterodox leaning,[1] the contributors including Boulter, afterwards Archbishop of Dublin, and the son of Bishop Burnet. But despite this attempt to keep the word Freethinking as a name for simple freedom from prejudice in secular affairs, the tendency to specialise it as aforesaid was irresistible. As names go, it was on the whole a good one ; and the bitterness with which it was generally

[1] Cp. Johnson on A. Philips in *Lives of the Poets*. Swift, too, issued his *Free Thoughts upon the Present State of Affairs* in 1714.

handled on the orthodox side showed that its implicit claim was felt to be disturbing, though some antagonists of course claimed from the first that they were as "free", under the law of right reason, as any sceptic.[1] At this time of day, the word may be allowed prescriptive standing, as having no more drawbacks than most other names for schools of thought or attitudes of mind, and as having been admitted into most European languages. The question-begging element is not greater in this than in many other terms of similar intention, such as Rationalism ; and it incurs no such charge of absurdity as lies against the invidious religious term, " Infidelity ".

For practical purposes, then, Freethought may be defined as a conscious reaction against some phase or phases of conventional or traditional doctrine in religion—on the one hand, a claim to think freely, in the sense not of disregard for logic but of special loyalty to it, on problems to which the past course of things has given a great intellectual and practical importance ; on the other hand, the actual practice of such thinking. This sense, which is substantially agreed on, will on one or other side sufficiently cover those phenomena of early or rudimentary Freethinking which wear the guise of simple concrete opposition to given doctrines or systems, whether by way of special demur or of the obtrusion of a new cult or doctrine. In either case, the claim to think in a measure freely is implicit in the criticism or the new affirmation : and such primary movements of the mind cannot well be separated, in psychology or in history, from the fully conscious practice of criticism in the spirit of pure truthseeking, or from the claim that such free examination is profoundly important to moral and intellectual health. Modern Freethought, specially so-called, is only one of the developments of the slight primary capacity of man to doubt, to reason, to improve on past thinking, to assert

---

[1] Thus Bentley, writing as *Phileleutherus Lipsiensis* against Collins, claims to have been "train'd up and exercis'd in *Free Thought* from my youth ".

his personality as against even sacrosanct and menacing authority. Concretely considered, it has proceeded by the support and stimulus of successive accretions of actual knowledge; and the modern consciousness of its own abstract importance emerged by way of an impression or inference from certain social phenomena, as well as in terms of self-asserting instinct. There is no break in its evolution from primitive mental states any more than in the evolution of the natural sciences from primitive observation. What particularly accrues to the state of conscious and systematic discrimination, in the one case as in the other, is just the immense gain in security of possession.

§ 2. *Previous Histories.*

It is somewhat remarkable that this phenomenon has thus far had no general historic treatment save at the hands of ecclesiastical writers who regarded it solely as a form of more or less perverse hostility to their own creed. The modern scientific study of religions, which has yielded so many instructive surveys, almost of necessity excludes from view the specific phenomenon of Freethought, which in the religion-making periods is to be traced rather by its religious results than by any record of its expression. All histories of philosophy, indeed, in some degree necessarily recognise it; and such a work as Lange's *History of Materialism* may be regarded as part—whether or not sound in its historical treatment—of a complete history of Freethought, dealing specially with general philosophic problems. But of Freethought as a revision or rejection of current religious doctrines by more or less practical people, we have no regular history by a professed Free-thinker, though there are many monographs.

The useful compilation of Mr. Charles Watts, entitled *Freethought: Its Rise, Progress, and Triumph* (n. d.), deals with Freethought in relation only to Christianity. Apart from treatises which broadly sketch the development of know-ledge and of opinion, the nearest approaches to a general historic treatment are the *Dictionnaire des Athées* of Sylvain Maréchal (1800 : 3e édit., par J. B. L. Germond, 1853) and the *Biographical Dictionary of Freethinkers* by the late Joseph Mazzini Wheeler. The quaint work of Maréchal, expanded by his friend Lalande, exhibits much learning, but is made partly fantastic by its sardonic plan of including a number of religionists (including Job, John, and Jesus Christ !) some of whose utterances are held to lead logically to Atheism. Mr. Wheeler's book is in every respect the more trustworthy.

In defence of Maréchal's method, it may be noted that the prevailing practice of Christian apologists had been to impute Atheism to heterodox theistic thinkers of all ages at every opportunity. The *Historia universalis Atheismi et Atheorum falso et merito suspectorum* of J. F. Reimmann (Hildesiæ, 1725) exhibits this habit both in its criticism and in its practice, as do the *Theses de Atheismo et Superstitione* of Buddeus (Trajecti ad Rhenum, 1716). These were the standard treatises of their kind for last century, and seem to be the earliest systematic treatises in the nature of a History of Freethought, excepting a *Historia Naturalismi* by A. Tribbechov (Jenae, 1700) and a *Historia Atheismi breviter delineata* by Jenkinus Thomasius (Basileæ, 1709). In the same year with Reimmann's *Historia* appeared J. A. Fabricius' *Delectus Argumentorum et Syllabus scriptorum qui veritatem religionis Christianæ adversus Atheos, Epicureos, Deistas, seu Naturalistas . . . . asseruerunt* (Hamburgi), in which it is contended (cap. viii) that many philosophers have been falsely described as Atheists; but in the *Freydenker Lexikon* of J. A. Trinius (Leipzig, 1759), planned as a supplement to the work of Fabricius, are included such writers as Sir Thomas Browne and Dryden.

The works of the late Rev. John Owen, *Evenings with the Skeptics, Skeptics of the Italian Renaissance*, and *Skeptics of the French Renaissance*, which, though not constituting a literary whole, collectively cover a great deal of historical ground, must be expressly excepted from the above characterisation of clerical histories of Freethought, in respect of their liberality of view.

In English, apart from studies of given periods and of the progress of science and culture, the only so-called Histories of Freethought are those of Bishop Van Mildert, the Rev. J. E. Riddle, and Mr. Adam Storey Farrar. Van Mildert's *Historical View of the Rise and Progress of Infidelity*[1] constituted the Boyle Lectures for 1802-5 ; Mr.

---

[1] Second ed. with enlarged Appendix (of authorities and references) 1808, 2 vols.

Riddle's *Natural History of Infidelity and Superstition in Contrast with Christian Faith* formed part of his Bampton Lectures for 1852; and Mr. Farrar produced his *Critical History of Freethought in reference to the Christian Religion* as the Bampton Lectures for 1862. All three were men of considerable reading, and their works give useful bibliographical clues; but the virulence of Van Mildert deprives his treatise of rational weight; Mr. Riddle, who in any case professes to give only a "Natural History" or abstract argument, and not a history proper, is only somewhat more constrainedly hostile to "infidelity"; and even Mr. Farrar, the most judicial as well as the most comprehensive of the three, proceeds on the old assumption that "unbelief" (from which he charitably distinguishes "doubt") generally arises from "antagonism of feeling, which wishes revelation untrue"—a thesis maintained with vehemence by the others.[1]

Writers so placed, indeed, could not well be expected to contemplate Freethought scientifically as an aspect of mental evolution common to all civilisations, any more than to look with sympathy on the Freethought which is specifically anti-Christian. The annotations to all three works, certainly, show some consciousness of the need for another temper and method than that of their text,[2] which is too obviously, perhaps inevitably, composed for the satisfaction of the ordinary orthodox animus of their respective periods; but even the best remains not so much a history as an indictment. In the present sketch, framed though it be from the rationalistic standpoint, it is proposed to draw up not a counter indictment, but a more or less dispassionate account of the main historical phases of Freethought, viewed on the one hand as expressions of the rational or critical spirit, playing on the subject matter of religion, and on the other hand as sociological phenomena conditioned by social forces, in particular the economic

---

[1] Farrar, pref., p, x; Riddle, p. 99; Van Mildert, i, 105, etc.
[2] Van Mildert even recast his first manuscript. See the *Memoir of Joshua Watson*, 1863, p. 35.

and political. The lack of any previous general survey of a scientific character will, it is hoped, be taken into account in passing judgment on its schematic defects as well as its inevitable flaws of detail.

§ 3. *The Psychology of Freethinking.*

Though it is no part of our business here to elaborate the psychology of doubt and belief, it may be well to anticipate a possible criticism on the lines of recent psychological speculation, and to indicate at the outset the practical conception on which the present survey broadly proceeds. Recent writers have pressed far the theorem that "will" enters as an element into every mental act, thus giving a momentary appearance of support to the old formula that unbelief is the result of an arbitrary or sinister perversity of individual choice. Needless to say, however, the new theorem applies equally to acts of belief; and it is a matter of the simplest concrete observation that in so far as will or wilfulness in the ordinary sense operates in the sphere of religion, it is at least as obvious and as active on the side of belief[1] as on the other. A moment's reflection on the historic phenomena of orthodox resistance to criticism will satisfy any student that, whatever may have been the stimulus on the side of heresy, the antagonism it arouses is largely the index of primary passion—the spontaneous resentment of the believer whose habits are disturbed. His will normally decides his action, without any process of judicial deliberation.

It is another way of stating the same fact, to point out the fallacy of the familiar assumption that Freethinking represents a bias to "negation". In the nature of the case, the believer has to do at least as much negation as his opponents; and if again we scan history in this

---

[1] Its legitimacy on that side is expressly contended for by Professor William James in his volume *The Will to Believe* (1897), the positions of which have been criticised by the present writer in the *University Magazine*, April and June, 1898.

connection we shall see cause to conclude that the
temperamental tendency to negation—which is a form of
variation like another—is abundantly common on the
side of religious conservatism.   Nowhere is there more
habitual opposition to new ideas as such.   At best the
believer, so-called, rejects a given proposition or suggestion because it clashes with something he already believes.
The proposition, however, has often been reached by way
not of preliminary negation of the belief in question, but
of constructive explanation, undertaken to bring observed
facts into theoretic harmony.   Thus the innovator has
only contingently put aside the old belief because *it*
clashes with something he believes in a more vital way;
and he has done this with circumspection, whereas his
opponent too often repels him without a second thought.
The phenomena of the rise of the Copernican astronomy,
modern geology, and modern biology, all bear out this
generalisation.

Nor is the charge of negativeness any more generally
valid against such Freethinking as directly assails current
doctrines.   There may be, of course, negative-minded
people on that side as on the other; and such may
fortuitously do something to promote Freethought, or
may damage it in their neighbourhood by their atmosphere.   But everything goes to show that Freethinking
normally proceeds by way of intellectual construction,
that is, by way of effort to harmonise one position with
another—to modify a special dogma to the general run of
one's thinking.   The attitude of pure scepticism on a
wide scale is really very rare—much rarer than the philosophic effort.   So far from Freethinkers being given to
"destroying without building up", they are as a rule
unable to destroy a dogma either for themselves or for
others without setting a constructive belief in its place—
a form of explanation, that is; such being much more
truly a process of construction than would be the imposition of a new scheme of dogma.   In point of fact, they
are often accused, and by the same critics, of an undue

tendency to speculative construction ; and the early Atheists of Greece and of the modern period did so err. But that is only a proof the more that their Freethinking was not a matter of arbitrary volition or an undue negativeness.

The only explanation which ostensibly countervails this is the old one above glanced at—that the unbeliever finds the given doctrine troublesome as a restraint, and so determines to reject it. It is to be feared that this view has survived Mr. A. S. Farrar. Yet it is very clear that no man need throw aside any faith, and least of all Christianity, on the ground of its hampering his conduct. To say nothing of the fact that in every age, under every religion, at every stage of culture from that of the negro or savage to that of the supersubtle decadent or mystic, men have practised every kind of misconduct without abandoning their supernatural credences—there is the special fact that the whole Christian system rests on the doctrine of forgiveness of sins to the believer. The theory of wilful disbelief on the part of the reprobate is thus entirely unplausible. Such disbelief in the terms of the case would be uneasy, as involving an element of incertitude ; and his fear of retribution could never be laid. On the other hand he has but inwardly to avow himself a sinner and a believer, and he has the assurance that repentance at the last moment will outweigh all his sins.

It is not, of course, suggested that such is the normal or frequent course of believing Christians ; but it has been so often enough to make the "libertine" theory of unbelief untenable. In all ages there have been antinomian Christians, whether of the sort that simply rest on the "seventy times seven" of the Gospel, or of the more articulately logical kind who dwell on the doctrine of faith versus works. For the rest, as the considerate theologian will readily see, insistence on the possibility of a sinister motive for the unbeliever brings up the equal possibility of a sinister motive on the part of the convert to Christianity, ancient or modern. At every turn, then, the charge of perversity of the will recoils on the advocate of belief; so that it would be the course of common prudence to abandon it, even were it not in itself, as a rule, so plainly an expression of irritated bias.

On the other hand, it need not be disputed that unbelief has been often enough found associated with some species of libertinism to give a passing color for the pretence of causal connection. The fact, however, leads us to a less superficial explanation, worth keeping in view here. Freethinking being taken to be normally a " variation " of intellectual type in the direction of a critical demand for consistency and credibility in beliefs, its social assertion will be a matter on the one side of force of character, and on the other hand of force of circumstances. The intellectual potentiality will be variously developed in different men and in different surroundings. If we ask ourselves how, in general, the critical tendency is to arise or to come into play, we are almost compelled to suppose a special stimulus as well as a special faculty. Critical doubt is made possible, broadly speaking, by the accumulation of ideas or habits of certain kinds which insensibly undo a previous state of homogeneity of thought: e.g., a community subsiding into peace and order from a state of warfare and plunder will at length find the ethic of its daily life at variance with the conserved ethic of its early religion of human sacrifice and special family or tribal sanctions; or a community which has accumulated a certain amount of accurate knowledge of astronomy will gradually find such knowledge irreconcilable with its primitive cosmology. A specially gifted individual will anticipate the general movement of thought; but even for him some standing ground must be supposed; and for the majority the advance in moral practice or scientific knowledge is the condition of any effective Freethinking.

Between top and bottom, however, there are all grades of vivacity, earnestness, and courage; and on the side of the normal resistance there are all varieties of political and economic circumstance. It follows, then, that the avowed Freethinker may be so in virtue either of special courage or of antecedent circumstances which make the attitude on his part less courageous. And it may even be granted to the quietist that the courage is at times that of ill-balanced judgment or heady temperament; just as it may be conceded to the conservative that it is at times that which goes with or follows on disregard of wise ways of life. It is well that the full force of this position be realised at the outset. When we find, as we shall, some historic Freethinkers displaying either extreme imprudence or personal indiscipline, we shall be prepared, in terms of this preliminary questioning, to realise anew that humanity has owed a great deal to some of its "unbalanced" types; and that, though discipline is nearly the last word of wisdom, indiscipline may at times be the morbid accompaniment or excess of a certain openness of view and spontaneity of action which are much more favorable to moral and intellectual advance than a cold prudence or a safe insusceptibility. As for the case of the man who, already at odds with his fellows in the matter of his conduct, may in some phases of society feel it the easier to brave them in the matter of his avowed creed, we have already seen that even this does not convict him of intellectual dishonesty. And were such cases relatively as numerous as they are scarce—were the debauched Deists even commoner than the vinous Steeles and Fieldings—the use of the fact as an argument would still be an oblique course on the side of a religion which claims to have found its first and readiest hearing among publicans and sinners.

It may, finally, help a religious reader to a judicial view of the phenomenon of Freethought if he is reminded that every step forward in the alleged historic evolution of his own creed would depend, in the case put, on the existence of persons capable of rejecting a current and prevailing code in favor of one either denounced as impious or marked off by circumstances as dangerous. The Israelites in Egypt, the prophets and their supporters, the Gospel Jesus and his adherents, all stand in some degree for positions of "negation", of hardy innovation, of disregard of things and persons popularly venerated; wherefore Collins, in the *Discourse* above mentioned, smilingly claimed at least the prophets as great Freethinkers. On that head it may suffice to say that some of the temperamental qualifications would probably be very much the same for those who of old brought about religious innovation in terms of supernatural beliefs, and those who in later times innovate by way of minimising or repudiating such beliefs, though the intellectual qualifications might be different. Bruno and Dolet and Vanini and Voltaire, faulty men all four, could at least be more readily conceived as prophets in ancient Jewry, or reformers under Herod, than as Pharisees or even Sadducees under either regimen.

Be that as it may, however, the issues between Freethought and Creed are ultimately to be settled only in virtue of their argumentative bases, as appreciable by men in society at any given time. It is with the notion of making the process of judicial appreciation a little easier, by historically exhibiting the varying conditions under which it has been undertaken in the past, that these pages are written.

CHAPTER II.

PRIMITIVE FREETHINKING.

§ 1.

To consider the normal aspects of primitive life, as we see them in savage communities and trace them in early literature, is to realise the enormous hindrance offered to critical thinking in the primary stages of culture by the mere force of habit. " The savage," says our leading anthropologist, " by no means goes through life with the intention of gathering more knowledge and framing better laws than his fathers. On the contrary, his tendency is to consider his ancestors as having handed down to him the perfection of wisdom, which it would be impiety to make the least alteration in. Hence among the lower races there is obstinate resistance to the most desirable reforms, and progress can only force its way with a slowness and difficulty which we of this century can hardly imagine."[1] It is hardly possible to estimate with any confidence the relative rates of progress; but though all are extremely slow, it would seem that reason could sooner play correctively on errors of secular practice[2] than on any species of proposition in religion—taking that word to connote at once mythology, early cosmology, and ritual ethic. In the long stage of lower savagery, then, the only approach to freethinking that would seriously affect general belief would presumably be that very credulity which gave foothold to religious beliefs to begin with. That is to say, without anything in the nature of general criticism of any story or doctrine, one

---

[1] Tylor, *Anthropology*, p. 439. Cp. Lang, *Custom and Myth*, ed. 1893, p. 72.
[2] Cp. Tylor, *Primitive Culture*, 3rd ed., i, 71, as to savage conservatism in handicraft.

such might to some extent supersede another, in virtue of the relative gift of persuasion or personal weight of the propounders. Up to a certain point, persons with a turn for myth or ritual-making would compete, and might even call in question each other's honesty, as well as each other's inspiration. Since the rise of scientific hierology, there has been a disposition among students to take for granted the good faith of all early religion-makers, and to dismiss entirely that assumption of fraud which used to be made by Christian writers concerning the greater part of every non-Christian system. When all systems are seen to be alike natural in origin, such charges are felt to recoil on the system which makes them. But a closer scrutiny suggests that wilful fraud must to some extent have entered into all religious systems alike, even in the period of primeval credulity, were it only because the credulity was so great. The leading hierologist of the day pronounces decisively as to an element of intentional deceit in the Koran-making of Mohammed[1]—a judgment which, if upheld, can hardly fail to be extended to some portions of all other Sacred Books. However that may be, we have positive evidence that wilful fraud enters at times into the doctrine of contemporary savages ;[2] and if we can point to deliberate imposture alike in the charm-mongering of contemporary negroes and in the sacred-book-making of the higher historical systems, it seems reasonable to surmise that conscious deceit, as distinguished from childlike fabrication, would chronically enter into the tale-making of primitive men, as into their simpler relations with each other. It is indeed difficult to conceive how a copious mythology could ever arise without the play of a kind of imaginativeness that is hardly compatible with strict veracity. Certain wild tribes here and there, living in a state of great simplicity,

---

[1] Tiele, *Outlines of the History of Religions*, Eng. tr., p. 96. Cp. Robertson Smith, *The Old Testament in the Jewish Church*, 2nd ed., p. 141, *note*.
[2] See the article by E. J. Glave, of Mr. Stanley's force, on *Fetishism in Congoland*, in the *Century Magazine*, April, 1891, p. 836.

ge of hypothesis in view of the entire absence of
tory proper in early Indian literature ; but we seem at
st to have the evidence of the Veda itself that while
vas being collected there were deniers of the existence
its Gods.[1]

The latter testimony alone may serve as ground for
sing afresh an old question which recent anthropology
somewhat inexactly decided—that, namely, as to
ether there are any savages without religious beliefs.

For old discussions on the subject, see Fabricius, *Delectus
argumentorum et Syllabus scriptorum*, Hamburgi, 1725, c. viii ;
cp. Swift, *Discourse concerning the mechanical operation of the Spirit*,
sec. 2. Sir John Lubbock (*Prehistoric Times*, 5th ed., pp. 574—
580 ; *Origin of Civilisation*, 5th ed., pp. 213—217) and Mr.
Spencer (*Principles of Sociology*, iii, § 583) have collected modern
travellers' testimonies as to the absence of religious ideas in
certain tribes. As Sir John Lubbock points out, the word
" religion " is by some loosely or narrowly used to signify only
a higher theology as distinct from lower supernaturalist beliefs.
Dr. Tylor (*Primitive Culture*, as cited, i, 417—425) and Dr. Max
Müller (*Introd. to the Science of Religion*, ed. 1882, p. 42 ff. ;
Natural Religion, 1889, pp. 81—89 ; *Anthropological Religion*, 1892,
pp. 428—435) have pressed the point as to the proved falsity of
many of the negative testimonies. The dispute, as it now
stands, mainly turns on the definition of religion. (Cp. Chantepie
de la Saussaye, *Manual of the Science of Religion*, Eng. tr. 1891,
pp. 16—18, where Lubbock's position is partly misunderstood.)
Dr. Tylor, while deciding that no tribes known to us are religionless, leaves open the question of their existence in the past.

The problem has been unduly narrowed to the issue
to whether there are any whole tribes so developed.
s obviously pertinent to ask whether there may not be
ersity of opinion within a given tribe. Such testi-
nies as those collected by Sir John Lubbock and
ers, as to the existence of religionless savages, are held

Rig-Veda, x, 121 (as translated by Muir, Müller, Dutt, and von Bradke) ;
x, 82 (Dutt's rendering). It is to be noted that the refrain " Who is the
whom we should worship ? " is entirely different in Ludwig's render-
f x, 121. Cp. Max Müller, *Natural Religion*, pp. 227-229, citing *R. V.*,
to, for an apparently undisputed case of scepticism. See again
ois's version of vi, 7, iii, 3 (p. 459). He cannot diverge more from
erman and English translators than they do from each other.

to be disposed of by further proof that tribes of savages
set down, on the evidence of some of themselves, as
religionless, had in reality a number of religious beliefs.
Undoubtedly the first view had in a number of cases been
hastily taken; but there remains the question, on all
hands surprisingly ignored, whether some of the savages
who disavowed all belief in things supernatural may not
have been telling the simple truth about themselves, or
even about their families and their comrades. A savage
asked by a traveller, " Do you believe" so-and-so, might
very well give a true negative answer for himself; and the
traveller's resulting misconception would be due to his
own arbitrary assumption that all members of any tribe
must think alike. Despite the social potency of primitive
custom, variation may be surmised to occur in the mental
as in the physical life at all stages; and what normally
happens in savagery and low civilisation appears to be a
frustration of the sceptical variation by the total circumstances—the strength of the general lead to supernaturalism, the plausibility of such beliefs to the average intelligence, and the impossibility of setting up sceptical
institutions to oppose the others. In civilised ages,
sceptical movements are repeatedly seen to dwindle for
simple lack of institutions, which however are spontaneously set up by and serve as sustainers of religious
systems. On the simpler level of savagery, sceptical
personalities would fail to affirm themselves as against
the institutions of ordinary savage religion—the seasonal
feasts, the ceremonies attending birth and death, the use
of rituals, images, charms, sorcery, all tending to stimulate
and conserve supernatural beliefs in general. Only the
abnormally courageous would dare outspokenly to doubt
or deny at all; and their daring would put them in special
jeopardy. The ancient maxim, *primus in orbe deos fecit
timor*, is verified by all modern study of primitive life. It
is a recent traveller who gives the definition : " Fetishism
is the result of the efforts of the savage intelligence seeking after a theory which will account for the apparent

hostility of nature to man."[1]   And this incalculable force of fear is constantly exploited by the religious bias from the earliest stages of sorcery.

The check to intellectual evolution would here be on all fours with some of the checks inferribly at work in early moral evolution, where the types with the higher ideals would seem often to be positively endangered by their peculiarity, and would thus be the less likely to multiply. And what happened as between man and man would further tend to happen at times as between communities. Given the possible case of a tribe so well placed as to be unusually little affected by fear of enemies and the natural forces, the influence of rationalistic chiefs or of respected tribesmen might set up for a time a considerable anti-religious variation, involving at least a minimising of religious doctrine and practices. But when such a tribe did chance to come into contact with others more religious, it would be peculiarly obnoxious to them ; and being in the terms of the case unwarlike, its chance of survival on the old lines would be small.

> Such a possibility is suggested with some vividness by the familiar contrast between the modern communities of Fiji and Samoa, the former cruel, cannibalistic, and religious, the latter much less austerely religious and much more humane. The ferocious Fijians " looked upon the Samoans with horror, because they had no religion, no belief in any such deities [as the Fijians'], nor any of the sanguinary rites which prevailed in other islands " (Spencer, *Study of Sociology*, pp. 293-294). The "no religion" is of course only relatively true. Mr. Lang has noticed the error of the phrase "the godless Samoans"; but while loosely suggesting that the facts are the other way, he admits that in their creed " the religious sentiment has already become self-conscious, and has begun to reason on its own practices " (*Myth, Ritual, and Religion*, ii, 34).

Taking the phenomena all along the line of evolution, we are led to the generalisation that the rationalistic tendency, early or late, like the religious tendency, is a

---

[1] E. J. Glave, art. cited, p. 825.   Cp. Lubbock, *Prehistoric Times*, pp. 582, 594.

variation which prospers at different times in different degrees relatively to the favorableness of the environment. This view will be set forth in some detail in the course of our history.

It is not, finally, a mere surmise that individual savages and semi-savages in our own time vary towards disbelief in the supernaturalism of their fellows. To say nothing of the rational scepticism exhibited by the Zulu converts of Bishop Colenso, which was the means of opening his eyes to the incredibility of the Pentateuch,[1] or of the rationalism of the African chief who debated with Sir Samuel Baker the possibility of a future state,[2]—or of the stories of spasmodic rationalism on the part of savages who lose patience with their fetishes[3]—we have the express missionary record that the forcible suppression of idolatry and tabu and the priesthood by King Rihoriho in the island of Hawaii, in 1819, was accomplished not only "before the arrival of any missionary", but on purely common-sense grounds, and with no thought of further-ing Christianity, though he had heard of the substitution of Christianity for the native religion by Pomare in Tahiti. Rihoriho simply desired to save his wives and other women from the cruel pressure of the tabu system, and to divert the priests' revenues to secular purposes; and he actually had some strong priestly support.[4] Had not the missionary system soon followed, however, the old worship, which had been desperately defended in battle at the instigation of the conservative priests, would in all probability have grown up afresh, though perhaps with modifications. The savage and semi-savage social con-ditions, taken as a whole, are fatally unpropitious to rationalism.

It is significant that in this and other cases of unbelief at higher levels of civilisation, it is only the high rank of

---

[1] *The Pentateuch*, vol. i, pref. p. vii; intro. p. 9.
[2] Spencer, *Principles of Sociology*, iii, § 583.
[3] Compare the quaint case of King Rum Bahadur of Nepaul, who cannonaded his Gods. Spencer, *Study of Sociology*, pp. 301-302.
[4] Ellis, *Polynesian Researches*, 1831 iv, 30-31, 126-128.

the doubter that secures publication for the fact of the doubt. In Hawaii, only a King's unbelief could make itself historically heard. So in the familiar story of the doubting Inca of Peru, who in public religious assembly is said to have avowed his conclusion that the deified Sun was not really a living thing, it is the status of the speaker that gives his words a record. The doubt had in all likelihood been long current among the wise men of Peru ; it is indeed ascribed to two or three different Incas ;[1] but save for the Incas' promulgation of it, history would bear no trace of Peruvian scepticism. In bare justice, we are bound to surmise that similar developments of rationalism have been fairly frequent in unwritten history.

There are to be noted, finally, the facts lately collected as to marked sceptical variation among children ;[2] and the express evidence that " it has not been found in a single instance that an uneducated deaf-mute has had any conception of the existence of a Supreme Being as the Creator and Ruler of the universe ".[3] These latter phenomena do not, of course, entitle us to accept Professor Gruppe's sweeping theorem that it is the religious variation that is abnormal, and that religion can have spread only by way of the hereditary imposition of the original insanity of one or two on the imagination of the many.[4] Deaf-mutes are not normal organisms. But all the facts together entitle us to decide that religion, broadly speaking, is but the variation that has chiefly flourished, by reason of its adaptation to the prevailing environment thus far ; and to reject as worse than unscientific the formulas which, even in the face of the rapidly spreading rationalism of the more civilised nations, still affirm supernaturalist beliefs to be a universal necessity of the human mind.

---

[1] Garcilasso, l. viii, c. 8 ; l. ix, c. 10 ; Herrera, Dec. v, l. iv, c. 4. See the passages in Réville's Hibbert Lectures, pp. 162-165.

[2] See Mr. James Sully's *Studies of Childhood*, 1895.

[3] Rev. S. Smith, *Church Work Among the Deaf and Dumb*, 1875, cited by Spencer, *Principles of Sociology*, iii, § 583. Cp. the testimony cited there from Dr. Kitto, *Lost Senses*, p. 200.

[4] *Die griechischen Culte und Mythen*, 1887, S. 263, 276, 277, etc.

CHAPTER III.

§ 1. *Early Association and Competition of Cults.*

WHEN religion has entered on the stage of quasi-civilised organisation, with fixed legends or documents, temples, and the rudiments of hierarchies, the increased forces of terrorism and conservatism are in nearly all cases seen to be in part countervailed by the simple interaction of the systems of different communities.   There is no more ubiquitous force in the whole history of the subject, operating as it does in ancient Assyria, in the life of Vedic India and Confucian China, and in the diverse histories of progressive Greece and relatively stationary Egypt, down through the Christian Middle Ages to our own period of comparative studies.

In ages when any dispassionate comparative study was impossible, religious systems appear to have been considerably modified by the influence of those of conquered peoples on those of their conquerors, and *vice versa.* Peoples who while at arm's length would insult and affect to despise each other's Gods, and would deride each other's myths,[1] appear frequently to have altered their attitude when one had conquered the other ; and this not because of any special growth of sympathy, but in virtue of the old motive of fear.   In the stage of natural polytheism, no nation really doubted the existence of the Gods of another ; at most, like the Hebrews of the early

---

[1] Cp. Mr. Lang (*Myth, Ritual, and Religion,* i, 91) as to the contemptuous disbelief of savages in Christian myths.   Mr Lang observes that this shows savages and civilised men to have " different standards of credulity ". That, however, does not seem to be the true inference.   Each order of believer accepts the myths of his own creed and derides others

historic period, it would set its own God above the others,
calling him "Lord of Lords". But, every community
having its own God, he remained a local power when his
own worshippers were conquered, and his cult and lore
were respected accordingly. This procedure, which has
been sometimes attributed to the Romans in particular as
a stroke of political sagacity, was the normal and natural
course of polytheism. Thus in the Hebrew books[1] the
Assyrian conquerer is represented as admitting that it is
necessary to leave a priest who knows "the manner of
the God of the land" among the new inhabitants he has
planted there. Similar cases have been noted in primitive
cults still surviving ;[2] and to the general tendency may be
conjecturally ascribed such phenomena as that of the
Saturnalia, in which masters and slaves changed places,
and the institution of the Levites among the Hebrews,
otherwise only mythically explained. But if conquerors
and conquered thus tended to amalgamate or associate
their cults, equally would allied tribes tend to do so ;
and when particular Gods of different groups were seen
to correspond in respect of special attributes, a further

---

[1] 2 Kings, xvii, 26. Cp. *Ruth*, i, 16, and *Judges*, xvii, 13. See also Tylor,
Primitive Culture, i, 113-115, and the able work of Mr. F. B. Jevons, *Introduction to the History of Religion*, 1896, pp. 36-40, where the fear felt by
conquering races for the occult powers of the conquered is limited to the
sphere of "magic". But when Mr. Jevons so defines magic as to admit of
his proposition (p. 38) that " the *hostility from the beginning* between religion
and magic is universally admitted", he throws into confusion the whole
phenomena of the early official-religious practice of magic, of which sacrifice and prayer are the type-forms that have best survived. And in the
end he upsets his definition by noting (p. 40) how magic, "*even where* its
relation to religion is one of avowed hostility", will imitate religion.
Obviously magic is a function or aspect or element of primitive religion
(cp. Sayce, pp. 315, 319, 327, and *passim*, and Tiele, *Egyptian Rel.*, pp. 22,
32) ; and any "hostility", far from being universal, is either a social or a
philosophical differentiation. In the opinion of Weber (*Ind. Lit.*, p. 264)
the magic arts "found a more and more fruitful soil as the religious
development of the Hindus progressed"; " so that they now, in fact, reign
almost supreme". See again Mr. Jevons' own later admission. p. 395,
where the exception of Christianity is somewhat arbitrary. On this
compare Kant, *Religion innerhalb der Grenzen der blossen Vernunft*, B. iv,
Apotome ii, Sect. 3.

[2] Cp. E. Higgins, *Hebrew Idolatry and Superstition*, 1893, pp. 20, 24;
Robertson Smith, *Religion of the Semites*, 1889, p. 77; Wellhausen, *Heidenthum*, S. 129, 183, cited by Smith, p. 79 ; Lang, *Making of Religion*, p. 65.

analysis would be encouraged.   Hence with every exten-
tion of every State, every advance in intercourse made in
peace or through war, there would be a further comparison of credences, a further challenge to the reasoning
powers of thoughtful men.

> This tendency did not exclude, but would in certain cases
> conflict with, the strong primitive tendency to associate every
> God permanently with his supposed original locality.   Tiele
> writes (*History of the Egyptian Religion*, Eng. tr. introd. p. xxvii)
> that in no case was a place given to the Gods of one nation in
> another's pantheon "if they did not wholly alter their form,
> character, appearance, and not seldom their very name".   This
> seems an over-statement.   What is clear is that local cults
> resisted the removal of their God's images ; and the attempt to
> deport such images to Babylon, thus affecting the monopoly
> of the God of Babylon himself, was a main cause of the fall of
> Nabonidos, who was driven out by Cyrus.   But the Assyrians
> invoked Bel Merodach of Babylon, after they had conquered
> Babylon, in terms of his own ritual ; even as Israelites often
> invoked the Gods of Canaan (Cp. Sayce, Hibbert Lectures, *On
> the Religion of the Ancient Babylonians*, p. 123).   A God could
> migrate with his worshippers from city to city (*Id*., p. 124) ; and
> the Assyrian scribe class maintained the worship of their
> special God Nebo wherever they went, though he was a local
> God to start with (*Id*., pp. 117, 119, 121).   And as to the recog-
> nition of the Gods of different Egyptian cities by politic kings,
> see Tiele's own statement, p. 36.   Cp. his *Outlines*, pp. 73, 84, 207.

A concrete knowledge of the multiplicity of cults,
then, was obtruded on the leisured and travelled men of
the early empires and of such a civilisation as that of
Hellas ; and when to such knowledge there was added a
scientific astronomy (the earliest to be constituted of the
concrete sciences) a revision of beliefs by such men was
inevitable.   It might take the form either of a guarded
scepticism or of a monarchic theology, answering to the
organisation of the actual earthly empire ; and the latter
view, in the nature of the case, would much the more
easily gain ground.   The Freethought of early civilisation,
then, would be practically limited for a long time to
movements in the direction of coördinating polytheism, to

the end of setting up a supreme though not a sole deity ;
the Chief God in any given case being apt to be the God
specially affected by the reigning monarch. Allocation of
spheres of influence to the principal deities would be the
working minimum of plausible adjustment, since only in
some such way could the established principle of the
regularity of the heavens be formally accommodated to
the current worship; and wherever there was monarchy,
even if the monarch were polytheistic, there was a lead
to gradation among the Gods.[1]   A pantheistic conception
would be the highest stretch of rationalism that could
have any vogue even among the educated class.   All the
while, every advance was liable to the ill-fortune of overthrow or arrest at the hands of an invading barbarism,
which even in adopting the system of an established
priesthood would be more likely to stiffen than to develop
it.   Early rationalism, in short, would share in the fluctuations of early civilisation; and achievements of thought
would repeatedly be swept away, even as were the
achievements of the constructive arts.

§ 2.   *The Process in India.*

The process thus deducible from the main conditions
is found actually happening in more than one of the
ancient cultures, as their history is now sketched.   In
the Rig Veda, which if not the oldest is the least altered
of the Eastern Sacred Books, the main line of change
is obvious enough.   It remains so far matter of conjecture
to what extent the early Vedic cults contain matter
adopted from non-Aryan Asiatic peoples; but no other
hypothesis seems to account for the special development
of the cult of Agni in India as compared with the content
and development of the other early Aryan systems, in
which, though there are developments of fire worship,

---

[1] Cp. Sayce, Hibbert Lectures, pp. 96, 121-122 ; Robertson Smith,
Religion of the Semites, p. 74; Tiele, *Egyptian Religion*, p. 36; and *Outlines*, p. 52.

the God Agni does not appear.[1] The specially priestly character of the Agni worship, and the precedence it takes in the Vedas over the solar cult of Mitra, who among the kindred Aryans of Eran receives in turn a special development, suggest some such grafting, though the relations between Aryans and the Hindu aborigines, as indicated in the Veda, seem to exclude the possibility of their adopting the fire-cult from the conquered inhabitants.[2] In any case the carrying on of the two main cults of Agni and Indra side by side points to an original and marked heterogeneity of racial elements ; while the varying combination with them of the worship of other deities, the old Aryan Varuna, the three forms of the Sun-God Aditya, the Goddess Aditi and the eight Adityas, the solar Mitra, Vishnu, Rudra and the Maruts, imply the adaptation of further varieties of hereditary creed. The outcome is a sufficiently chaotic medley, in which the attributes and status of the various Gods are reducible to no code.[3] Here, then, were the conditions provocative of doubt among the critical ; and while it is only in the later books of the Rig Veda that such doubt finds priestly expression, it must be inferred that it was current in some degree among laymen before the hymn-makers avowed that they shared it. It now seems to take the shape of a half-sceptical half-mystical questioning as to which, if any, God is real.

> From the Catholic standpoint, Dr. E. L. Fischer has argued that "Varuna is in the ontological, physical, and ethical relation the highest, indeed the unique God of ancient India "; and that the Nature-Gods of the Veda can belong only to a later period in the religious consciousness (*Heidenthum und Offen-*

[1] Cp. Tiele, *Outlines*, pp. 109-110, and Fischer, *Heidenthum und Offenbarung*, S. 59. Professor Max Müller's insistence that the lines of Vedic Religion could not have been "*crossed*" by trains of thought which started from China, from Babylon, or from Egypt " (*Physical Religion*, p. 251) does not affect the hypothesis put above. The Professor admits (p. 250) the exact likeness of the Babylonian fire-cult to that of Agni.

[2] But cp. Müller, *Anthropological Religion*, p. 164.

[3] Cp. Oldenberg, *Die Religion des Vedas*, 1894, S. 94, 98-9 ; Ghosha, *History of Hindu Civilisation as illustrated in the Vedas*, Calcutta, 1889, pp. 190-1 ; Max Müller, *Physical Religion*, 1891, pp. 197-8.

barung, 1878, S. 36-37). Such a development, had it really occurred, might be said to represent a movement of primitive Freethought from an unsatisfying monotheism to a polytheism that seemed better to explain natural facts. A more plausible view of the process, however, is that of Von Bradke, to the effect that " the old Indo-Germanic polytheism, with its pronounced monarchic apex, which . . . constituted the religion of the pre-Vedic [Aryan] Hindus, lost its monarchic apex shortly before and during the Rig-Veda period, and set up for itself the so-called Henotheism [worship of deities severally as if they were the only ones] which thus represented in India a time of religious decline ; a decline which, at the end of the period to which the Rig-Veda hymns belong, led to an almost complete dissolution of the old beliefs. The earlier collection of the hymns must have promoted the decline ; and the final redaction must have completed it. The collected hymns show only too plainly how the very deity before whom in one song all the remaining Gods bow themselves, in the next sinks almost in the dust before another. Then there sounds from the Rig-Veda (x, 121) the wistful question: Who is the God whom we should worship ? " (*Dyâus Asura, Ahuramazda, und die Asuras*, Halle, 1885, S. 115). On this view the growth of monotheism went on alongside of a growth of critical unbelief, but instead of expressing that, provoked it by way of reaction.

To meet such a doubt, a pantheistic view of things would naturally arise ;[1] and for ancient as for more civilised peoples such a doctrine had the attraction of nominally reconciling the popular cult with the scepticism it had aroused. Rising thus as Freethought, the pantheistic doctrine in itself became in India a dogmatic system, the monopoly of a priestly caste, whose training in mystical dialectic made them able to repel or baffle amateur scepticism. Such fortifying of a sophisticated creed by institutions—of which the Brahmanic caste system is perhaps the strongest type—is one of the main conditions of relative permanence for any set of opinions; yet even

---

[1] Cp. *Rig-Veda*, i, 164, 46, x, 90 (cited by Ghosha, pp. 191, 198); viii, 10 (cited by Müller, *Natural Religion*, pp. 227-9) ; and x, 82, 121, 129 (cited by Romesh Chunder Dutt, *History of Civilisation in Ancient India*, ed. 1893, i, 95-97) ; Tiele, *Outlines*, p. 125 ; Weber, *History of Indian Literature*, Eng trans., p. 5 ; Max Müller, *Physical Religion*, p. 187; Barth, *Religions of India* p. 8 ; Tylor, *Primitive Culture*, ii, 354.

within the Brahmanic system, in virtue presumably of the principle that the higher truth was for the adept, and need not interfere with the popular cult, there were again successive critical revisions of the pantheistic idea.

Of the nature of a Freethinking departure, among the early Brahmanists as in other societies, was the substitution of non-human for human sacrifices, a development of peaceful life-conditions which, though not primitive, must have ante-dated Buddhism. See Tiele, *Outlines*, pp. 126-7 and refs.; and Müller, *Physical Religion*, p. 101. Prof. Robertson Smith (*Religion of the Semites*, p. 346) appears to argue that animal sacrifice was never a substitute for human; but his ingenious argument, on analysis, is found to prove only that in certain cases the idea of such a substitution having taken place may have been un-historical. If it be granted that human sacrifices ever occurred, substitution would be an obvious way of abolishing them. Brahman thinkers went the further length of arguing against all blood sacrifices, but without practical success (Tiele, p. 126), until Buddhism triumphed (Mitchell, *Hinduism*, 1885, p. 106).

In the earliest Upanishads, the World-Being seems to have been figured as the totality of matter.[1] This view being open to all manner of anti-religious criticism, which it may have incurred even within the Brahmanic pale, there was evolved an ideal formula in which the source of all things is " the invisible, intangible, unrelated, color-less one, who has neither eyes nor ears, neither hands nor feet, eternal, all-pervading, subtile, and undecaying".[2]

The phenomenon of the schism represented by the two divisions of the Yazur Veda, the "White" and the "Black", is plausibly accounted for as the outcome of the tendencies of a new and an old school, who selected from their Brahmanas, or treatises of ritual and theology, the portions which respectively suited them. The implied critical movement would tend to affect official thought in general. This schism is held by Weber to

---

[1] Colebrooke's *Miscellaneous Essays*, ed. 1873, i, 375-6. Weber (*History*, p. 27) has advanced the view that the adherents of this doctrine, who gradually became stigmatised as heretics, were the founders of Buddhism. But the view of the universe as a self-existent totality appears to exist in the Brahmans Sankhya teaching, which is midway between the popular Nyaya system and the esoteric Vedanta (Ballantyne, *Christianity contrasted with Hindu Philosophy*, 1859, pp. xviii, 59, 61).
[2] Major Jacob's *Manual of Hindu Pantheism*, 1881, p. 3.

have arisen only in the period of ferment set up by Buddhism;
but other disputes seem to have taken place in abundance in
the Brahmanical schools before that time. (Cp. Tiele, *Outlines*,
p. 123; Weber, *History of Indian Literature*, pp. 10, 27, 232;
Max Müller, *Anthropological Religion*, 1892, pp. 36-37; and Rhys
Davids, *Buddhism*, p. 34.)   Again, the ascetic and penance-
bearing hermits, who were encouraged by the veneration paid
them to exalt themselves above all save the highest Gods,
would by their utterances of necessity affect the course of
doctrine.   Compare the same tendency as seen in Buddhism
and Jainism (Tiele, pp. 135, 140).

In the later form of the Vedânta, " the end of the Veda,"
this monistic and pantheistic teaching holds its ground in
our own day, after all the ups and downs of Brahmanism,
alongside of the aboriginal cults which Brahmanism
adopted in its battle with Buddhism; alongside, too, of the
worship of the Veda itself as an eternal and miraculous
document.   " The leading tenets [of the Vedânta] are
known to some extent in every village."[1]   But the
Vedantists, again, treat the Upanishads in turn as a
miraculous and inspired system,[2] and repeat in their
case the process of the Vedas: so sure is the law of
fixation in religious thought, while the habit of worship
subsists.

The highest activity of rationalistic speculation within
the Brahmanic fold is seen to have followed intelligibly
on the most powerful reaction against the Brahmans'
authority.   This took place when their sphere had been
extended from the region of the Punjaub, of which alone
the Rig-Veda shows knowledge, to the great kingdoms of
Southern India, pointed to in the Sutras,[3] or short digests
of ritual and law designed for general official use.   The
primary basis for rejection of a given system—belief in
another—made ultimately possible there the rise of an
atheistic system capable, wherever embraced, of annulling
the burdensome and exclusive system of the Brahmans,

[1] Major Jacob, as cited, *preface*.
[2] Max Müller, *Psychological Religion*, 1893, pp. 126, 295.
[3] Chunder Dutt, *History of Civilisation in Ancient India*, as cited, i, 112-3

which had been developed in its worst form[1] in the new
environment. Buddhism, though it can hardly have
arisen on one man's initiative in the manner claimed in
the legends, even as stripped of their supernaturalist
element, was in its origin essentially a movement of Freethought, such as could have arisen only in the atmosphere
of a much mixed society,[2] where the extreme Brahmanical
claims were on various grounds discredited, perhaps even
within their own newly adjusted body. The tradition
which makes the Buddha a prince suggests an upper-
class origin for the reaction; and there are traces of a
chronic resistance to the Brahmans'. rule among their
fellow-Aryans before the Buddhist period.

> "The royal families, the warriors, who, it may be supposed,
> strenuously supported the priesthood so long as it was a
> question of robbing the people of their rights, now that this
> was effected turned against their former allies, and sought to
> throw off the yoke that was likewise laid upon them. These
> efforts were, however, unavailing: the colossus was too firmly
> established. Obscure legends and isolated allusions are the
> only records left to us in the later writings of the sacrilegious
> hands which ventured to attack the sacred and divinely conse-
> crated majesty of the Brahmans; and these are careful to note
> at the same time the terrible punishments which befel those
> impious offenders " (Weber, *History*, p. 19).

The circumstances, however, that the Buddhist writings
were from the first in vernacular dialects, not in Sanskrit,[3]
and that the mythical matter which accumulated round the
story of the Buddha is in the main aboriginal, and largely
common to the myth of Krishna,[4] go to prove that
Buddhism spread specially in the non-Aryan sphere.[5] Its

---

[1] Prof. Weber (*Hist. Ind. Lit.*, p. 4) says the peoples of the Punjaub
never at all submitted to the Brahmanical rule and caste system. But the
subject natives there must at the outset have been treated as an inferior
order. Cp. Tiele, *Outlines*, p. 120, and refs.; and Rhys Davids, *Buddhism*, p. 23.
[2] Brahmanism had itself been by this time influenced by aboriginal
elements, even to the extent of affecting its language. Weber, as cited,
p. 177. Cp. Max Müller, *Anthropological Religion*, p 164.
[3] Weber, *History*, pp. 179, 299; Müller, *Natural Religion*, p. 299.
[4] See Senart, *Essai sur la légende de Buddha*, 2 e édit., p. 297 ff.
[5] Cp. Weber, p. 303.

practical (not theoretic)[1] Atheism seems to have rested
fundamentally on the conception of the transmigration of
the soul, or rather of the personality, through many
stages up to Nirvana ; and of this conception there is no
trace in the Vedas,[2] though it became a leading tenet of
Brahmanism.

> To the dissolvent influence of Greek culture may possibly
> be due some part of the success of Buddhism before our era,
> and even later.   Hindu astronomy in the Vedic period was but
> slightly developed (Weber, *Ind. Lit.*, pp. 246, 249, 250); and
> " it was Greek influence that first infused a real life into Indian
> astronomy " (*Id.*, p. 251; Cp. *Lib. Us. Kn. History of Astronomy*,
> c. ii).   This implies other interactions.   It is presumably to
> Greek stimulus that we must trace the knowledge by Aryabhata
> (Colebrooke's *Essays*, ed. 1873, ii, 404; cp. Weber, p, 257) of the
> doctrine of the earth's diurnal revolution on its axis; and the
> fact that in India as in the Mediterranean world the truth was
> later lost from men's hands, may be taken as one of the proofs
> that the two civilisations alike retrograded owing to evil poli-
> tical conditions.   In the progressive period (from about 320 B.C.
> onwards for perhaps some centuries) Greek ideas might well
> help to discredit traditionalism; and their acceptance at royal
> courts would be favorable to toleration of the new teaching.   At
> the same time, Buddhism must have been favored by the
> native mental climate in which it arose.

The main differentiation of Buddhism from Brahmanism,
again, is its ethical spirit, which sets aside formalism and
seeks salvation in an inward reverie and discipline ; and
this element in turn can hardly be conceived as arising
save in an old society, far removed from the warlike stage
represented by the Vedas.   Whatever may have been its
early association with Brahmanism,[3] then, it must be
regarded as essentially a reaction against Brahmanical
doctrine and ideals ; a circumstance which would account
for its early acceptance in the Punjaub, where Brahmanism had never attained absolute power and was jealously

---

[1] See Weber, p. 301 and *note*, and p. 307.
[2] Tiele, *Outlines*, p. 117.
[3] Cp. Weber, *History of Indian Literature*, pp. 27, 284-7 ; Max Müller.
Natural Religion, p. 555; Jacobi, as there cited; and Tiele, *Outlines*, pp. 135-6.

resisted by the free population.[1] And the fact that Jainism, so closely akin to Buddhism, has its sacred books in
a dialect belonging to the region in which Buddhism
arose, further supports the view that the reaction grew
out of the thought of a type of society differing widely
from that in which Brahmanism arose. The original
Atheism or Agnosticism of the Buddhist movement thus
appears as a product of a relatively high, because complex, moral and intellectual evolution.

" The fact cannot be disputed away that the religion of
Buddha was from the beginning purely atheistic. The idea
of the Godhead . . . . was for a time at least expelled from the
sanctuary of the human mind ; and the highest morality that
was ever taught before the rise of Christianity was taught by
men with whom the Gods had become mere phantoms, without
any altars, not even an altar to the Unknown God " (Max
Müller, *Introd. to the Science of Religion*, ed. 1882, p. 81).

" He [Buddha] ignores God in so complete a way that he
does not even seek to deny him ; he does not suppress him, but
he does not speak of him either to explain the origin and
anterior existence of man or to explain the present life, or to
conjecture his future life and definitive deliverance. The
Buddha knows God in no fashion whatever" (Barthélemy
Saint-Hilaire, *Le Bouddha et sa Religion*, 1866, p. v).

" Buddhism and Christianity are indeed the two opposite
poles with regard to the most essential points of religion :
Buddhism ignoring all feeling of dependence on a higher
power, and therefore denying the very existence of a supreme
Deity " (Müller, as last cited, p. 171).

" Lastly, the Buddha declared that he had arrived at [his]
conclusions, not by study of the Vedas, nor from the teachings
of others, but by the light of reason and intuition alone " (Rhys
Davids, *Buddhism*, p. 48). " The most ancient Buddhism
despises dreams and visions" (*Id.*, p. 177). "Agnostic Atheism
. . . . is the characteristic of his [Buddha's] system of philosophy " (*Id.*, p. 207).

On the other hand, the gradual coloring of Buddhism
with popular mythology, the reversion to adoration and
worship of the Buddha himself, and the final collapse of

---

[1] Weber, *History of Indian Literature*, pp. 4, 39.

the system in India before the pressure of Brahmanised Hinduism, all prove the potency of the sociological conditions of success and failure for creeds and criticisms. Buddhism took the monastic form for its institutions, thus incurring ultimate petrifaction alike morally and intellectually; and in any case the normal Indian social conditions of abundant population, cheap food, and general ignorance, involved an overwhelming vitality for the popular cults. These the Brahmans naturally took under their protection as a means of maintaining their hold over the multitude; and though their own highest philosophy has been poetically grafted on that basis, as in the epic of the Mahabharata and in the Bhagavat Gîta, the ordinary worship of the deities of these poems is perforce utterly unphilosophical, varying between a primitive sensualism and an emotionalism closely akin to that of popular forms of Christianity. Buddhism itself, where it still prevails, exhibits similar tendencies.

It is disputed whether the Brahman influence drove Buddhism out of India by physical force, or whether it decayed in virtue of maladaptation to its environment. Its vogue for some seven hundred years, from about 300 B.C. to about 400 A.C., seems to have been largely due to its protection and final acceptance as a State religion by the dynasty of Chandragupta (the Sandracottos of the Greek historians), whose grandson Asoka showed it special favor. His rock-inscribed edicts (for which see Max Müller, *Introd. to Science of Rel.*, pp. 5-6, 23; *Anthropological Religion*, pp. 40-43; Rhys Davids, *Buddhism*, pp. 220-228; Wheeler's *History of India*, vol. iii, app. i; Asiatic Society's *Journals*, vols. viii and xii; *Indian Antiquary*, 1877, vol. vi) show a general concern for natural ethics, and especially for tolerance, but his mention of " The Terrors of the Future " among the religious works he specially honors, shows (if genuine) that already normal superstition had affected the system. Under Asoka, however, it was powerful enough to react somewhat on the West, then in contact with India as a result of the Alexandrian conquest (Cp. Mahaffy, *Greek World under Roman Sway*, ch. ii; Weber's lecture on Ancient India, Eng. trans., pp. 25-6, *Indische Skizzen*, p. 28 [cited in the present writer's *Christ and Krishna*, p. 34] and Weber's *History*, p. 255 and p. 309, *note*); and the fact that after his time it entered on a long conflict with Brahmanism proves that it remained practically dangerous to that system. In the fifth and sixth centuries of our era, Buddhism in India "rapidly declined "—a circumstance hardly intelligible save as a result of violence. Tiele, after expressly asserting the " rapid decline " (*Outlines*, p. 139), in the next breath asserts that there are no satisfactory proofs of such violence, and that " on the contrary, Buddhism appears to have pined away *slowly*" (p. 140 : contrast his *Egyptian Religion*, p. xxi). But compare Rhys Davids, *Buddhism* p. 246; Max Müller, *Anthrop. Rel.*, p. 43. Internal decay appears to have made the work of suppression easier. Already in Gautama's own life there were doctrinal disputes within his party, according to the legends (Müller, *A. R.*, p. 38) ; and soon heresies and censures abounded (*Introd. to Sc. of Rel.*, p. 23), till schisms arose and no fewer than eighteen sects took shape (Davids, pp. 213-218). Of the nature of the influence of Buddhism in Burmah, where it has prospered, a vivid and thoughtful account is given in the recent work of H. Fielding, *The Soul of a People*, 1898. At its best, the cult there deifies the Buddha; elsewhere it is interwoven with aboriginal polytheism and superstition (Davids, pp. 207-211 ; Müller, *A. R.*, p. 132).

Within Brahmanism, again, there have been at different times attempts to set up partly naturalistic reforms in religious thought ; *e.g.*, that of Chaitanya in the 16th century; but these have never been pronouncedly freethinking, and Chaitanya preached a "surrender of all to Krishna ", very much in the manner of evangelical Christianity. Finally he has been deified by his followers. (Müller *Nat. Rel.*, p. 100 ; *Phys. Rel.*, p. 356.)

More definitely freethinking was the monotheistic cult set up among the Sikhs in the fifteenth century, as the history runs, by Nanak, who had been influenced both by Parsees and by Mohammedans, and whose ethical system repudiated caste. But though Nanak objected to any adoration of himself, he and all his descendants have been virtually deified by his devotees, despite their profession of a theoretically pantheistic creed. (Cp. De la Saussaye, *Manual*, pp. 659-662; Müller, *Phys. Rel.*, p. 355.) Trumpp (*Die Religion der Sikhs*, 1881, S. 123) tells of other Sikh sects, including one of a markedly Atheistic character belonging to the present century ; but all alike seem to sink towards Hinduism.

Similarly among the Jainas, who compare with the Buddhists in their nominal atheism as in their tenderness to animals and in some other respects, there has been decline and compromise ; and their numbers appear steadily to dwindle, though in India they survived while Buddhism disappeared

(Cp. De la Saussaye, *Manual*, pp. 557-563; Rev. J. Robson, *Hinduism*, 1874, pp. 80-86; Tiele, *Outlines*, p. 141). Finally the Brahmo-Somaj movement of the present century appears to have come to little in the way of rationalism (Mitchell, *Hinduism*, pp. 224-246; De la Saussaye, pp. 669-671; Tiele, p. 160).

§ 3. *Mesopotamia*.

The nature of the remains we possess of the ancient Babylonian and Assyrian religions is not such as to yield a direct record of their development; but they suffice to show that there, as elsewhere, a measure of rationalistic evolution occurred. Were there no other ground for the inference, it might not unreasonably be drawn from the post-exilic monotheism of the Hebrews, who, drawing so much of their cosmology and temple ritual from Babylon, may be presumed to have been influenced by the higher Semitic civilisations in other ways also. But there is concrete evidence. What appears to have happened in Babylonia and Assyria, whose religious systems were grafted on that of the more ancient Akkadian civilisation, is a gradual subordination of the numerous local gods (at least in the thought of the more philosophic, including some of the priests), to the conception of one all-pervading power. This process would be assisted by that of imperialism, while on the other hand it would be resisted by the strength of the traditions of the Babylonian cities, all of which had ancient cults before the later empires were built up.[1] The result was a set of compromises in which the provincial and foreign deities were treated either genealogically or grouped in family or other relations with the chief God or Gods of the time being.[2] Certain cults, again, were either kept always at a higher ethical level than the popular one, or were treated by the more refined and more critical worshippers in an elevated spirit; and this tendency seems again to have led to conceptions of purified deities who underlay or transcended the popular types, the names ot

---

[1] Sayce, Hibbert Lectures, pp. 121, 213, 215; E. Meyer, *Geschichte des Alterthums*, 1884, i, 161 (§ 133).
[2] Sayce, pp. 219, 344; Lenormant, *Chaldean Magic*, Eng. ed., p. 127.

the latter being held to point to one who was misconceived under their grosser aspects.[1] Astronomical knowledge, again, gave rise to cosmological theories which pointed to a ruling and creating God,[2] who as such would have a specially ethical character. In some such way was reached a conception of a Creator-God as the unity represented by the fifty names of the Great Gods, who lost their personality when their names were liturgically given to him[3]—a conception which in some statements even had a pantheistic aspect[4] among a "group of priestly thinkers", and in others took the form of an ideal theocracy.[5] There is record that the Babylonian schools were divided into different sects,[6] and their science was likely to make some of these rationalistic.[7]

It may be almost taken for granted, further, that disbelief would be set up by such a primitive fraud as the pretence of the priests of Bel Merodach that the God cohabited nightly with the concubine set apart for him (Herodotos, i, 181-2), as was similarly pretended by the priests of Amun at Thebes. Herodotos could not believe the story; and there must have been some such sceptics within the sphere of the cults in question, to say nothing of the priests who carried on the fraud.

As regards Freethinking in general, much would depend on the development of the Chaldæan astronomy. That science, growing out of primitive astrology (cp. Whewell, *History of the Inductive Sciences*, 3rd. ed. i, 108), would tend to discredit, among its experts, much of the prevailing religious thought; and they seem to have carried it so far as to frame a scientific theory of comets (Seneca, citing Apollonius Myndius, *Quaest. Nat.*, vii, 3; cp. Lib. Use. Kn. *History of Astronomy*, c. 3; E. Meyer, *Gesch. des Alterthums*, i, 186; and Weber, *Ind. Lit.*, p. 248). Such knowledge would greatly favor scepticism, as well as monotheism and pantheism. It was sought to be astrologically applied; but as the horoscopes varied, this was again a source of un-

---

[1] Sayce, pp. 129, 267-8; Cp. Kuenen, *Religion of Israel*, Eng. tr., i, 91; Menzies, *History of Religion*, 1895, p. 171.

[2] Sayce, p. 331, ff., 367, ff.; Lenormant, *Chaldean Magic*, p 112.

[3] Sayce, p. 305. Cp. Robertson Smith, *Religion of the Semites*, p. 452.

[4] Sayce, pp. 191-2, 367; Lenormant, pp. 112, 113, 119, 133.

[5] Tiele, *Outlines*, p. 78; Sayce, *Ancient Empires of the East*, pp. 152-153. Cp. Rawlinson, *Five Great Monarchies*, 2nd. ed., iii, 13.

[6] Strabo, xvi, c. 1, § 6.

[7] Cp. Rawlinson, *Five Great Monarchies*, i, 110; iii, 12-13.

belief (Meyer, S. 179). Medicine, again, made little progress (Herodot. i, 197).

It can hardly be doubted, finally, that in Babylonia and Assyria there were idealists who, like the Hebrew prophets, repudiated alike image-worship and the religion of sacrifices. The latter repudiation occurs frequently in later Greece and Rome. There, as in Jerusalem, it could make itself heard in virtue of the restrictedness of the power of the priests, who in Babylonia and Assyria, on the other hand, might be trusted to suppress or override any such propaganda, as we have seen was done in Brahmanical India.

Concerning image-worship, apart from the proved fact of pantheistic doctrine, and the parallels in Egypt and India, it is to be noted that Isaiah actually puts in the mouth of the Assyrian king a tirade against the "kingdoms of the idols" or "false Gods", including in these Jerusalem and Samaria (Isa. x, 10, 11). The passage is dramatic, but it points to the possibility that in Assyria just as in Israel a disbelief in idols could arise from reflection on the spectacle of their multitude.

The chequered political history of Babylon and Assyria, however, made impossible any long-continued development of critical and philosophical thought. Their amalgamations of creeds and races had in a measure favored such development;[1] but the inevitably subject state of the mass of the people, and the chronic military upset of the government, were conditions fatally favorable to ordinary superstition. Culture remained wholly in the hands of the priestly and official class.[2] Accordingly we find the early religion of sorcery maintaining itself in the literature of the advanced empires.[3] The attitude of the Semitic priests and scribes towards the old Akkadic as a sacred language was in itself, like the use of Sacred Books in general, long a check upon new thought;[4] and though the Assyrian culture seems to have set this check aside, in virtue of the lack of a culture class in Assyria, the later Babylonian kingdom which rose on the fall of Assyria was too short-lived to profit much by the gain, being in turn overthrown in the second genera-

---

[1] Sayce, pp. 192, 345.
[2] E. Meyer, *Geschichte des Alterthums*, i, 187, and *note*.
[3] Sayce, pp. 316, 320, 322, 327 ; Meyer, S. 183 ; Lenormant, p. 110.
[4] Sayce, pp. 326, 341.

tion by Cyrus. It is significant that the conqueror was welcomed by the Babylonian priests as against their last king, the innovating Nabonidos[1] (Nabounahid), who had aimed at a monarchic polytheism or quasi-monotheism. It is thus clear that Cyrus, who restored the old state of things, was no strict monotheist of the later Persian type, but a schemer who relied everywhere on popular religious interests, and conciliated the polytheists of Babylon as he did the Yahweh-worshipping Jews. The Persian quasi-monotheism and anti-idolatry, however, already existed, and it is conceivable that they may have been intensified by the peculiar juxtaposition of cults set up by the Persian conquest.

> Mr. Sayce's dictum (Hibbert Lectures, p. 314) that the later ethical element in the Akkado-Babylonian system is "necessarily" due to Semitic race elements, is seen to be fallacious in the light of his own subsequent admission (p. 353) as to the lateness of the development among the Semites. The difference between early Akkadian and later Babylonian was simply one of culture-stage. See Mr. Sayce's own remarks on p. 300; and compare E. Meyer (*Geschichte des Alterthums*, i, 178, 182, 183) who entirely rejects the claim made for Semitic ethics. See again Tiele, *Outlines*, p. 78, and Mr. Sayce's own account (*Ancient Empires of the East*, p. 202) of the *Phoenician* religion as "impure and cruel". The explanation of such arbitrary judgments seems to be that the Semites are assumed to have had a primordial religious gift as compared with "Turanians"; and that the Hebrews in turn are assumed to have been so gifted above other Semites. We shall best guard against *a priori* injustice to the Semites themselves, in the conjunctures in which they really advanced civilisation, by entirely discarding the unscientific method of explaining the history of races in terms of hereditary character.

§ 4. *Ancient Persia.*

The Mazdean system, or worship of Ahura Mazda (Ormazd), of which we find in Herodotos positive historical record as an anti-idolatrous and nominally monotheistic

[1] *Id.*, pp. 85-91 : *Ancient Empires of the East*, p. 245.

creed[1] in the fifth century B.C., is the first to which these
aspects can be ascribed with certainty. As the Jews are
found represented in the Book of Jeremiah[2] (assumed to
have been written in the sixth century B.C.), worshipping
numerous Gods with images; and as polytheistic and
idolatrous practices are still described in the Book of
Ezekiel[3] (assumed to have been written during or after the
Babylonian Captivity), it is inadmissible to accept the
unauthenticated writings of ostensibly earlier prophets as
proving even a propaganda of monotheism on their part,
the so-called Mosaic law with that character being known
to be of late invention.   In any case the mass of the people
were clearly image-worshippers.   The Persians on the
other hand can be taken with certainty to have had an
imageless worship (though images existed for other purposes), with a Supreme God set above all others, in the
sixth century.   The Magian or Mazdean creed, as we have
seen, was not very devoutly held by Cyrus, but Dareios a
generation later is found holding it with zeal; and it cannot
have grown in a generation to the form it then bore.   It
must therefore be regarded as a development of the
religion of some section of the " Iranian " race, centring
as it does round some deities common to the Vedic
Aryans.

The Mazdean system, as we first trace it in history, was
the religion of the Medes, a people joined with the Persians
proper under Cyrus; and the Magi or priests figure as one
of the seven tribes of the Medes.[4]   It may thus be con-
jectured that they were a people who previously conquered
or were conquered by the Medes, who had then adopted
their religion, as did the Persians after their conquest by
or union with the Medes.   Cyrus, a semi-Persian, may well
have regarded the Medes with some racial distrust, and,
while using them as the national priests, would naturally
not be devout in his adherence at a time when the two
peoples were still mutually jealous.   When, later, after the

---

[1] Herod. i, 131.   [2] Jer. xi, 13, etc.   [3] Ezek. cc. vi, viii.
[4] Herodotos i, 101.

assassination of his son Smerdis (Bardes, or Bardija), by
the elder son, King Cambyses, and the death of the latter,
the Median and Magian interest set up the "false
Smerdis", Persian conspirators overthrew the latter and
crowned the Persian Dareios Hystaspis, marking their sense
of hostility to the Median and Magian element by a general
massacre of Magi.[1] Those Magi who survived would
naturally cultivate the more their priestly influence, the
political being thus for the time destroyed; though they
seem to have stirred up a Median insurrection in the next
century against Dareios II.[2] However that may be,
Dareios I became a zealous devotee of their creed,[3] doubtless
finding that a useful means of conciliating the Medes in
general, who at the outset of his reign seem to have given
him much trouble.[4] The richest part of his dominions[5]
was East-Iran, which appears to have been the original
home of the worship of Ahura-Mazda.[6]

Such is the view of the case derivable from Herodotos, who
remains the main authority; but recent critics have raised
some difficulties. That the Magians were originally a non-
Median tribe seems clear; Dr. Tiele (*Outlines*, pp. 163, 165)
even decides that they were certainly non-Aryan. Compare
Ed. Meyer (*Geschichte des Alterthums* i, 530, *note*, 531, §§ 439, 440),
who holds that the Mazdean system was in its nature not
national but abstract, and could therefore take in any race.
Several modern writers, however (Canon Rawlinson, ed. of
Herodotos, i, 426-431; *Five Great Monarchies*, ii, 345-355, iii,
402-4; Lenormant, *Chaldean Magic*, Eng. tr., pp. 197, 218-239;
Sayce, *Ancient Empires of the East*, p. 248), represent the Magians
as not only anti-Aryan (= anti-Persian) but opposed to the
very worship of Ormazd which is specially associated with
their name. It seems difficult to reconcile this view with the
facts: at least it involves the assumption of two opposed sets
of Magi. The main basis for the theory seems to be the
allusion in the Behistun inscription of Dareios to some acts of

[1] *Id.* iii, 79.
[2] Cp. Grote, *History of Greece*, Part ii, ch. 33 (ed. 1888, iii, 442), *note*.
[3] E. Meyer, *Geschichte des Alterthums*, i, 505 (§ 417), 542 (§ 451), 617 (§ 515);
Tiele, *Outlines*, p, 164.
[4] Herod. i, 130.
[5] Cp. Herod. iii, 94, 98; Grote, vol. iii, p. 448.
[6] E. Meyer, as cited, i, 505, 530 (§ 439); Tiele, *Outlines*, pp. 163, 165.

temple-destruction by the usurping Magian Gomates, brother
and controller of the pretended Smerdis. (See the inscription
translated in *Records of the Past*, i, 111-115.) This Meyer sets aside
as an unsettled problem, without inferring that the Magians
were anti-Mazdean (cp. §449 and §511, *note*). As to the massacre,
however, Meyer decides (i, 613) that Herodotus blundered,
magnifying the killing of "the Magus" into a slaughter of
"the Magi". But this is one of the few points at which
Herodotos is corroborated by Ktesias (cp. Grote, iii, 440, *note*).
A clue to a solution may perhaps be found in the facts that
while the priestly system remained opposed to all image-
worship, Dareios made emblematic images of the Supreme
God (Meyer, i, 213, 617) and of Mithra; and that Artaxerxes
Mnemon later put an image of Mithra in the royal temple of
Susa, besides erecting many images to Anaitis. (Rawlinson,
Five Great Monarchies, 2nd ed., iii, 320-1, 360-1). There may
have been opposing tendencies; the conquest of Babylon being
likely to have introduced new influences. The Persian art now
arising shows the most marked Assyrian influences.

The religion thus imposed on the Persians seems to
have been imageless by reason of the simple defect of art
among its cultivators;[1] and to have been monotheistic
only in the sense that its chief Deity was supreme over all
others, including even the great Evil Power, Ahriman
(Angra Mainyu). Its God-group included Mithra, once the
equal of Ahura-Mazda,[2] and later more prominent than he,[3]
as well as a Goddess, Anahita, apparently of Akkadian
origin. Before the period of Cyrus, the eastern part of
Persia seems to have been but little civilised;[4] and it was
probably there that its original lack of images became an
essential element in the doctrine of its priests. As we find
it in history, and still more in its sacred book, the Zendavesta, which as we have it represents a late liturgical
compilation,[5] Mazdeism is thus a priest-made religion,
rather than the work of Zarathustra or any one reformer;

---

[1] Meyer, i, 528 (§ 438).
[2] Darmesteter, *The Zendavesta* (in "Sacred Books of the East" series),
vol. i, introd., p. lx (1st ed.).
[3] Rawlinson, *Religions of the Ancient World*, p. 105; Meyer, § 417, 450-1.
[4] Meyer, as cited, i, 507 (§ 418).
[5] Cp. Meyer, i, 506-8; Renan, as cited by him, S. 508; Darmesteter, as
cited, cc. iv-ix, 2nd ed.; Tiele, *Outlines*, p. 165.

and its rejection of images, however originated, is to be counted to the credit of its priests, like the pantheism or nominal monotheism of the Mesopotamian, Brahmanic, and Egyptian religions. The original popular faith had clearly been a normal polytheism.[1] For the rest, the Mazdean ethic has the usual priestly character as regards the virtue it assigns to sacrifice;[2] but otherwise compares favorably with Brahmanism.

As to this cult being priest-made, see Meyer, i, 523, 540, 541, Tiele (*Outlines*, pp. 167, 178) assumes a special reformation such as is traditionally associated with Zarathustra, holding that either a remarkable man or a sect must have established the monotheistic idea. Meyer (i, 537) holds with M. Darmesteter that Zarathustra is a purely mythical personage, made out of a Storm-God. Dr. Menzies (*History of Religion*, p. 384), holds strongly by his historic actuality. The problem is analogous to those of Moses and Buddha; but the historic case of Mohammed bars a confident decision in the negative.

There is no reason to believe, however, that among the Persian peoples the higher view of things fared any better than elsewhere.[3] The priesthood, however enlightened it may have been in its inner culture, never slackened the practice of sacrifice and ceremonial; and the worship of subordinate spirits and the propitiation of demons figured as largely in their beliefs as in any other. In time the cult of the Saviour-God Mithra came to the front very much as did that of Jesus later; and in the one case as in the other, despite ethical elements, superstition was furthered. When, still later, the recognition of Ahriman was found to endanger the monotheistic principle, an attempt seems to have been made under the Sassanian dynasty, in our own era, to save it by positing a deity who was father of both Ahura-Mazda and Angra-mainyu;[4] but this last slight

[1] Meyer, i, 520 (§ 428).
[2] *Id.* i, 524 (§ 433); Tiele, *Outlines*, p. 178; Darmesteter, *Ormazd et Ahriman*, 1877, pp. 7-18.
[3] Meyer, § 450 (i, 541).
[4] Tiele, *Outlines*, p. 167. Cp. Lenormant (*Chaldean Magic*, p. 229), who attributes the heresy to immoral Median Magi; and Spiegel (*Aves.a*, 1852, i, 271), who considers it a derivation from Babylon.

effort of freethinking speculation come to nothing.   Social
and political obstacles determined the fate of Magian as of
other ancient rationalism.

> According to Rawlinson, Zoroastrianism under the Parthian
> (Arsacide) empire was gradually converted into a complex
> system of idolatry, involving a worship of ancestors and dead
> kings (*Sixth Oriental Monarchy*, p. 399; *Seventh Monarchy*, pp.
> 8-9, 56). Gutschmid, however, following Justin (xli, 3, 5-6),
> pronounces the Parthians zealous followers of Zoroastrianism,
> dutifully obeying it in the treatment of their dead (*Geschichte
> Irans von Alexander bis zum Untergang der Arsakiden*, 1888,
> S. 57-58)—a law not fully obeyed even by Dareios and his
> dynasty (Heeren, *Asiatic Nations*, Eng. tr. i, 127). Rawlinson
> on the contrary says the Parthians burned their dead—an
> abomination to Zoroastrians.   Certainly the name of the
> Parthian King Mithradates implies acceptance of Mazdeism.
> At the same time, Rawlinson admits that in Persia itself, under
> the Parthian dynasty, Zoroastrianism remained pure (*Seventh
> Monarchy*, pp. 9-10), and that even when ultimately it became
> mixed up with normal polytheism, the Dualistic faith and the
> supremacy of Ormazd were maintained (*Five Monarchies*, 2nd
> ed. iii, 362-3 ; Cp. Darmesteter, *Zendavesta*, i, lxvi, 2nd. ed.).

§ 5.   Egypt.

The relatively rich store of memorials left by the
Egyptian religions yields us hardly any more direct light
on the growth of religious rationalism than do those of
Mesopotamia, though it supplies much fuller proof that
such a growth took place.   All that is clear is that the
comparison and competition of henotheistic cults there as
elsewhere led to a measure of relative scepticism, which
took doctrinal shape in a loose monism or pantheism.
The alternate ascendancy of different dynasties, with
different Gods, forced on the process, which included, as
in Babylon, a priestly grouping of deities in families and
triads.[1]   It involved also an esoteric explanation of the
God-myths as symbolical of natural processes, or else of
mystical ideas.[2]   At the beginning of the New Kingdom

---

[1] E. Meyer, *Geschich e des Alterthums*, i, 83.
[2] *Id.*, S. 81 (§ 66) ; Tiele, *History of the Egyptian Religion*, Eng. tr., pp.
119, 154.

(B.C. 1500) it had been fully established for all the priest-hoods that the Sun-God was the one real God, and that it was he who was worshipped in all the others.[1] He in turn was conceived as a pervading spiritual force, of anthropomorphic character and strong moral bias. This seems to have been by way of a purification of one pre-eminent compound deity, Amun-Ra, to begin with, whose model was followed in other cults.[2] " Theocrasies of this kind could not have been formed unconsciously. Men knew perfectly well that they were taking a great step in advance of their fathers."[3] There had occurred, in short, among the educated and priestly class a considerable development, going on through many centuries, alike in philosophical and in ethical thought, the ethics of the Egyptian " Book of the Dead " being quite as altruistic as those of any portion of the much later Christian gospels.[4] Such a development could only arise in long periods of peace and law-abiding life. And yet all this was done " without ever sacrificing the least particle of the beliefs of the past ".[5] The popular polytheism, resting on absolute ignorance, was indestructible; and the most philosophic priests seem never to have dreamt of unsettling it.

It is contended, as against the notion of an esoteric and an exoteric doctrine, that the scribes " did not, as is generally supposed, keep their new ideas carefully concealed, so as to leave to the multitude nothing but coarse superstitions. The contrary is evident from a number of inscriptions which can be read by anybody, and from books which anyone can buy."[6] But the assumption that " any one " could read or buy books in ancient Egypt is a serious misconception. Even in our own civilisation, where

[1] Meyer, *Geschichte des alten Egyptens*, in Oncken's series, 1877, B. iii, Kap. 3, S. 249; *Geschichte des Alterthums*, i, 109; Tiele, *Egyptian Religion*, pp. 149, 151, 157.
[2] Tiele, pp. 153, 155, 156.
[3] *Id.*, p, 157.
[4] Tiele, pp. 226-230; Brugsch, *Religion und Mythologie der alten Aegypter*, 1884, 16; 1 Hälfte, S. 90-1; Kuenen, *Religion of Israel*, Eng. tr. i, 395-7.
[5] *Id.*, pp. 114, 118, 154. Cp. Meyer, *Geschichte des Alterthums*, i, 101-2 (§ 85).
[6] Tiele, *Egyptian Religion*, p. 157 Cp. p. 217.

" anyone " can presumably buy Freethought journals or works on anthropology and the history of religions, the mass of the people are so placed that only by chance does such knowledge reach them ; and multitudes are so little cultured that they would pass it by with uncomprehending indifference were it put before them. In ancient Egypt, however, the great mass of the people could not even read; and no man thought of teaching them.

> This fact alone goes far to harmonise the ancient Greek testimonies as to the existence of an esoteric teaching in Egypt with Tiele's contention to the contrary. See the pros and cons set forth and confusedly pronounced upon by Professor Chantepie de la Saussaye, *Manual of the Science of Religion*, Eng tr. pp. 400-1. We know from Diodoros (i, 81), what we could deduce from our other knowledge of Egyptian conditions, that apart from the priests and the official class, no one received any literary culture save in some degree the higher grades of artificers, who needed some little knowledge of letters for their work in connection with monuments, sepulchres, mummy-cases, and so forth. Even the images of the higher Gods were shown to the people only on festival-days (Meyer, *Gesch. des Alterthums*, i, 82).

The Egyptian civilisation was thus, through all its stages, definitely conditioned by its material basis, which in turn ultimately determined its polity, there being no higher contemporary civilisation to lead it otherwise. An abundant, cheap, and regular food supply maintained in perpetuity a dense and easily exploited population, whose lot through thousands of years was toil, ignorance, political subjection, and a primitive mental life. For such a population general ideas had no light and no comfort : for them was the simple human worship of the local natural Gods or the presiding Gods of the kingdom, alike confusedly conceived as great powers, figured often as some animal, which for the primeval mind signified indefinite capacity and unknown possibility of power and knowledge.[1] Myths and not theories, magic and not ethics, were their spiritual food, albeit their peaceful animal lives conformed suf-

[1] Meyer, i, 72.

ficiently to their code. And the life-conditions of the mass
determined the policy of priest and king. The priestly
revenue came from the people, and the king's power rested
on both orders.

This was fully seen when King Chuenaten, = Amun-
hotep (or Amenophis) IV, moved by monotheistic fanaticism, departed so far from the customary royal policy as to
put under the ban all deities save that he had chosen for
himself, repudiating the God-name Amun in his own name,
and taking that of his chosen God, Aten, for whom he
built a new capital city. Though the king enforced his
will while he lived, his movement "bore no fruit whatever", his policy being speedily reversed, and his own
monuments and capital city razed to the ground by orthodox
successors.[1] In the same way the earlier attempt of the
alien Hyksos to suppress the native polytheism and image-
worship had come to nothing.[2]

As the centuries lapsed, the course of popular religion
was rather downward than upward, if it can be measured
by the multiplication of superstitions. The priests, who
held the allegorical key to mythology, seem to have been
the main multipliers of magic and fable, mummery, ceremonial, and symbol; and they jealously guarded their
specialty against lay competition.[3] Esoteric and exoteric
doctrine flourished in their degrees side by side,[4] the
instructed apparently often accepting or acting upon both;
primitive rites all the while flourishing on the level of the
lowest civilisations,[5] though the higher ethical teaching
even improves, as in India.

Conflicts, conquests, and changes of dynasties seem to
have made little difference in the life of the common
people. Religion was the thread by which any ruler could

[1] Meyer, *Geschichte des alten Aegyptens*, B. iii, Kap. 4, 5; *Gesch. des Alterthums*, i, 271-4; Tiele, pp. 161-5. The history of Chuenaten is a discovery
of the later Egyptology. Sharpe has no mention of it.
[2] Tiele, p. 144. Cp. Meyer, *Gesch. des Alt.* i, 135.
[3] Tiele, pp. 180-182; Meyer, *Gesch. des Alt.* i, 140-143.
[4] Tiele, pp. 184-5, 196, 217.
[5] Herodotos, ii, 48, 60-64, etc.

lead them ; and after the brief destructive outbreak of
Cambyses,[1] himself at first tolerant, the Persian conquerors
allowed the old faiths to subsist, caring only, like their
predecessors, to prevent strife between the cults which
would not tolerate each other.[2] The Ptolemies are found
adopting and using the native cults as the native kings had
done ages before them;[3] and in the learned Greek-speaking
society created by their dynasty at Alexandria there can
have been at least as little concrete belief as prevailed in
the priesthood of the older civilisation. It developed a
pantheistic philosophy which ultimately, in the hands of
Plotinus, compares very well with that of the Upanishads
and of later European systems. But this was a hot-house
flower ; and in the open world outside, where Roman rule
had broken the power of the ancient priesthood and Greek
immigration had overlaid the native element, Christianity
found an easy entrance, and in a declining society flourished
at its lowest level.[4] The ancient ferment, indeed, produced
many stirrings of relative Freethought in the form of
Christian heresies to be noted hereafter ; the sanest of all
being that of Arius, who like his antagonist Athanasius
was an Alexandrian. But the cast of mind which elaborated
the dogma of the Trinity is as directly an outcome of
Egyptian culture-history as that which sought to rationalise
the dogma by making the popular deity a created person ;
and the long and manifold internecine struggles of the
sects were the due duplication of the older strifes between
the worshippers of the various sacred animals in the several
cities.[5] In the end, the entire population was but so much
clay to take the impress of the Árab conquerors, with their
new fanatic monotheism, standing for the minimum of
rational thought.

[1] The familiar narrative of Herodotos is put in doubt by the monuments. Sayce, *Ancient Empires*, p. 246. But cp. Meyer, i, 611 (§ 508).
[2] Tiele, p. 158.
[3] See figures 209, 212, 221, 235, 242, 249, 250, in vol. i of Sharpe's
History of Egypt, 7th ed.
[4] Cp. Sharpe, ii, 287-295.
[5] These fights had not ceased even in the time of Julian (Sharpe ii, 280).
Cp. Juvenal, *Sat.* xv, 33 ff.

Apart from this normal tendency to identify Gods called by the same title (a state of things which, however, in ancient as in modern Catholic countries, tended at the same time to set up special adoration of a given image) there is seen in the later religion of Phoenicia a spirit of syncretism which operated in a manner the reverse of that seen in later Jewry. In the latter case the national God was ultimately conceived, however fanatically, as universal, all others being negated: in commercial Phoenicia, many foreign Gods were adopted,[1] the tendency being finally to conceive them as all manifestations of one Power.[2] And there is reason to suppose that in the cosmopolitan world of the Phoenician cities the higher intelligence reached a yet more subversive, though still fallacious, theory of religion. The pretended ancient Phoenician cosmogony of Sanchoniathon, preserved by Eusebius,[3] while worthless as a record of the most ancient beliefs, may be taken as representing views current not only in the time and society of Philo of Byblos (A.C. 100), who had pretended to translate it, but in a period considerably earlier. This cosmogony is, as Eusebius complains, deliberately atheistic; and it further systematically explains away all God stories as being originally true of remarkable men.

Where this primitive form of atheistic rationalism originated, we cannot now tell. But it was in some form current before the time of the Greek Evêmeros, who systematically developed it about 300 B.C.; for in a monotheistic application it more or less clearly underlies the redaction of much of the Hebrew Bible, where both patriarchal and regal names of the early period are found to be old God names; and where the Sun-God Samson is made a "judge".[4] In the Byblian writer, however, the

[1] Meyer, *Geschichte des Alterthums*, i, 251, § 209; Tiele, *Outlines*, p. 84.
[2] Rawlinson, *Hist. of Phoenicia*, p. 340; Sayce, *Ancient Empires*, p. 204; Menzies, *Hist. of Religion*, p. 168.
[3] *Præparatio Evangelica*, B. i, c. 9-10.
[4] Cp. Sayce, Hibbert Lectures, p. 159, as to Persian methods of the same kind.

purpose is not monotheistic but atheistic ; and the problem
is whether this or that was the earlier development of the
method.   The natural presumption seems to be that the
Hebrew adaptors of the old mythology used an already
applied method, as the Christian Fathers later used the
work of Evêmeros; and the citation from Thallos by
Lactantius[1] suggests that the method had been applied in
Chaldea. It is in any case credible enough that among
the much-travelling Phoenicians, with their open pantheon,
an atheistic Evêmerism was thought out by the sceptical
types before Evêmeros; and that the latter really drew
his principles from Phoenicia.[2] At any rate, they were
there received, doubtless by a select few, as a means of
answering the customary demand for "something in place
of" the rejected Gods.

> The Byblian cosmogony may be conceived as an atheistic
> refinement on those of Babylon, adopted by the Jews. It
> connects with the curious theogony of Hesiod (which has
> Asiatic aspects), in that both begin with Chaos, and the Gods
> of Hesiod are born later. But whereas in Hesiod Chaos
> brings forth Erebos and Night (Eros being causal force), and
> Night bears Æther and Day to Erebos, while Earth virginally
> brings forth Heaven (Uranos) and the Sea, and then bears the
> first Gods in union with Heaven, the Phoenician fragment
> proceeds from black chaos and wind, after long ages, through
> Eros or Desire, to a kind of primeval slime, from which arise
> first animals without intelligence, who in turn produce some
> with intelligence. The effort to expel Deity must have been
> considerable, for sun and moon and stars seem to arise un-
> created, and the sun's action spontaneously produces further
> developments. The first man and his wife are created by
> male and female principles of wind, and their offspring proceed
> to worship the Sun, calling him Beel Samin. The other Gods
> are explained as eminent mortals deified after their death. See
> the details in Cory's *Ancient Fragments*, Hodges' ed., pp. 1-22.

At the same time there are signs even in Phoenician
worship of an effort after an ethical as well as an intellectual purification of the common religion.   To call

---

[1] *Div. Inst.* i, 23.   [2] So Sayce, *Ancient Empires*, p. 204.

"the" Phoenician religion "impure and cruel"[1] is to obscure the fact that in all civilisations certain types and cults vary from the norm. In Phoenicia as in Israel there were humane anti-sensualists who either avoided or impugned the sensual and the cruel cults around them; as well as ascetics who stood by human sacrifice while resisting sexual license. That the better types remained the minority is to be understood in terms of the balance of the social and cultural forces of their civilisation, not of any racial bias or defect, intellectual or moral.

The remark of Meyer (*Gesch. des Alt.* i, 211, § 175) that an ethical or mystical conception of the God was "entirely alien" to "the Semite", reproduces the old fallacy of definite race-characters; and Mr. Sayce, in remarking that "the immorality performed in the name of religion was the invention of the Semitic race itself" (*Anc. Emp.* p. 203; contrast Tiele, *Outlines*, p. 83), after crediting the Semitic race with an ethical faculty alien to the Akkadian (above, p. 39), suggests another phase of the same error. There is nothing special to the Semites in the case save degree of development, similar phenomena being found in many savage religions, in Mexico, and in India. On the other hand there was a chaste as well as an unchaste worship of the Phoenician Ashtoreth. Ashtoreth Karnaim, or Tanit, the Virgin, as opposed to Atergates and Annit, the Mother-Goddesses, had the characteristics of Artemis. Cp. Tiele, *Religion comparée*, as cited, pp. 318-9; Menzies, *History of Religion*, pp. 159, 168-171; Tiele, *Religion of Israel*, i, 91. Smith, *Religion of the Semites*, pp. 292, 458. For the rest, the cruelty of the Phoenician cults, in the matter of human sacrifice, was fully paralleled among the early Teutons. See Tiele, *Outlines*, p. 199.

§ 7. Ancient China.

Of all the ancient Asiatic systems, that of China yields us the first clear biographical trace of a practical rationalist, albeit a rationalist stamped somewhat by Chinese conservatism. Confucius (*Kung-fu-tse* = the Master Kung) is a tangible person, despite some mythic accretions,

[1] Sayce, *Ancient Empires*, p. 302.

whereas Zarathustra and Buddha are but doubtful possibilities, and even Lao-Tsze is elusive.

Before Confucius, it is evident, there had been a slackening in religious belief among the governing classes. It is claimed for the Chinese, as for so many other races, that they had anciently a " pure " monotheism;[1] but the ascription as usual is misleading. They saw in the expanse of Heaven the " Supreme " Power, not as a result of reflection on the claims of other deities among other races, but simply as expressing their primordial tribal recognition of that special God, before contact with the God-ideas of other peoples. Monotheistic in the modern sense they could not be. Concerning them as concerning the Semites we may say that the claim of a primary monotheism for them " is also true of all primitive totemistic or clannish communities. A man is born into a community with such a divine head, and the worship of that God is the only one possible to him."[2] Beside the belief in the Heaven-God there stood beliefs in heavenly and earthly spirits, and in ancestors, who were worshipped with altars.[3]

> The remark of Professor Legge (*Religions of China*, p. 11) that the relation of the names Shang-Ti = Supreme Ruler, and T'ien = the sky, "has kept the monotheistic element prominent in the religion proper of China *down to the present time*," may serve to avert disputation. It may be agreed that the Chinese were anciently "monotheists" in the way in which they are at present, when they worship spirits innumerable. When, however, Professor Legge further says (p. 16) that the ancient monotheism five thousand years ago was "in danger of being corrupted " by nature worship and divination, he puts in doubt the meaning of the other expression above cited. He states several times (pp. 46, 51, 52) that the old monotheism remains; but speaks (p. 84) of the mass of the people as " cut off from the worship of God for themselves ". And see p. 91 as to ancestor-worship by the Emperor. Tiele (*Outlines*, p. 27) in

[1] Legge, *Religions of China*, 1880, pp. 11, 16; Douglas, *Confucianism and Taouism*, 1879, pp. 12, 82.
[2] Menzies, *History of Religion*, p. 158.
[3] Legge, pp. 12, 19, 23, 25, 26; Tiele, *Outlines*, p. 27; Douglas, p. 79.

comparison somewhat overstresses the polytheistic aspect of the Chinese religion in his opening definition; but he adds the essential facts. Dr. Legge's remark that "the idea of revelation did not shock" the ancient Chinese (p. 13) is obscure. He is dealing with the ordinary Akkado-Babylonian astrology.

As regards ancestral worship, we have record of a display of disregard for it by the lords of Lû in Confucius' time;[1] and the general attitude of Confucius himself, religious only in his adherence to old ceremonies, is incompatible with a devout environment. It has been disputed whether he makes a "sceptic denial of any relation between man and a living God";[2] but an authority who disputes this, complains that his "avoiding the personal name of Tî, or God, and only using the more indefinite term Heaven," suggests "a coldness of temperament and intellect in the matter of religion".[3] He was indeed above all things a moralist; and concerning the spirits in general he taught that "To give one's self to the duties due to men, and while respecting spiritual beings, to keep aloof from them, may be called wisdom".[4] He would never express an opinion concerning the fate of souls,[5] or encourage prayer;[6] and in his redaction of the old records he seems deliberately to have eliminated mythological expressions.[7]

The view that there was a very early "arrest of growth" in the Chinese religion (Menzies, *History of Religion*, p. 108), "before the ordinary developments of *mythology* and doctrine, priesthood," etc., had "time to take place", seems untenable as to the mythology. The same writer had just before spoken (p. 107) of the Chinese system before Confucius as having "already *parted with* all savage and irrational elements", That Confucius would seek to eliminate these seems likely enough, though the documentary fact is disputed.

[1] Legge, p. 142.
[2] See the citations made by Legge, p. 5.
[3] *Id.*, p. 139. Cp. Menzies, p. 109.
[4] Legge, p. 140; cp. p. 117; Douglas, p. 81.
[5] Legge, p. 117; Douglas, p. 68; Tiele, *Outlines*, p. 29.
[6] Tiele, p. 31; Legge, p. 143.
[7] Tiele, pp. 31-2; Douglas, pp. 68, 84. But cp. Legge, pp. 123, 137.

In the elder contemporary of Confucius, Lao-Tsze
("Old Boy"), the founder of Taouism, may be recognised
another and more remarkable early Freethinker of a
different stamp, in some essential respects much less conservative, and in intellectual cast markedly more original.
Where Confucius was an admirer and student of antiquity,
Lao-Tsze expressly put such concern aside,[1] seeking a law
of life within himself, in a manner suggestive of much
Indian and other oriental thought. His personal relation
to Confucius was that of a self-poised sage, impatient of
the other's formalism and regard to prescription and
precedent. Where they compare is in their avoidance of
supernaturalism, and in the singular rationality of their
views of social science; in which latter respect, however,
they were the recipients and transmitters of an already
classic tradition. It is not going too far to say that no
ancient people appears to have produced sane thinkers
and scientific moralists earlier than the Chinese. The
Golden Rule, repeatedly formulated by Confucius, seems
to be but a condensation on his part of doctrine he found
in the older classics;[2] and as against Lao-Tsze he is
found maintaining the practical form of the principle of
reciprocity. The older man, like some later teachers,
preached the rule of returning kindness for evil, without
leaving any biographical trace of such practice on his own
part. Confucius, dealing with human nature as it
actually is, argued that evil should be met by justice,
and kindness with kindness, else the evil were as much
fostered as the good.[3]

It is to be regretted that Christian writers should keep up
the form of condemning Confucius (so Legge, p. 144;
Douglas, p. 144) for a teaching the practice of which is
normally possible, and is never transcended in their own
church, where the profession of returning good for evil merely
constitutes one of the great hypocrisies of civilisation. How
little effect the self-abnegating teaching of Lao-Tsze, in turn,

---

[1] Douglas, pp. 179, 184.   [2] Legge, p. 137.
[3] Legge, p. 143; Douglas, p. 144.

has had on *his* followers may be gathered from their very legends concerning him (Douglas, p. 182). There is a fallacy, further, in the Christian claim that Confucius put the Golden Rule in a lower form than that of the Gospels, in that he gave it the negative form, " Do *not* that which ye would *not* have done unto you ". This is really the rational and valid form of the Rule. The positive form, unless construed in the restrictive sense, would merely prescribe a non-moral doing of favors in the hope of receiving favors in return.

Lao-Tsze, on his part, had reduced religion to a minimum. "There is not a word in the Tâo Têh King [by Lao-Tsze] of the sixth century B.C. that savors either of superstition or religion."[1] But the quietist and mystical philosophy of Lao-Tsze and the practicality of Confucius alike failed to check the growth of superstition among the ever-increasing ignorant Chinese population. " In the works of Lieh-tsze and Chwang-tsze, followers of Lao-Tsze, two or three centuries later, we find abundance of grotesque superstition, though we are never sure how far those writers really believed the things they relate "— the old fatality, seen in Brahmanism, in Buddhism, in Egypt, in Islam, and in Christianity. Confucius himself was soon worshipped.[2] A reaction against him set in after a century or two, doctrines of pessimism on the one hand and of universal love on the other finding a hearing;[3] but the influence of the great Confucian teacher Mencius (Meng-tse) carried his school through the struggle. " In his teaching, the religious element retires still further into the background "[4] than in that of Confucius; and he is memorable for his insistence on the remarkable principle of Confucius, that " the people are born good "; that they are the main part of the State;

[1] Legge, p. 164. We do find, however, an occasional allusion to deity, as in the phrase " the Great Architect " (Chalmers' trans., 1868, c. lxxiv, p. 57), and "Heaven" is spoken of in a somewhat personalised sense. Still, Dr. Chalmers complains (p. xv) that Lao-Tsze did not recognise a personal God, but put "an indefinite, impersonal and unconscious Tau" above all things (c. iv).

[2] Legge, p. 147; Tiele, *Outlines*, p. 33.

[3] Legge, *Life and Works of Mencius*, 1875, pp. 29, 50, 77, etc.

[4] Tiele, p. 33.

and that it is the ruler's fault if they go astray.[1] But Mencius put his finger on the central force in Chinese history when he taught that " it is only men of education who, without a certain livelihood, are able to maintain a fixed heart. As to the people, if they have not a certain livelihood, it follows that they will not have a fixed heart."[2] So clearly was the truth seen in China over two thousand years ago. But whether under feudalism or imperialism, under anarchy or under peace—and the teachings of Lao-Tsze and Mencius combined to discredit militarism[3]—the Chinese mass always pullulated on cheap food, at a low standard of comfort, and in a state of utter ignorance. Hence the cult of Confucius was maintained among them only by recognising their normal superstition; but on that basis it has remained secure, despite competition and even a term of early persecution. One iconoclastic emperor, the founder of the Ch'in or Ts'in dynasty (B.C. 221 or 212), sought to extirpate Confucianism as a means to a complete reconstruction of the government; but the effort came to nothing.

In the same way Lao-Tsze came to be worshipped as a God[4] under the religion called Taoism, a title sometimes mistranslated as Rationalism, "a name admirably calculated to lead the mind astray as to what the religion is".[5] The Taoists or Tao-sse " do their utmost to be as unreasonable as possible".[6] They soon reverted from the philosophic mysticism of Lao-Tsze, after a stage of indifferentism,[7] to a popular supernaturalism,[8] which "the cultivated Chinese now regard with unmixed contempt";[9] the crystallised common-sense of Confucius on the other hand, allied as it is with the official spirit of ceremonial-

---

[1] Legge, *Life and Works of Mencius,* pp. 44, 47, 56, 57, etc.
[2] *Id.,* p, 49 ; cp. p. 48.
[3] Cp. Legge's *Mencius,* pp. 47, 131 ; Chalmers' *Lao-Tsze,* pp. 23, 28, 53, 58 (cc. xxx, xxxi, xxxvi, lxvii, lxxiv) ; Douglas, *Taouism,* cc. ii, iii.
[4] Legge, *Religions of China,* p. 159.   [5] *Id.,* p. 60.
[6] Tiele, p. 37.   [7] Douglas, p. 222.   [8] *Id.,* p. 239.
[9] Tiele, p. 35; Douglas, p. 287. Taoism, however, has a rather noteworthy ethical code. See Douglas, ch. vi.

ism, retaining its hold as an esoteric code for the learned.

Nowhere perhaps is our sociological lesson more clearly to be read than in China. Centuries before our era it had a rationalistic literature, an ethic no less earnest and far more sane than that of the Hebrews, and a line of teachers as remarkable in their way as those of ancient Greece, who flourished about the same period. But where even Greece, wrought upon by all the other cultures of antiquity, retrograded till, under Christianity, it stayed at a Chinese level of unprogressiveness for a thousand years, isolated China, helped by no neighbouring culture adequate to the need, has stagnated as regards the main mass of its life, despite some political and other fluctuations, till our own day. Its social problem, like that of India, is now more or less dependent on the solutions that may be reached in Europe, where the problem is only relatively more mature, not fundamentally different.

§ 8'. *Mexico and Peru.*

In the religions of pre-Christian Mexico and Peru we have peculiarly interesting examples of " early " religious systems, flourishing at some such culture-level as the ancient Akkadian, in full play at the time of the European Renaissance. In Mexico a " high " ethical code, as the phrase goes, was held concurrently with the most frightful indulgence in human sacrifice, sustained by the continuous practice of indecisive war and the interest of a vast priesthood. In this system had been developed all the leading features of those of the Old World—the identification of all the Gods with the Sun ; the worship of fire, and the annual renewal of it by special means ; the conception of God-sacrifice and of communion with the God by the act of eating his slain representative; the belief in a Virgin-Mother-Goddess; the connection of humanitarian ethic with the divine command; the opinion that celibacy, as a state of superior virtue, is incumbent on most priests and on all would-be saints; the substitution of a sacramental bread for the "body and blood" of the God-Man; the idea of an interceding Mother-God; the hope of a Coming Saviour; the regular practice of prayer; exorcism, special indulgences, confession, absolution, fasting, and so on.[1] In Peru, also, many of those conceptions were in force; but the limitation of the power and numbers of the priesthood by the imperial system of the Incas, and the state of peace normal in their dominions, prevented the Mexican development of human sacrifice.

It seems probable that the Toltecs, conquered and for the most part driven out by the Aztecs a few centuries before Cortes, were a less warlike and more humane people, with an unbloody worship. Their God Quetzalcoatl, retained through fear by the Aztecs,[2] was a benign deity opposed to human sacrifice, apparently rather a late purification or partial rationalisation of an earlier God-type than a primitively harmless conception.[3] In that case their overthrow would stand for the military inferiority of the higher and more rational civilisation[4] to the lower and more religious, which in turn, however, was latterly being much weakened by its enormously burdensome military and priestly system, and may even be held to have been ruined by its own superstitious fears.[5]

Among the recognisable signs of normal progress in the ordinary Aztec religion were (1) the general recognition of the Sun as the God really worshipped in all the temples of the deities with special names;[6] (2) the substi-

---

[1] Details are given in the author's lecture on *The Religions of Ancient America* in *Religious Systems of the World*, 2nd ed.

[2] Réville, Hibbert Lectures *On the Native Religions of Mexico and Peru*, 1884, pp. 62-67.

[3] H. H. Bancroft, *Native Races of the Pacific States*, iii, 279. (Passage cited in author's lecture, p. 365; where is also noted Dr. Tylor's view that Quetzalcoatl was a real personage.)

[4] Cp. Prescott, *Conquest of Mexico*, Kirk's ed, 1890, p. 41.

[5] Réville, p. 66.

[6] *Id.*, p. 46. Dr. Réville speaks of the worship of the unifying deity as pretty much "effaced" by that of the lower Gods. It seems rather to have been a priestly effort to syncretise these. As to the alleged monotheism of Nezahuatl, see Lang, *Making of Religion*, p. 270, *note*, and p. 282.

tution in some cults of baked bread-images for a crucified human victim. With such beginnings made, the Aztecs might conceivably have risen above their system of human sacrifices, as the Aryan Hindus had done in an earlier age. Their material civilisation was unquestionably much superior to that which the Spaniards put in its place ; and their priesthood, being a leisured and wealthy class with a marked ethical bias, might have developed intellectually as did the Brahmans.[1] In the Hindu case the reform of sacrifices seems to have resulted from the reaction of a southern and vegetarian population on a flesh-eating one ; but as regards human sacrifice there needed in Mexico only a development of the physiological recoil, which would have been greatly furthered by a state of peace, could that have been attained.

In Peru, again, we find civilisation advancing in respect of the innovation of substituting statuettes for wives and slaves in the tombs of the rich ; and we have already noted[2] the remarkable records of the avowed unbelief of several Incas in the divinity of the nationally worshipped Sun. For the rest, there was the dubious quasi-monotheistic cult of the Creator-God, Pachacamac, concerning whom every fresh discussion raises fresh doubt.[3]

> Mr. Lang, as usual, leans to the view that Pachacamac stands for a primordial and " elevated " monotheism (*Making of Religion*, pp. 263-270) while admitting the slightness of the evidence. Garcilasso, the most eminent authority, who, however, is contradicted by others, represents that the conception of Pachacamac as Creator, needing no temple or sacrifice, was " philosophically " reached by the Incas and their wise men (Lang, p. 262). The historical fact seems to be that a race subdued by the Incas, the Yuncas, had one temple to this deity ; and that the Incas adopted the cult. Garcilasso says the Yuncas had human sacrifices and idols, which the Incas

---

[1] As to the capabilities of the Aztec language, see Bancroft, *Native Races*, ii, 727-8 (quoted in lecture cited, p. 373, *note*).

[2] Above, p. 22. Cp. Lang, as last cited, pp. 263, 282.

[3] Cp. Kirk's ed. of Prescott's *Conquest of Peru*, 1889, p. 44 ; Réville, pp. 189-190 ; Lang, as cited below.

abolished, setting up their monotheistic cult in that one temple.
This is sufficiently unlikely; and it may very well have been
the fact that the Yuncas had offered no sacrifices. But if they
did not, it was because their material conditions, like those of
the Australians and Fuegians, had not facilitated the practice;
and in that case their " monotheism " likewise would merely
represent the ignorant simplicity of a clan cult. (Compare
Tylor, *Primitive Culture*, ii, 335, ff.; Brinton, *Myths of the
New World*, p. 52.) On the other hand, *if* the Incas had set up
a cult without sacrifices to a so-called One God, their idea
would be philosophical, as taking into account the multitude
of clan-cults as well as their own national worships, and
transcending these.

But the outstanding sociological fact in Incarial Peru
was the absolute subjection of the mass of the people;
and though its material development and political organisation were comparable to those of ancient Persia under
the Akhamenidæ, so that the Spanish Conquest stood for
mere destruction, there is no reason to think that at the
best its intellectual life could have risen higher than that
of pre-Alexandrian Egypt, to which it offers so many
resemblances. The Incas' schools were for the nobility
only.[1] Rationalistic Incas and high priests might have
ruled over a docile unlettered multitude, gradually softening
their moral code, in connection with their rather highly-
developed doctrine (resembling the Egyptian) of a future
state. But these seem the natural limits, in the absence
of contact with another civilisation not too disparate for
a fruitful union.

In Mexico, on the other hand, an interaction of native
cultures had already occurred to some purpose; and the
strange humanitarianism of the man-slaying priests, who
made free public hospitals of part of their blood-stained
temples,[2] suggests a possibility of esoteric mental culture
among them. They had certainly gone relatively far in
their moral code, as apart from their atrocious creed of

---

[1] Réville, p. 152, citing Garcilasso. See same page for a story of resistance to the invention of an alphabet.

[2] Réville, p. 50, citing Torquemada, l. viii, c. 20, *end*.

sacrifice, even if we discount the testimony of the benevolent priest Sahagun ;[1] and they had the beginnings of a system of education for the middle classes.[2] Their murdered civilisation is thus the "great perhaps" of sociology : the priesthood itself being at once the most promising and the most sinister factor in the problem.

§ 9. *The Common Forces of Degeneration.*

It is implied more or less in all of the foregoing summaries that there is an inherent tendency in all systematised and instituted religion to degenerate intellectually and morally, save for the constant corrective activity of freethought. It may be well, however, to note specifically the forms or phases of the tendency.

1. Dogmatic and ritual religion being, to begin with, a more or less general veto on fresh thinking, it lies in its nature that the religious person is as such less intelligently alive to all problems of thought and conduct than he otherwise might be—a fact which at least outweighs, in a whole society, the gain from imposing a terrorised conformity on the less well-biassed types. Wherever conduct is a matter of sheer obedience to a superhuman code, it is *ipso facto* uncritical and unprogressive. Thus the history of most religions is a record of declines and reformations, each new affirmation of freethought *ad hoc* being in turn erected into a set of sheer commands. To set up the necessary ferment of corrective thought even for a time there seems to be needed (*a*) a provocation to the intelligence, as in the spectacle of conflict of cults ; and (*b*) a provocation to the moral sense and to self-interest through a burdensome pressure of rites or priestly exactions. An exceptional personality of course counts for much in the making of a movement.

2. The fortunes of such reactions are determined by

---

[1] *History of the Affairs of New Spain*, French trans., 1880, l. vi, c. 7, pp. 342-3. Cp. Prescott, *Conquest of Mexico*, Kirk's ed., pp. 31, 33.
[2] Prescott, p. 34.

socio-economic or political conditions. They are seen to
be at a minimum, as to energy and social effect, in the
conditions of greatest social invariability, as in ancient
Egypt, where progress in thought, slow at best, was
confined to the priestly and official class, and never
affected popular culture.

3. In the absence of social conditions fitted to raise
popular levels of life and thought, every religious system
tends to worsen intellectually in the sense of adding to its
range of superstition—that is, of irrational belief. Credulity
has its own momentum. Even the possession of limitary.
Sacred Books cannot check this tendency—e.g., Hinduism,
Judaism, Mohammedanism, Mazdeism, Christianity up
till the age of doubt and science, and the systems of
ancient Egypt, Babylon, and post-Confucian China.
This worsening can take place alongside of a theoretic
purification of belief within the sphere of the educated
theological class.

> Christian writers have undertaken to show that such
> deterioration went on continuously in India from the beginning
> of the Vedic period, popular religion sinking from Varuna to
> Indra, from Indra to the deities of the Atharva Veda, and from
> these to the Puranas (Cp. Dr. J. Murray Mitchell, *Hinduism
> Past and Present*, 1885, pp. 22, 25, 26, 54). The argument,
> being hostile in bias from the beginning, ignores or denies the
> element of intellectual advance in the Upanishads and other
> later literature ; but it holds good of the general phenomena.
> It holds good equally, however, of the history of Christianity in
> the period of the supremacy of ignorant faith and absence of
> doubt and science ; and is relatively applicable to the religion
> of the uneducated mass at any time and place.
>
> On the other hand, it is not at all true that religious history
> is from the beginning, in any case, a process of mere degenera-
> tion from a pure ideal. Simple statements as to primitive
> ideas are found to be misleading because of their simplicity.
> They *can* connote only the ethic of the life conditions of the
> worshipper. Now, we have seen (pp. 16-17) that primitive
> peoples living at peace and in communism, or in some respects
> well placed, may be on that account in some moral respects
> superior to the average or mass of more civilised and more
> intelligent peoples. [As to the kindliness and unselfishness of

some savages, living an almost communal life, and as to the
scrupulous honesty of others, there is plenty of evidence—*e.g.*
as to Andaman islanders, Max Müller, *Anthrop. Relig.*, citing
Colonel Cadell, p. 177; as to Malays and Papuans, Dr. Russel
Wallace, *Malay Archipelago*, p. 595 (but compare pp. 585, 587,
589) ; Reclus, *Primitive Folk*, pp. 15, 37, 115 (but cp. pp. 41-2).
In these and other cases unselfishness within the tribe is the
concomitant of the communal life, and represents no conscious
ethical volition, being concurrent with phases of the grossest
tribal egoism.   In the case of the preaching of unselfishness to
the young by the old among the Australians, where Lubbock
and his authorities see " the selfishness of the old " (*Origin of
Civilisation*, 5th ed., pp. 451-2) Mr. Lang sees a pure primeval
ethic.   Obviously the other is the true explanation.]   The
transition from that state to one of war and individualism is in
a sense degeneration ; but, broadly speaking, it is by that path
that progress in civilisation has been made, the large military
states ultimately securing within themselves some of the conditions for special development of thought, arts, and knowledge.
The residual truth is that the simple religion of the harmless
tribe is *pro tanto* superior to the instituted religion of the more
civilised nation with greater heights and lower depths of life,
the popular religion in the latter case standing for the worse
conditions.   But the simple religion did not spring from any
higher stage of knowledge.   The recent theorem of Mr. A.
Lang (*The Making of Religion*, 1898) as to religion having
originally been a pure and highly ethical monotheism, from
which it degenerated into animism and non-moral polytheism,
is at best a misreading of the facts just stated.   Mr. Lang
never asks what " Supreme Being " and " monotheism " mean
for savages who know nothing of other men's religions : he
virtually takes all the connotations for granted.   For the rest,
his theory is demonstrably wrong in its ethical interpretation
of many anthropological facts, and as it stands is quite irreconcilable with the law of evolution, since it assumes an abstract
monotheism as primordial.   In general it approximates scientifically to the last century doctrine of the superiority of savagery
to civilisation.

4. Even primary conditions of material well-being, if
not reacted upon by social science or a movement of
freethought, may in a comparatively advanced civilisation
promote religious degeneration.   Thus abundance of food
is favorable to multiplication of sacrifice, and so to

priestly predominance.[1]   The possession of domesticated
animals, so important to civilisation, lends itself to sacrifice
in a specially demoralising degree.   But abundant cereal
food-supply, making abundant population, may in a
country habitually at war, greatly promote human sacrifice
—e.g., Mexico.

The error of Mr. Lang's method is seen in the use he makes
(Work cited, pp. 286-289, 292) of the fact that certain "low"
races—as the Australians, Andamanese, Bushmen, and Fuegians—offer no animal sacrifice.   He misses the obvious significance of the facts that these unwarlike races have as a rule
no domesticated animals and no agriculture, and that their
food supply is thus in general precarious.   The Andamanese,
sometimes described (Malthus, *Essay on Population*, ch. iii, and
refs.) as very ill-fed, appear to be well supplied with fish and
game (Peschel, *Races of Mankind*, p. 147; M. Müller, *Anthrop.
Rel.*, citing Cadell, p. 177); but in any case they have no agriculture.   The Australians and Fuegians, again, have often great
difficulty in feeding themselves (Peschel, pp. 148, 159, 334;
Darwin, *Voyage*, c. 10).   In the case, however, of the primitive
Vedic Aryans, well supplied with animals, sacrifices were
abundant, and tended to become more so (Müller, *Nat. Relig.*,
pp. 136, 185; *Physical Relig.*, p. 105; but cp. pp. 98, 101;
Mitchell, *Hinduism*, p. 43   Lefmann, *Geschichte des alten Indiens*,
in Oncken's series, 1890, S. 49, 430-1).   Of these sacrifices, that
of the horse seems to have been in Aryan use in a most remote
period (Cp. M. Müller, *Nat. Rel.*, pp. 524-5; H. Böttger, *Son-
nencult der Indogermanen*, Breslau, 1891, S. 41-44; Preller,
Römische Mythologie, ed. Köhler, S. 102, 299, 323; *Griechische
Mythologie*, 2te Aufg. i, 462; Frazer, *Golden Bough*, ii, 65-66).
Dr. Müller's remark (*Physical Religion*, p. 106) that "the idea of
sacrifice did not exist at a *very* early period " because there is
no common Aryan term for it, counts for nothing, as he admits
(p. 107) that the Sanskrit word cannot be traced back to any
more general root; and he admits the antiquity of the *practice.*
On this cp. Mitchell, *Hinduism*, pp. 37-38.   The reform in Hindu
sacrifice, consummated by Buddhism, has been noted above.

5.   Even scientific knowledge, while enabling the
thoughtful to correct their religious conceptions, in some

---

[1] "The priest says, 'the spirit is hungry', the fact being that he himself is hungry.   He advises the killing of an animal" (Müller, *Anthropological Religion*, p. 307).

forms lends itself easily to the promotion of popular superstition. Thus the astronomy of the Babylonians, while developing some scepticism, served in general to encourage divination and fortune-telling; and seems to have had the same effect when communicated to the Chinese, the Hindus, and the Hebrews, all of whom, however, practised divination previously on other bases.

6. Finally, the development of the arts of sculpture and painting, unaccompanied by due intellectual culture, tends to keep religion at a low anthropomorphic level, and worsens its psychology by inviting image-worship.[1] It is not that the earlier and non-artistic religions are not anthropomorphic, but that they give more play for intellectual imagination than does a cult of images. But where the arts have been developed, idolatry has always arisen save when resisted by a special activity or revival of freethought to that end; and even in Protestant Christendom, where image-worship is tabooed, religious pictures now promote popular credulity as they did in the Italian Renaissance. So manifold are the forces of intellectual degeneration—degeneration, that is, from an attained ideal or stage of development, not from any primordial knowledge.

---

[1] On the general tendency cp. Chantepie de la Saussaye, *Manual of the Science of Religion*, pp. 77-84.

CHAPTER IV.

RELATIVE FREETHOUGHT IN ISRAEL.

THE modern critical analysis of the Hebrew Sacred Books has made it sufficiently clear that in Jewish as in all other ancient history progress in religion was by way of evolving an ethical and unique deity out of normal primeval polytheism. What was special to the Hebrews was the set of social conditions under which the evolution took place. Through these conditions it was that the relative Freethought which rejected normal polytheism was so far favored as to lead to a pronounced monotheistic cultus, though not to a philosophic monotheism.

§ 1.

As seen in their earliest historical documents (especially portions of the Book of Judges) the Hebrews are a group of agricultural and pastoral but warlike tribes of Semitic speech, with household Gods and local deities,[1] living among communities at the same or a higher culture stage. Their ancestral legends show similar religious practice. Of the Hebrew tribes, some may have sojourned for a time in Egypt; but this is uncertain, the written record being a late and in large part deliberately fictitious construction. At one time, twelve such tribes appear to have confederated, in conformity with a common ancient superstition, seen in Arab and Greek history as well as in the Jewish, as to the number twelve. As they advanced in civilisation, on a basis of city life existing among a population settled in Canaan before them, parts of which

[1] Jud. xvii, xviii.　　　[2] Gen. xxxi, 19, 34, 35.

they conquered, one of their public cults, that of Yahu or Yahweh, finally fixed at Jerusalem, became politically important. The special worshippers of this God (supposed to have been at first a Thunder-God or Sun-God) were in that sense monotheists; but not otherwise than kindred neighbouring communities such as the Ammonites and Moabites and Edomites, each of which had its special God, like the cities of Babylonia and Egypt. But that the earlier conceptions of the people had assumed a multiplicity of Gods is clear from the fact that even in the later literary efforts to impose the sole cult of Yahweh on the people, the plural name *Elohim*, " Powers " or " Gods " (in general, things to be feared),[1] is retained, either alone or with that of Yahweh prefixed, though cosmology had previously been written in Yahweh's name. The Yahwists did not scruple to combine an Elohistic narrative, varying from theirs in cosmology and otherwise, with their own.[2]

As to the original similarity of Hebraic and other Canaanite religions cp. E. Meyer, *Geschichte des Alterthums*, §§ 309-311 (i, 372-376); Kuenen, i, 223; Wellhausen, *Israel*, p. 440; Réville, *Prolégomènes de l'Histoire des Religions*, 1881, p. 85. " Before being monotheistic, Israel was simply *monolatrous*, and even that only in its religious *élite* " (Réville). " Their [the Canaanites'] worship was the same in principle as that of Israel, but it had a higher organisation " (Menzies, *History of Religion*, p. 179 : Cp. Tiele, *Outlines*, pp. 85-89). On the side of the traditional view, Mr. Lang, while sharply challenging most of the propositions of the higher critics, affirms that "*we know* that Israel had, in an early age, the conception of the

[1] The word is applied to the apparition of Samuel in the story of the Witch of Endor (1 Sam. xxviii, 13).

[2] The unlearned reader may here be reminded that in Gen. i the Hebrew word translated "God" is "Elohim", and that the phrase in Gen. ii rendered "the Lord God" in our versions is in the original "Yahweh-Elohim". The first chapter, with its plural deity, is, however, probably the later as well as the more dignified narrative, and represents the influence of Babylonian quasi-science. See, for a good general account of the case, *The Witness of Assyria*, by C. Edwards, 1893, c. ii. Cp. Wellhausen, *Prolegomena to the History of Israel*, Eng. tr., pp. 296-308; E. J. Fripp, *The Composition of the Book of Genesis*, 1892, *passim;* Driver, *Introd. to the Lit. of the Old Testament*, 1891, pp. 18-19.

moral Eternal; we know that, at an early age, the conception
was contaminated and anthropomorphised; and we know that
it was rescued, in a great degree, from this corruption, while
always retaining its original ethical aspect and sanction"
(*Making of Religion*, p. 295). If " we know " this, the discussion
is at an end. But Mr. Lang's sole documentary basis for the
assertion is just the fabricated record, reluctantly abandoned
by theological scholars as such. When this is challenged,
Mr. Lang falls back on the position that such low races as the
Australians and Fuegians have a "moral Supreme Being",
and that therefore Israel "must" have had one (p. 309). It
will be found however that the ethic of these races is perfectly
primitive, on Mr. Lang's own showing, and that his estimate is
a misinterpretation. As to their Supreme Beings it will suffice
to compare Mr. Lang's *Making of Religion*, cc. ix, xii, with his
earlier *Myth, Ritual, and Religion*, i, 168, 335, ii, 6, etc. He has
now merely added the ambiguous and misleading epithet
" Supreme ", stressing it indefinitely, to the ordinary God-idea
of the lower races. (Cp. Cox, *Mythology of the Aryan Races*, ed.
1882, p. 155; and K. O. Müller, *Introd. to Scientific Mythology*,
Eng. tr., p. 184.)

There being thus no highly imagined "moral Eternal" in
the religion of primitive man, the Hebrews were originally in
the ordinary position. Their early practice of human sacrifice
is implied in the legend of Abraham and Isaac, and in the
story of Jephthah. (Cp. Micah, vi, 7, and Kuenen on the
passage, i, 237.) In their reputed earliest prophetic books we
find them addicted to divination (Hosea, iv, 12; Micah v, 12.
Cp. the prohibition in Lev. xx. 6; also 2 Kings xxiii, 24, and
Isa. iii, 2 : as to the use of the ephod, teraphim, and urim and
thummim, see Kuenen, *Religion of Israel*, Eng. trans. i, 97-100
and to polytheism. (Amos, v. 26, viii, 14; Hosea, i, 13, 17,
etc. Cp. Jud. viii, 27; 1 Sam. vii. 3). These things Mr. Lang
seems to admit (p. 309, *note*) despite his previous claim; but
he builds (p. 332) on the fact that the Hebrews showed little
concern about a future state—that " early Israel, having, so
far as we know, a singular lack of interest in the future of the
soul, was born to give himself up to developing, undisturbed,
the theistic conception, the belief in a righteous Eternal "—
whereas later Greeks and Romans, like Egyptians, were much
concerned about life after death. Mr. Lang's own general
theory would really require that *all* peoples at a certain stage
should act like the Israelites; but he suspends it in the interest
of the orthodox view as to the early Hebrews. At the same
time he fails to explain why the Hebrews failed to adopt the

future-state creed when they were "contaminated"—a pro-
position hardly reconcilable with the sentence just quoted.
The solution, however, is simple. Israel was not at all
"singular" in the matter. The *early* Greeks and Romans (cp.
as to Hades the *Iliad, passim; Odyssey*, B. xi, *passim ;* Tiele,
Outlines, p. 209, as to the myth of Persephone ; and Preller,
Römische Mythologie, ed. Köhler, 1865, S. 452-5 as to the early
Romans) like the early Vedic Aryans (Tiele, *Outlines*, p. 117 ;
Müller, *Anthropol. Relig.*, p. 269), and the early Babylonians and
Assyrians (Meyer, *Geschichte des Alterthums*, i, 181-2 ; Sayce,
Hibbert Lectures, p. 364) took little thought of a future state.
This attitude has again been erroneously regarded (*e.g.* Dickin-
son, *The Greek View of Life*, p. 35) as peculiar to the Greeks.
Mr. Lang's assumption may in fact be overthrown by the single
case of the Phoenicians, who showed no more concern about a
future life than did the Hebrews (see Canon Rawlinson's
History of Phoenicia, 1889, pp. 351-2), but who are not pretended
to have given themselves up much to "developing, undisturbed,
the belief in a righteous Eternal". The truth seems to be
that in all the early progressive and combative civilisations the
main concern was as to the continuance of *this* life. On that
head the Hebrews were as solicitous as any (cp. Kuenen, i,
65) ; and they habitually practised divination on that score.
Further, they attached the very highest importance to the
continuance of the individual in his offspring. The idea of a
future State is first found highly developed in the long-lived
cults of the long-civilised but unprogressive Egyptians ; and
the Babylonians were developing in the same direction. Yet
the Hebrews took it up (see the evidence in Schürer, *Jewish
People in the time of Jesus*, Eng. tr., Div. II, vol. ii, p. 179) just
when, according to Mr. Lang, their cult was "rescued, in a
great degree, from corruption " ; and, generally speaking, it
was in the stage of maximum monotheism that they reached
the maximum of irrationality. For the rest, belief in immortality is found highly developed in a sociologically "degenerate"
or unprogressive people such as the Tasmanians (Müller,
Anthrop. Rel., p. 433), who are yet primitively pure on Mr.
Lang's hypothesis.

This primary polytheism is seen to the full in that
constant resort of Israelites to neighbouring cults, against
which so much of the Hebrew doctrine is directed. To
understand their practice, the modern reader has to get
rid of the hallucination imposed on Christendom by its

idea of revelation. The cult of Yahweh was no primordial Hebrew creed, deserted by backsliding idolators, but a finally successful tyranny of one local cult over others. Therefore, without begging the question as to the moral sincerity of the prophets and others who identified Yahwism with morality, we must always remember that they were on their own showing devotees of a special local worship, and so far fighting for their own influence. Similar prophesying may conceivably have been carried on in connection with the same or other God-names in other localities, and the extant prophets freely testify that they had Yahwistic opponents; but the circumstance that Yahweh was worshipped at Jerusalem without any image might be an important cause of differentiation in the case of that cult. In any case, it must have been through simple " exclusivism " that they reached any form of " monotheism ".[1]

The inveterate usage, in the Bible-making period, of forging and interpolating ancient or pretended writings, makes it impossible to construct any detailed history of the rise of Yahwism. We can but proceed upon data which do not appear to lend themselves to the purposes of the later adaptors. In that way we see cause to believe that at one early centre the so-called ark of Yahweh contained various objects held to have super-natural virtue.[2] In the older historic documents it has, however, no such sacredness as accrues to it later,[3] and no great traditional prestige. This ark, previously moved from place to place as a fetish,[4] is said to have been transferred to Jerusalem by the early King David,[5] whose story, like that of his predecessor Saul and his son Solomon, is in part blended with myth.

As to David, compare 1 Sam. xvi, 18, with xvii, 33, 42. Daoud (= Dodo = Dumzi = Tammuz = Adonis) was a

[1] Cp. Meyer, *Geschichte des Alterthums*, i, 398.
[2] See the myth of the offerings put in it by the Philistines (1 Sam. vi)
[3] 1 Sam. iii, 3.   Cp. ch. ii, 12-22.   Contrast Lev. xvi, 2, ff.
[4] 1 Sam. iv, 3-11.   Cp. v, vii, 2.   [5] 2 Sam., vi.

Semitic deity (Sayce, Hib. Lect., pp. 52-57 and art. *The Names of the first three Kings of Israel*, in *Modern Review*, Jan. 1884) whom David resembles as an inventor of the lyre (Amos, vi, 5; cp. Hitzig, *Die Psalmen*, 2 Theil, 1836, S. 3). But Saul and Solomon also were God-names (Sayce, as cited), as was Samuel (*Id.*, pp. 54, 181; cp. Lenormant, *Chaldean Magic*, Eng. tr., p. 120); and when we note these data, and further the plain fact that Samson is a solar myth, being a personage Evemerised from Samas, the Sun-God, we are prepared to find further traces of Evemeristic redaction in the Hebrew books. To say nothing of other figures in the Book of Judges, we find that Jacob and Joseph were old Canaanitish deities (Sayce, Lectures, p. 51; Records of the Past, New Series, v, 48); and that Moses, as might be expected, was a name for more than one Semitic God (*Id.* Lect., pp. 46-47) and in particular stood for a Sun-God. Abraham, in turn, appears to be an ancient deity (Meyer, *Gesch. des Alt.*, i, 374, § 309). Miriam was probably in similar case. The Arabs even had a tradition (Tabari, ed. Paris, 1867, i, 396, cited by Baring Gould, *Legends of Old Test. Characters*, 1871, ii, 138) that Joshua was the son of Miriam, whence we may almost surmise another reduction of an ancient cult to the form of history, perhaps obscuring the true original of the worship of Mary and Jesus. It seems probable, finally, that such figures as Elijah, who ascends to heaven in a fiery chariot, and Elisha, the "bald head" and miracle-worker, are similar constructions of personages out of Sun-God lore. In such material lies part of the refutation of the thesis of Renan (*Histoire des langues sémitiques*, 2e édit. pp. 7, 485) that the Semites were natural monotheists, devoid of mythology. [Renan is followed in whole or in part by Nöldeke, *Sketches from Eastern History*, Eng. tr., p. 6; Soury, *Religion of Israel*, Eng. tr., pp. 2, 10; Spiegel, *Erânische Alterthumskunde*, i, 389; also Roscher, Draper, Peschel, and Bluntschli, as cited by Goldziher, *Mythology among the Hebrews*, Eng. tr., p. 4, *note*. On the other side compare Goldziher, ch. i; Steinthal's *Prometheus and Samson*, Eng. tr. (with Goldziher) pp. 391, 428, etc., and his *Geschichte der Sprachwissenschaft bei den Griechen und den Römern*, 1863, S. 15-17; Kuenen, *Religion of Israel*, i, 225; Smith, *Rel. of the Semites*, p. 49; Ewald, *History of Israel*, Eng. tr., 4th ed., i, 38-40; Müller, *Nat. Rel.*, p. 314.] Renan's view seems to be generally connected with the assumption that life in a "desert" makes a race for ever unimaginative or unitary in its thought. The *Arabian Nights* might be supposed a sufficient proof to the contrary. The historic truth seems to be that, stage for stage, the ancient Semites were as mythological as any

other race; but that (to say nothing of the Babylonians and
Assyrians) the mythologies of the Hebrews and of the Arabs
were alike suppressed as far as possible in their monotheistic
stage. Compare Renan's own admissions, pp. 27, 110, 475,
and *Histoire du Peuple d'Israël*, i, 49-50.

At other places, however, Yahweh was symbolised and
worshipped in the image of a young bull,[1] a usage associated with the neighbouring Semitic cult of Molech, but
probably indigenous, or at least early, in the case of
Yahweh also. A God, for such worshippers, needed to
be represented by something, if he were to be individualised
as against others ; and where there was not an ark or a
sacred stone or special temple or idol there could be no
cult at all. " The practices of ancient religion require a
fixed meeting place between the worshippers and their
God."[2] The pre-exilic history of Yahweh-worship seems
to be in large part that of a struggle between the
devotees of the imageless worship fixed to the temple at
Jerusalem, and other worships, with or without images,
at other and less influential shrines.

So far as can be gathered from the documents, it was
long before monotheistic pretensions were made in connection with Yahwism. They must in the first instance
have seemed not only tyrannical but blasphemous to the
devotees of the old local shrines, who in the earlier
Hebrew writings figure as perfectly good Yahwists ; and
they clearly had no durable success before the period of
the Exile. Some three hundred years after the supposed
period[3] of David, and again eighty years later, we meet
with ostensible traces[4] of a movement for the special
aggrandisement of the Yahweh cult and the suppression
of the others which competed with it, as well as of certain
licentious and vicious practices carried on in connection
with Yahweh-worship. Concerning these, it could be
claimed by those who had adhered to the simpler tradition

[1] I Kings, xii, 28 ; Hosea viii, 4-6. Cp. Jud. viii, 27; Hosea viii, 5.
[2] Smith, *Religion of the Semites*, p. 196. But see above, p. 50.
[3] 11th cent. B.C.   [4] 2 Kings, xviii, 4, 22 ; xxiii, 48.

of one of the early worships that they were foreign importations.   They were in fact specialities of a rich ancient society, and were either native to Canaanite cities which the Hebrews had captured, or copied by them from such cities.   But the fact that they were thus, on the showing of the later Yahwistic records, long associated with Yahwist practice, proves that there was no special elevation about Yahwism originally.

Even the epithet translated "Holy" *(Kadosh)* had originally no high moral significance. It simply meant "set apart", "not common" (Cp. Kuenen, *Religion of Israel*, i, 43; Wellhausen, *Israel*, in *Prolegomena* vol., p. 499); and the special substantive *(Kadesh* and *Kedeshah)* was actually the name for the most degraded ministrants of both sexes in the licentious worship (see Deut. xxiii, 17, 18, and *marg.* Rev. Vers. Cp. 1 Kings, xiv, 25; xv, 12; 2 Kings, xxiii, 7). On the question of early Hebrew ethics it is somewhat misleading to cite Wellhausen (so Mr. Lang, *Making of Religion*, p. 304) as saying *(Israel*, p. 437) that religion inspired law and morals in Israel with exceptional purity.   In the context Wellhausen has said that the starting-point of Israel was normal; and he writes in the *Prolegomena* (p. 302) that "good and evil in Hebrew mean primarily nothing more than salutary and hurtful: the application of the words to virtue and sin is a secondary one, these being regarded as serviceable or hurtful in their effects".

§ 2.

Given the co-existence of a multitude of local cults, and of various local Yahweh-worships, it is conceivable that the Yahwists of Jerusalem, backed by a priest-ridden king, should seek to limit all worship to their own temple, whose revenues would thereby be much increased.   But insoluble perplexities are set up as to the alleged movement by the incongruities in the documents.   Passing over for the moment the prophets Amos and Hosea and others who ostensibly belong to the eighth century B.C., we find the second priestly reform,[1] consequent on a finding or framing of "the law", represented as occurring

[1] 2 Kings, xxiii.

early in the reign of Josiah (641—610 B.C.). But later in
the same reign are placed the writings of Jeremiah, who
constantly contemns the scribes, prophets and priests in
mass, and makes light of the ark,[1] besides declaring[2] that
in Judah there are as many Gods as towns, and in
Jerusalem as many Baal-altars as streets. The difficulty
is reduced by recognising the quasi-historical narrative as
a later fabrication; but other difficulties remain as to the
prophetic writings; and for our present purpose it is
necessary briefly to consider these.

1. The "higher criticism", seeking solid standing
ground at the beginning of the tangible historic period,
the eighth century, singles out[3] the books of Amos and
Hosea, setting aside, as dubious in date, Nahum and
Joel; and recognising in Isaiah a composite of different
periods. If Amos, the "herdsman of Tekoa", could be
thus regarded as an indubitable historical person, he
would be a remarkable figure in the history of Freethought, as would his nominal contemporary Hosea.
Amos is a monotheist, worshipping not a God of Israel
but a Yahweh or Elohim of Hosts, called also by the
name Adon or Adonai, "the Lord," who rules all the
nations and created the universe. Further, the prophet
makes Yahweh "hate and despise" the feasts and burnt-
offerings and solemn assemblies of his worshippers;[4] and
he meddles impartially with the affairs of the kingdoms
of Judah and Israel. In the same spirit, Hosea menaces
the solemn assemblies, and makes Yahweh desire "mercy
and not sacrifice".[5] Similar doctrine occurs in the
reputedly genuine or ancient parts of Isaiah,[6] and in
Micah.[7] Isaiah too disparages the Sabbath and solemn
meetings, staking all upon righteousness.

2. These utterances, so subversive of the priestly
system, are yet held to have been preserved through the

---

[1] Jer. i, 18; iii, 16; vi, 13; vii, 4-22; viii, 8; xviii, 18; xx, 1, 2; xxiii, 11.
[2] Jer. ii, 28; xi, 13.
[3] So Kuenen, vol. i, App. i to Ch. 1.   [4] Amos v, 21, 22.
[5] Hosea ii, 11; vi, 6.   [6] Isa. i, 11-14.   [7] Mic. vi, 6-8.

ages—through the Assyrian conquest, through the Babylonian Captivity, through the later period of priestly reconstruction—by the priestly system itself. In the state of things pictured under Ezra and Nehemiah, only the zealous adherents of the priestly law can at the outset have had any letters, any literature; it must have been they, then, who treasured the anti-priestly and anti-ritual writings of the prophets—unless indeed the latter were preserved by the Jews remaining at Babylon.

3. The perplexity thus set up is greatly deepened when we remember that the period assigned to the earlier prophets is near the beginning of the known age of alphabetic writing,[1] and before the known age of writing on scrolls. A herdsman of Judea, with a classic and flowing style, is held to have written out his hortatory addresses at a time when such writing is not certainly known to have been practised anywhere else; and the pre-eminent style of Isaiah is held to belong to the same period.

> "His [Amos's] language, with three or four insignificant exceptions, is pure, his style classical and refined. His literary power is shown in the regularity of structure which often characterizes his periods . . . . as well as in the ease with which he evidently writes. . . . . Anything of the nature of roughness or rusticity is wholly absent from his writings" (Driver, *Introd. to Lit. of Old Testament*, c. vi, § 3, p. 297, ed. 1891). Isaiah, again, is in his own narrow field one of the most gifted and skilful writers of all antiquity. The difficulty is thus nearly as great as that of the proposition that the Hebrew of the Pentateuch is a thousand years older than that of the latest prophetical books, whose language is substantially the same. (Cp. Andrews Norton, *The Pentateuch*, ed. 1863, pp. 47-48; Renan, *Histoire des langues sémitiques*, 2e édit., p. 118.)

4. The specialist critics, all trained as clergymen, and

---

[1] Cp. M. Müller, *Natural Religion*, pp. 560-1; *Psychological Religion*, pp. 30-32; Wellhausen, *Israel*, p. 465. If the Moabite Stone be genuine—and it is accepted by Stade (*Geschichte des Volkes Israel*, in Oncken's Series, 1881, i, 86)—the Hebrew alphabetic writing is carried back to the 9th century B.C. An account of the Stone is given in *The Witness of Assyria*, by C. Edwards, ch. xi. See again Mommsen, *History of Rome*, B. i, ch. 14, Eng. tr., 1894, i, 280, for a theory of the extreme antiquity of the alphabet.

loth to yield more than seems absolutely necessary to scepticism, have surrendered the antiquity claimed for Joel, recognising that the arguments for that are "equally consistent with a date *after* the Captivity".[1] One of the conclusions here involved is that "Egypt is probably mentioned only as the *typical instance* of a power hostile to Judah ". Thus, when we remember the later Jewish practice of speaking of Rome as "Babylon ", allusions by Amos and Hosea to "Assyria " have no evidential force. The same reasoning applies to the supposed ancient portions of Isaiah.

5. Even on the clerical side, among the less conservative critics, it is already conceded that there are late "insertions" in Amos. Some of these insertions are among, or analogous to, the very passages relied on by Kuenen to prove the lofty monotheism of Amos. If these passages, however, suggest a late date, no less do the others disparaging sacrifices. The same critics find interpolations and additions in Hosea. But they offer no proof of the antiquity of what they retain.

> The principal passages in Amos given up as insertions by Canon Cheyne are :—iv, 13 ; v, 8-9 ; ix, 5-6 ; and ix, 8-15. See his introduction to 1895 ed. of Prof. Robertson Smith's *Prophets of Israel*, p. xv. Compare Kuenen, i, 46, 48. Dr. Cheyne regards as insertions in Hosea the following ; i, 10-ii, 1 ; "and David their King " in iii, 5 ; viii, 14 ; and xiv, 1-9 (as cited, pp. xviii-xix). Obviously these admissions entail others.

6. The same school of criticism, while adhering to the traditional dating of Amos and Hosea, has surrendered the claim for the Psalms, placing most of these in the same age with the books of Job, Proverbs, Ecclesiastes, and Ecclesiasticus.[2] Now, the sentiment of opposition to burnt-offerings is found in some of the Psalms in

---

[1] Driver, *Introd. to Lit. of Old Testament*, c. vi, § 2 (p. 290, ed. 1891). Cp. Kuenen, *Religion of Israel*, i, 86; and Robertson Smith, art. *Joel*, in *Encyc. Brit.*

[2] Cp. Wellhausen, *Israel*, p. 501 : Driver, c. vii (pp. 352 ff., esp. pp. 355, 361, 362, 365); Stade, *Gesch. des Volkes Israel*, i, 85.

language identical with that of the supposed early prophets.[1] Instead of taking the former for late echoes of the latter, we may reasonably suspect that they belong to the same culture-stage.

> The principle is in effect recognised by Canon Cheyne when he writes : "Just as we infer from the reference to Cyrus in xliv, 28, xlv, 1, that the prophecy containing it proceeds from the age of the conqueror, so we may infer from the fraternal feeling towards Egypt and Assyria (Syria) in xix, 23-25 that the epilogue was written when hopes of the union and fusion of Israelitish and non-Israelitish elements first became natural for the Jews, *i.e.* in the early Greek period " (*Introd. to the Book of Isaiah*, 1895, pp. 109-110).

7. From the scientific point of view, finally, the element of historical prediction in the prophets is one of the strongest grounds for presuming that they are in reality late documents. In regard to similar predictions in the Gospels (Matt. xxiv, 15 ; Mark xiii, 2 ; Luke, xxi, 20) rational criticism decides that they were written after the event. No other course can consistently be taken as to early Hebrew predictions of captivity and restoration ; and the adherence of many Biblical scholars at this point to the traditional view is psychologically on a par with their former refusal to accept a rational estimate of the Pentateuchal narrative.

> On some points, such as the flagrant pseudo-prediction in Isaiah xix, 18, even conservative critics surrender. Thus " König sees rightly that xix, 18 can. only refer to Jewish colonies in Egypt, and *refrains from the arbitrary supposition that Isaiah was supernaturally informed* of the future establishment of such colonies" (Cheyne, Introd. to Smith's *Prophets of Israel*, p. xxxiii). But in other cases Dr. Cheyne's own positions involve such an " arbitrary supposition ", as do Kuenen's; and Smith explicitly posited it as to the prophets in general. And even as to Isaiah xix, 18, whereas Hitzig, as Havet later, rightly brings the date down to the actual historic time of the establishment of the temple at Heliopolis by Onias (Josephus, *Ant.* xiii, 3, 1 ; *Wars* vii, 10, 2), about 160 B.C., Dr. Cheyne (*Introd.*

---

[1] *E.g.*, Ps. l, 8-15 ; li, 16-17, where v. 19 is obviously a priestly addition, meant to countervail vv. 16, 17.

to the Book of Isaiah, p. 108) compromises by dating it about
B.C. 275.

The lateness of the bulk of the prophetical writings has been
ably argued by Ernest Havet (*Le Christianisme et ses Origines*,
vol. iv, 1878, ch. 6; and in the posthumous vol. *La Modernité
des Prophètes*, 1891), who supports his case by many cogent
reasonings. For instance, besides the argument as to
Isa. xix, 18, above noted :—(1) The frequent prediction of the
ruin of Tyre by Nebuchadnezzar (*Isa.*, ch. xxiii; Jer. xxv, 22;
Ezek. xxvi, 7, ch. xxvii), false as to him (a fact which might be
construed as a proof of the fallibility of the prophets and the
candor of their transcribers), is to be understood in the light
of other post-predictions as referring to the actual capture of
the city by Alexander. (2) Hosea's prediction of the fall of
Judah as well of Israel, and of their being united, places the
passage after the exile, and may even be held to bring it down
to the period of the Asmoneans. So with many other details:
the whole argument deserves careful study. M. Havet's views
were of course scouted by the conservative specialists, as their
predecessors scouted the entire hypothesis of Graf, now taken
in its essentials as the basis of sound Biblical criticism. M.
Scherer somewhat unintelligently objected to him (*Etudes sur la
litt. contemp.*, vii, 268) that he was not a Hebraist. There is no
question of philology involved. It was non-Hebraists who first
pointed out the practical incredibility of the central Pentateuchal narrative, on the truth of which Kuenen himself long
stood with other Hebraists. (Cp. Wellhausen, *Prolegomena*,
pp. 39, 347; also his (4th) ed. of Bleek's *Einleitung in das alte
Testament*, 1878, S. 154; and Kuenen, *Hexateuch*, Eng. tr., pp. xv,
43.) Colenso's argument, in the gist of which he was long
preceded by lay Freethinkers, was one of simple common-sense.
The weak side of M. Havet's case is his undertaking to bring
the prophets bodily down to the Maccabean period. This is
claiming too much. But his negative argument is not affected
by the reply (Darmesteter, *Les Prophètes d'Israël*, 1895, pp.
128-131) to his constructive theory.

It is true that where hardly any documentary datum
is intrinsically sure, it is difficult to prove a negative for
one more than for another. The historical narratives
being systematically tampered with by one writer after
another, and even presumptively late writings being interpolated by still later scribes, we can never have demonstrative proof as to the original date of any one prophet.

Thus it is arguable that fragments of utterance from
eighth century prophets may have survived orally and
been made the nucleus of later documents. This view
would be reconcilable with the fact that the prophets
Isaiah, Hosea, Amos, and Micah are all introduced with
some modification of the formula that they prophesied " in
the days of Uzziah, Jotham, Ahaz, and Hezekiah, kings of
Judah," Jeroboam's name being added in the cases of
Hosea and Amos. But that detail is also reconcilable
with absolute fabrication. To say nothing of sheer bad
faith in a community whose moral code said nothing
against fraud save in the form of judicial perjury, the
Hebrew literature is profoundly compromised by the
simple fact that the religious development of the people
made the prestige of antiquity more essential there for
the purposes of propaganda than in almost any other
society known to us. Hence an all-pervading principle
of literary dissimulation ; and what freethinking there was
had in general to wear the guise of the very force of unreasoning traditionalism to which it was inwardly most
opposed. Only thus could new thought find a hearing
and secure its preservation at the hands of the tribe of
formalists. Even the pessimist Koheleth, wearied with
science yet believing nothing of the doctrine of immortality, must needs follow precedent and pose as the
fabulous King Solomon, son of the mythic David.

§ 3.

We are forced, then, to regard with distrust all
passages in the "early" prophets which express either a
disregard of sacrifice and ritual or a universalism incon
gruous with all that we know of the native culture of
their period. The strongest ground for surmising a really
"high" development of monotheism in Judah before the
Captivity is the stability of the life there as compared
with northern Israel.[1] In this respect the conditions

[1] Cp Kuenen, i, 156; Wellhausen, *Prolegomena*, p. 139; *Israel*, p. 478.

might indeed be considered favorable to priestly or other culture ; but, on the other hand, the records themselves exhibit a predominant polytheism. The presumption then is strong that the "advanced" passages in the prophets concerning sacrifice belong to an age when such ideas had been reached in more civilised nations, with whose thought travelled Jews could come in contact.

It is true that some such ideas were current in Egypt many centuries before the period under notice—a fact which alone discounts the ethical originality claimed for the Hebrew prophets. *E.g.*, the following passage from the papyrus of Ani, belonging to the Nineteenth Dynasty, not later than 1288 B.C.:— " That which is detestable in the sanctuary of God is noisy feasts ; if thou implore him with a loving heart of which all the words are mysterious, he will do thy matters, he hears thy words, he accepts thine offerings " (*Religion and Conscience in Ancient Egypt*, by W. M. Flinders Petrie, 1898, p. 160). The word " mysterious " here may mean " solemn " or " liturgical ", or may merely prescribe privacy. But in any case we must look for later culture-contacts as the source of the later Hebrew radicalism under notice, though Egyptian sources are not to be wholly set aside. See Kuenen, i, 395 ; and Brugsch, as there cited ; but cp. Wellhausen, *Israel*, p. 440.

It is clear that not only did they accept a cosmogony from the Babylonians, but they were influenced by the lore of the Zoroastrian Persians, with whom, as with the monotheists or pantheists of Babylon, they would have grounds of sympathy. It is an open question whether their special hostility to images does not date from the time of Persian contact.[1] Concerning the restoration, the later critical view is that only a few Jewish exiles returned to Jerusalem " both under Cyrus and under Darius " ; and that, though the temple was rebuilt under Darius Hystaspis, the builders were not the *Gola* or returned exiles, but that part of the Judahite population which had

---

[1] As to a possible prehistoric connection of Hebrews and Perso-Aryans, see Kuenen, i, 254, discussing Tiele and Spiegel, and iii, 35, 44, treating of Tiele's view, set forth in his *Godsdienst van Zarathustra*, that fire-worship was the original basis of Yahwism. Cp. Land's view, discussed p. 398 ; and Renan, *Hist. des langues sémit.*, p. 473.

not been deported to Babylon.[1] Thus the separatist spirit of the narratives of Ezra and Nehemiah (which in any case tell of an opposite spirit) is not to be taken as a decisive clue to the character of the new religion. For the rest, the many Jews who remained in Babylon or spread elsewhere in the Persian empire, and who developed their creed on a non-local basis, were bound to be in some way affected by the surrounding theology. And it is tolerably certain not only that was the notion of angels derived by the Jews from either the Babylonians or the Persians, but that their rigid Sabbath and their weekly synagogue meetings came from one or both of these sources.

That the Sabbath was an Akkado-Babylonian and Assyrian institution is now well established (G. Smith, *Assyrian Eponym Canon*, 1875, p. 20; Sayce, Hibbert Lectures, p. 76, and in Variorum Teacher's Bible, ed. 1885, *Aids*, p. 71). It was before the fact was ascertained that Kuenen wrote of the Sabbath (i, 245) as peculiar to Israel. The Hebrews may have had it before the Exile; but it was clearly not then a great institution; and the mention of Sabbaths in Amos (viii, 5) and Isaiah (i, 13) is one of the reasons for doubting the antiquity of those books. The custom of synagogue meetings on the Sabbath is post-exilic, and may have arisen either in Babylon itself (so Wellhausen, *Israel*, p. 492) or in imitation of Parsee practice (so Tiele, cited by Kuenen, iii, 35). The same alternative arises with regard to the belief in angels, usually regarded as certainly Persian in origin (cp. Kuenen, iii. 37; Tiele, *Outlines*, p. 90; and Sack, *Die altjüdische Religion*, 1889, S. 133). This also could have been Babylonian (Sayce, in Var. Bible, as cited, p. 71); even the demon Asmodeus in the Book of Tobit, usually taken as Persian, being of Babylonian derivation (*id.*). Cp. Darmesteter's introd. to *Zendavesta*, 2nd ed., ch. v. On the other hand, the conception of Satan, the Adversary, as seen in 1 Chr. xxi, 1; Zech. iii, 1, 2, seems to come from the Persian Ahriman, though the Satan of Job has not Ahriman's status. Such a modification would come of the wish to insist on the supremacy of the good God. And this quasi-monotheistic view, again, we are led to regard, in the case of the prophets, as a possible Babylonian derivation, or at least as a

---

[1] Cheyne, *Introd. to Isaiah*, Prol. pp. xxx, xxxviii, following Kosters.

result of the contact of Yahwists with Babylonian culture. To
a foreign influence, finally, must be definitely attributed the
later Priestly Code, over-ruling Deuteronomy, lowering the
Levites, setting up a high priest, calling the dues into the
sanctuary, resting on the Torah the cultus which before was
rested on the patriarchs, and providing cities and land for the
Aaronidae and the Levites (Wellhausen, *Prolegomena*, pp. 123,
127, 147, 149, 347; *Israel*, pp. 495, 497)—the latter an arrangement impossible in mountainous Palestine, as regards the
land-measurements (*Id. Proleg.* p. 159, following Gramberg and
Graf), and clearly deriving from some such country as Babylonia or Persia. As to the high-priest principle in Babylon
and Assyria, see Sayce, Hibbert Lectures, pp. 59-61.

Of the general effect of such contacts we have clear
trace in two of the most remarkable of the later books of
the Old Testament, Job and Ecclesiastes, both of which
clearly belong to a late period in religious development.
The majority of the critics still confidently describe Job
as an original Hebrew work, mainly on the ground,
apparently, that it shows no clear marks of translation,
though its names and its local color are all non-Jewish.
In any case it represents, for its time, a cosmopolitan
culture, and contains the work of more than one hand.

Compare Cheyne, *Job and Solomon*, 1887, p. 72; Bradley,
Lectures on the Book of Job, p. 171; Bleek-Wellhausen, *Einleitung*,
§ 268 (291), ed. 1878, S. 542; Driver, *Introduction*, p. 405-8.
Renan's dating of the book six or seven centuries before Ecclesiastes (*L'Ecclésiaste*, p. 26; *Job*, pp. xv-xliii) is oddly uncritical.
Dr. Cheyne notes that in the sceptical passages the name
Yahweh is very seldom used (only once or twice, as in xii, 9;
xxviii, 28); and Dr. Driver admits that the whole book not only
abounds in Aramaic words, but has a good many "explicable
only from the Arabic". Other details in the book suggest the
possible culture-influence of the Himyarite Arabs, who had
reached a high civilisation before 500 B.C. Dr. Driver's remark
that "the thoughts are thoroughly Hebraic" burkes the entire
problem as to the manifest innovation the book makes in
Hebrew thought and literary method alike. Cp. Renan, *Job*,
1859, p. xxv, where the newness of the whole treatment is
admitted.

What marks off the book of Job from all other Hebrew

literature is its dramatic and reflective handling of the ethical problem of theism, which the prophets either evade or dismiss by declamation against Jewish sins. Not that it is solved in Job, where the rôle of Satan is an inconclusive resort to the Persian dualistic solution, and where the Deity is finally made to answer Job's freethinking by sheer literary thunder, much less ratiocinative though far more artistic than the theistic speeches of the friends. But at least the writer or writers of Job's speeches consciously grasped the issue ; and the writer of the epilogue evidently felt that the least Yahweh could do was to compensate a man whom he had allowed to be wantonly persecuted. The various efforts of ancient thought to solve the same problem will be found to constitute the motive power in many later heterodox systems, theistic and atheistic.

In certain aspects the Book of Job speaks for a further reach of early freethinking than is seen in Ecclesiastes (Koheleth), which unquestionably derives from late foreign influence. By an increasing number of students, though not yet by common critical consent, it is dated about 200 B.C., when Greek influence was stronger in Jewry than at any previous time.

> Grätz even puts it as late as the time of Herod the Great. But compare Tyler, *Ecclesiastes*, 1874, p. 31; Plumptre's *Ecclesiastes*, 1881, introd., p. 34; Renan, *L'Ecclésiaste*, 1882, pp. 54-59; Kuenen, *Religion of Israel*, iii, 82 : Driver, *Introduction*, pp. 446-7; Bleek-Wellhausen, *Einleitung*, S. 527. Cheyne, and some others, still put the date before 332 B.C.

But the thought of the book is, as Renan says, profoundly fatigued; and the sombre avowals of the absence of divine moral government are balanced by sayings, probably interpolated by other hands, averring an ultimate rectification even on earth. What remains unqualified is the deliberate rejection of the belief in a future life, .couched in terms that imply the currency of the doctrine; [1]

---

[1] Eccles. iii, 19-21.

and the deliberate caution against enthusiasm in religion.
Belief in a powerful but remote Deity, with a minimum of
worship and vows, is the outstanding lesson.[1]

That there was a good deal of this species of tired or
stoical semi-rationalism among the Jews of the Hellenistic
period may be inferred from various traces.   It is told in
the Talmud that in the Maccabean period there came
into use the formula, " Cursed be the man that cherisheth
swine ; and cursed be the man that teacheth his son the
wisdom of the Greeks"; and there is preserved the saying
of Rabbi Simeon, son of Gamaliel, that in his father's
school five hundred learnt the law, and five hundred the
wisdom of the Greeks.[2]   Before Gamaliel, the Greek
influence had affected Jewish philosophic thought ; and it
is very probable that among the Sadducees who resisted
the doctrine of resurrection there were some thinkers of
the Epicurean school.   But of Greek or other atheism
there is no direct trace in the Hebrew literature ;[3] and
the rationalism of the Sadducees, who were substantially
the priestly party,[4] was like the rationalism of the
Brahmans and the Egyptian priests—something esoteric
and withheld from the multitude.   In the apocryphal
Wisdom of Solomon, which belongs to the 1st century A.C.,
the denial of immortality, so explicit in Ecclesiastes, is
treated as a proof of utter immorality, though the deniers
are not represented as atheists.[5]   They thus seem to have
been still numerous, and the imputation of wholesale
immorality to them is of course not to be credited ;[6] but

---

[1] Ch. v.   Renan's translation lends lucidity.
[2] Biscoe, *History of the Acts of the Apostles*, ed. 1829, p. 80, following
Selden and Lightfoot.
[3] The familiar phrase in the Psalms (xiv, i ; liii, 1), " The fool hath said
in his heart, there is no God," supposing it to be evidence for anything,
clearly does not refer to any reasoned unbelief.   Atheism could not well
be quite so general as the phrase, taken literally, would imply.
[4] Cp. W. R. Sorley, *Jewish Christians and Judaism*, 1881, p. 9 : Robertson
Smith, *Old Testament in the Jewish Church*, ed. 1892, pp. 48-49.   These writers
somewhat exaggerate the novelty of the view they accept.   Cp. Biscoe,
On the Acts, ed. 1829, p. 101.
[5] *Wisdom*, c. 2.
[6] Cp. the implications in *Ecclesiasticus* vi, 4-6, xvi, 11-12, as to the ethics
of many believers.

there is no trace of any constructive teaching on their part.

So far as the literature shows, save for the confused Judaic-Platonism of Philo of Alexandria, there is practically no rational progress in Jewish thought after Koheleth till the time of contact with revived Greek thought in Saracen Spain. The mass of the people, in the usual way, are found gravitating to the fanatical and the superstitious levels of the current creed. The book of Ruth, written to resist the separatism of the post-exilic theocracy,[1] never altered the Jewish practice, though allowed into the canon. The remarkable Levitical legislation providing for the periodical restoration of the land to the poor never came into operation,[2] any more than the very different provision giving land and cities to the children of Aaron and the Levites. None of the more rationalistic writings in the canon seems ever to have counted for much in the national life. To conceive of "Israel", in the fashion still prevalent, as being typified in the monotheistic prophets, whatever their date, is as complete a misconception as it would be to see in Mr. Ruskin the expression of the every-day ethic of commercial England. The anti-sacrificial and universalist teachings in the prophets and in the Psalms never affected, for the people at large, the sacrificial and localised worship at Jerusalem ; though they may have been esoterically received by some of the priestly or learned class there, and though they may have promoted a continual exodus of the less fanatical types, who turned to other civilisations. Despite the resistance of the Sadducees and the teaching of Job and Ecclesiastes, the belief in a resurrection rapidly gained ground[3] in the two or three centuries before the rise of Jesuism, and furnished a basis for the new creed ; as did the Messianic hope and the belief in a speedy

---

[1] Kuenen, ii, 242-3.
[2] Kalisch, Comm. on *Leviticus* xxv, 8, Eng. tr., Pt. ii, p. 548.
[3] In the *Wisdom of Solomon*, iii, 13, iv, 1, the old desire for offspring is seen to be in part superseded by the newer belief in personal immortality.

ending of the world, with both of which Jewish fanaticism sustained itself under the long frustration of nationalistic faith before the Maccabean interlude and after the Roman conquest. With the major hallucination thus in full possession, the subordinate species of superstition flourished as in Egypt and India; so that at the beginning of our era the Jews were among the most superstitious peoples in the world.[1] When their monotheism was fully established, and placed on an abstract footing by the destruction of the temple, it seems to have had no bettering influence on the practical ethics of the Gentiles, though it may have furthered the theistic tendency of the Stoic philosophy. Juvenal exhibits to us the Jew proselyte at Rome as refusing to show an unbeliever the way, or guide him to a spring.[2] Sectarian monotheism was thus in part on a rather lower ethical and intellectual[3] plane than the polytheism, to say nothing of the Epicureanism or the Stoicism, of the society of the Roman Empire.

It cannot even be said that the learned Rabbinical class carried on a philosophic tradition while the indigent multitude thus discredited their creed. In the period after the fall of Jerusalem, the narrow nationalism which had always ruled there seems to have been even intensified. In the Talmud "the most general representation of the Divine Being is as the chief Rabbi of Heaven; the angelic host being his assessors. The heavenly Sanhedrim takes the opinion of living sages in cases of dispute. Of the twelve hours of the day, three are spent by God in study, three in the government of the world (or rather in the exercise of mercy), three in providing food for the world, and three in playing with Leviathan. But since the destruction of Jerusalem, all amusements were banished from the courts of heaven, and three hours were employed

---

[1] See *Supernatural Religion*, 6th ed., i, 97-100, 103-121 ; Mosheim, *Commentaries on Christian Affairs before Constantine*, Vidal's trans., i, 70 ; Schürer, *Jewish People in the Time of Jesus*, Eng. tr., Div. II, Vol. iii, p. 152.
[2] Sat. xvi, 96-106.   [3] Cp. Horace, I Sat. v, 100.

in the instruction of those who had died in infancy."[1] So little can a nominal monotheism avail, on the basis of a completed Sacred Book, to keep thought sane when freethought is lacking.

[1]Rev. A. Edersheim, *History of the Jewish Nation after the Destruction of Jerusalem*, 1856, p. 462, citing the *Avoda Sara*, a treatise directed against idolatry! Other Rabbinical views cited by Dr. Edersheim as being in comparison "sublime" are no great improvement on the above—*e.g.*, the conception of deity as "the prototype of the high-priest, and the king of kings" "who created everything for his own glory". With all this in view, Dr. Edersheim thought it showed "spiritual decadence" in Philo Judæus to speak of Persian magi and Indian gymnosophists in the same laudatory tone as he used of the Essenes, and to attend "heathenish theatrical representations" (p. 372).

CHAPTER V.

FREETHOUGHT IN GREECE.

THE highest of all the ancient civilisations, that of Greece, was naturally the product of the greatest possible complex of culture-forces;[1] and its rise to pre-eminence begins after the contact of the Greek settlers in Æolia and Ionia with the higher civilisations of Asia Minor. The great Homeric epos itself stands for the special conditions of Æolic and Ionic life in those colonies;[2] even Greek religion, spontaneous as were its earlier growths, was soon influenced by those of the East;[3] and Greek philosophy and art alike draw their first inspirations from Eastern contact.[4] Whatever reactions we may make against the tradition of Oriental origins,[5] it is clear that the higher civilisation of antiquity had Oriental (including in that term Egyptian) roots. It matters not whether we hold the Phrygians and Karians of history to have been originally an Aryan stock, related to the Hellenes, and thus to have acted as intermediaries between Aryans and Semites, or to have been originally Semites, with whom Greeks intermingled.[6] On either view, the intermediaries represented Semitic influences, which they passed on to the Greek-speaking race.

A Hellenistic enthusiasm has led a series of eminent

---

[1] Cp. Tiele, *Outlines*, pp. 205, 207, 212.
[2] Cp. K. O. Müller, *Literature of Ancient Greece*, ed. 1847, p. 77.
[3] Duncker, *Geschichte des Alterthums*, 2 Aufl. iii, 209-210, 252-4, 319 ff.
[4] E. Curtius, *Griechische Geschichte*, 1858, i, 28, 29, 35, 40, 41, 101, 203, etc.
[5] See the able and learned essay of M. Reinach, *Le Mirage Orientale*, reprinted from *L'Anthropologie*, 1893. I do not find that its arguments affect any of the positions here taken up. See pp. 40-41.
[6] Cp. K. O. Müller, *History of the Doric Race*, Eng. tr., 1830, i, 8-10, Busolt, *Griechische Geschichte*, 1885, i, 33 ; Grote, *History of Greece*, 10-vol. ed., 1888, iii, 3-5, 35-44; Duncker, iii, 136, *n.*; E. Meyer, *Geschichte des Alterthums*, i, 299-310 (§§ 250-258) ; E. Curtius, i, 29.

scholars to carry so far their resistance to the tradition of Oriental beginnings as to take up the position that Greek thought is "autochthonous."[1] If it were, it could not conceivably have progressed as it did. Only the tenacious psychological prejudice as to race-characters and racial "genius" could so long detain so many students at a point of view so much more nearly related to super-naturalism than to science. It is safe to say that if any people is ever seen to progress in thought, art, and life, with measurable rapidity, its progress is due to the reactions of foreign intercourse. The primary civilisa-tions, or what pass for such, as those of Akkad and Egypt, are immeasurably slow in accumulating culture-material; the relatively rapid developments always involve the stimulus of old cultures upon a new and vigorous civilisa-tion, well-placed for social evolution for the time being. There is no point in early Greek evolution, so far as we have documentary trace of it, at which foreign impact or stimulus is not either patent or inferrible.[2] In the very dawn of history, the Greeks are found to be a composite stock, growing still more composite; and the very begin-nings of its higher culture are traced to the non-Grecian people of Thrace,[3] who worshipped the Muses. The later supremacy of the Greek culture is thus to be explained in terms not of an abnormal "Greek genius", but of the special evolution of intelligence in the Greek-speaking stock, firstly through constant crossing with others, and secondarily through its furtherance by the

---

[1] Cp. on one side, Ritter, *History of Ancient Philosophy*, Eng. tr., i, 151; Zeller, *History of Greek Philosophy*, Eng. tr., 1881, i, 43-49; and on the other Ueberweg, *Hist. of Philos.*, Eng. tr., i, 31, and the weighty criticism of Lange, *History of Materialism*, Eng. tr., i, 9, *note* 5.

[2] Cp. Curtius, i, 125.

[3] As to the primary mixture of "Pelasgians" and Hellenes, cp. Busolt, 1, 27-32; Curtius, i, 27; Thirlwall, *History of Greece*, ed. 1839, i, 51-2, 116. K. O. Müller (*Doric Race*, Eng. tr., i, 10) and Thirlwall, who follows him (i, 45-47) decide that the Thracians cannot have been very different from the Hellenes in dialect, else they could not have influenced the latter as they did. This position is clearly untenable, whatever may have been the ethnological facts. It would entirely negate the possibility of reaction between Greeks, Kelts, Egyptians, Semites, Romans, Persians, and Hindus

special social conditions of the more progressive Greek
city-states, of which conditions the most important were
their geographical dividedness, and their own consequent
competition and interaction.

§ 1.

By the tacit admission of one of the ablest opponents
of the theory of foreign influence, Hellenic religion as
fixed by Homer for the Hellenic world was partly determined by Asiatic influences.   Ottfried Müller decided not
only that Homer the man (in whose personality he
believed) was probably a Smyrnean, whether of Æolic or
Ionic stock,[1] but that Homer's religion must have represented a special selection from the manifold Greek
mythology, necessarily representing his local bias.[2]   Now,
the Greek cults at Smyrna, as in the other Æolic and
Ionic cities of Asia Minor, would be very likely to reflect
in some degree the influence of the Karian or other Asiatic
cults around them.[3]   The early Attic conquerors of Miletos
allowed the worship of the Karian Sun-God there to be
carried on by the old priests ; and the Attic settlers of
Ephesos in the same way adopted the neighbouring
worship of the Lydian Goddess (who became the Artemis
or " Great Diana " of the Ephesians), and retained the
ministry of the attendant priests and eunuchs.[4]   Smyrna
was apparently not like these a mixed community, but
one founded by Achaians from the Peloponnesos ; but the
general Ionic and Æolic religious atmosphere, set up by
common sacrifices,[5] must have been represented in an
epic brought forth in that region.   The Karian civilisation

[1] *Lit. of Anc. Greece*, pp. 41-47.
[2] *Introduction to Scientific Mythology*, Eng. tr., pp. 180, 181, 291.   Cp.
Curtius, i, 126.
[3] Cp. Curtius, i, 107, as to the absence in Homer of any distinction
between Greeks and barbarians; and Grote, 10-vol. ed., 1888, iii, 37-8, as
to the same feature in Archilochos.
[4] Duncker, *Gesch. des Alt.* as cited, iii, 209-210; S. 257, 319 ff.   Cp. K. O.
Müller, as last cited, pp. 181, 193; Curtius, i, 43-49, 53, 54, 107, 365, 373,
377, etc. ; and Grote, iii, 39-41.
[5] Duncker, iii, 214; Curtius, i, 155, 121; Grote, iii, 279-280.

had at one time spread over a great part of the Ægean, including Delos and Cyprus.[1] Such a civilisation must have affected that of the Greek conquerors, who only on that basis became civilised traders.[2]

It is not necessary to ask how far exactly the influence may have gone in the Iliad : the main point is that even at that stage of comparatively naïf Hellenism the Asiatic environment, Karian or Phoenician, counted for something, whether in cosmogony or in furthering the process of God-grouping, or in conveying the cult of Cyprian Aphrodite,[3] or haply in lending some characteristics to Zeus and Apollo and Athene,[4] an influence none the less real because the genius of the poet or poets of the Iliad has given to the whole Olympian group the artistic stamp of individuality which thenceforth distinguishes the Gods of Greece from all others. But soon the Asiatic influence becomes clearly recognisable. There is reason to hold with Schrader that the belief in a blissful future state, as seen even in the Odyssey[5] and in Hesiod, is "a new belief which is only to be understood in view of oriental tales and teaching".[6] In Hesiod, again, the Semitic element increases,[7] Kronos for instance being a Semitic figure; while Semelê, if not Dionysos, appears to be no less so.[8] But we may further surmise that in Homer, to begin with, the conception of Okeanos, the earth-sur-

---

[1] Busolt, *Griechische Geschichte*, 1885, i, 171-2. Cp. S. 32-34; and Curtius, i, 42.

[2] On the general question cp. Gruppe, *Die griechische Culte und Mythen*, S. 151 ff., 157, 158 ff., 656 ff., 672 ff.

[3] Preller, *Griechische Mythologie*, 2 Aufl. i, 260 ; Tiele, *Outlines*, p. 211 ; R. Brown, Jr., *Semitic Influence in Hellenic Mythology*, 1898, p. 130.

[4] See Tiele, *Outlines*, pp. 210, 212. Cp., again, Curtius, *Griechische Geschichte*, i, 95, as to the probability that the "twelve Gods" were adjusted to the confederations of twelve cities, and again S. 126.

[5] iv, 561 ff.

[6] *Prehistoric Antiquities of the Aryan Peoples*, Eng. tr., p. 423. Williamowitz holds that the verses *Od.* xi, 566-631 are interpolations made later than 600 B.C.

[7] Tiele, *Outlines*, p. 209 ; Preller, S. 263.

[8] Sayce, Hibbert Lectures, pp. 54, 181. Cp. Cox, *Mythology of the Aryan Nations*, p. 260, *note*. It has not however been noted in the discussions on Semelê that *Semlje* is the Slavic name for the Earth as Goddess. Ranke, *History of Servia*, Eng. tr., p. 43.

rounding Ocean-stream, as the origin of all things[1] comes from some Semitic source; and that Hesiod's more complicated scheme of origins from Chaos is a further borrowing of Oriental thought—both notions being found in ancient Babylonian lore, whence the Hebrews derived their combination of Chaos and Ocean in the first verses of Genesis.[2] It thus appears that the earliest Oriental[3] influence upon Greek thought was in the direction of developing religion, with only the germ of rationalism conveyed in the idea of an existence of matter before the Gods, which we shall later find scientifically developed.

§ 2.

In the Iliad there is no thought of the possibility of religious scepticism, though the Gods are so wholly in the likeness of men that the lower deities fight with heroes and are worsted. In the Odyssey there is a bare hint of possible speculation in the use of the word *atheos;* but it is applied only in the phrase οὐκ ἀθεεί, "not without a God",[4] in the sense of similar expressions in other passages and in the Iliad.[5] The idea was that sometimes the Gods directly meddled. When Odysseus accuses the suitors of not dreading the Gods,[6] he has no thought of accusing them of unbelief.[7] Homer has indeed been supposed to have exercised a measure of relative free-thought in excluding from his song the more offensive

---

[1] *Iliad*, xiv, 201, 302.

[2] Sayce, Hibbert Lectures, p. 367 ff.; *Ancient Empires*, p. 158. Note p. 387 in the Lectures as to the Assyrian influence, and p. 391 as to the Homeric notion in particular.

[3] It is unnecessary to examine here the view of Herodotos that many of the Greek cults were borrowed from Egypt. Herodotos reasoned from analogies, with no exact historical knowledge.

[4] *Od*. xviii, 352.   [5] *Od*. vi, 240; *Il*. v., 185.   [6] *Od*. xxii, 39.

[7] In *Od*. xiv, 18, αντίθεοι means not "opposed to the Gods" but "god-like", in the ordinary Homeric sense of noble-looking or richly attired. Cp. vi, 241. Yet a Scholiast on the former passage took it in the sense of God-opposing. Clarke's ed. *in loc.* Liddell and Scott give no use of ἄθεος, in the sense of denying the Gods, before Plato (*Apol.* 26 C, etc.), or in the sense of ungodly before Pindar (P. iv, 288) and Æschylus (*Eumen.* 151).

myths about the Gods,[1] but such exclusion may be sufficiently explained on the score that the epopees were chanted in aristocratic dwellings, before womenkind, without surmising any process of doubt on the poet's part.

It is in Pindar (B.C. 518-442) that we first find such a mental process avowed by a believer. In his first Olympic Ode he plainly declares the need for bringing afterthought to bear on poetic lore, that so men may speak nought unfitting of the Gods; and he protests that he will never tell the tale of the blessed ones banqueting on human flesh.[2] In the ninth Ode he again protests that his lips must not speak blasphemously of such a thing as strife among the immortals.[3] Here the critical motive is ethical, though while repudiating one kind of scandal about the Gods, Pindar placidly accepts others no less startling to the modern sense. For such a development we are not of course forced to assume a foreign influence : mere progress in refinement and in mental activity could bring it about; yet none the less it is probable that foreign influence did quicken the process. The period of Pindar and Æschylus follows on one in which Greek thought, stimulated on all sides, had taken the first great stride in its advance beyond all antiquity. Egypt had been fully thrown open to the Greeks in the reign of Psammetichus[4] (B.C. 650); and a great historian who contends that the " sheer inherent and expansive force " of " the " Greek intellect, " aided but by no means either impressed or provoked from without," was the true cause, yet concedes that inter-

---

[1] Lang, *Myth, Ritual, and Religion*, i, 11. E. Curtius (*G. G.* i, 126) goes so far as to ascribe a certain irony to the portraiture of the Gods (Ionian Apollo excepted) in Homer, and to trace this to Ionian levity. To the same cause he assigns the lack of any expression of a sense of stigma attaching to murder. This sense he holds the Greek people had, though Homer does not hint it. Cp. Grote (i, 24), whose inference Curtius implicitly impugns.

[2] Ol. i, 42-57, 80-85.   [3] Ol. ix, 54-61.

[4] A ruler of Libyan stock, and so led by old Libyan connections to make friends with Greeks. He reigned over fifty years, and the Greek connection grew very close. Curtius i, 344-5. Cp. Grote, i, 144-155.

course with Egypt " enlarged the range of their thoughts
and observations, while it also imparted to them that
vein of mysticism which overgrew the primitive simplicity
of the Homeric religion," and that from Asia Minor in
turn they had derived " musical instruments and new
laws of rhythm and melody ", as well as " violent and
maddening religious rites ".[1] And others making similar
a priori claims for the Greek intelligence are forced
likewise to admit that the mental transition between
Homer and Herodotos cannot be explained save in terms
of " the influence of other creeds, and the necessary
operation of altered circumstances and relations ".[2] In
the *Persae* of Æschylus we even catch a glimpse of direct
contact with foreign scepticism,[3] though in the poet's
own thought there has occurred only an ethical judgment
of the older creeds, and a growth of pessimism[4] that
hints of their final insufficiency.   But these developments
in Æschylus and Pindar had been preceded by the great
florescence of early Ionian philosophy in the sixth
century, a growth which constrains us to look for the
effective fructification of the Greek inner life rather in
Asia Minor than in Egypt.

§ 3.

The Greeks varied from the general type of culture-
evolution seen in India, Persia, Egypt, and Babylon, and
approximated somewhat to that of ancient China, in that
their higher thinking was done not by an order of priests,
pledged to cults, but by independent laymen.   In Greece
as in China this line of development is to be understood
as a result of early political conditions—in China, those
of a multiplicity of independent feudal States; in Greece,

---

[1] Grote, 10-vol. ed., 1888, i, 307, 326, 329, 413.   Cp. i, 27-30; ii, 52;
iii, 39-41, etc.
[2] K. O. Müller, *Introd. to Mythology*, p. 192.
[3] " Then one [of the Persians] who before had in nowise believed in
[*or*, recognised the existence of] the Gods, offered prayer and supplication,
doing obeisance to Earth and Heaven " (*Persae*, 497-9).
[4] *Prometheus*, 247-251.

those of a multiplicity of City-States, set up first by the geographical structure of Hellas, and reproduced in the colonies of Asia Minor and Magna Graecia by reason of the acquired ideal and the normal state of commercial competition. Such conditions prevented the growth of a priestly caste or organisation.[1] Neither China nor Pagan Greece was imperialised till there had arisen enough of rationalism to prevent the rise of a powerful priesthood; and the later growth of a priestly system in Greece in the Christian period is to be explained in terms first of a positive social degeneration, accompanying a complete transmutation of political life, and secondly of the imposition of a new cult, on the popular plane, specially organised on the model of the political system that adopted it. Under imperialism, however, the two civilisations ultimately presented a singular parallel of unprogressiveness.

In the great progressive period, the possible gains from the absence of a priesthood are seen in course of realisation. For the Greek-speaking world in general there was no dogmatic body of teaching, no written code of theology and moral law, no Sacred Book.[2] Each local cult had its own ancient ritual, often ministered by priestesses, with myths, often of late invention, to explain it; only Homer and Hesiod, with perhaps some of the now lost epics, serving as a general treasury of myth-lore. The two great epopees ascribed to Homer, indeed, had a certain Biblical status; and the Homerids or other bards who recited them did what in them lay to make the old poetry the standard of theological opinion; but they too lacked organised influence, and could not hinder higher thinking. The special priesthood of Delphi, wielding the oracle, could maintain their political influence only by holding their function above all apparent self-seeking or effort at domination. It only needed, then, such civic

---

[1] As to ancient beginnings of such an organisation, see E. Curtius, i, 92-94, 97.
[2] K. O. Müller, *Introd. to Mythology*, pp. 188-192, 195; Curtius, i, 384 387, 389; Duncker, iii, 340, 519-521, 563; Thirlwall, i, 200-204.

conditions as should evolve a leisured class, with a lead
towards study, to make possible a growth of lay philosophy.
Those conditions first arose in the Ionian cities;
because there first did Greek citizens attain commercial
wealth,[1] in virtue of adopting the older commercial civilisation whose independent cities they conquered, and of
the greater rapidity of development which belongs to
colonies in general.[2] There it was that, in matters of
religion and philosophy, the comparison of their own
cults with those of their foreign neighbours first provoked
their critical reflection, as the age of primitive warfare
passed away. And there it was, accordingly, that on a
basis of primitive Babylonian science there originated
with Thales of Miletos, a Phoenician by descent,[3] the
higher science and philosophy of the Greek-speaking race.

It is historically certain that Lydia had an ancient and
close historical connection with Babylonian and Assyrian
civilisation, whether through the "Hittites" or otherwise
(Sayce, *Ancient Empires of the East*, 1884, pp. 217-229; Curtius,
Griechische Geschichte, i, 63, 207; Meyer, *Geschichte des Alterthums*, i, 166, 277, 299, 305-310, Soury; *Bréviaire de l'histoire du
matérialisme*, 1881, pp. 30, 37 ff. Cp. as to Armenia, Edwards,
The Witness of Assyria, 1893, p. 144); and in the seventh
century the commercial connection between Lydia and Ionia,
long close, was presumably friendly up to the time of the first
attacks of the Lydian Kings, and even afterwards (Herodotos,
i, 20-23), Alyattes having made a treaty of peace with Miletos,
which thereafter had peace during his long reign. This brings
us to the time of Thales (640-548 B.C.) At the same time, the
Ionian settlers of Miletos had from the first a close connection
with the Karians (Herod. 1, 146, and above, p. 93), whose
near affinity with the Semites, at least in religion, is seen in
their practice of cutting their foreheads at festivals (*Id*. ii, 61 ;.
cp. Grote, ed. 1888, 1, 27, *note*; E. Curtius, i, 36, 42 ; Busolt, i,
33 ; and Spiegel, *Eranische Alterthumskunde*, i, 228). Thales
was thus in the direct sphere of Babylonian culture before the
conquest of Cyrus; and his Milesian pupils or successors,
Anaximandros and Anaximenes, stand for the same influences.
Herakleitos in turn was of Ephesus, an Ionian city in the same

---

[1] Curtius, i, 112.
[2] *Id*. i, 201, 204, 205, 381 ; Grote, iii, 5 ; Lange, *Hist. of Materialism*, i, 33.
[3] Herodotos, i, 170 ; Diogenes Laërtius, *Thales*, c. i.

culture-sphere; Anaxagoras was of Klazomenai, another Ionian city, as had been Hermotimos, of the same philosophic school; the Eleatic school, founded by Xenophanes and carried on by Parmenides and the elder Zeno, come from the same matrix, Elea having been founded by exiles from Ionian Phokaia on its conquest by the Persians; and Pythagoras, in turn, was of the Ionian city of Samos, in the same sixth century. Finally, Protagoras and Demokritos were of Abdera, an Ionian colony in Thrace; Leukippos, the teacher of Demokritos, was either an Abderite, a Milesian, or an Elean; and Archelaos, the pupil of Anaxagoras and a teacher of Sokrates, is said to have been a Milesian. Wellhausen, (*Israel*, p. 473 of vol. of *Prolegomena*, Eng. tr.) has spoken of the rise of philosophy on the "threatened and actual political annihilation of Ionia" as corresponding to the rise of Hebrew prophecy on the menace and the consummation of the Assyrian conquest. As regards Ionia this may hold in the sense that the stoppage of political freedom threw men back on philosophy, as happened later at Athens. But Thales philosophised before the Persian conquest.

§ 4.

THALES, like Homer, starts from the Babylonian conception of a beginning of all things in water; but in Thales the motive and the sequel are strictly cosmological and in nowise theological. The phrase attributed to him, that "all things are full of Gods",[1] clearly meant that in his opinion the forces of things inhered in the cosmos, and not in personal powers who spasmodically interfered with it.[2] To the later doxographists he "seems to have lost belief in the Gods".[3] From the mere second-hand and often unintelligent statements which are all we have in his case, it is hard to make sure of his system; but that it was pantheistic[4] and physicist seems clear. He conceived that matter not only came from but was resolvable into water; that all phenomena were ruled by

---

[1] *The First Philosophers of Greece*, by A. Fairbanks, 1898, pp. 2, 3, 6. This compilation usefully supplies a revised text of the ancient philosophic fragments, with a translation of these and of the passages on the early thinkers by the later, and by the epitomists.

[2] Cp. Lange, *History of Materialism*, Eng. tr, i, 8, *note*. Mr. Benn, usually one of the best of guides, seems to me not to put the right construction on the phrase (*The Greek Philosophers*, i, 8).

[3] Fairbanks, p. 4.   [4] Diogenes Laërtius, *Thales*, c. 9.

law or "necessity"; and that the sun and planets
(commonly regarded as deities), were bodies analogous
to the earth, which he held to be spherical but "resting
on water".[1] For the rest, he speculated in meteorology
and in astronomy, and is credited with having predicted
a solar eclipse[2]—a clear proof of his knowledge of
Chaldean science—and with having introduced geometry
into Greece from Egypt.[3] To him too is ascribed a
wise counsel to the Ionians in the matter of political
federation,[4] which, had it been followed, might have
saved them from the Persian conquest; and he is one
of the many early moralists who laid down the Golden
Rule as the essence of the moral law.[5] With his maxim,
"Know thyself," he seems to mark a new departure in
ancient thought: the balance of energy is shifted from
myth and theosophy and poesy to analysis of consciousness and the cosmic process.

From this point, Greek rationalism is continuous,
despite reactions, till the Roman conquest. ANAXI-
MANDROS, pupil and companion of Thales, was like him
an astronomer, geographer, and physicist, seeking for a
first principle (for which he invented the name); affirming an infinite material cause, without beginning and
indestructible,[6] with an infinite number of worlds; and
—still showing the Chaldean impulse—speculating curiously on the descent of man from something aquatic, as
well as on the form of the earth (figured by him as a
cylinder[7]), and the nature and motions of the solar system,
and thunder and lightning.[8]

[1] Fairbanks, pp. 3, 7.   [2] Herodotos, i, 74.   [3] Diog. Laërt., c. 3.
[4] Herod. i, 170. Cp. Diogeres, c. 3.   [5] Diog. Laërt., c. 9.
[6] Fairbanks, pp. 9-10. Mr. Benn (*Greek Philosophers*, i, 9) decides that
the early philosophers, while realising that *ex nihilo nihil fit*, had not
grasped the complementary truth that nothing can be annihilated. But
even if the teaching ascribed to Anaximandros be set aside as contradictory
(since he spoke of generation and destruction within the infinite), we have
the statement of Diogenes Laërtius (B. ix, c. 9) that Diogenes of Apollonia,
pupil of Anaximenes, gave the full Lucretian formula.
[7] Diogenes Laërtius, however, (ii, 2) makes him agree with Thales.
[8] Fairbanks, pp. 9-16. Diogenes makes him the inventor of the gnomon
and of the first map and globe, as well as a maker of clocks. Cp. Grote,
i. 330, *note*.

ANAXIMENES, yet another Milesian, pupil in turn of Anaximandros, speculates similarly, making his infinite and first principle the air, in which he conceives the earth to be suspended; theorises on the rainbow, earthquakes, the nature and the revolution of the heavenly bodies (which, with the earth, he supposed to be broad and flat); and affirms the eternity of motion and the perishableness of the earth.[1] It is after a generation of such persistent questioning of Nature that we find in HERAKLEITOS of Ephesus—still in the Ionian culture-sphere—a positive and aggressive criticism of the prevailing beliefs. He has stern sayings about "bringing forth untrustworthy witnesses to confirm disputed points", and about eyes and ears being " bad witnesses for men, since their souls lack understanding".[2] "What can be seen, heard, and learned, this I prize," is one of his declarations; and he is credited with contemning book-learning, as having failed to give wisdom to Hesiod, Pythagoras, Xenophanes, and Hekataios.[3] The belief in progress, he roundly insists, stops progress.[4] From his cryptic utterances it may be gathered that he too was a pantheist;[5] and from his insistence on the immanence of strife in all things,[6] as from others of his sayings, that he was of the stoic mood. It was doubtless in resentment of immoral religion that he said[7] Homer and Archilochos deserved flogging; as he is severe on the phallic worship of Dionysos[8] and on popular pietism in general.[9] One of his sayings, $\ddot{\eta}\theta o\varsigma$ $\dot{\alpha}\nu\theta\rho\dot{\omega}\pi\omega$ $\delta\alpha\dot{\iota}\mu\omega\nu$,[10] " character is a man's dæmon," seems to

---

[1] Fairbanks, pp. 17-22.
[2] Polybios, iv, 40; Sextus Empiricus, *Adversus Mathematicos*, viii, 126.
—Fairbanks, pp. 25, 27; Frag. 4, 14. Cp. 92, 111, 113.
[3] Diog. Laërt. ix, 1, § 2.
[4] Fairbanks, Fr. 134.
[5] *Id.*, Frag. 36, 67.   [6] *Id.*, Frag, 43, 44, 46, 62.
[7] If indeed the saying (Diog. Laërt. last cit.) be his, and not from Herakleides. See Fairbanks, Fr. 119 and note.
[8] Clemens Alexandrinus, *Exhortation to the Heathen*, c. 2, Wilson's trans., p. 41. The passage is obscure, but Mr. Fairbanks' translation (Fr. 127) is excessively so.
[9] Clemens, as cited, p. 32; Fairbanks, Fr. 124, 125, 130.
[10] Fairbanks, Fr. 121.

be the definite assertion of rationalism in affairs as against the creed of special providences.

But while thought was travelling so much faster in Ionia than in the Greek motherland, it was travelling still faster in the colonies planted from Ionia in Italy and Thrace. About 550 B.C. was founded the city of Elea (Hyela, or Velia), on the western Italian coast, south of Paestum, by unsubduable Phokaians seeking a new home after the Persian conquest, and after they had been further defeated in the attempt to live as pirates in Corsica.[1] Thither came XENOPHANES of Kolophon, aged about thirty, likewise seeking freedom. In that hardy polity, freedom of thought and of speech must have gone hand in hand; for the Ionic pantheism of Xenophanes[2] expressed itself in an attack on anthropomorphic religion, no less direct and much more ratiocinative than that of any Hebrew prophet upon idolatry. "Mortals," he wrote, in a famous passage, "suppose that the Gods are born, and wear man's clothing and have voice and body. But if cattle or lions had hands, so as to paint with their hands and make works of art as men do, they would paint their Gods and give them bodies like their own—horses like horses, cattle like cattle."[3] On Homer and Hesiod, the myth-singers, his attack is no less stringent: "they attributed to the Gods all things that with men are of ill-fame and blame : they told of them countless nefarious things, thefts, adulteries, and deception of each other".[4] And when the Eleans, somewhat shaken by such criticism,[5] asked him whether they should sacrifice and sing a dirge to Leukothea, the child-bereft Sea-Goddess, he bade them not to sing a dirge if they thought her divine, and not to

---

[1] Herodotos, i, 163-7 ; Grote, iii, 421.
[2] Fairbanks, pp. 79, 80.
[3] Fairbanks, p. 67, Fr. 5, 6 ; Clemens Alex., *Stromata*, B. v., Wilson's tr., ii, 285-6. Cp. B. vii, c. 4.
[4] Fairbanks, Fr. 7.
[5] In his poetry he is gravely religious, standing for respect to deity as against the old myths. See the extract in Athenæus, B. xi, c. 7; Fairbanks, Fr 21.

sacrifice if she were human.[1] Beside this ringing
radicalism, not yet out of date, the physics and philosophy of the Eleatic freethinker are less noticeable, the
physics being weak, though the philosophy was not
unsubtle nor unoriginal ; but it is interesting to find him
reasoning from fossil-marks that what was now land had
once been sea-covered, and been left mud.

A limit was doubtless soon set to free speech even in
Elea ; and the Eleatic school after Xenophanes, in the
hands of PARMENIDES, ZENO, and MELISSOS, is found
turning first to deep metaphysic and then to verbal
dialectic, to discussion on being and not-being, and the
impossibility of motion, and the frivolous problem of
Achilles and the tortoise. From Parmenides, the most
philosophic mind of all,[2] there is a rapid descent to
professional verbalism, popular life the while proceeding
on the old levels. The social difference between Greece
and the monarchic civilisations was after all only one of
degree : there as elsewhere the social problem was finally
unsolved ; and the limits to Greek progress were soon
approached. But the evolution went far in many places,
and it is profoundly interesting to trace it.

§ 5.

Compared with the early Milesians and with Xenophanes, the elusive PYTHAGORAS is not so much a rationalistic as a theosophic freethinker ; but to Freethought
his name belongs in so far as the system connected with
it did rationalise and discarded mythology. If the bio-
graphic data be in any degree trustworthy, it starts like
Milesian speculation from Oriental precedents. Pythagoras
was of Samos in the Ægean ; and the traditions have it
that he was a pupil of Pherekydes the Syrian, and that
before settling at Krôton in Italy he travelled in Egypt,

---

[1] Aristotle, *Rhetoric*, ii, 23, § 27. A similar saying is attributed to
Herakleitos, on slight authority (Fairbanks, p. 54).
[2] See good estimates of him in Benn's *Greek Philosophers*, i, 17-19 ; and
Zeller, i, 580 ff.

and had intercourse with the Chaldean Magi. Some
parts of the Pythagorean code of life, at least, point to an
Eastern derivation.

The striking resemblances between the doctrine and
practice of the Pythagoreans and those of the Jewish Essenes
has led Zeller to argue (*Philosophie der Griechen*, Th. iii. Abth.
2), that the latter were a branch of the former. Bishop Lightfoot, on the other hand, noting that the Essenes did not hold
the specially prominent Pythagorean doctrines of numbers and
of the transmigration of souls, traces Essenism to Zoroastrian
influence (Ed. of *Colossians*, Appendix on the Essenes, pp.
150-1). This raises the issue whether both Pythagoreanism
and Essenism were not of Persian derivation; and Dr. Schürer
(*Jewish People in the time of Jesus*, Eng. tr., Div. II, vol. ii, p. 218)
pronounces in favor of an Oriental origin for both. The new
connection between Persia and Ionia just at or before the time
of Pythagoras (fl. 530 B.C. ?) squares with this view; but it is
further to be noted that the phenomenon of monasticism,
common to Pythagoreans and Essenes, arises in Buddhism
about the Pythagorean period; and as it is hardly likely that
Buddhism in the sixth century B.C. reached Asia Minor, there
remains the possibility of some special diffusion of the new
ideal from the Babylonian sphere after the conquest by Cyrus,
there being no trace of a Persian monastic system. As to
Buddhism, the argument for a Buddhist origin of Essenism
shortly before our era (cp. A. Lillie, *Buddhism in Christendom*
and *The Influence of Buddhism on Primitive Christianity*; E.
Bunsen, *The Angel - Messiah ; or, Buddhists, Essenes, and
Christians*—all three to be read with much caution) does not
meet the case of the Pythagorean precedents for Essenism.

As regards the mystic doctrine that numbers are as
it were the moving principle in the cosmos, we can but
pronounce it a development of thought *in vacuo*, and
look further for the source of Pythagorean influence in
the moral and social code of the movement, in its science,
in its pantheism,[1] its contradictory dualism,[2] and perhaps
in its doctrine of transmigration of souls. On the side
of natural science, its absurdities[3] point to the fatal lack
of observation which so soon stopped progress in Greek

---

[1] Fairbanks, pp. 145, 151, 155, etc.   [2] *Id.*, p. 143.   [3] *Id.*, p. 154.

physics and biology. Yet in the fields of astronomy, mathematics, and the science of sound, the school seems to have done good scientifie work. It is recorded that Philolaos, the successor of Pythagoras, was the first to teach openly the true doctrine of the motion of the earth[1]—which, however, was also said to have been previously taught by Anaximandros[2] (from whom some incline to derive the Pythagorean theory of numbers in general[3]) and by Iketas of Syracuse.[4] As to its politics, finally, it seems hard to solve the paradox that Pythagoras is pronounced the first teacher of the principle of community of goods,[5] and that his adherents at Krôton formed an aristocratic league, so detested by the people for its anti-democratism that its members were finally massacred in their meeting place, their leader, according to one tradition, being slain with them. The solution seems to be that the early movement was in no way monastic or communistic; that it was however a secret society; and that, whatever its doctrines, its members were mostly of the upper class.[6] If they held by the general rejection of popular religion attributed to Pythagoras, they would so much the more exasperate the demos; for though at Krôton as in the other Grecian colonial cities there was considerable freedom of thought and speech, the populace can nowhere have been free-thinking. In any case, it was after its political over-throw, and still more in the Italian revival of the second century B.C., that the mystic and superstitious features of Pythagoreanism were most multiplied; and doubtless the master's teachings were often much perverted by his devotees. Thus we find the later Pythagoreans laying it down as a canon that no story once fully current concerning the Gods was to be disbelieved[7]—the com-

---

[1] Diog. Laërt., *Philolaos*. (B. viii, c. 7).   [2] *Hist. of Astron.* cited, p. 20.
[3] See Benn, *Greek Philosophers*, i, 11.
[4] Diog. Laërt., in Life of *Philolaos*.
[5] Diog. Laërt., viii, i, 8.
[6] The whole question is carefully sifted by Grote, iv, 76-94.
[7] Grote, *Plato and the other Companions of Sokrates*, ed. 1885, iv, 163

plete negation of philosophical freethought. It must have
taken a good deal of decadence to bring an innovating
sect to that pass; and even about 200 B.C. we find the
freethinking Ennius at Rome calling himself a Pythagorean;[1] but the course of things in Magna Graecia was
mostly downward after the sixth century; the ferocious
destruction of Sybaris by the Krotoniates helping to
promote the decline.[2] Intellectual life, in Magna Graecia
as in Ionia, obeyed the general tendency.

Before the decadence comes, however, the phenomenon of rationalism occurs on all hands in the colonial
cities, older and younger alike. At Syracuse we find the
great comic dramatist EPICHARMOS, about 470 B.C., treating the deities on the stage in a spirit of such audacious
burlesque[3] [as must be held to imply unbelief. Aristophanes at Athens, indeed, shows a measure of the same
spirit while posing as a conservative in religion; but
Epicharmos was professedly something of a Pythagorean
and philosopher,[4] and was doubtless protected by Hiero,
at whose court he lived, against any religious resentment
he may have aroused. The story of SIMONIDES' answer to
Hiero's question as to the nature of the Gods—first
asking a day to think, then two days, then four, then
avowing that meditation only made the problem harder[5]
—points to the prevalent tone among the cultured.

§ 6.

At last the critical spirit finds utterance, in the great
Periklean period, at Athens, but first by way of importation from Ionia. ANAXAGORAS of Klazomenai is the first
freethinker historically known to have been legally
prosecuted and condemned for his freethought ; and it
was in the Athens of Perikles, despite Perikles' protection,
that the attack was made. Coming of the Ionian line of

---

[1] Ennii *Fragmenta*, ed. Hesselius, 1707, pp. 1, 4-7 ; Horace, Epist. ii,
i, 52 ; Persius, Sat. vi.
[2] Grote, *History*, iv, 97.
[3] K. O. Müller, *Dorians*, Eng. tr., ii, 365-8 ; Mommsen, iii, 113.
[4] Grote, i, 333, *note*.   [5] Cicero, *De natura Deorum*, i, 22.

thinkers, and himself a pupil of Anaximenes of Miletos, he held firmly by the scientific view of the cosmos, and taught that the sun, instead of being animated and a deity as the Athenians believed, was "a red hot mass many times larger than the Peloponnesos "'—and the moon a fiery solid body having in it plains and mountains and valleys—this while asserting that infinite mind was the source and introducer of all the motion in the infinite universe ;[2] infinite in extent and infinitely divisible. This "materialistic" doctrine as to the heavenly bodies was propounded, as Sokrates tells in his defence, in books that anyone could buy for a drachma ; and the anti-Periklean party, striking at the statesman through his friends, had him indicted for blasphemy, as the Athenian laws fully entitled them to do. Saved by Perikles from the death punishment, he either was exiled or chose to leave the intolerant city ; and he made his home at Lampsakos, where, as the story runs, he won from the municipality the favor that every year the children should have a holiday in the month in which he died.[3]

In this memorable episode we have a finger-post to the road travelled later by Greek civilisation. At Athens itself the bulk of the free population was ignorant and bigoted enough to allow of the law being used by any fanatic or malignant partisan against any professed rationalist ; and there is no sign that Perikles, himself a freethinker,[4] saw or dreamt of applying the one cure for the evil—the systematic bestowal of rationalistic instruction on all. The fatal maxim of ancient scepticism, that religion is a necessary restraint upon the multitude, brought it about that everywhere, in the last resort, the unenlightened multitude became a restraint upon reason and freethought. In the more aristocratically ruled colonial cities, as we have seen, philosophic speech was

---

[1] Fairbanks, pp. 245, 255, 261 ; Diog. Laërt., *Anaxagoras* (B. ii, c. 3, § 4).
[2] Fairbanks, pp. 239-245. Cp. Grote, *Plato*, i, 54, and Ueberweg, i, 66, as to the nature of the *Nous* of Anaxagoras.
[3] Diog. Laërt., *Anaxagoras*, §§ 9, 10.   [4] Plutarch, *Perikles*, c. 32.

substantially free: it was the Athenian democracy that
brought religious intolerance into Greek life, playing
towards science, in form of law, the part that the fanatics
of Egypt and Palestine had played towards the worshippers of other Gods than their own. To no man,
apparently, did it occur to resist the religious spirit by
systematic propaganda : that, like the principle of
representative government, was to be hit upon only in a
later age. And the spirit of pious persecution, once
generated, went from bad to worse, crowning itself with
crime, till at length the overthrow of Athenian self-
government wrought liberty of scientific speech at the
cost of liberty of political action.

> While the people menaced freethinking in religion, the
> aristocracies opposed freethinking in politics. Thus under the
> Thirty Tyrants all intellectual teaching was forbidden; and
> Kritias, himself accused of having helped to parody the
> mysteries, sharply interdicted the political rationalism of
> Sokrates. (Grote, vi, 476-7.) Meantime, Freethinkers of culture
> were numerous enough. ARCHELAOS, the most important
> disciple of Anaxagoras, taught the social origin and basis of
> morals; and another disciple, METRODOROS, of Lampsakos,
> (Grote, i, 374: not to be confused with METRODOROS of Chios,
> and METRODOROS of Lampsakos the friend of Epicurus, both
> also freethinkers; Cp. Cudworth, ed. Harrison, i, 32; Grote, i,.
> 395, n.) offered an allegorical interpretation of Homer, making
> Zeus stand for mind, and Athênê for art.

While Athens was gaining power and glory and beauty
without popular wisdom, the colonial city of Abdera, in
Thrace, founded by Ionians, had like others carried on
the great impulse of Ionian philosophy, and had produced
in the fifth century some of the great thinkers of the race.
Concerning the greatest of these, DEMOKRITOS, and the
next in importance, PROTAGORAS, we have no sure dates ;[1]
but it is probable that the second, whether older or
younger, was influenced by the first, who indeed has
influenced all philosophy down to our own day. How

[1] See the point discussed by Lange, i, 39, note.

much he learned from his master LEUKIPPOS cannot now
be ascertained.[1] Logically continuing the non-theistic
line of thought, Demokritos either struck out or
assimilated one of the most fruitful of all scientific
principles, the Atomic theory. That this idea again is a
direct development from Babylonian science is not
impossible : at least there seems to be no doubt that
Demokritos had travelled far and wide,[2] whether or not
he had been brought up, as the tradition goes, by Persian
magi ;[3] and that he told how the cosmic views of
Anaxagoras, which scandalised the Athenians, were
current in the East.[4] His atomic theory, held in conjunction with a conception of " mind-stuff " similar to
that of Anaxagoras, may be termed the high-water mark
of ancient scientific thought ; and it is noteworthy that in
the same age EMPEDOKLES of Agrigentum, another
product of the freer colonial life, threw out a certain
glimmer of the Darwinian conception that adaptations
prevail in nature just because the adaptations fit organisms
to survive, and the non-adapted perish.[5] In his teaching,
too, the doctrine of the indestructibility of matter is clear
and firm :[6] and the denial of anthropomorphic deity is
explicit.[7] But Empedokles wrought out no clear system :
" half-mystic and half-rationalist, he made no attempt to
reconcile the two inconsistent sides of his intellectual
character ";[8] and his explicit teaching of metempsychosis[9]
and other Pythagoreanisms gave foothold for more
delusion than he ever dispelled. Demokritos, again,
shunned dialectic and discussion, and founded no school ;
and although his atomism was later adopted by Epicurus,
it was no more developed on a basis of investigation and
experiment than was the biology of Empedokles. Greek

[1] Cp. Ueberweg, i, 68-69.
[2] Lange, i. 17 ; Clem. Alex. Stromata, i, 15 ; Diog. Laër. B. ix, c. vii, 2 (§ 35).
[3] On this also see Lange, i, 15, note.   [4] Diog. Laërt., B. ix, c. vii, 2 (§ 34).
[5] Fairbanks, pp. 189-191. The idea is not put with any such definiteness
as is suggested by Lange, i, 33, 35, and Ueberweg, Hist. of Philos., Eng tr.,
i, 62, n. But Ueberweg's exposition is illuminating.
[6] Fairbanks, pp. 136, 169.   [7] Id., p. 201.   [8] Benn, i, 28.
[9] Fairbanks, p. 205.

society failed to set up the conditions needed for progress
beyond the point gained by its unguided forces.

Thus when Protagoras ventured to read, at the house
of the freethinking EURIPIDES, a treatise of his own
beginning with the avowal that he offered no opinion
as to the existence of the Gods, life being too short for
the enquiry,[1] the remark got wind, and he had to fly for
his life, though Euripides and most of the guests must
have been very much of the same way of thinking.[2] In
the course of his flight, the philosopher was drowned ;
and his book was publicly burned—the earliest known
instance of censorship of the press.[3] Partisan malice was
doubtless at work in his case as in that of Anaxagoras ;
for the philosophic doctrine of Protagoras became common
enough. It is not impossible, though the date is
doubtful, that the attack on him was one of the results of
the great excitement in Athens in the year 415 B.C. over
the sacrilegious mutilation of the figures of Hermes, the
familial or boundary-God, in the streets by night. It was
at that time that the poet DIAGORAS of Melos was
prosecuted for atheism, he having declared that the non-
punishment of a certain act of iniquity proved that there
were no Gods.[4] It has been surmised, with some reason,
that the iniquity in question was the slaughter of the
Melians by the Athenians in 416 B.C.[5] For some time
after 415, the Athenian courts made strenuous efforts to
punish every discoverable case of impiety ; and parodies
of the Eleusinian mysteries (resembling the mock Masses
of Catholic Europe) were alleged against Alkibiades and
others.[6] Diagoras, who was further charged with divulging
the Eleusinian and other mysteries, and with making
firewood of an image of Herakles,[7] became thenceforth one of the proverbial atheists of the ancient

[1] Diogenes Laërtius, B. ix, c. viii, § 3 (51) ; cp. Grote, vii, 49, *note*.
[2] For a defence of Protagoras against Plato, see Grote, vii, 43-54.
[3] Beckmann, *History of Inventions*, Eng. tr., 1846, ii, 513.
[4] Diod. Sic., xiii, 6 ; Hesychius, cit. in Cudworth, ed. Harrison, i, 131.
[5] Ueberweg, i, 80 ; Thukydides, v, 116.
[6] Grote, vi, 13, 32, 33, 42-45.   [7] Athenagoras, *Apol.* c. 4.

world,[1] and a reward of a silver talent was offered for killing him, and of two talents for his capture alive;[2] despite which he seems to have escaped. But no antidote was found or sought to the bane of fanaticism; and the most famous publicist in Athens was the next victim.

§ 7.

The wide subject of the teaching of SOKRATES, PLATO, and ARISTOTLE, must here be briefly noticed with a view only to our special enquiry. All three must be inscribed in any list of ancient Freethinkers; and yet all three furthered Freethought only indirectly, the two former being in different degrees supernaturalists, while the last touched on religious questions only as a philosopher, avoiding all question of practical innovation.

The same account holds good of the best of the so-called Sophists, as GORGIAS the Sicilian, who was a nihilistic sceptic; HIPPIAS of Elis, who impugned the political laws and prejudices which estranged men of thought and culture; and PRODIKOS of Cos, author of the fable of Herakles at the Parting of the Ways, who seems to have privately criticised the current Gods as mere deifications of useful things and forces, and was later misconceived as teaching that the things and forces were Gods. Cp. Cicero, De nat. Deorum, i, 42; Ueberweg, vol. i, p. 78.

I. SOKRATES was fundamentally and practically a Freethinker in that in all things he thought for himself, definitely turning away from the old ideal of mere transmitted authority in morals.[3] Being, however, preoccupied with public life and conduct, he did not carry his critical thinking far beyond that sphere. In regard to the extension of solid science, one of the prime necessities of Greek intellectual life, he was quite reactionary, drawing a line between the phenomena which he thought intelligible and traceable and those which he

---

[1] Cicero, De natura Deorum, i, 1, 23, 42; iii, 37 (the last reference gives proof of his general rationalism); Lactantius, De irâ Dei, c. 9. In calling Sokrates "the Melian", Aristophanes (Clouds, 830) was held to have virtually called him "the atheist".

[2] Diod., xiii, 6; Suidas, s.v. Diagoras; Aristophanes, Birds, 1073.

[3] Zeller, Socrates and the Socratic Schools, Eng. tr., 3d. ed., p. 227; Hegel, as there cited; Grote, Plato, ed. 1885, i, 423.

thought past finding out. "Physics and astronomy, in
his opinion, belonged to the divine class of phenomena
in which human research was insane, fruitless, and
impious."[1] The sound scientific view led up to by so
many previous thinkers was set forth, even in religious
phraseology, by his great contemporary Hippokrates,[2]
and he opposed it. While separating himself in practice
from the popular worships, he held by the belief in
omens, though not in all the ordinary ones; and in one
of the Platonic dialogues he is made to say he holds by
the ordinary versions of all the myths, on the ground
that it is an endless task to find rational explanations
for them.[3] He hoped, in short, to rationalise conduct
without seeking first to rationalise creed—the dream of
Plato and of a thousand religionists since.

Taken as illustrating the state of thought in the
Athenian community, the trial and execution of Sokrates
for "blasphemy" and "corrupting the minds of the
young", goes far to prove, however, that there prevailed
in Athens nearly as much hypocrisy in religious matters
as exists in the England of to-day. Doubtless he was
liable to death from the traditionally orthodox Greek
point of view,[4] having practically turned aside from the
old civic creed and ideals; but then most educated
Athenians had in some degree done the same. EURIPIDES
is so frequently critical of the old theology and mythology
in his plays[5] that he too could easily have been indicted;
and Aristophanes, who attacked Euripides in his comedies
as unscrupulously as he did Sokrates, would no doubt
have been glad to see him prosecuted.[6] The psychology

---

[1] Grote, *History*, i, 334 ; Xenophon, *Memorabilia*, i, 1, §§ 6-9.
[2] Grote, i, 334-5 ; Hippokrates, *De Aeribus, Aquis, Locis*, c. 22 (49).
[3] Plato, *Phaedrus*, Jowett's trans., 3rd ed., i, 434 ; Grote, *History*, i, 393.
[4] Zeller, *Socrates and the Socratic Schools*, as cited, p. 231. The case
against Sokrates is bitterly urged by Forchhammer, *Die Athenen und
Sokrates*, 1837 ; see in particular S. 8-11. Cp. Grote, *Hist.*, vii, 81.
[5] See many of the passages cited by Bishop Westcott in his *Essays in
the Hist. of Relig. Thought in the West*, 1891, pp. 102-127. Cp. Dickinson,
The Greek View of Life, pp. 46-49 ; Grote, *Hist.*, i, 346-8.
[6] See Aristophanes' *Frogs*, 888-894.

of Aristophanes, who freely ridiculed and blasphemed the
Gods in his own comedies while reviling all men who did
not believe in them, is hardly intelligible[1] save in the
light of parts of the English history of our own time,
when unbelieving indifferentists on the Conservative side
have been seen ready to join in turning the law against a
freethinking publicist for purely party ends. Indeed in
the case of Sokrates, not only party malice but the
individual dislikes he so industriously set up[2] must have
counted for much in securing the small majority of the
Dikastery that pronounced him guilty; and his own clear
preference for death over any sort of compromise did the
rest.[3] He was old, and little hopeful of social betterment;
and the temperamental obstinacy which underlay his
perpetual and pertinacious debating helped him to choose
a death that he could easily have avoided. But the fact
remains that he was not popular; that the mass of the
voters as well as of the upper class disliked his constant
cross-examination of popular opinion, which must often
have led logical listeners to carry on criticism where he
left off; and that after all his ratiocination he left Athens
substantially irrational on some essential issues. His
dialectic method has done more to educate the later
world than it did for Greece. But in view of his own
limitations it is not surprising that through all Greek
history educated men (including Aristotle) continued to
believe firmly in the deluge of Deukalion[4] and the invasion
of the Amazons[5] as solid historical facts.

---

[1] Nor is it easy to comprehend the mental state of the populace who
listened and laughed. The Athenian faith, as M. Girard remarks (*Essai
sur Thucydide*, 1884, pp. 258-9), "was more disposed to suffer the buffooneries
of a comedian than the serious negation of a philosopher" It seemed to
think that jocular impiety did no harm, where serious negation might
cause divine wrath.

[2] "Nothing could well be more unpopular and obnoxious than the task
which he undertook of cross-examining and convicting of ignorance
every distinguished man whom he could approach" (Grote, vii, 95. Cp.
pp. 141-144). Cp. also Trevelyan's *Life of Macaulay*, ed. 1881, p. 316.

[3] On the desire of Socrates to die, see Grote, vii, 152-164.

[4] Grote, *History*, i, 94.

[5] *Id.*, i, 194. Not till Strabo do we find this myth disbelieved; and
Strabo was surprised to find most men holding by the old story while
admitting that the race of Amazons had died out. *Id.*, p. 197.

Such beliefs, of course, are on all fours with those current in the modern religious world down till the present century: we shall in fact best appraise the rationality of Greece by making such comparisons. The residual lesson is that where Greek reason ended, modern social science had better be regarded as only beginning. THUKYDIDES, the greatest of all the ancient historians, and one of the great of all time, treated human affairs in a spirit so strictly rationalistic that he might reasonably be termed an atheist on that score even if he had not earned the name as a pupil of Anaxagoras.[1] But his task was to chronicle a war which proved that the Greeks were to the last children of instinct for the main purposes of life, and that the rule of reason which they are credited with establishing[2] was only an intermittent pastime.

2. The decisive measure of Greek accomplishment is found in the career of PLATO. One of the great prose writers of the world, he has won by his literary genius— that is, by his power of continuous presentation as well as by his style—no less than by his service to supernaturalist philosophy in general, a repute above his deserts as a thinker. In the history of Freethought he figures as a man of genius formed by Sokrates and reflecting his limitations, developing the Sokratic dialectic on the one hand and finally emphasising the Sokratic dogmatism to the point of utter bigotry. If the Athenians are to be condemned for putting Sokrates to death, it must not be forgotten that the spirit if not the letter of the *Laws* drawn up by Plato in his old age fully justified them.[3] That code, could it ever have been put in force, would have wrought the death of every honest freethinker as well as of most of the ignorant believers within its sphere. Alone among the great serious writers of Greece does he

[1] Life of Thukydides, by Marcellinus, c. 22, citing Antyllas. Cp. Girard, *Essai sur Thucydide*, p. 239; and the prefaces of Hobbes and Smith to their translations.

[2] Girard, p. 3.

[3] Cp. Grote, *Plato*, iv, 162, 381.

implicate Greek thought in the gospel of intolerance
passed on to modern Europe from antiquity. It is recorded
of him[1] that he wished to burn all the writings of
Demokritos that he could collect, and was dissuaded only
on the score of the number of the copies.

What was best in Plato, considered as a Freethinker,
was his early love of ratiocination, of " the rendering and
receiving of reasons ". Even in his earlier dialogues,
however, there are signs enough of an arbitrary temper,
as well as of an inability to put science in place of religious
prejudice. The obscurantist doctrine which he put in
the mouth of Sokrates in the *Phaedrus* was also his own,
as we gather from the exposition in the *Republic*. In
that brilliant performance he objects, as so many believers
and freethinkers had done before him, to the scandalous
tales in the poets concerning the Gods and the sons of
Gods ; but he does not object to them as being all untrue.
His position is that they are unedifying.[2] For his own
part he proposes to frame new myths which shall edify
the young : in his Utopia it is part of the business of the
legislator to frame or choose the right fictions ;[3] and the
systematic imposition of an edifying body of pious fiction
on the general intelligence is part of his scheme for the
regeneration of society.[4] Honesty is to be built up by fraud,
and reason by delusion. What the Hebrew Bible-makers
actually did, Plato proposed to do. The one thing to be
said in his favor is that by thus telling how the net is to
be spread in the sight of the bird he put the decisive
obstacle—if any were needed—in the way of his plan. It
is indeed inconceivable that the author of the *Republic*
and the *Laws* ever dreamt that either polity as a whole
would ever come into existence. He had failed com-

---

[1] Diog. Laert., B. ix, c. vii, § 8 (40).

[2] *Republic*, B. ii and iii ; Jowett's trans, 3d. ed., iii, 60 ff., 68 ff. In B. x.
it is true, he does speak of the poets as unqualified by knowledge and
training to teach truth (Jowett's trans., iii, 311 ff.) ; but Plato's " truth " is
not objective but idealistic, or rather fictitious-didactic.

[3] *Id.*, B. ii and iii ; Jowett, pp. 59, 69, etc.

[4] *Id.*, B. iii ; Jowett, pp. 103-105.

pletely as a statesman in practice :¹ as a schemer he does
not even posit the first conditions of success.

None the less, the prescription of intolerance in the
*Laws*² classes Plato finally on the side of fanaticism, and
indeed ranks him with the most sinister figures on that
side, since his earlier writing shows that he would be
willing to punish men for rejecting what he knew to be
untruths.³ His psychology is as strange as that of Aristophanes, but strange with a difference. He seems to
have practised "the will to believe" till he grew to be a
fanatic on the plane of the most ignorant of orthodox
Athenians; and after all that science had done to
enlighten men on that natural order the misconceiving of
which had been the foundation of their creeds, he
inveighs furiously in his old age against the impiety of
those who dared to doubt that the sun and moon and
stars were deities, as every nurse taught her charges.⁴
And when all is said, his Gods satisfy no need of the
intelligence, for he insists that they only partially rule the
world, sending the few good things but not the many evil⁵
—save in so far as evil may be a beneficent penalty and
discipline. At the same time, while advising the imprisonment or execution of heretics who did not believe
in the Gods, Plato regarded with even greater detestation
the man who taught that they could be persuaded or
propitiated by individual prayer and sacrifice.⁶ Thus he
would have struck alike at the freethinking few and at

---

¹ See the story of his and his pupil's attempts at Syracuse (Grote,
History, ix, 37-123). The younger Dionysius, whom they had vainly
attempted to make a model ruler, seems to have been an audacious
unbeliever to the extent of plundering the temple of Persephone at Locris,
one of Jupiter in the Peloponnesos, and one of Æsculapius at Epidaurus.
It was noted that nevertheless he died in his bed. Cicero (*De nat. Deorum*,
iii, 33, 34) and Valerius Maximus (i, 1) tell the story of the elder
Dionysius; but of him it cannot be true. In his day the plunder of the
temples of Demêtêr and Persephone in Sicily by the Carthaginians was
counted a deadly sin. See Freeman, *History of Sicily*, iv, 125-147.

² *Laws*, x ; Jowett, v, 295-298.

³ *Republic*, ii, iii, as cited. Cp. *Laws*, ii, iii; Jowett, v, 42, 79.

⁴ *Laws*, Jowett's trans , 3rd ed., v, 271-2. Compare the comment of
Benn, i, 271-2.

⁵ *Republic*, B. ii ; Jowett, iii, 62.

⁶ *Laws*. x, 906-7, 910 ; Jowett, v, 293-4, 297-8.

the multitude who held by the general religious beliefs of
Greece, dealing damnation on all save his own clique, in
a way that would have made Torquemada blench.[1] In
the face of such teaching as this, it may well be said that
"Greek philosophy made incomparably greater advances
in the earlier polemic period [of the Ionians] than after
its friendly return to the poetry of Homer and Hesiod "[2]
—that is, to their polytheistic basis. It is to be said for
Plato finally that his embitterment at the downward
course of things in Athens is a quite intelligible source for
his own intellectual decadence : a very similar spectacle
being seen in the case of our own great modern Utopist,
Sir Thomas More. But Plato's own writing bears witness
that among the unbelievers against whom he declaimed
there were wise and blameless citizens;[3] while in the act
of seeking to lay a religious basis for a good society he
admitted the fundamental immorality of the religious
basis of the whole of past Greek life.

3. Of ARISTOTLE it may here suffice to say that like
Sokrates he rendered rather an indirect than a direct
service to Freethought. Where Sokrates gave the critical
or dialectic method or habit, "a process of eternal value
and of universal application,"[4] Aristotle supplied the
great inspiration of system, partly correcting the Sokratic
dogmatism on the possibilities of science by endless
observation and speculation, though himself falling into
scientific dogmatism only too often. That he was an
unbeliever in the popular and Platonic religion is clear.
Apart from the general rationalistic tenor of his
works,[5] there was a current understanding that the
Peripatetic school denied the utility of prayer and
sacrifice ;[6] and though the attempt of the anti-

---

[1] On the general inconsistency of the whole doctrine. see Grote's *Plato*,
iv, 379-397.
[2] Ueberweg, *Hist. of Philos.*, Eng. tr., i, 25. Cp. Lange, i, 52-4. See,
however, Mr. Benn's final eulogy of Plato as a thinker, i, 273.
[3] *Laws*, x, 908 : Jowett, v, 295.
[4] Grote, *History*, vii, 168.
[5] Cp. Grote, *Aristotle*, 2nd ed., p. 10.
[6] Origen, *Against Celsus*, ii, 13 ; cp. i, 65 ; iii, 75 ; vii, 3.

Macedonian party to impeach him for impiety may have turned largely on his hyperbolic hymn to his dead friend Hermeias (who was a eunuch, and as such held peculiarly unworthy of being addressed as on a level with semi-divine heroes[1]) it could hardly have been undertaken at all unless he had given solider pretexts. The threatened prosecution he avoided by leaving the city, dying shortly afterwards.

It is clear, further, that he was a monotheist, but a monotheist with no practical religion. " Excluding such a thing as divine interference with nature, his theology of course excludes the possibility of revelation, inspiration, miracles, and grace."[2] His influence must thus have been to some extent, at least, favorable to rational science, though unhappily his own science is too often a blundering reaction against the surmises of earlier thinkers with a greater gift of intuition than he, who was rather a methodizer than a discoverer.[3] What was worst in his doctrine was its tendency to apriorism, which made it in a later age so adaptable to the purposes of the Roman Catholic Church. For the rest, while guiltless of Plato's fanaticism, he had no scheme of reform whatever, and was as far as any other Greek from the thought of raising the mass by instruction. His own science, indeed, was not progressive; and his political ideals were rather reactionary; his clear perception of the nature of the population problem leaving him in the earlier attitude of Malthus, and his lack of sympathetic energy making him a defender of slavery when other men had condemned it.[4] He was in some aspects the greatest brain of the

---

[1] Grote, *Aristotle*, p. 13.
[2] Benn, *The Greek Philosophers*, i, 352. Mr. Benn refutes Sir A. Grant's view that Aristotle's creed was a " vague pantheism "; but that phrase loosely conveys the idea of its non-religiousness, so to speak. It might be called a Lucretian monotheism. Cp. Benn, i, 294.
[3] Cp. the severe criticisms of Benn, vol. i, ch. 6, and Lange, i, 82-90. But see Lange's summary, p. 91, also p. 11, as to the unfairness of Whewell; and ch. v of Soury's *Bréviaire de l'histoire du Matérialisme*, 1881, esp. *end*.
[4] *Politics* i, 2

ancient world; and he left it, at the close of the great Grecian period, without much faith in man, while positing for the modern world its vague conception of Deity.

The lack of fresh science, which was the proximate cause of the stagnation of Greek thought, has been explained like other things as a result of race qualities : " the Athenians," says Mr. Benn (i, 42) " had no genius for natural science : none of them were ever distinguished as savans. . . . . It was, they thought, a miserable trifling waste of time. . . . . Pericles, indeed, thought differently. . . . . " On the other hand Lange decides (i, 11) that " with the freedom and boldness of the Hellenic mind was united . . . . the gift of scientific deduction ". These contrary views seem alike arbitrary. If Mr. Benn means that other Hellenes had what the Athenians lacked, the answer is that only special social conditions could have set up such a difference, and that it could not be innate, but must be a mere matter of usage. The Chaldeans were forward in astronomy because their climate favored it to begin with, and religion and their superstitions did so later. Hippokrates of Cos became a great physician because, with natural capacity, he had the opportunity to compare many practices. The Athenians failed to carry on the sciences not because the faculty or the taste was lacking among them—Perikles cannot have been alone in his attitude; and the " miserable trifling " must, in the terms of the case, have been done by some native Athenians as well as by immigrants—but because their political and artistic interests, for one thing, preoccupied them, e.g. Sokrates and Plato ; and because, for another, their popular religion, popularly supported, menaced the students of physics. But the Ionians, who had savans, failed equally to progress after the Alexandrian period ; the explanation being again not stoppage of faculty but the advent of conditions unfavorable to the old intellectual life, which in any case, as we saw, had been first set up by Babylonian contacts. On the " faculty " theory, we should have to decide that somehow all the Hellenes with such a faculty had happened to go to Ionia or Sicily. (Compare, on the ethnological theorem of Cousin, Guillaume Bréton, Essai sur la poésie philosophique en Grèce, 1882, p. 10.) On the other hand, Lange's theory of gifts " innate " in the Hellenic mind in general, merely reverses the fallacy. Potentialities are " innate " in all populations, according to their culture stage, and it was their total environment that specialised the Greeks as a community.

§ 8.

The overthrow of the "free" political life of Athens
was followed by a certain increase in intellectual activity,
the result of throwing back the remaining store of energy
on the life of the mind.   The new schools of philosophy
founded by ZENO the Stoic and EPICURUS, whatever their
defects, compare not ill with those of Plato and Aristotle,
exhibiting greater ethical sanity and sincerity if less metaphysical subtlety.   Of metaphysics there had been enough
for the age : what it needed was a rational philosophy of
life.   But the loss of political freedom, although thus for
a time turned to account, was fatal to continuous progress.
The first great thinkers had all been free men in a
politically free environment : the atmosphere of cowed
subjection, especially after the advent of the Romans,
could not breed their like ; and originative energy of the
higher order soon disappeared.   Sane as was the moral
philosophy of Epicurus, and austere as was that of Zeno,
they are alike static or quietist, the codes of a society
seeking a regulating and sustaining principle rather than
hopeful of new achievement or new truth.   And the
universal scepticism of PYRRHO has the same effect of
suggesting that what is wanted is not progress but balance.

Considered as Freethinkers, all three men tell at once
of the critical and of the reactionary work done by the
previous age.   Pyrrho was the universal doubter ; Zeno
was substantially a monotheist ; Epicurus, adopting but
not greatly developing the science of Demokritos,[1] turned
the Gods into a far-off band of glorious spectres, untroubled
by human needs, dwelling for ever in immortal calm,
neither ruling nor caring to rule the world of men.[2]   This
strange retention of the theorem of the existence of Gods,
with a flat denial that they did anything in the universe,

---

[1] See, however, Wallace's *Epicureanism* ("Ancient Philosophies" series),
1880, pp. 176 ff., 186 ff., p. 266, as to the scientific merits of the system.
[2] The Epicurean doctrine on this and other heads is chiefly to be
gathered from the great poem of Lucretius.   Prof. Wallace's excellent
treatise gives all the clues.   See p. 202 as to the Epicurean God-idea.

might be termed the great peculiarity of average ancient
rationalism, were it not that what makes it at all intelligible for us is just the similar practice of modern
non-Christian theists. The Gods of antiquity were
non-creative, but strivers and meddlers and answerers of
prayer; and ancient rationalism relieved them of their
striving and meddling, leaving them no active or governing
function whatever, but for the most part cherishing their
phantasms. The God of modern Christendom had been
at once a creator and a governor, ruling, meddling,
punishing, rewarding, and hearing prayer; and modern
theism, unable to take the atheistic or agnostic plunge,
relieves him of all interference in things human or cosmic,
but retains him as a creative abstraction who somehow
set up "law", whether or not he made all things out of
nothing. The psychological process in the two cases
seems to be the same—an erection of aesthetic habit into
a philosophic dogma.

Whatever may have been the logical and psychological
crudities of Epicureanism, however, it counted for much
as a deliverance to men from superstitious fears; and
nothing is more remarkable in the history of ancient
philosophy than the affectionate reverence paid to the
founder's memory[1] on this score through whole centuries.
The powerful Lucretius sounds his highest note of praise
in telling how this Greek had first of all men freed human
life from the crushing load of religion, daring to pass the
flaming ramparts of the world, and by his victory putting
men on an equality with heaven.[2] The laughter-loving
Lucian two hundred years later grows gravely eloquent
on the same theme.[3] And for generations the effect of
the Epicurean check on orthodoxy is seen in the whole
intellectual life of the Greek world, already predisposed
in that direction. The new schools of the Cynics and

---

[1] Compare Wallace, *Epicureanism*, pp. 64-71, and ch. xi; and Mackintosh,
On the Progress of Ethical Philosophy, 4th ed., p. 29.

[2] *De rerum natura*, i, 62-79.

[3] *Alexander seu Pseudomantis*, cc. 25, 38, 47, 61, cited by Wallace, pp.
249-250.

the Cyrenaics had alike shown the influence in their
perfect freedom from all religious preoccupation, when
they were not flatly dissenting from the popular beliefs.
ANTISTHENES, the founder of the former school
(fl. 400 B.C.), though a pupil of Sokrates, had been
explicitly anti-polytheistic.[1] ARISTIPPOS of Cyrene, also
a pupil of Sokrates, who a little later founded the Hedonic
or Cyrenaic sect, seems to have put theology entirely
aside; and one of the later adherents of the school,
THEODOROS, was like Diagoras labelled "the Atheist"[2]
by reason of the directness of his opposition to religion;
and in the Rome of Cicero he and Diagoras are the
notorious atheists of history.[3]   To Theodoros is attributed an influence over the thought of Epicurus,[4] who,
however, took the safer position of a verbal Theism.
The atheist is said to have been menaced by Athenian
law in the time of Demetrius Phalereus, who protected him; and there is even a story that he was condemned to drink hemlock[5]; but he was not of the type
that meets martyrdom, though he might go far to
provoke it.[6]

In the same age the same freethinking temper is seen
in STILPO of Megara, of the school of Euclides, who is
said to have been brought before the Areopagus for the
offence of saying that the Pheidian statue of Athênê was
"not a God", and to have met the charge with the jest
that she was in reality not a God but a Goddess; whereupon he was exiled.[7]   Yet another professed atheist was
BION of Borysthenes, pupil of Theodoros, of whom it is
told, in a fashion familiar to our own time, that in sickness

---

[1] Cicero, *De natura Deorum*, i, 13.
[2] Diogenes Laërtius, B. ii, c. viii, §§ 7, 14 (86, 100).
[3] Cicero, *De natura Deorum*, i, 1, 23, 42.
[4] Diogenes, as cited, § 12 (97).
[5] *Id.*, §§ 15, 16 (101-2).
[6] Prof. Wallace's account of the court of Lysimachos of Thrace as a
"favourite resort of emancipated freethinkers" (*Epicureanism*, p. 42) is
hardly borne out by his authority, Diogenes Laërtius, who represents
Lysimachos as unfriendly towards Theodoros.   Hipparchia the Cynic,
too, opposed rather than agreed with the atheist.
[7] *Id.*, B. ii, c. xii, § 5 (116).

he grew pious through fear.[1] In the other schools, SPEUSIPPUS, the nephew of Plato, leant to monotheism[2]; STRATO, the Peripatetic, called "the Naturalist", taught sheer pantheism[3]; DIKAIARCHOS, another disciple of Aristotle, denied the existence of separate souls;[4] and ARISTO and CLEANTHES, disciples of Zeno, varied likewise in the direction of pantheism; the latter's monotheism, as expressed in his famous hymn, being one of several doctrines ascribed to him.[5]

Contemporary with Epicurus and Zeno and Pyrrho, too, was EVEMEROS (Euhemerus), whose peculiar propaganda against Godism seems to imply theoretic atheism. His lost work, of which only a few extracts remain, undertook to prove that all the Gods had been simply famous men, deified after death ; the proof, however, being by way of a fiction about old inscriptions found in an imaginary island.[6] As above noted,[7] the idea may have been borrowed from sceptical Phoenicians, the principle having already been monotheistically applied by the Bible-making Jews.[8] In any case, it seems to have had considerable vogue in the Hellenistic world ; but with the effect rather of paving the way for new cults than of setting up scientific rationalism in place of the old ones.

In Athens, indeed, the democracy, restored in a subordinate form by Demetrius Poliorkêtes (B.C. 307) tried to put down the philosophic schools, all of which, but the Aristotelian in particular, were anti-democratic, and doubtless also comparatively irreligious. THEOPHRASTOS, the head of the Aristotelian school, was indicted for

---

[1] *Id.*, last cit. (117) and B. iv, c. vii, §§ 4, 9, 10 (52, 54, 55).

[2] Cicero, *De natura Deorum*, i, 13.

[3] *Id., ib.; Acad. Quæst.* iv, 38.

[4] Cicero, *Tusculans*, i, c. x, 21 ; c. xxxi, 77.

[5] Sir A. Grant's trans. of the hymn is given in Capes' *Stoicism* ("Chief Ancient Philosophies" series), 1880, p. 41 ; and the Greek text by Mahaffy, *Greek Life and Thought*, p. 262. Cp. Cicero, *De nat. Deor.*, i, 14.

[6] Eusebius, *Praep. Evang*, B. ii, c. 2 ; Plutarch, *Isis and Osiris*, c. 23.

[7] Pp. 51-2.

[8] It may count for something that Diogenes the Babylonian, a follower of Chrysippus, is found applying the principle to Greek mythology. Cicero, *De natura Deorum*, i, 15.

impiety, which seems to have consisted in denouncing
animal sacrifice.[1] These repressive attempts, however,
failed; and no others followed at Athens in that era;
though in the next century the Epicureans seem to have
been expelled from Lythos in Crete and from Messenê in
the Peloponnesos, nominally for their atheism, in reality
probably on political grounds.[2] Thus Zeno was free to
publish a treatise in which, besides far out-going Plato in
schemes for dragooning the citizens into an ideal life, he
proposed a State without temples or law courts or
gymnasia.[3] In the same age there is trace of " an
interesting case of Rationalism even in the Delphic
oracle ".[4] The people of the island of Astypalaia, plagued
by hares or rabbits, solemnly consulted the oracle, which
briefly advised them to keep dogs and take to hunting.

It was in keeping with this general but mostly placid
and non-polemic rationalism that the New Academy, the
second birth of the Platonic school, in the hands of
ARKESILAOS and KARNEADES, and later of the Carthaginian
KLITOMACHOS, should be marked by that species of
scepticism thence called Academic—a scepticism which
urged the doubtfulness of current religious beliefs without
going the Pyrrhonian length of denying that any beliefs
could be proved. On this basis, in a healthy environment,
science and energy might have reared a constructive
rationalism; and for a time astronomy, in the hands of
ARISTARCHOS of Samos (3rd cent. B.C.), ERATOSTHENES
of Cyrene, the second keeper of the great Alexandrian
library (2nd century B.C.), and above all of HIPPARCHOS
of Nikæa, the greatest of the Alexandrian school, was
carried to a height of perfection which could not be
maintained, and was only re-attained in modern times.[5]

---

[1] Mahaffy, *Greek Life and Thought*, 1887, pp. 133-135 ; Diogenes.
Laërtius, B. ii, c. v, § 5 (38).
[2] Wallace, *Epicureanism* (pp. 245-6), citing Suidas, *s.v. Epicurus.*
[3] Diogenes Laërtius, B. vii, c. i, § 28 (33); Cp. Origen, *Against Celsus,.*
B. i, c. 5.
[4] Mahaffy, as cited, p. 135, *n.;* Athenæus, ix, 400.
[5] *History of Astronomy* before cited, ch. vi.

" History records not one astronomer of note in the three centuries between Hipparchos and Ptolemy ; " and Ptolemy retrograded into error. Other science mostly did likewise. The Greek world, already led to lower intellectual levels by the sudden ease and wealth opened up to it through the conquests of Alexander and the rule of his successors, was cast still lower by the Roman conquest. In the air of imperialism, stirred by no other, original thought could not arise ; and the mass of the Greek-speaking populations, rich and poor, gravitated to the level of the intellectual[1] and emotional life of more or less well-fed slaves. In this society there rapidly multiplied private religious associations — *thiasoi, eranoi, orgeonoi*—in which men and women, denied political life, found new bonds of union and grounds of division in cultivating worships, mostly Oriental, which stimulated the religious sense and sentiment.[2] Such was the soil in which Christianity took root and flourished; while philosophy, after the freethinking epoch following on the fall of Athenian power, gradually reverted to one or other form of mystical theism or theosophy, of which the most successful was the Neo-Platonism of Alexandria.[3] When the theosophic Julian rejoiced that Epicureanism had disappeared,[4] he was exulting in a symptom of the intellectual decline that made possible the triumph of the faith he most opposed.

Here and there, through the centuries, the old intellectual flame burns whitely enough : the noble figure of EPICTETUS in the first century of the new era, and that of the brilliant LUCIAN in the second, in their widely different ways remind us that the evolved faculty was still there if the circumstances had been such as to evoke it.

---

[1] Lucian's dialogue *Philopseudes* gives a view of the superstitions of average Greeks in the second century of our era. Cp. Mr. Williams' note to the first *Dialogue of the Dead* in his trans., p. 87.

[2] See M. Foucart's treatise, *Des associations religieuses chez les Grecs*, 1873, 2e partie.

[3] On the early tendency to orthodox conformity among the unbelieving Alexandrian scholars, see Mahaffy, *Greek Life and Thought*, pp. 260-1.

[4] Frag. cited by Wallace, p. 258.

MENIPPUS in the first century B.C. had played a similar
part to that of Lucian, in whose freethinking dialogues he
so often figures; but with less of subtlety and intel-
lectuality. But the moral doctrine of Epictetus is one of
endurance and resignation; and the almost unvarying
raillery of Lucian, making mere perpetual sport of the
now moribund Olympian Gods, was hardly better fitted
than the all-round scepticism of SEXTUS EMPIRICUS to
inspire positive and progressive thinking.

Sextus, it is true, strikes at ill-founded beliefs, and so
makes for reason : but he has no idea of a method which
shall reach sounder conclusions. Lucian, again, thought
soundly and sincerely on life ; his praise of the men whose
memories he respected, as Epicurus and Demonax (if
the Life of Demonax attributed to him be really his), is
grave and heartfelt ; and his ridicule of the discredited
Gods was perfectly right so far as it went. In the period
of declining pagan belief, the maxim that superstition was
a good thing for the people must have wrought a quantity
and a kind of corruption that no amount of ridicule of
religion could ever approach. Polybios (fl. B.C. 150)
agrees with his complacent Roman masters that their
greatness is largely due to the carefully cultivated superstition of their populace ; and charges with rashness and
folly those who would uproot the growth;[1] and Strabo,
writing under Tiberius, confidently lays down the same
principle of governmental deceit.[2] So far had the doctrine
evolved since Plato preached it. But to counteravail it
there needed more than a ridicule which after all reached
only the class who had already cast off the beliefs derided,
leaving the multitude unenlightened. The lack of the
needed machinery of enlightenment was of course part of
the general failure of the Græco-Roman civilisation ; and

---

[1] Polybios, B. vi, c. 56. Cp. B. xvi, Frag. 5 (12), where he speaks.
impatiently of the miracle-stories told of certain cults, and, repeating his
opinion that some such stories are useful for preserving piety among the
people, protests that they should be kept within bounds.
[2] B. i, c. 2, § 8. Plutarch (*Isis* and *Osiris*, c. 8) puts the more decent
principle that all the apparent absurdities have good occult reasons.

no one man's efforts could have availed, even if any man of the age could have grasped the whole situation. The historic fact is that the higher life of Greece finally followed the fortunes of that of Rome; and it is thither that we must look for the last records of the decadent rationalism of the old Mediterranean world.

CHAPTER VI.

FREETHOUGHT IN ANCIENT ROME.

§ 1.

THE Romans, so much slower and later than the Greeks in their intellectual development, were in some respects peculiarly apt to accept freethinking ideas when Greek rationalism at length reached them. After receiving from their Greek neighbours in Southern Italy, in the pre-historic period, the germs of higher culture, in particular the alphabet, they rather retrograded than progressed for centuries, the very alphabet degenerating for lack of literary activity[1] in the absence of any culture class, and under the one-idea'd rule of the landowning aristocracy, whose bent to military aggression was correlative to the smallness of the Roman facilities for commerce. In the early republican period, the same conditions of relative poverty, militarism, and aristocratic emulation prevented any development of the priesthood beyond the rudimentary stage of a primitive civic function ; and the whole of these conditions in combination kept the Roman Pantheon peculiarly shadowy, and the Roman mythology abnormally undeveloped.

The character of the Roman religion has been usually explained in the old manner, in terms of their particular " genius " and lack of genius. On this view the Romans primordially tended to do whatever they did—to be slightly religious in one period, and highly so in another. By no writer has the subject been more unphilosophically treated than by

---

[1] Mommsen, *History of Rome*, B. i, c. 14 (Eng. tr. 1894, vol. i, pp. 282-283). Mommsen's opinion of the antiquity of writing among the Latins (p. 280) is hardly intelligible. He places its introduction about or before 1000 B.C. ; yet he admits that they got their alphabet from the Greeks, and he can show no Greek contacts for that period. Cp. pp. 167-8 (ch. 10).

Mommsen, whose chapter on Roman religion (vol. i, ch. 12) is an insoluble series of contradictions. The differentiation of Greek and Roman religion is to be explained by the culture-history of the two peoples; and that, in turn, was determined by their geographical situation and their special contacts. Roman life was made systematically agricultural and militarist by its initial circumstances, where Greek life in civilised Asia Minor became industrial, artistic, and literary. The special "genius" of Homer, or of various members of an order of bards developed by early colonial-feudal Grecian conditions, would indeed count for much by giving permanent artistic definiteness of form to the Greek Gods, where the early Romans, leaving all the vocal arts mainly to the conservative care of their women and children as something beneath adult male notice, missed the utilisation of poetic genius among them till they were long past the period of romantic simplicity (cp. Mommsen, B. i, c. 15, Eng. tr. 1894, vol. i. pp. 285-300). Hence the comparative abstractness of their unsung Gods (cp. Boissier, *La religion romaine d'Auguste aux Antonins*, 4e édit. i, 8), and the absence of such a literary mythology as was evolved and preserved in Greece by local patriotisms under the stimulus of the great epopees and tragedies. The doctrine that "the Italian is deficient in the passion of the heart", and that *therefore* "Italian" literature has "never produced a true epos or a genuine drama" (Mommsen, c. 15, vol. i, p. 284), is one of a thousand samples of the fallacy of explaining a phenomenon in terms of itself. On the same verbalist method, Mommsen decides as to the Etruscan religion that "the mysticism and barbarism of their worship had their foundation in the essential character of the Etruscan people" (ch. 12, p. 232).

Thus when Rome, advancing in the career of conquest, had developed a large aristocratic class, living a city life, with leisure for intellectual interests, and had come in continuous contact with the conquered Grecian cities of Southern Italy, its educated men underwent a literary and a rationalistic influence at the same time, and were the more ready to give up all practical belief in their own slightly defined Gods when they found Greeks explaining away theirs. Indeed Greek rationalism was already old when the Romans began to develop a written and artistic literature : it had even taken on the popular form given to it by Evêmeros a century before the Romans took it up. Doubtless there was scepticism among the latter before Ennius : such a piece of religious procedure as the invention of a God of Silver (*Argentinus*), son of the God of Copper (*Æsculanus*), on the introduction of a silver currency, B.C. 269, must have been smiled at by the more intelligent.[1]

> Mommsen states (ii, 70) that at this epoch the Romans kept "equally aloof from superstition and unbelief", but though superstition was certainly the rule, there are traces of rationalism. On the next page, the historian himself admits that the faith of the people had already been shaken by the interference allowed to the priestly colleges in political matters; and in another chapter (B. ii, c. 13; vol. ii, 112) he recalls that a consul of the Claudian gens had jested openly at the auspices in the first Punic war, B.C. 249. The story is told by Cicero, *De natura Deorum*, ii, 3. The sacred poultry on being let out of their coop would not feed, so that the auspices could not be taken; whereupon the consul caused them to be thrown into the water, *etiam per jocum Deos inridens*, saying they might drink if they would not eat. His colleague Junius in the same war also disregarded the auspices; and in both cases, according to Balbus the Stoic in Cicero's treatise, the Roman fleets were duly defeated; whereupon Claudius was condemned by the people, and Junius committed suicide. Cp. Valerius Maximus, l. i, c. iv, § 3. Such stories would fortify the agelong superstition as to auspices and omens, which was in full force among Greek commanders as late as Xenophon, when many cultured Greeks were rationalists. But it was mainly a matter of routine, in a sphere where freethought is slow to penetrate. Cato, who would never have dreamt of departing from a Roman custom, was the author of the saying (Cicero, *De Div.* ii, 24) that haruspices might well laugh in each other's faces. He had in view the Etruscan practice, being able to see the folly of that, though not of his own. Cp. Mommsen, iii, 116.

But it is with the translation of the *Sacred History* of Evêmeros by ENNIUS, about 200 B.C., that the literary history of Roman Freethought begins. In view of the

---

[1] Mommsen, B. ii, c. 8, Eng. tr. ii, 70. Such creation of deities by mere abstraction of things and functions had been the rule in the popular as distinguished from the civic religion. Cp. Augustine, *De civitate Dei*, iv, 16, 23; vi, 9, etc.

position of Ennius as a teacher of Greek and *belles lettres* (he being of Greek descent, and born in Calabria), it cannot be supposed that he would openly translate an anti-religious treatise without the general acquiescence of his aristocratic patrons. Cicero says of him that he " followed " as well as translated Evêmeros;[1] and his favorite Greek dramatists were the freethinking Euripides and Epicharmos, both of whom he translated.[2] The popular superstitions, in particular those of soothsaying and divination, he sharply attacked.[3] If his patrons all the while stood obstinately to the traditional usages of official augury and ritual, it was in the spirit of political conservatism that belonged to their class and their civic ideal, and on the principle that religion was necessary for the control of the multitude. In Etruria, where the old culture had run largely to mysticism and soothsaying on oriental lines, the Roman government took care to encourage it, by securing the theological monopoly of the upper-class families,[4] and thus set up a standing hot-bed of superstition. In the same spirit they adopted from time to time popular cults from Greece, that of the Phrygian Mother of the Gods being introduced in the year 204 B.C. The attempt to suppress the Bacchic mysteries, B.C. 186, of which a distorted and extravagant account[5] is given by Livy, was made on grounds of policy and not of religion ; and even if the majority of the senate had not been disposed to encourage the popular appetite for emotional foreign worships, the multitude of their own accord would have introduced the latter, in resentment of the exclusiveness of the patricians in keeping the old

---

[1] *De natura Deorum*, i, 42.

[2] Mr. Shuckburgh (*History of Rome*, 1894, p. 401, *note*) cites a translated passage in his fragments (Cicero, *De Div*. ii, 50 ; *De nat. Deorum*, iii, 32), putting the Epicurean view that the Gods clearly did not govern human affairs, " which he probably would have softened if he had not agreed with it ". Cp. Mommsen, iii, 113 (B. ii, c 13).

[3] *Fragmenta*, ed. Hesselius, p. 226 ; Cicero, *De Divinat one*, i, 58.

[4] Mommsen, i, 301, ii, 71 ; iii, 117 (B. i, c. 15 ; B. ii, c. 8 ; B. iii, c. 13). Cicero, *De Div*. i, 41.

[5] Livy, xxix, 18.

domestic and national cults in their own hands.[1] As new
Eastern conquests multiplied the number of foreign slaves
and residents in Rome, the foreign worships multiplied
with them; and with the worships came such forms of
Freethought as then existed in Greece, Asia Minor, and
Egypt.[2] The general social tendency being downwards,
it was only a question of time when the rationalism should
be overgrown by the superstition.

§ 2.

While self-government lasted, rationalism among the
cultured classes was fairly common. The great poem of
LUCRETIUS, *On the Nature of Things*, with its enthusiastic
exposition of the doctrine of Epicurus, remains to show
to what a height of sincerity and ardor a Roman freethinker could rise. No Greek utterance that has come
down to us makes so direct and forcible an attack as his
on religion as a social institution. He is practically the
first systematic freethinking propagandist; so full is he of
his purpose that after his stately prologue to *alma Venus*,
who is for him but a personification of the genetic forces
of Nature, he plunges straight into his impeachment of
religion as a foul tyranny from which thinking men were
first freed by Epicurus. The sonorous verse vibrates with
an indignation such as Shelley's in *Queen Mab :* religion is
figured as *horribili super aspectu mortalibus instans ;* a little
further on its deeds are denounced as *scelerosa atque impia*,
"wicked and impious," the religious term being thus
turned against itself ; and a moving picture of the sacrifice
of Iphigeneia justifies the whole. "To so much of evil
could religion persuade." It is with a bitter consciousness of the fatal hold of the hated thing on most men's

[1] Cp. Boissier, *La religion romaine d'Auguste aux Antonins*, ed. 1892, i,
39, 346.
[2] The decree carried by the Catonic party in the Senate against the
Greek rhetors, *uti Romae ne essent* (Aulus Gellius, xv, 11), was passed on
grounds of general conservatism, as was the later decree against the Latin
rhetors. Both failed in their purpose. Cp. Shuckburgh, p. 520.

ignorant imagination that he goes on to speak of the fears[1]
so assiduously wrought upon by the *vates*, and to set up
with strenuous speed the vividly imagined system of
Epicurean science by which he seeks to fortify his friend
against them. That no thing comes from nothing or
lapses into nothing ; that matter is eternal ; that all things
proceed " without the Gods " by unchanging law, are
his insistent themes ; and for nigh two thousand years a
religious world has listened with a reluctant respect.

And yet throughout the whole powerful poem we have
testimony to the pupillary character of Roman thought in
relation to Grecian. However much the earnest student
may outgo his masters in emphasis and zeal of utterance,
he never transcends the original irrationality of asserting
that " the Gods " exist, albeit it is their glory to do
nothing. It is in picturing their ineffable peace that he
reaches his finest strains of song,[2] though in the next
breath he repudiates every idea of their control of things
cosmic or human. He swears by their sacred breasts,
proh sancta deum pectora, and their life of tranquil joy,
when he would express most vehemently his scorn of the
thought that it can be they who hurl the lightnings which
haply destroy their own temples and strike down alike
the just and the unjust.

The explanation of the anomaly seems to be twofold.
In the first place, Roman thought had not lived long
enough—it never did live long enough—to stand confidently on its own feet and criticise its Greek teachers.
In Cicero's treatise *On the Nature of the Gods*, the
Epicurean and the Stoic in turn retail their doctrine as
they had it from their school, the Epicurean affirming the
existence and the inaction of the Gods with equal confidence, and repeating without a misgiving the formula
about the Gods having not bodies but quasi-bodies with

[1] Cp. v, 1166.
[2] *De rerum natura*, ii, 646-650 (the passage cited by Mr. Gladstone in
the House of Commons in one of the Bradlaugh debates, with a confession
of its noble beauty) ; and again ii, 1090-1105, and iii, 18-22.

not blood but quasi-blood ; the Stoic, who stands by most
of the old superstitions, professing to have his philosophical reasons for them.   Each sectarian derides the
beliefs of the other ; neither can criticise his own creed.
It would seem as if in the habitually militarist society,
even when it turns to philosophy, there must prevail a
militarist ethic and psychology in the intellectual life ;
each man chosing a flag or a leader and fighting through
thick and thin on that side thenceforth.   On the other
hand the argumentation of the high-priest Cotta in the
dialogue turns to similar purpose the kindred principle of
civic tradition.   He argues in turn against the Epicurean's
science and the Stoic's superstition, contesting alike the
claim that the Gods are indifferent and the claim that
they govern ; and in the end he brazenly affirms that
while he sees no sound philosophic argument for religious
beliefs and practices, he thinks it is justifiable to maintain
them on the score of prescription or ancestral example.
Here we have the senatorial or conservative principle.[1]
In terms of that ideal, which prevailed alike with believers
and indifferentists,[2] and mediated between such rival
schools as the Epicurean and Stoic, we may partly
explain the Epicurean theorem itself.   For the rest, it is
to be understood as an outcome partly of surviving sentiment and partly of forced compromise in the case of its
Greek framers, and of the habit of partisan loyalty in the
case of its Roman adherents.

In the arguments of Cotta, the unbelieving high-priest,
we presumably have the doctrine of CICERO himself.[3] With
his vacillating character, his forensic habit, and his genius

----

[1] See the account of the doctrine of the high-priest Scaevola, preserved
by Augustine, *De civ. Dei*, iv, 27.   He and Varro (*Id.*, iv, 31 ; vi, 5-7)
agreed in rejecting the current myths, but insisted on the continued civic
acceptance of them.   On the whole question compare Boissier, *La religion
romaine*, i, 47-63.

[2] Thus the satirist LUCILIUS, who ridiculed the popular beliefs, was
capable, in his capacity of patriot, of crying out against the lack of respect
shown to religion and the Gods. (Boissier, pp. 51-52.)   The purposive
insanity set up in their thinking by such men must of course have been
destructive to character.

[3] Cp. the *De Divinatione*, i, 2.

for mere speech, he could not but betray his own lack of intellectual conviction; and such weakness as his found its natural support in the principle of use and wont, the practice and tradition of the commonwealth. On that footing, he had it in him to boast like any pedigree'd patrician of the historic religiousness of Rome, he himself the while being devoid cf all religious belief. Doubtless he gave philosophic color to his practice by noting the hopeless conflict of the creeds of the positive sects, very much as in our own day conservative dialectic finds a ground for religious conformity in the miscarriages of the men of science.[1] But Cicero does not seem even to have had a religious sentiment to cover the nakedness of his political opportunism. In his treatise *On Divination* he shows an absolute disbelief in all the recognised practices, including the augury which he himself officially practised; and his sole excuse is that they are to be retained "on account of popular opinion and of their great public utility".[2] In his countless private letters, again, he shows not a trace of religious feeling,[3] or even of interest in the questions which in his treatises he declares to be of the first importance.[4] Even the doctrine of immortality, to which he repeatedly returns, seems to have been for him only a forensic theme, never a source of the private consolation he ascribed to it.[5]

In the upper-class Rome of Cicero's day, his type seems to have been predominant,[6] the women alone being in the mass orthodox,[7] and in their case the tendency was to add new superstitions to the old. In the supreme figure of JULIUS CÆSAR we see the Roman brain at its strongest; and neither his avowed unbelief in the already

---

[1] *E.g.*, Mr. A. J. Balfour's *Foundations of Belief.*
[2] *De Divinatione*, ii, 33, 34, Cp. ii, 12 ; and *De nat. Deorum*, i, 22.
[3] Boissier, i, 58.
[4] *De nat. Deorum*, ii, 1.
[5] Boissier, p. 59.
[6] " It seems to me that on the whole, among the educated and the rich, the indifferent must have been in the majority " (Boissier, p. 61).
[7] *Id.*, p. 59.

popular doctrine of immortality,[1] nor his repeatedly
expressed contempt for the auspices,[2] withheld him from
holding and fulfilling the function of high pontiff. The
process of scepticism had been rapid among the men of
action. The illiterate Marius carried about with him a
Syrian prophetess ; of Sulla, who unhesitatingly plundered
the temple of Delphi, it was said, with no great probability, that he carried a small figure of Apollo as an
amulet ;[3] of Cæsar, unless in so far as it may be true that
in his last years, like Napoleon, he grew to believe in
omens as his powers failed, under the stress of perpetual
conflict,[4] it cannot be pretended that he was aught but a
convinced freethinker.[5] The greatest and most intellectual man of action in the ancient world had no part in
the faith which was supposed to have determined the
success of the most powerful of all the ancient nations.

Dean Merivale, noting that Cæsar "professed without
reserve the principles of the unbelievers", observes that "freethinker as he was, he could not escape from the universal
thraldom of superstition in which his contemporaries were
held " (History of the Romans under the Empire, ed. 1865, ii,
424). The reproach, from a priest, is piquant, but misleading.
All the stories on which it is founded apply to the last two or
three years of Cæsar's life ; and supposing them to be all true,
which is very doubtful, they would but prove what has been
suggested above, that the overstrained soldier, rising to the
dizzy height of a tremendous career, partly lost his mental
balance, like so many another. Such is the bearing of the
doubtful story (Pliny, Hist. Nat. xxviii, 2) that after the breaking
down of a chariot (presumably the casualty which took place
in his fourfold triumph : see Dion, xliii, 21) he never mounted
another without muttering a charm. M. Boissier (i, 70) makes
the statement of Pliny apply to Cæsar's whole life ; but
although Pliny gives no particulars, even Dean Merivale

---

[1] Sallust, Bellum Catilin., c. 51.
[2] Suetonius, Julius, cc. 59, 77 ; Cicero, De Divinatione, ii, 24. Cp.
Merivale, History of the Romans under the Empire, ed. 1865, ii, 424.
[3] Plutarch, Sulla, c. 29 ; Marius, c. 16.
[4] Compare the fears which grew upon Cromwell in his last days.
[5] Pompeius on the other hand had many seers in his camp ; but after
his overthrow expressed natural doubts about Providence. Cicero,
De Div. ii, 24, 47 ; Plutarch, Pompeius, c. 75.

(p. 372) connects it with the accident in the triumph. To the same time belongs the less challengeable record (Dion Cassius, lx, 23) of his climbing on his knees up the steps of the Capitol to propitiate Nemesis. The very questionable legend, applied so often to other captains, of his saying, *I have thee, Africa*, when he stumbled on landing (*Sueton. Jul.* 59), is a proof not of superstition but of presence of mind in checking the superstitious fears of the troops ; and was so understood by Suetonius ; as was the rather flimsy story of his taking with him in Africa a man nicknamed Salutio (Sueton. *ibid.*) to neutralise the luck of the opposing Cornelii. The whole turn given to the details by the clerical historian is arbitrary and unjudicial. Nor is he accurate in saying that Cæsar " denied the Gods" in the Senate. He actually swore by them, *per Deos immortales*, in the next sentence to that which he denied a future state. The assertion of the historian (p. 423) that in denying the immortality of the soul Cæsar denied " the recognised foundation of all religion", is a no less surprising error. The doctrine never had been so recognised in ancient Rome. A Christian ecclesiastic might have been expected to remember that the Jewish religion, believed by him to be divine, was devoid of the " recognised foundation" in question, and that the canonical book of Ecclesiastes expressly discards it. Of course Cæsar offered sacrifices to Gods in whom he did not believe. That was the habitual procedure of his age.

§ 3.

It is significant that the decay of rationalism in Rome begins and proceeds with the Empire. Augustus, whose chosen name was sacerdotal in its character,[1] made it part of his policy to restore as far as possible the ancient cults, many of which had fallen into extreme neglect, between the indifference of the aristocratic class[2] and the devotion of the populace to the more attractive worships introduced from Egypt and the East. That he was himself a habitually superstitious man seems certain ;[3] but even had he not been, his policy would have been natural from the

---

[1] Boissier, i, 73.

[2] See the citation from Varro in Augustine, *De civ. Dei*, vi, 2. Cp. Suetonius, *Augustus*, 29.

[3] The only record to the contrary is the worthless scandal as to his " suppers of the Twelve Gods " (Sueton. *Aug.* 70).

Roman point of view. A historian of two centuries later puts in the mouth of Mæcenas an imagined counsel to the young emperor to venerate and enforce the national religion, to exclude foreign cults, to put down alike atheism and magic, to control divination officially, and to keep an eye on the philosophers.[1] What the empire sought above all things was stability ; and a regimen of religion, under imperial control, seemed one of the likeliest ways to keep the people docile. Julius himself had seemed to plan such a policy,[2] though he also planned to establish public libraries, which would hardly have promoted faith among the educated.

Augustus, however, aimed at encouraging public religion of every description, repairing or rebuilding eighty-two temples at Rome alone, giving them rich gifts, restoring old festivals and ceremonies, reinstituting priestly colleges, encouraging special foreign worships, and setting up new civic cults ; himself playing high pontiff and joining each new priesthood, to the end of making his power and prestige so far identical with theirs ;[3] in brief, anticipating the later ruling principle of the Church of Rome. The natural upshot of the whole process was the imperial apotheosis, or raising of each emperor to Godhead at death. The usage of deifying living rulers was long before common in the East,[4] and had been adopted by the conquering Spartan Lysander in Asia Minor as readily as by the conquering Alexander. Julius Cæsar seems to have put it aside as a nauseous flattery ;[5] but Augustus wrought it into his policy. It

---

[1] Dion Cassius, lii, 36.
[2] *E.g.* his encouragement of a new college of priests founded in his honor. Dion, xliv, 6.
[3] Boissier, pp. 67-108.
[4] L'Abbé Beurlier, *Le Culte Impérial*, 1891, introd. and ch. 1 ; Boissier, ch. 2.
[5] It would seem that the occasion on which he enraged the Senate by not rising to receive them (Sueton. *Jul.* 78) was that on which they came to announce that they had made him a God, Jupiter Julius, with a special temple and a special priest. See Long, *Decline of the Roman Republic*, v, 418. He might very well have intended to rebuke their baseness. But cp. Boissier, i, 122, citing Dion, xlvi, 6.

was the consummation of the old political conception of religion.

In a society so managed, all hope of return to self-government having ceased, the level of thought sank accordingly. There was practically no more active freethought. HORACE, with his *credat Judæus Apella*, and his frank rejection of the fear of the *Deos tristes*,[1] was no believer, but he was not one to cross the emperor;[2] OVID could satirise[3] the dishonest merchant who prayed to the Gods to absolve his frauds; but he hailed Augustus as the sacred founder and restorer of temples,[4] and prayed for him as such, and busied himself with the archæology of the cults; VIRGIL, at heart a pantheist with rationalistic leanings,[5] but sadly divided between Lucretius and Augustus, his poetical and his political masters,[6] tells all the transition from the would-be scientific to the newly-credulous age in the two wistful lines—

> Felix qui potuit rerum cognoscere causas . . . .
> Fortunatus et ille, Deos qui novit agrestes ;[7]

" happy he who has learned the causes of things ; fortunate also he who has known the rural Gods ". The Gods, rural and other, entered on their due heritage in a world of decadence ; Virgil's epic is a religious celebration of antiquity ; and Livy's history is written in the credulous spirit or at least in the tone of an older time, with a few concessions to recent common-sense.[8] In the next generation, SENECA's monotheistic aversion to the popular superstitions is the high-water mark of the period, and represents the elevating power of the higher Greek Stoicism. On this score he belongs to the freethinking age, while his theistic apriorism belongs to the next.[9]

As the empire proceeds, the echoes of the old free-

---

[1] 1 Sat., v, 98-103.
[2] As to the conflict between Horace's bias and his policy, cp. Boissier, i, 193-201.
[3] *Fasti*, v, 673-692.
[4] *Fasti*, ii, 61-66.
[5] Æneid, vi, 724-7.   [6] Cp, Boissier, i, 228-9.   [7] *Georgics*, ii, 490, 493.
[8] Cp. Boissier, i, 193.   [9] Cp. Boissier, ii, 84-92.

thought become fewer and fewer. It is an entire misconception to suppose that Christianity came into the
Roman world as a saving counterforce to licentious
unbelief. Unbelief had practically disappeared before
Christianity made any headway ; and that creed came as
one of many popular cults, succeeding in virtue of its
various adaptations to the special conditions, moral and
economic. It was easy for the populace of the empire to
deify a man : at Rome it was the people, now so largely
of alien stock, who had most insisted on deifying Cæsar.[1]
But the upper class soon kept pace with them in the zest
for religion. In the first century, the elder PLINY recals
the spirit of Lucretius by the indignant eloquence with
which he protests against the burdensome belief in immortality; but though Seneca and others reject the fear
of future torment, Pliny is the last writer to repudiate
with energy the idea of a future state.[2] A number of
epitaphs still chime with his view ; but already the
majority are on the other side ;[3] and the fear of hell was
normally as active as the hope of heaven ; while the belief
in an approaching end of the world was proportionally as
common as it was later under Christianity.[4] Thus,
whatever may be the truth as to the persecutions of the
Christians in the first two centuries of the empire, the
motive was in all cases certainly political or moral, as in
the earlier case of the Bacchic mysteries, not hostility to
its doctrines as apart from Christian attacks on the
established worships.

Some unbelievers there doubtless were after PETRONIUS,
whose perdurable maxim that " Fear first made Gods in
the world ",[5] adopted in the next generation by STATIUS,[6]
was too pregnant with truth to miss all acceptance among

---

[1] Suetonius, *Jul.* 88.
[2] *Hist. nat.* vii, 55 (56). Cp. Boissier, i, 300.
[3] *Id.*, pp. 301-3.
[4] See the praiseworthy treatise of Mr. J. A. Farrer, *Paganism and
Christianity*, 1891, cc. 5, 6, and 7.
[5] *Primus in orbe deos fecit timor.* Frag. xxii, ed. Burmanni. The whole
passage is noteworthy.
[6] *Thebaïd*, iii, 661.

thinking men. The fact that Statius in his verse ranked
Domitian with the Gods made its truth none the less
pointed. The Alexandrian rationalist CHAEREMON, who
had been appointed one of the tutors of Nero, had
explained the Egyptian religion as a mere allegorising of
the physical order of the universe.[1] It has been remarked
too that in the next century the appointment of the freethinking Greek Lucian by Marcus Aurelius to a post of
high authority in Egypt showed that his writings gave no
great offence at court,[2] where indeed, save under the two
great Antonines, religious seriousness was rare. These,
however, were the exceptions : the whole cast of mind
developed under the autocracy, whether in the good
or in the bad, made for belief and acquiescence or
superstition rather than for searching doubt and sustained
reasoning.

The statement of Mosheim or of his commentators (*Eccles.
Hist.*, Cent. I, Pt. I. c. i, § 21, *note* ; Murdock's trans., Reid's ed.)
that JUVENAL (Sat. xiii, 86) "complains of the many atheists at
Rome" is a perversion of the passage cited. Juvenal's allusion
to those who put all things down to fortune and deny a moral
government of the world, begins with the phrase "*sunt qui*",
"there are (some) who" ; he makes far more account of the
many superstitious, and never suggests that the atheists are
numerous in his day. Neither does he "complain" : on the
contrary his allusion to the atheists as such is non-condemnatory
as compared with his attacks on pious rogues, and is thus part of
the ground for holding that he was himself something of a Freethinker—one of the last among the literary men. In the tenth
Satire (346 ff.) he puts the slightly theistic doctrine, sometimes
highly praised (ed. Ruperti, 1817, *in loc.*), that men should not
pray for anything, but leave the decision to the Gods, to whom
man is dearer than to himself. There too occurs the famous
doctrine (356) that if anything is to be prayed for it should be
the *mens sana in corpore sano*, and the strong soul void of the
fear of death. The accompanying phrase about offering "the
intestines and the sacred sausages of a whitish pig" is flatly
contemptuous of religious ceremonial; and the closing lines,

---

[1] Porphyry, *Epistle to Anebo* (with Jamblichus). Chaeremon, however,
regarded comets as divine portents. Origen, *Against Celsus*, B. i, c. 59.
[2] Prof. C. Martha, *Les moralistes sous l'empire romain*, ed. 1881, p. 341.

placing the source of virtue and happiness within, are strictly
naturalistic. In the two last :

> Nullum numen habes, si sit prudentia ; nos [*or* sed] te
> Nos facimus, Fortuna, Deam, cœloque locamus,

the frequent reading *abest* for *habes* seems to make the better
sense : " No divinity is wanting, if there be prudence ; but it is
we, O Fortune, who make thee a Goddess, and throne thee in
heaven." In any case, the insistence is on man's lordship
of himself. (The phrase occurs again in Sat. xiv, 315.)

As regards the general tone of Roman literature from the
first century onwards, the summing up of Renan is substantially
just :—"The freethinkers . . . . diminish little by little and
disappear . . . . Juvenal alone continues in Roman society,
down to the time of Hadrian, the expression of a frank
incredulity . . . Science dies out from day to day. From the
death of Seneca, it may be said that there is no longer a
thoroughly rationalistic scholar. Pliny the Elder is inquisitive
but uncritical. Tacitus, Pliny the Younger, Suetonius, avoid
commenting on the inanity of the most ridiculous inventions.
Pliny the Younger (Ep. vii, 27) believes in puerile stories of
ghosts; Epictetus (xxxi, 5) would have all practise the
established worship. Even a writer so frivolous as Apuleius
feels himself bound to take the tone of a rigid conservative
about the Gods (*Florida*, i, 1 ; *De magia*, 41, 55, 56, 63). A
single man, about the middle of this century, seems entirely
exempt from supernatural beliefs; that is Lucian. The scientific
spirit, which is the negation of the supernatural, exists only in
a few; superstition invades all, enfeebling all reason " (*Les
Evangiles*, ed. 1877, pp. 406-7).

§ 4.

One element of betterment there was in the life of
declining Rome, until the Roman ideals were superseded
by Oriental. Even the Augustan poets, Horace and Ovid,
had protested like the Hebrew prophets, and like Plato
and like Cicero, against the idea that rich sacrifices
availed with the Gods above a pure heart ; and such
doctrine prevailed more and more.[1] The men who grew
up under the autocracy, though inevitably feebler and

---

[1] Plato, 2 *Alcib.;* Cicero, *Pro Cluentio*, c. 68 ; Horace, *Carm.*, iii, 23, 17 ;
Ovid, *Heroides, Acont. Cydipp.*, 191-2 ; Persius, *Sat.* ii, 69 ; Seneca, *De
Beneficiis*, i, 6.   Cp. Diod. Sic. xii, 20 ; Varro, in Arnobius, *Adv. Gentes*, vii, 1.

more credulous in their thinking than those of the commonwealth, developed at length a concern for conduct, public and private, which lends dignity to the later philosophic literature, and lustre to the imperial rule of the' Antonines. This concern it was that, linking Greek theory to Roman practice, produced a code of rational law which could serve Europe for a thousand years. This concern too it was, joined with the high moral quality of their theism, that ennobled the writing of Seneca[1] and Epictetus and Maximus of Tyre; and irradiates the words as well as the rule of Marcus Aurelius. In them was anticipated all that was good[2] in the later Christian ethic, even as the popular faiths anticipated the Christian dogmas; and they cherished a temper of serenity that the Fathers fell far short of. To compare their pages with those of the subsequent Christian fathers—Seneca with Lactantius, "the Christian Seneca"; Maximus with Arnobius; Epictetus with Tertullian; the admirable Marcus, and his ideal of the "dear city of Zeus", with the shrill polemic of Augustine's *City of God* and the hysteria of the *Confessions*—is to prove a rapid descent in magnanimity, sanity, self-command, sweetness of spirit, and tolerance. Any prosecution of Christians under the Antonines was certainly on the score of political turbulence or malpractices, not on that of heresy; a crime created only by the Christians themselves, in their own conflicts. The scientific account of the repellent characteristics of the Fathers, of course, is not that their faith made them what they were, but that the ever-worsening social and intellectual conditions assorted such types into their ecclesiastical places, and secured for them their influence over the types now prevailing among the people. The new church organisation was above all things a great economic

[1] On Seneca's moral teaching, cp. Martha, *Les Moralistes sous l'empire romain*, pp. 57-66; Boissier, *La religion romaine*, ii, 80-82. M. Boissier further examines fully the exploded theory that Seneca received Christian teaching.
[2] Seneca was so advanced in his theoretic ethic as to consider all war on a level with homicide. *Epist.* xcv, 30.

endowment for a class of preachers, polemists and propagandists; and between the closing of the old spheres of public life and the opening of the new,[1] the new faith was established as much by political and economic conditions as by its intellectual adaptation to an age of mental twilight.

Of the religion of the educated Pagans in its last forms, it is finally to be said that it was markedly rationalistic as compared with the Christianity which followed, and has been on that ground stigmatised by Christian orthodoxy down till our own day. The religion of Marcus Aurelius is self-reverence, self-study, self-rule, plus faith in Deity; and it is not to be gainsaid that he remains the noblest monarch in history; the nearest parallel being the more superstitious but still ethically rationalistic Julian, the last of the great Pagans. In such rulers the antique philosophy was justified of its children; and if it never taught them to grapple with the vast sociological problem set up by the Empire, and so failed to preserve the antique civilisation, it at least did as much for them in that regard as the new faith did for its followers.

---

[1] It is to be noted that preaching had begun among the moralists of Rome in the first century; and was carried on by the priests of Isis in the second; and that in Egypt monasticism had long been established. Martha, as cited, p. 67; Boissier, i, 356-9. Cp. Mosheim, Cent. II, Pt. II, c. iii, § § 13, 14, as to monasticism.

CHAPTER VII.

ANCIENT CHRISTIANITY AND ITS OPPONENTS.

§ 1.

THE Christian Gospels, broadly considered, stand for a certain measure of freethinking reaction against the Jewish religion, and are accordingly to be reckoned with in the present enquiry; albeit their practical outcome was only an addition to the world's supernaturalism and traditional dogma. To estimate aright their share of Freethought, we have but to consider the kind and degree of demand they made on the reason of the ancient listener, as apart, that is, from the demand made on their basis for the recognition of a new Deity. When this is done, it will be found that they express in parts a process of reflection which outwent even critical common-sense in a kind of ecstatic Stoicism, an Oriental repudiation of the tyranny of passions and appetites; in other parts a mysticism that proceeds as far beyond the credulity of ordinary faith. Socially considered, they embody a similar opposition between an anarchistic and a partly orthodox or regulative ideal. The plain inference is that they stand for many independent movements of thought in the Græco-Roman world.

Any attentive study of the Gospels discloses not merely much glossing and piecing and interpolating of documents but a plain medley of doctrines, of ideals, of principles; and to accept the mass of disconnected utterances ascribed to "the Lord", many of them associated with miracles, as the oral teaching of any one man, is a proceeding so uncritical that in no other study could it now be followed. The simple fact that Paul's Epistles show *no* knowledge of any Jesuine miracles

(145)

or teachings whatever, except as regards the Last Supper (1 Cor. xi, 24-25,—a passage obviously interpolated after the Synoptics), admits of only three possible interpretations:—(1) *his* Jesus had not figured as a teacher at all; *or* (2) Paul gave no credit or attached no importance to reports of his teachings. Either of these views (of which the first is plainly the more plausible) admits of (3) the further conclusion that Paul's Jesus was not the Gospel Jesus, but an earlier one—a likely enough hypothesis; but on that view the mass of Dominical utterances in the Gospels is only so much the less certificated. When, then, it is admitted by all open-minded students that the *events* in the narrative are in many cases fictitious, even when they are not miraculous, it is wholly inadmissible that the *sayings* should be trustworthy, as one man's teachings.

Analysing them in collation we find even in the Synoptics, and without taking into account the Fourth Gospel, such wide discrepancies as the following :—

1. The doctrine : "the Kingdom of God is within you" (Lk. xvii, 21), side by side with promises of the speedy arrival of the Son of Man, whose coming = the Kingdom of God (Cp. Matt. iii, 2, 3 ; iv, 17 ; Mk. i, 15).

2. The frequent profession to supersede the Law (Mt. v, 21, 33, 38, 43, etc.) ; and the express declaration that not one jot or tittle thereof is to be superseded (Mt. v, 17-20).

3. Proclamation of a Gospel for the poor and the enslaved (Lk. iv, 18) ; with the tacit acceptance of slavery (Lk. xvii, 7, 9, 10; where the word translated "servant" in the A.V., and let pass by McClellan, certainly means "slave").

4. Stipulation for the simple fulfilment of the Law as a passport to eternal life, with or without further self-denial (Matt. xix, 16-21 ; Lk. x. 28); on the other hand a stipulation for simple benevolence, as in the Egyptian ritual (Mt. xxv; cp. Lk, ix, 48); and yet again stipulations for blind faith (Mt. x, 15) and for blood redemption (Mt. xxvi, 28).

5. Alternate promise (Mt. vi, 33 ; xix, 29) and denial (Mt. x, 34-39) of temporal blessings.

6. Alternate commands to secrecy (Mt. xii, 16; viii, 4 ; ix, 30; Mk. iii, 12 ; v, 43; vii, 36) and to publicity (Mt. vii, 7-8; Mk. v, 19) as to miracles, with a frequent record of their public performance.

7. Specific restriction of salvation to Israelites (Mt. x, 5, 6; xv, 24 ; xix, 28) ; equally specific declaration that the Kingdom of God shall be to another nation (Mt. xxii, 43) ; no less specific assurance that the Son of

Man (not the Twelve as in Mt. xix, 28) shall judge all nations, not merely Israel (Mt. xxv, 32 ; cp. viii, 11).

8. Profession to teach all, especially the simple and the childlike (Mt. xviii, 3 ; xi, 25, 28-30; Mk. x, 15) ; on the contrary a flat declaration (Mt. xiii, 10-16: Mk. iv, 11 ; Lk. viii, 10 ; cp. Mk. iv, 34) that the saving teaching is only for the special disciples ; yet again (Mt. xv, 16 ; Mk. vi, 52 : viii, 17, 18) imputations of lack of understanding on them.

9. Companionship of the teacher with "publicans and sinners" (Mt. ix, 10) ; and on the other hand a reference to the publicans as falling far short of the needed measure of loving kindness (Mt. v, 46).

10. Explicit contrarieties of phrase, not in context (Mt. xii, 30 ; Lk. ix, 50).

11. Flat contradictions of narrative as to the teacher's local success (Mt. xiii, 54-58 ; Lk. iv, 23).

12. Insistence that the Mesiah is of the Davidic line (Mt. i; xxi, 15; Lk. i, 27 ; ii, 4) and that he is not (Mt. xxii, 43-45 ; Mk. xii, 35-37 ; Lk. xx).

13. Contradictory precepts as to limitation and non-limitation of forgiveness (Mt. xviii, 17, 22).

Such variously serious discrepancies count for more than even the chronological and other divergences of the records concerning the Birth, the Supper, the Crucifixion, and the Resurrection, as proofs of diversity of source; and they may be multiplied indefinitely. The only course for criticism is to admit that they stand for the ideas of a variety of sects or movements, or else for an unlimited manipulation of the documents by individual hands. Many of them may very well have come from various so-called " Lords " and " Messiahs " ; but they cannot be from a single teacher.

It remains to note the so-far rationalistic character of such teaching as the protests against ceremonialism, the favoring of the poor and the outcast, the extension of the future life to non-Israelites, and the express limitation of prayer (Mt. vi, 9 ; Lk. xi, 2) to a simple expression of religious feeling—a prescription which has been absolutely ignored through the whole history of the Church, despite the constant use of the one prayer prescribed—itself a compilation of current Jewish phrases.

The expression in the Dominical prayer translated "Give us this day [or day by day] our daily bread" (Mt. vi, 11 ; Lk. xi, 3) is pointless and tautological as it stands in the

English and other Protestant versions. In verse 8 is the
assurance that the Father knows beforehand what is needed ;.
the prayer is therefore to be a simple process of communion
or advocation, free of all verbiage ; then, to make it specially
ask for the necessary subsistence, without which life would
cease, and further to make the demand each day, when in the
majority of cases there would be no need to offer such a
request, is to stultify the whole. If the most obvious necessity
is to be urged, why not all the less obvious ? The Vulgate
trans., " Give us to-day our super-substantial· bread," though.
it has the air of providing for the Mass, is presumptively
the original sense ; and is virtually supported by McClellan
(*N.T.* 1875, ii, 645-7), who notes that the repeated use of the
article, τὸν ἄρτον ἡμῶν τὸν ἐπιούσιον, implies a special meaning,
and remarks that of all the suggested translations " *daily* " is
" the very one which is most manifestly and utterly condemned ". Compare the bearing of the verses Mt. vi, 25-26,.
31-34, which expressly exclude the idea of prayer for bread,.
and Luke xi, 13. Naturally the average theologian (*e.g.*, Dr..
Lightfoot, cited by McClellan) clings to the conception of a.
daily appeal to the God for physical sustenance ; but in so-
doing he is utterly obscuring the original doctrine. Properly
interpreted, the prayer forms a curious parallel to the close of
the tenth satire of Juvenal, above cited, where all praying for
concrete boons is condemned, on the ground that the Gods.
know best, and that man is dearer to them than to himself ;.
but where there is permitted (of course illogically) an appeal
for soundness of mind and spiritual serenity. The documents.
would be nearly contemporary, and, though independent,.
would represent kindred processes of ethical and rational
improvement on current religious practice. On the other
hand the prayer " lead us not into temptation, but deliver us
from evil "—which again rings alien to the context—would
have been scouted by Juvenal as representing a bad survival
of the religion of fear.

It may or may not have been that this rationalisation
of religion was originally preached by the same sect or
school as gave the exalted counsel to resist not evil and
to love enemies—a line of thought found alike in India
and in China and, in the moderate form of a veto on
retaliation, in Greece and Rome.[1] But it is inconceivable

---

[1] *Eg.*, Plato, *Crito*, Jowett's tr. 3d. ed., ii, 150 ; Seneca, *De Ira*, ii, 32.
Valerius Maximus (iv, 2,˙4) even urges the returning of benefits for injuries.

that the same sect originally laid down the doctrines of
the blood sacrifice and the final damnation of those who
did not accept the Messiah (Mt. x).   The latter dogmas,
with the myths, naturally became the practical creed of
the later Church, for which the counsel of non-solicitous
prayer and the love of enemies were unimaginable ideals.[1]
Equally incapable of realisation by a State Church was
the anti-Pharisaical and " Bohemian " attitude ascribed
to the founder, and the spirit of independence towards
the reigning powers.   For the rest, the crazy doctrine
that a little faith might suffice to move mountains—a
development from the mysticisms of the Hebrew prophets
—could count for nothing save as an incitement to
prayer in general.   The freethinking elements in the
Gospels, in short, were precisely those which historic
Christianity inevitably cast aside.

§ 2.

Already in the Epistles the incompatibility of the
original critical spirit with sectarian policy has become
clear.   Paul—if the first epistle to the Thessalonians be
his—exhorts his converts to " prove all things, hold fast
what is good "[2]; and by way of making out the Christist
case against unpliable Jews he argues copiously in his
own way; but as soon as there is a question of "another
Jesus "[3] being set up, he is the sectarian fanatic pure
and simple ; and he no more thinks of applying the
counsel of criticism to his dogma[4] than of acting on his
prescription of love in controversy.   The attitude
towards slavery now becomes a positive fiat in its
support[5]; and all political freethinking is superseded by

---

[1] It is impossible to find in the whole patristic literature a single
display of the "love" in question.   In all early Christian history there
is nothing to represent it save the attitude of martyrs towards their
executioners—an attitude seen often in Pagan literature.   (Cp. Aelian,
Var. Hist. xii, 49.)
    [2] I Thess. v, 21.   [3] 2 Cor. xi, 4.   [4] Cp. Rom. ix, 14-21.
    [5] I Cor. vii, 20-24 (where the phrase translated in English " use it
rather " unquestionably means " rather continue " = remain a slave.   Cp.
Eph. vi, 5, and Variorum Teacher's Bible in loc.

a counsel of conformity.[1] The slight touch of rationalism
in the Judaic epistle of James, where the principle of
works is opposed to that of faith, is itself quashed by an
anti-rational conception of works.[2]

§ 3.

When the new creed, spreading through the Empire,
comes actively in contact with Paganism, the rationalistic
principle of anti-idolatry, still preserved by the Jewish
impulse, comes into prominence; and in so far as they
criticised Pagan myths and Pagan image-worship, the
early Christians may be said to have rationalised.[3] As
soon as the cult was joined by lettered men, the primitive
rationalism of Evêmeros was turned by them to account;
and a series of Fathers, including Clement of Alexandria,
Arnobius, Lactantius, and Augustine, pressed the case
against the Pagan creeds with an unflagging malice
which, if exhibited by later rationalists towards their own
creed, Christians would characterise in strong terms.
But the practice of criticism towards other creeds was
with the religious as with the philosophical sects, no help
to self-criticism.   The attitude of the Christian mass
towards Pagan idols and the worship of the Emperor was
rather one of frenzy[4] than of intellectual superiority[5];
and the Fathers never seem to have found a rationalistic
discipline in their polemic against Pagan beliefs.   Where
the unbelieving Lucian brightly banters, they taunt and
asperse, in the temper of barbarians deriding the Gods of
the enemy.   None of them seems to realise the bearing

---

[1] *Rom.* xiii, 1. Cp. *Tit.* iii, 1. The anti-Roman spirit in the Apocalypse
is Judaic, not Gentile-Christian; the book being of Jewish origin.
[2] *James* ii, 21.
[3] The Apology of Athenagoras (2d. c.) is rather a defence of monotheism
than a Christian document; hence no doubt its speedy neglect by the
Church.
[4] Cp. Tertullian, *De Idolatria*, passim, and *Ad Scapulam*, c. 5.
[5] For the refusal to worship men as Gods, they had of course abundant
Pagan precedent.   Cp. Plutarch, *Isis and Osiris*, cc. 23, 24; Arrian,
Alexander's Expedition, iv, 11; Curtius, viii, 5-8; Plutarch, *Artaxerxes*, c. 22;
Herodotos, vii, 136.

against his own creed of the Pagan argument that to die
and to suffer is to give proof of non-deity.[1] In the end,
the very image-worship which had been the main ground
of their rational attack on Paganism became the universal
usage of their own church ; and its worship of saints and
angels, of Father, Son, and Virgin Mother, made it
more truly a polytheism than the creed of the later
Pagans had been.[2] It is therefore rather to the heresies
within the Church than to its attacks on the old
polytheism that we are to look for early Christian
survivals of ancient rationalism; and for the most part,
after the practically rationalistic refusal of the early
Ebionites to accept the doctrine of the Virgin Birth,
these heresies were but combinations of other theosophies
with the Christian.

Already in the spurious Epistles to Timothy we have
allusion to the "antitheses of the *gnosis*"[4] or pretended
occult knowledge ; and to early Gnostic influences may
plausibly be attributed those passages in the Gospel,
above cited, which affirm that the Messiah's teaching is
not for the multitude but for the adepts.[5] All along,
Gnosticism[6] stood for the influence of older systems on
the new faith ; an influence which among Gentiles, un-
trained to the cult of sacred books, must have seemed
absolutely natural. In the third century, Ammonios
Saccas, of Alexandria, said to have been born of Christian
parents, set up a school which sought to blend the
Christian and the Pagan systems of religion and philo-

---

[1] *E.g.* Tertullian, *De Testimonio Animæ*, c. 1 ; Arnobius, *Adversus Gentes*,
i, 41, etc.; Lactantius, *Divine Institutes*, c. xv ; *Epit.* c. vii.
[2] Cp. Farrer, *Paganism and Christianity*, ch. 7.
[3] Irenæus, *Against Heresies*, i, 26. Cp. Hagenbach, *Lehrbuch der Dogmengeschichte*, 3te Aufl., § 23, 4 (S. 37), as to Cerinthus.
[4] 1 *Tim.* vi, 20. The word persistently translated "oppositions " is a
specific term in Gnostic lore. Cp. R. W. Mackay, *Rise and Progress of
Christianity*, 1854, p. 115, *note.*
[5] Cp. Harnack, *Outlines of the History of Dogma*, Mitchell's trans., p. 77
(c. 6), p. 149 (B. ii, c. 6) ; Gieseler, *Comp. of Eccles. Hist.* i, § 63, Eng. tr. i,
234, as to the attitude of Origen.
[6] The term Gnostic, often treated as if applicable only to heretical
sects, was adopted by Clemens of Alexandria as an honorable title. Cp.
Gieseler, p. 241, as cited.

sophy into a pantheistic whole, in which the old Gods
figured as subordinate daimons or as allegorical figures,
and Christ as a reformer.[1] The special leaning of the
school to Plato, whose system, already in vogue among
the scholars of Alexandria, had more affinity to Christianity than any of its rivals,[2] secured for it adherents of
many religious shades,[3] and enabled it to develop an
influence which permanently affected Christian theology;
this being the channel through which the doctrine of the
Trinity entered. According to Mosheim, almost no other
philosophy was taught at Alexandria down to the sixth
century.[4] Only when the regulative zeal of the Church
had began to draw the lines of creed definitely[5] on anti-
philosophic lines did the syncretic school, as represented
by Plotinus, Porphyry, and Hierocles,[6] declare itself
against Christianity.

Among the church sects, as distinguished from the
philosophic, the syncretic tendency was hardly less the
vogue. Some of the leading Fathers of the second century,
in particular Clement of Alexandria and Origen, show the
Platonic influence strongly,[7] and are given, the latter in
particular, to a remarkably free treatment of the sacred
books, seeing allegory wherever credence had been made
difficult by previous science,[8] or inconvenient by accepted
dogma. But in the multiplicity of Gnostic sects is to be
seen the main proof of the effort of Christians, before the
complete collapse of the ancient civilisation, to think with

---

[1] Mosheim, *Eccles. Hist.*, Cent. II, Pt. II, c. i, §§ 4-12. Cp., however,
Abbé Cognat, *Clément d'Alexandrie*, 1859, pp. 421-3, and Ueberweg, i, 239, as
to the obscurity resting on the original teaching of Ammonios.
[2] Cp. Gieseler, *Compendium*, i, § 52 (trans. vol. i, p. 162).
[3] *Id.*, §§ 54, 55, pp. 186-190.
[4] *E. H.*, Cent. III, Pt. II, c. i, §§ 2-4.
[5] As to the earlier latitudinarianism, cp. Gieseler as cited, p. 166.
[6] Gieseler, § 55.
[7] Mosheim, *E. H.*, Cent. III, Pt. II, c. iii, §§ 1-7; Gieseler, as cited,
§ 52, pp. 162-5; Eusebius, *Eccles. Hist.* vi, 19; B. Saint-Hilaire, *De
l'·cole d'Alexandrie*, 1845, p. 7; Baur, *Church History*, Eng. tr. ii, 3-8. But
cp. Cognat, *Clément d'Alexandrie*, l. v, ch. 5.
[8] Cp. Mosheim on Origen, *Comm. de rebus Christ. ante Const.*, §§ 27, 28,
summarised in Schlegel's note to *Ec. Hist.*, Reid's ed., pp. 100-1; Gieseler,
§ 63; Renan, *Marc-Aurèle*, pp. 114, 140.

some freedom on their religious problems.[1] In the terms
of the case—apart from the Judaising of the Elcesaites
and Clemens Romanus—the thought is an adaptation of
Pagan speculation, chiefly Oriental and Egyptian; and
the commonest characteristics are, (1) in theology, an
explanation of the moral confusion of the world by
assuming two opposed Powers,[2] or by setting a variety of
good and bad subordinate powers between the world and
the Supreme Being; and (2) in ethics, an insistence either
on the inherent corruptness of matter or on the incompatibility of holiness with physical pleasure.[3] The sects
influenced chiefly from Asia teach as a rule a doctrine of
two great opposing Powers; those influenced from Egypt
seek rather the solution of graduation of power under
one chief God. All alike showed some hostility to the pretensions of the Jews. Thus:—

1. Saturninus of Antioch (2nd c.) taught of a Good and an Evil Power,
and that the world and man were made by the seven planetary spirits,
without the knowledge or consent of either Power; both of whom, however, sought to take control, the Good God giving men rational souls, and
subjecting them to seven Creators, one of whom was the God of the Jews.
Christ was a spirit sent to bring men back to the Good God; but only
their asceticism could avail to consummate the scheme. (Irenæus, *Against
Heresies*, i, 24; Epiphanius, *Hæreses*, xxiii.)

2. Similarly Marcion (son of a bishop of Pontus) placed between the
good and bad Powers the Creator of the lower world, who was the God
and Lawgiver of the Jews, a mixed nature, but just; the other nations
being subjects of the Evil Power. Jesus, a divine spirit sent by the

---

[1] "Gnosis was an attempt to convert Christianity into philosophy; to
place it in its widest relation to the universe, and to incorporate with it the
ideas and feelings approved by the best intelligence of the times." Mackay,
Rise and Progress of Christianity, p. 109. But cp. the *per contra* on p. 110:
"it was but a philosophy in fetters, an effort of the mind to form for itself
a more systematic belief in its own prejudices". Again (p. 115): "a
reaction towards freethought was the essence of Gnosis".

[2] This view could be supported by the Platonists from Plato, *Laws*,
B. x. Cp. Chaignet, *La vie et les écrits de Platon*, 1871, p. 422; and Milman,
Hist. of Christianity, B. ii, c. v, ed. Paris, 1840, i, 288. It is explicitly set
forth by Plutarch, *I. and O.*, cc. 45-49.

[3] On the subject in general cp. Mosheim, *E. H.*, Cent. II, Pt. II. c. v;
also his *Commentaries on the Affairs of the Christians before Constantine*, Eng.
tr. vol. ii; Harnack, *Outlines of the Hist. of Dogma*, ch. 4; King, *The Gnostics
and their Remains;* Mackay, *Rise and Progress of Christianity*, Part III, §§ 10,
11, 12; Renan, *L'Eglise Chrétienne*, ch. ix, x; Milman, *Hist. of Christianity*,
B. ii, c. 5; Lardner, *Hist. of Heretics*, in *Works*, ed. 1835, vol. viii; Baur,
Church History, Pt. III.

Supreme God to save men, was opposed by both the God of the Jews and
the Evil Power; and asceticism is the way to carry out his saving purpose.
Of the same cast were the sects of Bardesanes and Tatian. (Irenæus, *Against
Heresies*, 1, 27, 28; Epiphanius, *Hæreses*, c. 56; Eusebius, *Eccles. Hist.*, iv, 30.
Mosheim, *E. H.*, Cent. II, Pt. II, ch. v, §§ 7-9. As to Marcion see Harnack, *Outlines*, ch. 5; Mackay, *Rise and Progress of Christianity*, Part III,
§§ 7, 12, 13; Irenæus, iv, 29, 30; Tertullian, *Against Marcion*.)

3. The Manichean creed (attributed to the Persian Mani or Manichæus, 3rd c.) proceeded on the same dualistic lines. In this the human
race had been created by the Power of Evil or Darkness, who is the God
of the Jews, and hence the body and its appetites are primordially evil, the
good element being the rational soul, which is part of the Power of Light.
By way of combining Christism and Mithraism, Christ is virtually identified with Mithra, and Manichæus claims to be the promised Paraclete.
Ultimately the Evil Power is to be overcome, and kept in eternal darkness,
with the few lost human souls. Here again the ethic is extremely ascetic, and
there is a doctrine of purgatory. (Milman, *Hist. of Christianity*, B. iii. ch. i;
Mosheim, *E. H.*, Cent. III, Pt. II, c. 5, §§ 2-11; Beausobre, *Hist. Critique de
Manichée et du Manichéisme*, 1734; Lardner, *Cred. of the Gospels*, Pt. II, ch. 63.)

4. Among the Egyptian Gnostics, again, Basilides taught that the one
Supreme God produced seven perfect secondary Powers, called Æons (Ages),
two of whom, Dynamis and Sophia (Power and Wisdom) procreated superior
angels, who built a heaven, and in turn produced lower grades of angels,
which produced others, till there were 365 grades, all ruled by a Prince
named Abraxas (whose name yields the number 365). The lowest grade
of angels, being close to eternal matter (which was evil by nature), made
thereof the world and men. The Supreme God then intervened, like the
Good Power in the Oriental system, to give men rational souls, but left
them to be ruled by the lower angels, of whom the Prince became God of
the Jews. All deteriorated, the God of the Jews becoming the worst.
Then the Supreme God sent the Prince of the Æons, Christ, to save men's
souls. Taking the form of the man Jesus, he was slain by the God of the
Jews. Despite charges to the contrary, this system too was ascetic, though
lenient to paganism. Similar tenets were held by the sects of Carpocrates
and Valentinus, all rising in the 2nd century; Valentinus setting up Thirty
Æons, male and female, in pairs, with four unmarried males, guardians of
the Pleroma or Heaven, namely Horus, Christ, the Holy Spirit, *and* Jesus.
The youngest Æon, Sophia, brought forth a daughter, Achamoth (*Scientia*),
who made the world out of rude matter, and produced Demiourgos, the
Artificer, who further manipulated matter. (Irenæus, B. i, cc. 24, 25; B. ii.)
These sects in turn split into others, with endless peculiarities.

Such was the relative Freethought of credulous
theosophic fantasy,[1] turning fictitious data to fresh

---

[1] "Mysticism itself is but an insane Rationalism" (Hampden, Bampton
Lect. on *Scholastic Philosophy*, 3d. ed. intr. p. liii). It may be described as
free thought without regard to evidence—that "lawless thought" which
Christian polemists are wont to ascribe to rationalists.

purpose by way of solving the riddle of the painful earth. The problem was to account for evil consistently with belief in a Good God; and the Orientals, inheriting a dualistic religion, adapted that ; while the Egyptians, inheriting a syncretic monotheism, set up grades of Powers between the All-Ruler and men, on the model of the grades between the Autocrat, ancient or modern, and his subjects. The Manichæans, the most thoroughly organised of all the outside sects, appear to have absorbed many of the adherents of the great Mithraic religion, and held together for centuries, despite fierce persecution and hostile propaganda, their influence subsisting till the Middle Ages.[1] The other Gnosticisms fared much worse. Lacking sacred books, often setting up a severe ethic as against the frequently loose practice of the Churches,[2] and offering a creed unsuited to the general populace, all alike passed away before the competition of the organised Church, which founded on the Canon[3] and the concrete dogmas, with many Pagan rites and beliefs[4] and a few great Pagan abracadabras added.

§ 4.

More persistently dangerous to the ancient Church were the successive efforts of the struggling spirit of reason within to rectify in some small measure its most arbitrary dogmas. Of these efforts the most prominent were the quasi-Unitarian doctrine of ARIUS (4th c.) and

[1] Gieseler, §§ 61, 86 (pp. 228, 368, 370).
[2] In the fourth century and later, however, the gospel of asceticism won great orthodox vogue through the writings of the so-called Dionysius the Areopagite (Mosheim, Cent. IV, Pt. II, c. iii, § 12).
[3] Compare the process by which the Talmudic system unified Judaism. Wellhausen, *Israel*, as cited, pp. 541-2 ; Milman, *History of Christianity*, B. ii, c. 4. Ed. Paris, 1840, i, 276.
[4] " There is good reason to suppose that the Christian bishops multiplied sacred rites for the sake of rendering the Jews and the pagans more friendly to them " (Mosheim, *E. H.*, Cent. II, Pt. II, c. iv. Cp. c. iii, § 17 ; c. iv, §§ 3-7; Cent. IV, Pt. II, c. iii, §§ 1-3 ; c. iv, §§ 1-2; Cent. V, Pt. II, c. iii, § 2.) This generalisation is borne out by nearly every other church historian. Cp. Harnack, *Outlines*, Pt. II, B. i, c. 1 ; Milman, B. iv, c. 5, pp. 367-374 ; Gieseler, §§ 98, 99, 101, 104 ; Renan, *Marc-Aurèle*, 3e. edit., p. 630. Baur, *Church History*, Eng. tr. ii, 285-9.

the opposition by PELAGIUS and his pupil CÆLESTIUS
(early in 5th c.) to the doctrine of hereditary sin—a
Judaic conception dating from Tertullian and unknown
to the Greeks.[1]

The former was the central and one of the most
intelligible conflicts in the vast medley of early discussion
over the nature of the Person of the Founder—a theme
susceptible of any conceivable formula, when once the
principle of deification was adopted. Between the
Gnosticism of Athenagoras, which made the Logos the
direct manifestation of Deity, and the Judaic view that
Jesus was "a mere man", for stating which the Byzantine
Theodotos was excommunicated at Rome by Bishop
Victor[2] in the third century, there were a hundred possible
fantasies of discrimination[3]; and the record of them is a
standing revelation of the intellectual delirium in the
ancient Church. Arianism itself, when put on its defence,
pronounced Jesus to be God, after beginning by declaring
him to be merely the noblest of created beings, and thus
became merely a modified mysticism, fighting for the
conception *homoiousios* (of similar nature) as against that
of *homoousios* (of the same nature).[4] Even at that, the
sect split up, its chief dissenters ranking as semi-Arians,
and many of the latter at length drifting back to Nicene
orthodoxy.[5] At first strong in the East, where it persecuted when it could, it was finally suppressed, after
endless strifes, by Theodosius at the end of the fourth
century; only to reappear in the West as the creed of

---

[1] Gieseler, § 87, p. 373 ; Hagenbach, *Lehrbuch der Dogmengeschichte*, 3te
Aufl. § 108.

[2] Gieseler, § 60, p. 218.

[3] Cp. Gieseler, §§ 80-83, pp. 328-353 ; Harnack, *Outlines*, Pt. II, B. i,
esp. pp. 201-2.

[4] In the end the doctrine declared orthodox was the opposite of what
had been declared orthodox in the Sabellian and other controversies
(Mosheim, Cent. IV, Pt. II, c. v, § 9) ; and all the while " the Arians and
the orthodox embraced the same theology in substance " (Murdock, note
on Mosheim, Reid's ed., p. 161). An eminent modern Catholic, however,
has described Arianism as " a deistic doctrine which *had not the courage to
bury itself in the fecund obscurities of dogma* " (Ozanam, *La Civilisation chrétienne
chez les Francs*, 1849, p. 35).

[5] Gieseler, § 83, p. 345.

the invading Goths and Lombards. In the East it had stood for ancient monotheism; in the West it prospered by early missionary chance till the Papal organisation triumphed. Its suppression meant the final repudiation of rationalism; though it had for the most part subsisted as a fanaticism, no less than did the Nicene creed.

Pelagianism, which unlike Arianism was not an ecclesiastical but a purely theological division,[1] fared better, the problem at issue involving the permanent crux of religious ethics. Augustine, whose supreme talent was the getting up of a play of dialectic against every troublesome movement in turn, without regard to his previous positions,[2] undertook to confute Pelagius and Cælestius as he did every other innovator; and his influence was such that after they had been acquitted of heresy by a church council in Palestine and by the Roman pontiff, the latter was induced to change his ground and condemn them, whereupon many councils followed suit, eighteen Pelagian bishops being deposed in Italy. But though the movement in its first form was thus crushed, and though in later forms it fell considerably short of the measure of ethical rationalism seen in the first, it soon took fresh shape in the form of so-called semi-Pelagianism, and so held its ground while any culture subsisted[3]; while Pelagianism on the subject of the needlessness of " prevenient grace ", and the power of man to secure salvation of his own will, has been chronic in the Church.

For a concise view of the Pelagian tenets see Murdock's note on Mosheim, following Walch and Schlegel (Reid's edition, pp. 208-9). They included (1) denial that Adam's sin was inherited; (2) assertion that death is strictly natural, and

---

[1] " Pelagianism is Christian rationalism " (Harnack, *Outlines*, Pt. II., B. ii, c. iv, § 3, p. 364.

[2] He was first a Manichean; later an anti-Manichean, denying predestination; later, as an opponent of the Pelagians, an assertor of predestination. Cp. Mackay, *Rise and Progress of Christianity*, Pt. V, § 15. As to his final Manicheanism, see Milman, *Hist. of Latin Christianity*, 3rd ed., i, 152.

[3] Cp. Harnack, *Outlines*, Pt. II, B. II, c. v, § 1 (p. 386).

not a mere punishment for Adam's sin; (3) denial that children and virtuous adults dying unbaptized are damned, a middle state being provided for them; (4) assertion that good acts come of a good will, and that the will is free; grace being an enlightenment of the understanding, and not indispensable to all men. The relative rationalism of these views is presumptively to be traced to the facts that Pelagius was a Briton and Cælestius an Irishman, and that both were Greek scholars. (When tried in Palestine they spoke Greek, like the council, but the accuser could speak only Latin.) They were thus bred in an atmosphere not yet laden with Latin dogma. In "confuting" them, Augustine developed the doctrine (intelligible as that of an elderly polemist in a decadent society) that all men are predestined to salvation or damnation by God's "mere good pleasure"—a demoralising formula which he at times hedged with illogical qualifications. (Cp. Murdock's note on Mosheim, as cited, p. 210; Gieseler, § 87.) But an orthodox champion of Augustine describes him as putting the doctrine without limitations (Rev. W. R. Clarke, St. Augustine, in "The Fathers for English Readers" series, p. 132.) It was never adopted in the East (Gieseler, p. 387); but became part of Christian theology, especially under Protestantism. On the other hand the Council of Trent erected several Pelagian doctrines into articles of faith; and the Protestant churches have in part since followed. See Sir W. Hamilton's Discussions on Philosophy and Literature, 1852, pp. 493-4, note; and Milman, Hist. of Latin Christianity, i, 142, 149.

The Latin Church thus finally maintained in religion the tradition of sworn adherence to sectarian formulas which has been already noted in the Roman philosophic sects, and in so doing reduced to a minimum the exercise of the reason, alike in ethics and in philosophy. Its dogmatic code was shaped under the influence of (1) Irenæus and Tertullian, who set Scripture above reason and, when pressed by heretics, tradition above even Scripture,[1] and (2) Augustine, who had the same tendencies, and whose incessant energy secured him an enormous influence. That influence was used not only to dogmatise every possible item of the faith but to

---

[1] Cp. Hampden, Bampton Lectures on The Scholastic Philosophy, 1848, pp. xxxv-xxxvi, and refs.

enforce in religion another Roman tradition, formerly confined to politics—that of systematic coercion of heretics. Before Augustine there had indeed been abundant mutual persecution of the bitterest kind between the parties of the Church; the Donatists in particular, with their organisation of armed fanatics, the Circumcelliones, had inflicted and suffered at intervals all the worst horrors of civil war in Africa during a hundred years; and the slaying of the Pagan girl-philosopher Hypatia[1] by the Christian monks of Alexandria is one of the vilest episodes in the whole history of religion. On the whole it is past question that the amount of homicide wrought by all the Pagan persecution of the earlier Christians was not a tithe of that wrought by their successors in their own quarrels. But the spirit which had so operated, and which had been repudiated even by the bitter Tertullian, was raised by Augustine to the status of a Christian dogma,[2] which of course had sufficient support in the Sacred Books, Judaic and Jesuist, and which henceforth inspired such an amount of murderous persecution in Christendom as the ancient world had never seen. When, the temple revenues having been already confiscated, the Pagan worships were finally overthrown and the temples appropriated by the edict of Honorius in the year 408, Augustine " though not entirely consistent, disapproved of the forcible demolition of the temples".[3] But he had nothing to say against the forcible suppression of their worship, and of the festivals.

Under the Eastern Empire, when once a balance of creed was attained in the Church, the same coercive

---

[1] Sokrates, *Eccles. Hist.*, B. vii, c. 15.
[2] *Epist.* 93. Cp. Schlegel's notes on Mosheim, in Reid's ed., pp. 159, 198; Rev. W. R. Clarke, *Saint Augustine*, pp. 86-87 (a defence); Milman, *History of Latin Christianity*, B. ii, c. 2, 3d. ed., i, 163; Boissier, *La fin du paganisme*, 2e édit., i, 69-79. Harnack's confused and contradictory estimate of Augustine (*Outlines*, Pt. II, B. II, cc. iii, iv) ignores this issue. He notes, however, (pp. 362-3) some of Augustine's countless self-contradictions.
[3] Milman, *Hist. of Christianity*, B. iii, c. 8; ed. cited, ii, 182, 188, and *note*. For the views of Ambrose, see p. 184. In Gaul, St. Martin put down the old shrines by brute force. *Id.*, p. 179. Temples had previously been robbed and demolished by bands of monks in the East. Libanius, *Orat. pro Templis.*

ideal was enforced, with differences in the creed insisted
on. Whichever phase of dogma was in power, persecution
of the others went on as a matter of course.[1] Athanasians
and Arians, Nestorians and Monophysites, used the same
weapons to the utmost of their scope ; Cyril of Alexandria led his fanatics to the pillage and expulsion of the
Jews as his underling Peter led them to the murder of
Hypatia; other bishops wrought the destruction of temples
throughout Egypt ;[2] Theodosius, Marcian, St. Leo, Zeno,
Justinian, all used coercion against every heresy without a
scruple, affirming every verbal fantasy of dogma at the point
of the sword. It was due to no survival of the love of
reason that some of the more stubborn heresies, driven
into communion with the new civilisation of the Arabs,
were the means of carrying some of the seeds of ancient
thought down the ages, to fructify ultimately in the
mental soil of modern Europe.

§ 5.

Against the orthodox creed, apart from social and
official hostility, there had early arisen critics who reasoned in terms of Jewish and Pagan beliefs, and in terms
of such rationalism as survived. Of the two former sorts,
some remains have been preserved, despite the tendency
of the Church to destroy their works. Of the latter,
apart from Lucian, we have traces in the Fathers and in
the Neo-Platonists.

Thus Tertullian (*De Testimonio Animæ*, c. 2) speaks of
some who believe in a non-active and passionless God, and
disdain those who turn Christian out of fear of a hereafter;
and again (c. 3) of Stoics who deride the belief in demons.
Jamblichos, too (*On the Mysteries*, B. x, c. 2), speaks of
opponents of the worship of the Gods in his day (early in
4th c.). Cp. Minucius Felix (2nd c.), *Octavius*, c. 5. In the fifth
century, again, Salvian makes a polemic against those who
in Christian Gaul denied that God exercised any government

---

[1] Gibbon, c. 47. Bohn ed. v, 211-252, 264, 268, 272.
[2] Milman, as cited, p. 178.

on earth. (*De Gubernatione Dei, l.* 4.) They seem, however, to
have been normal Christians driven to this view by the
barbarian invasions. Fronto, the tutor of Marcus Aurelius,
seems to have attacked the Christians partly as rationalist,
partly as conservative. See Renan, *L'Eglise Chrétienne*, p. 493.
As to Crescens, the enemy of Justin Martyr (2 *Apol.*, c. 3), see
id., p. 492. Cp. Arnobius, *Adversus Gentes, passim*, as to pagan
objections. What remains of Porphyry will be found in
Lardner's *Testimonies of the Heathen*, ch. 37.

The *Dialogue with Trypho* by Justin Martyr (about 150)
is a mere documental discussion between a Christian and
a Jew, each founding on the Hebrew Scriptures, and the
Christian doing nearly all of the argument. There is
not a scintilla of independent rationalism in the whole
tedious work.[1] Justin was a type of the would-be
"philosopher" who confessedly would take no trouble to
study science or philosophise, but who found his sphere
in an endless manipulation of the texts of Sacred Books.
But the work of the learned Origen *Against Celsus*
preserves for us a large part of the *True Discourse* of Celsus,
a critical and extremely well-informed argument against
Christianity by a Pagan of the Platonic[2] school in the
time of Hadrian,[3] on grounds to a considerable extent
rationalistic.[4] The line of rejoinder followed by Origen, one
of the most cultured of the Christian Fathers, is for the
most part otherwise. When Celsus argues that it makes
no difference by what name the Deity is called, Origen
answers[5] that on the contrary certain God-names have a
miraculous or magical virtue for the casting out of evil
spirits; that this mystery is known and practised by the
Egyptians and Persians; and that the mere name of
Jesus has been proved potent to cast out many such
demons. When on the other hand Celsus makes a Jew

---

[1] The *Controversy between Jason and Papiscus regarding Christ*, mentioned
by Origen (*Ag. Celsus*, B. iv, c. 4) seems to have been of the same nature.
[2] Origen repeatedly calls him an Epicurean ; but this is obviously false.
The Platonising Christian would not admit that a Platonist was anti-
Christian.
[3] So Origin. Kain, however, dates the treatise 177-8.
[4] Cp. Renan, *Marc-Aurèle*, 3e édit., pp. 346-371.
[5] B. i, cc. 24, 25.

argue against the Christist creed on the basis of the
Jewish story that the founder's birth was illegitimate,[1] the
Father's answer begins in sheer amiable ineptitude,[2]
which soon passes into shocked outcry.[3] In other
passages he is more successful, as when he convicts
Celsus' Jew of arguing alternately that the disciples were
deceived and that they were deceivers.[4] This part of the
discussion is interesting chiefly as showing how educated
Jews combated the Gospels in detail, at a level of
criticism not always above that of the believers. Sometimes the Jew's case is shrewdly put, as when he asks,[5]
" Did Jesus come into the world for this purpose, that we
should not believe him ? "—a challenge not to be met by
Origen's theology. One of the acutest of Celsus' thrusts
is the remark that Jesus himself declared that miracles
would be wrought after him by followers of Satan, and
that the argument from miracles is thus worthless.[6] To
this the rejoinder of Origen is suicidal; but at times the
assailant, himself a believer in all manner of miracles,
gives away his advantage completely enough.

Of a deeper interest are the sections in which Celsus
(himself a believer in a Supreme Deity and a future state,
and in a multitude of lower Powers, open to invocation)
rests his case on grounds of general reason, arguing that
the true Son of God must needs have brought home his
mission to all mankind[7]; and sweeps aside as foolish the
whole dispute between Jews and Christians,[8] of which he
had given a sample. Most interesting of all are the
chapters[9] in which the Christian cites the Pagan's
argument against the homocentric theory of things.
Celsus insists on the large impartiality of Nature, and repudiates the fantasy that the whole scheme is adjusted
to the well-being and the salvation of man. Here the
Christian, standing for his faith, may be said to carry on,
though in the spirit of a new fanaticism, the anti-

---

[1] B. i, cc. 28, 32.   [2] c. 32.   [3] cc. 37, 39.
        [4] B. ii, c. 26.   [5] B. ii, c. 78.   [6] B. ii, c. 49.
[7] B. ii, c. 30.   [8] B. iii, c. i.   [9] B. iv, cc. 23-30, 54-60, 74.

scientific humanism first set up by Sokrates; while the
Pagan, though touched by religious apriorism and prone
to lapse from logic to mysticism in his turn, approaches
the scientific standpoint of the elder thinkers who had
set religion aside.[1] Not for fifteen hundred years was his
standpoint to be regained among men. His protest
against the cultivation of blind faith,[2] which Origen tries
to meet on rationalistic lines, would in a later age be
regarded as conveying no imputation. Even the simple
defensive subtleties of Origen are too rationalistic for the
succeeding generations of the orthodox. The least embittered of the Fathers, he is in his way the most
reasonable; and in his unhesitating resort to the principle
of allegory wherever his documents are too hard for belief,
we see the last traces of the spirit of reason as it had
been in Plato, not yet paralysed by faith. Henceforth,
till a new intellectual life is set up from without,
Christian thought is more and more a mere disputation
over the unintelligible, in terms of documents open
always to opposing constructions.

Against such minds, the strictest reason would be
powerless; and it was fitting enough that LUCIAN, the
last of the great Freethinkers of the Hellenistic world,
should merely turn on popular Christianity some of his
serene satire[3]—more, perhaps, than has come down to us;
though on the other hand his authorship of the *De Morte
Peregrini*, which speaks of the "crucified sophist", has
been called in question.[4] The forcible-feeble dialogue
Philopatris, falsely attributed to Lucian, but clearly
belonging to the reign of Julian, is the last expression of
general scepticism in the ancient literature. The writer,
a bad imitator of Lucian, avows disbelief alike in the

---

[1] Cp. A. Kind, *Teleologie und Naturalismus in der altchristlichen Zeit*, 1875;
Soury, *Breviaire de l'histoire du Matérialisme*, pp. 331-340.
[2] B. i, cc. 9-11.   [3] Cp. Renan, *Marc-Aurèle*, pp. 373-7.
[4] Christian excisions have been suspected in the *Peregrinus*, § 11, (Ber-
nays, *Lucian und die Kyniker*, 1879, S. 107). But see Mr. J. M. Cotterill's *Peregrinus Proteus*, Edinburgh, 1879, for a theory of the spuriousness of the
treatise, which is surmised to be a fabrication of Henri Etienne.

old Gods and in the new, and professes to respect, if any, the "Unknown God" of the Athenians; but he makes no great impression of intellectual sincerity. Apart from this, and the lost anti-Christian work of Hierocles, governor of Bithynia under Diocletian, the last direct literary opponents of ancient Christianity were Porphyry and Julian. As both were believers in many Gods, and opposed Christianity because it opposed these, neither can well rank on that score as a Freethinker, even in the sense in which the speculative Gnostics were so. The bias of both, like that of Plutarch, seems to have been to the utmost latitude of religious belief; and, apart from personal provocations, it was the exiguity of the Christian creed that repelled them. Porphyry's treatise, indeed, was answered by four Fathers,[1] all of whose replies have disappeared, doubtless in fulfilment of the imperial edict for the destruction of Porphyry's book—a dramatic testimony to the state of mental freedom under Theodosius II.[2] The answer of Cyril to Julian has survived probably in virtue of Julian's status. His argumentations against the unworthy elements, the exclusiveness, and the absurdities of the Jewish and Christian faith are often reasonable enough, as doubtless were those of Porphyry;[3] but his own theosophic positions are hardly less vulnerable; and Porphyry's were probably no better, to judge from his preserved works. Yet it is to be said that the habitual tone and temper of the two men compares favorably with that of the polemists on the other side. They had inherited something of the elder philosophic spirit, which is so far to seek in patristic literature, outside of Origen.

After Julian, open rationalism being already extinct, anti-Christian thought was simply tabooed; and though the leading historians for centuries were Pagans, they

---

[1] Methodius, Eusebius, Apollinaris, and Philostorgius.
[2] Cod. Justin., *De Summa Trinitate*, l. I, tit. i, c. 3.
[3] Cp. Mackay, *Rise and Progress of Christianity*, p. 160. Chrysostom (*De Mundi Creatione*, vi, 3) testifies that he "led many away from the faith". He ably anticipated the "higher criticism" of the Book of Daniel.

only incidentally venture to betray the fact.   With public
lecturing forbidden, with the philosophic schools at Athens
closed and plundered by imperial force,[1] with heresy
ostracised, with Pagan worship, including the strong rival
cult of Mithraism, suppressed by the same power,[2] unbelief was naturally little heard of after the fifth century.
About its beginning we find Chrysostom boasting[3] that the
works of the anti-Christian writers had persuaded nobody,
and had almost disappeared.   It was only too true.   Save
for a few quasi-rational heresies, such as that of the
Unitarian Anomeans or Eunomians, who condemned
the worship of relics,[4] and whom Chrysostom himself
denounced as unbelievers, the spirit of sane criticism
had gone, with science, with art, with philosophy,
with culture.   But the verdict of time is given in the
persistent recoil of the modern spirit from the literature
of the age of faith to that of the elder age of nascent
reason ; and the historical outcome of the state of
things in which Chrysostom rejoiced was the re-establish-
ment of universal idolatry and practical polytheism in
the name of the creed he had preached.

§ 6.

It might safely have been inferred, but it is a matter
of proved fact, that while the higher intellectual life was
thus being paralysed, the primary intellectual virtues were
attainted.   As formerly in Jewry, so now in Christendom,

[1] By Justinian, in 529.   The banished thinkers were protected by
Chosroes in Persia, who secured them permission to return (Finlay, *Hist.
of Greece*, ed. Tozer, i, 277, 287).   Theodosius II had already forbidden all
public lectures by independent teachers (*Id.*, pp. 282-3).

[2] Theodosius I, Arcadius, and Theodosius II (379-450) successively
passed laws forbidding and persecuting Paganism (Finlay i, 286).   Mith-
raism was suppressed in the same period (Jerome, *Epist.* cvii, *ad Laetam* ,
Sokrates, *Eccles. Hist.* B. v, c. 16).   It is to be remembered that Constans
and Constantius, the sons of Constantine, had commenced to persecute
Paganism as soon as their father's new creed was sufficiently established
(Cod. Theod. xvi, 10, 2, 4), and this with the entire approval of the whole
Church.   It was not their fault that it subsisted till the time of Theodosius
II (Cp. Gieseler, § 75, pp. 306-8).   On the edict of Theodosius I, see
Milman, B. iii, c. 8, as cited, p. 186.

[3] *In S. Babylam, contra Julianum*, c. ii.   Cp. his Hom. iv on 1st Cor., Eng.
tr. 1839, p. 42.   [4] Jerome, *Adv. Vigilantium*, cc. 9, 11.

the practice of pious fraud became normal : all early
Christian literature, and most of the ecclesiastical history
of many succeeding centuries, is profoundly compromised
by the habitual resort to fiction, forgery, and interpola-
tion.   The mystical poetry of the Pagans, the Jewish
history of Josephus, the Gospels, the Epistles, all were
interpolated in the same spirit as had inspired the production of new Gospels, new Epistles, new books of
Acts, new Sibylline verses.   And even where to this
tendency there was opposed the growing demand of the
organised Church for a faithful text, when the documents
had become comparatively ancient, the disposition to
invent and suppress, to reason crookedly, to delude and
mislead, was normal among Churchmen.   This is the
verdict of orthodox ecclesiastical history, a dozen times
repeated.[1]   It of course carries no surprise for those who
have noted the religious doctrine of Plato, of Polybios,
of Cicero, of Varro, of Strabo, of Dion Cassius.

While intelligence thus retrograded under the reign
of faith, it is impossible to maintain, in the name of
historical science, the conventional claim that the faith
wrought a countervailing good.   What moral betterment
there was in the decaying Roman world was a matter of
the transformed social conditions, and belongs at least as
much to Paganism as to Christianity : even the asceticism
of the latter, which in reality had no reformative virtue
for society at large, was a pre-Christian as well as an
anti-Christian phenomenon.   It is indeed probable that in
the times of persecution the Christian community would
be limited to the more serious and devoted types[2]—that

---

[1] Mosheim, *E. H.*, Cent. II, Pt. II, c. iii, § 8 ; c. iv, § 15 ; Cent. III,
Pt. I, c. ii, § 5 ; Pt. II, c. iii, §§ 10, 11 ; Cent. IV., Pt. II, c. iii, §§ 3, 16 ;
Gieseler, § 63, p. 235 ; Waddington, *Hist. of the Church*, 1833, pp. 38-39 ;
Milman, *Hist. of Chr.*, B. iv, c. 3, ed. cited, ii, 337.   Cp. Mackay, *Rise and
Progress of Christianity*, pp. 11-12.

[2] Cp. the explicit admissions of Mosheim, *E. H.*, Cent. II, Pt. II, c. iv,
§ 16 ; Cent. III, Pt. II, c. ii, §§ 4, 6 ; Cent. IV, Pt. II, c. ii, § 8 ; c. iii, § 17 ;
Gieseler, § 103, vol. ii, p. 56.   It is to be noted, however, that even the
martyrs were at times bad characters who sought in martyrdom remission
for their sins (Gieseler, § 74, p. 296 ; De Wette, as there cited).

is to say, to those who would tend to live worthily under any creed. But that the normal Christian community was superior in point of morals is a poetic hallucination, set up by the legends concerning the martyrs and by the vauntings of the Fathers, which are demonstrably untrustworthy. The assertion, still at times made by professed Positivists, that the discredit of the marriage tie in Roman life necessitated a new religion, and that the new religion was regenerative, is only a quasi-scientific variation of the legend.

The evidence as to the failure of the faith to reform its adherents is continuous from the first generation onwards. Paul complains bitterly of the sexual licence among his first Corinthian converts (1 Cor. v, 1, 2) and seeks to check it by vehement commands, some mystical (*id. v.* 5) some prescribing ostracism (*vv.* 9-13) — a plain confession of failure, and a complete reversal of the prescription in the Gospel (Mt. xviii, 22) If that could be set aside, the command as to divorce could be likewise. Justin Martyr (*Dial. with Trypho*, c. 141) describes the orthodox Jews of his day as of all men the most given to polygamy and arbitrary divorce. (Cp. Deut. xxiv, 1; Edersheim, *History*, p. 294). Then the Christian assumption as to Roman degeneration and Eastern virtue cannot be sustained.

At the beginning of the third century, we have the decisive evidence of Tertullian that many of the charges of immorality made by serious Pagans against Christians were in large part true. First he affirms (*Ad Nationes*, B. i, c. 5) that the Pagan charges are not true of all, "*not even* of the greatest part of us". In regard to the charge of incest (c. 16) instead of denying it as the earlier apologist Minucius Felix had done, in the age of persecution, he merely argues that the same offence occurs *through ignorance* among the Pagans. The chapter concludes by virtually admitting the charge, with regard to misconduct in "the mysteries". Still later, when he has turned Montanist, Tertullian explicitly charges his former associates with sexual licence (*De Jejuniis* cc. 1, 17; *De Virginibus Velandis*, c. 14); pointing now to the heathen as showing more regard for monogamy than do the Christians (*De Exhort. Castitatis*, c. 13).

From the fourth century onward, the history of the Church reveals at every step a conformity on the part of its members to average pagan practice. The third canon of the Nicene Council forbids clerics of all ranks from keeping as companions or housekeepers women who are not their close blood relations. In the fifth century Salvian denounces the Christians alike of Gaul and Africa as being boundlessly licentious in comparison with the Arian barbarians (*De Gubernatione Dei, lib.* 5, 6, 7). They do not even, he declares, deny the charge, contenting themselves with claiming superior orthodoxy. (Cp. Bury, *Hist. of the Later Roman Empire*, i, 198-9, and Finlay, ii, 219, for another point of view.) On all hands, heresy was reckoned the one deadly sin (Gieseler, § 74, p. 295, and refs.), and all real misdeeds came to seem venial by comparison. As to sexual vice and crime among the Christianised Germans, see Gieseler, § 125, vol. ii, 158-160.

In the East, the conditions were the same. The story of the indecent performances of Theodora on the stage (Gibbon, c. 40), probably untrue of her, implies that such practices openly occurred. Milman (*Hist. of Chr.*, B. iv, c. ii, ed. cited, ii, 327) recognises general indecency, and notes that Zosimus charged it on Christian rule. Salvian speaks of unlimited obscenity in the theatres of Christian Gaul (*De Gub. Dei*, l. 6). Cp. Gibbon as to the character of the devout Justinian's minister Trebonian ; who, however, was called an atheist. (Suidas, *s.v.*) On the collapse of the iconoclastic movement, license became general (Finlay, *Hist. of Greece*, ed. Tozer, ii, 162). But even in the fourth century, Chrysostom's writings testify to the normality of all the vices, as well as the superstitions, that Christianity is supposed to have banished ; the churches figuring, like the ancient temples, as places of assignation. (Cp. the extracts of Lavollée, *Les Mœurs Byzantines*, in *Essais de littérature et d'histoire*, 1891, pp. 48-62, 89 ; the S. P. C. K.'s *St. Chrysostom's Picture of his Age*, 1875, pp. 6, 94, 96, 98, 100, 102-4, 108, 194 ; Chrysostom's *Homilies*, Eng. tr. 1839, Hom. xii on 1st. Cor., pp. 159-164 ; Jerome, *adv. Vigilantium*, cited by Gieseler, ii, 66, note 19, and in Gilly's *Vigilantius and his Times*, 1844, pp. 406-7.) The clergy were among the most licentious of all, and Chrysostom had repeatedly to preach against them (Lavollée, ch. 4 ; Mosheim, as last cited ; Gibbon, c. 47, Bohn ed. iv. 232). The position of women was practically what it had been in post-Alexandrian Greece and Asia-Minor (Lavollée, ch. 5 ; cp. *St. Chrysostom's Pict. of his Age*, pp. 180-2) ; and the practice corresponded. Indeed the supposition that the population of Constantinople as we see it under Justinian, or that of Alexandria in the same age, could have been morally austere, is fantastic.

It would indeed be unintelligible that intellectual decline without change of social system should put morals on a sound footing. The very asceticism which seeks to mortify the body is an avowal of the vice from which it recoils, and in so far as this has prevailed under Christianity it has specifically hindered general temper-ance,[1] inasmuch as the types capable of self-rule thus leave no offspring.

On the other hand, with the single exception of the case of the gladiatorial combats (which had been de-nounced in the first century by the Pagan Seneca,[2] but lasted in Rome long after Christianity had become the State religion;[3] while the no less cruel combats of men with wild beasts were suppressed only when the finances of the falling Empire could no longer maintain them),[4] the vice of cruelty seems to have been in no serious degree cast out.[5] Cruelty to slaves was certainly not less than in the Rome of the Antonines; and Chrysostom[6] denounces just such atrocities by cruel mistresses as had been described by Horace and Juvenal. The story of the slaying of Hypatia, indeed, is decisive as to Christian ferocity.[7]

In fine, the entire history of Christian Egypt, Asia, and Africa, progressively decadent till their easy conquest by the Saracens, and the entire history of the Christian Byzantine empire, at best stagnant in mental and material life during the thousand years of its existence, serve conclusively to establish the principle that in the absence of Freethought no civilisation can progress. More completely than any of the ancient civilisations to which they succeeded, they cast out or were denuded of

---

[1] Cp. Gieseler, ii, 67-8.

[2] *Epist.* vii, 5; xcv, 33. Cp. Cicero, *Tusculans*, ii. 17.

[3] Cp. the Bohn ed. of Gibbon, note by clerical editor, iii, 359.

[4] The express declaration of Salvian, *De Gubernatione Dei*, l. 6. On the general question compare Mr. Farrer's *Paganism and Christianity*, ch. 10; Milman, as last cited, p. 331; and Gieseler, ii, 71, note 6.

[5] As to the specially cruel use of judicial torture by the later Inquisiti see H. C. Lea, *Superstition and Force*, 3d. ed, p. 452.

[6] Lavollée, as cited, p. 92. Cp. *St. Chrysostom's Picture of his Age*, p. 112, and the admissions of Milman, B. iv, c. 1.

[7] As to the spirit of hatred roused by controversy among believers, see Gieseler, § 104, vol. ii, pp. 64-67.

the spirit of free reason.   The result was strictly con-
gruous.   The process, of course, was in terms of socio-
political causation throughout; and the rule of dogma
was the symptom or effect of the process, not the
extraneous cause.   But that is only the clinching of the
sociological lesson.

CHAPTER VIII.

FREETHOUGHT UNDER ISLAM.[1]

§ I.

THE Freethinking of Mohammed may be justly said to begin and end with his rejection of popular' polytheism, and his acceptance of the idea of a single God. That idea he held as a kind of revelation, not as a result of any traceable process of reasoning; and he affirmed it from first to last as a fanatic. One of the noblest of fanatics he may be, but hardly more.

That the idea, in its most vivid form, reached him in middle age by way of a vision, is part of the creed of his followers; and that it derived in some way from Jews, or Persians, or Christians, as the early unbelievers declared,[2] is probable enough. But there is evidence that among his fellow-Arabs the idea had taken some slight root before his time, even in a rationalistic form, and it is clear that there were before his day many believers, though also many unbelievers, in a future state.[3] The Moslems themselves preserved a tradition that one Zaid, who died five years before the Prophet received his first inspiration, had of his own accord renounced idolatry without becoming either Jew or Christian; but on being

---

[1] The strict meaning of this term, given by Mohammed ("the true religion with God is Islam": Sura iii, 17) is "submission"—such being the attitude demanded by the Prophet. "Moslem" means one who accepts Islam. Koran means strictly, not "book", but "reading" or recitation.

[2] Rodwell's trans. of the Koran, ed. 1861, Pref. p. xv.

[3] Sale, *Preliminary Discourse* to trans. of the Koran, ed. 1833, i, 42. Cp. Freeman, *History and Conquests of the Saracens*, 1856, p. 35. The late Prof. Palmer, in introd. to his trans. of the Koran (Sacred Books of the East series), i, p. xv, says that "By far the greater number had ceased to believe in anything at all"; but this is an extravagance, confuted by himself in other passages—*e.g.* p. xi.

told by a Jew to become a *Hanyf*,[1] that is to say, of the
religion of Abraham, who worshipped nothing but God,
he at once agreed.[2] In the oldest extant biography of
Mohammed, an address of Zaid's has been preserved, of
which six passages are reproduced in the Koran ;[3] and
there are other proofs[4] that the way had been partly
made for Mohammedanism before Mohammed. He uses
the term *Hanyf* repeatedly as standing for his own
doctrine.[5] The doctrine of a Supreme God was indeed
general ;[6] and Mohammed's insistence on the rejection of
the lesser deities or "companions of God" was but a
preaching of unitarianism to half-professed Monotheists
who yet practised polytheism and idolatry. The Arabs
at his time, in short, were on the same religious plane as
the Christians, but with a good deal of unbelief; and the
Prophet used traditional ideas to bring them to his
unitary creed. The several tribes were further to some
extent monolatrous,[7] somewhat as were the Semitic tribes
of Palestine ; and before Mohammed's time a special
worshipper of the star Sirius sought to persuade the
Koreish, Mohammed's tribe, to give up their idols and
adore that star alone. Thus between their partially

---

[1] The word means either convert or pervert : in Heb. and Syr. "heretic" ;
in Arabic, "orthodox". It must not be confounded with *Hanyfite*, the
name of an orthodox sect, founded by one Hanyfa.

[2] See Rodwell's trans. of the Koran, ed. 1861, pref. pp. xvi, xvii ; and
Sura xvi (lxxiii in Rodwell's chron. arrangement) *v.* 121, p. 252, note 2.

[3] Sprenger, *Das Leben und die Lehre des Mohammad*, i, 83, ff. Cp. 60, ff.

[4] Rodwell, p. 497, note to Sura iii (xcvii) 19 ; and pref. p. xvi ; Caussin
de Perceval, *Essai sur l'histoire des Arabes avant l'Islamisme*, 1847, i, 321-6.
"To the great mass of the citizens of Mecca, the new doctrine was simply
the Hanyfism to which they had become accustomed ; and they did not at
first trouble themselves at all about the matter." Palmer, introd. to trans.
of Koran, i, p. xxiv. Cp. Sprenger, as cited, i, 46-60, 65.

[5] The word *Hanyf* or *Hanif* recurs in Sura ii, 129 ; iii, 60, 89 ; iv, 124 ;
vi, 79, 162 ; x, 105 ; xvi, 121 ; xxii, 32 ; xxx, 29. Cp. H. Derenbourg, *La
science des religions et l'Islamisme*, 1886, pp. 42-3. Palmer's translation, marred
as it unfortunately is by slanginess, is on such points specially trustworthy.
Rodwell's does not always indicate the use of the word *hanyf*; but the
German version of Ullman, the French of Kasimirski, and Sale's, do not
indicate it at all. Sprenger, (S. 43) derives the *Hanyfs* from Essenes who
had almost lost all knowledge of the Bible.

[6] Cp. Sale's *Prelim. Discourse*, as cited, i, 38 ; and Palmer, introd., p. xv.

[7] Sale, pp. 39-41.

developed monotheism, their partial familiarity with *Hanyf* monotheism, and their common intercourse with the nominally monotheistic Jews and Christians, the Arabs were in a measure prepared for the Prophet's doctrine ; which, for the rest, embodied many cf their own traditions and superstitions as well as many orally received from Christians and Jews.

"The Koran itself is, indeed, less the invention or conception of Mohammed than a collection of legends and moral axioms borrowed from desert lore and couched in the language and rhythm of desert eloquence, but adorned with the additioned charm of enthusiasm. Had it been merely Mohammed's own invented discourses, bearing only the impress of his personal style, the Koran could never have appealed with so much success to every Arab-speaking race as a miracle of eloquence."[1]

The final triumph of the religion, however, was due neither to the elements of its Sacred Book nor to the moral or magnetic power of the Prophet. This power it was that won his first adherents, who were mostly his friends and relatives, or slaves to whom his religion was a species of enfranchisement.[2] From that point forward his success was military—thanks, that is, to the valor of his followers—his fellow citizens never having been won in mass to his teaching. Such success as his might conceivably be gained by a mere military chief. Nor could the spread of Islam after his death have taken place save in virtue of the special opportunities for conquest lying before its adherents—opportunities already seen by Mohammed, either with the eye of statesmanship or with that of his great general, Omar.[3] It is an error to assume, as is habitually done, that it was the unifying and inspiring power of the religion that wrought the

---

[1] Palmer, introd. to his *Haroun Alraschid*, 1881, p. 14. Cp. Derenbourg, *La science des religions et l'islamisme*, p. 44, controverting Kuenen.

[2] Rodwell, note to Sura xcvi (K. i), 10.

[3] Renan ascribes the idea wholly to Omar. *Etudes d'histoire et de critique*, ed. 1862, p. 250. The faithful have preserved a sly saying that " Omar was many a time of a certain opinion, and the Koran was then revealed accordingly". Nöldeke, *Enc. Brit.* art. on Koran, in *Sketches from Eastern History*, 1892, p. 28. On the other hand, Sedillot decides (*Histoire des Arabes*, 1854, p. 60) that " in Mohammed it is the political idea that dominates ".

Saracen conquests. Warlike northern barbarians overran the Western Empire without any such stimulus; the
prospect of booty, and racial kinship,[1] sufficed them for
the conquest of a decadent community; and the same
conditions existed for the equally warlike Saracens, who
also, before Mohammed, had learned something of the
military art from the Graeco-Romans.[2] Their religious
ardor would have availed them little against the Pagan
legions of unbelieving Caesar; and as a matter of fact
they could never conquer, though they curtailed, the
comparatively weak Byzantine Empire; its moderate
economic resources and traditional organisation sufficing
to sustain it, despite intellectual decadence, till the age of
Saracen greatness was over. Nor did their faith ever
unify them save ostensibly, for purposes of common
warfare against the racial foe—a kind of union attained
in all ages and with all varieties of religion. Deadly
domestic strifes broke out as soon as the Prophet was
dead. It would be as true to say that the common racial
and military interest against the Graeco - Roman and
Persian States unified the Moslem parties, as that Islam
unified the Arab tribes and factions. Apart from the
inner circle of converts, indeed, the first conquerors were
in mass not at all deeply devout, and many of them
maintained to the end of their generation, and after his
death, the unbelief which from the first met the Prophet
at Mecca.[3] A general fanaticism grew up later. But
had there been no Islam, enterprising Arabs would
probably have overrun Syria and Persia and Africa and
Spain all the same. Attila went further, and he is not
known to have been a monotheist or a believer in
Paradise. Nor were Jenghiz Khan and Tamerlane indebted to religious faith for their conquests.

---

[1] On the measure of racial unity set up by Abyssinian attacks as well as
by the pretensions of the Byzantine and Persian empires, see Sedillot,
pp. 30, 38.
[2] Prof. Stanislas Guyard, *La Civilisation Musulmane*, 1884, p. 22.
[3] Renan, *Etudes*, pp. 257-266.

On the other hand, when a Khalifate was anywhere established by military force, the faith would indeed serve as a nucleus of administration, and further as a means of resisting the insidious propaganda of the rival faith, which might have been a source of political danger. It was their Sacred Book and Prophet that saved the Arabs from accepting the religion of the states they conquered as did the Goths and Franks. The faith thus so far preserved their military polity when that was once set up; but it was not the faith that made the polity possible, or gave the power of conquest, as is conventionally held. At most it partly facilitated their conquests by detaching a certain amount of purely superstitious support from the other side.

2.

It may perhaps be more truly claimed for the Koran that it was the basis of Arab scholarship; since it was in order to elucidate its text that the first Arab grammars and dictionaries and literary collections were made.[1] Here again, however, the reflection arises that some such development would have occurred in any case, on the basis of the abundant pre-Islamic poetry, given but the material conquests. The first conquerors were illiterate, and had to resort to the services and the organisation of the conquered[2] for all purposes of administrative writing, using for a time even the Greek and Persian languages. There was nothing in the Koran itself to encourage literature; and the first conquerors either despised or feared that of the conquered.[3]

When the facts are inductively considered, it appears that the Koran was from the first rather a force of intel-

---

[1] Prof. Guyard, as cited, pp. 16, 51 ; C. E. Oelsner, *Des effets de la religion de Mohammed*, etc., 1810, p. 130.

[2] Guyard, p. 21 ; Palmer, *Haroun Alraschid*, introd. p. 19.

[3] Whether Omar caused the destruction of the library of Alexandria is still a disputed point. See Gibbon, c. 51, (Bohn ed., vi, 65). But the act would be in keeping with the tone of early Islam, and even with later acts. Cp. Oelsner, as cited, pp. 142-3.

lectual fixation than one of stimulus. As we have seen, there was a measure of rationalism as well as of monotheism among the Arabs before Mohammed; and the Prophet set his face violently against all unbelief. The word unbeliever or infidel in the Koran normally signifies merely rejector of Mohammed; but a number of passages show that there were specific unbelievers in the doctrine of a future state as well as in miracles; and his opponents put to him challenges which showed that they rationally disbelieved his claim to inspiration.[2] Hence, clearly, the scarcity of miracles in his early legend, on the Arab side. On a people thus partly "refined, sceptical, incredulous,"[3] whose poetry showed no trace of religion,[4] the triumph of Islam gradually imposed a tyrannous dogma, entailing abundance of primitive superstition under the ægis of monotheistic doctrine. Some moral service it did compass, and for this the credit seems to be substantially due to Mohammed; though here again he was not an innovator. Like previous reformers,[5] he vehemently denounced the horrible practice of burying alive girl children; and when the Koran became law his command took effect. His limitation of polygamy, too, may have counted for something, despite the unlimited practice of his latter years. For the rest he prescribes, in the traditional Eastern fashion, liberal almsgiving; this, with normal integrity and patience, and belief in "God and the Last Day, and the Angels, and the Scriptures, and the Prophets"[6] is the gist of his ethical and religious code, with much stress on hell-fire and the joys of Paradise, and at the same time on predestination, and with no reasoning on either issue.

---

[1] Sura vi, 25, 29; xix, 67; xxvii, 68-70; liv, 2; lxxxiii, 10-13. According to lviii, 28, however, some polytheists denied the future state.

[2] Cp. Renan, *Etudes d'histoire et de critique*, pp. 232-4;

[3] Renan, as cited, p. 232.

[4] *Id.*, p. 235.

[5] Sedillot, p. 39.

[6] See the passage cited with praise by the sympathetic Mr. Bosworth Smith (Sura ii) in his *Mohammed and Mohammedanism*, 2d ed., p. 181; where also delighted praise is given to the "description of Infidelity" in Sura xxiv, 39-40. The "infidels" in question were simply non-Moslems.

§ 3.

The history of Saracen culture is the history of the attainment of saner ideas and a higher plane of thought. Within a century of the Hejra[1] there had arisen some rational scepticism in the Moslem schools, as apart from the chronic schisms and strifes of the faithful. A school of theology had been founded by Hasan-al-Basri at Bassorah; and one of his disciples, Wasil ibn Attâ, rejected the predestination doctrine of the Koran as inconsistent with the future judgment; arguing for free-will and at the same time for the humane provision of a purgatory. From this beginning dates the Motazileh or class of Motazilites (or Mu'tazilites),[2] the freethinkers of Islam. Other sects of a semi-political character had arisen even during the last illness of the Prophet, and others soon after his death.[3] One party sought to impose on the faithful the "Sunna" or "traditions", which really represented the old Arabian ideas of law, but were pretended to be unwritten sayings of Mohammed.[4] To this the party of Ali (the Prophet's cousin) objected; whence began the long dispute between the Shiah or Shîites, the anti-traditionists, and the Sunnites; the conquered Persians tending to stand with the former, and generally, in virtue of their own thought, to supply the heterodox element under the later Khalifates.[5] Thus Shîites were apt to be Motazilites.[6] On Ali's side, again, there broke away a great body of Kharejites or Separatists, who claimed that the Imaum or head of the Faith should be chosen by election, while the Shîites stood for

---

[1] The Flight (of the Prophet from Mecca, in 622), from which begins the Mohammedan era.

[2] Weil, *Geschichte der Chalifen*, ii, 261-4 ; Dugat, *Histoire des philosophes et des théologiens Musulmans*, 1878, pp. 48-55 ; H. Steiner, *Die Mu'taziliten, oder die Freidenker im Islam*, 1865, S. 49-50 ; Guyard, p. 36. The term Motazila broadly means " dissenter ", or " belonging to a sect ".

[3] Steiner, S. 1.

[4] Palmer, introd. to *Haroun Alraschid*, p. 14.

[5] As to the Persian influence on Arab thought, cp. A. Müller, *Der Islam*, i, 469 ; Palmer, as last cited ; and Weil, *Geschichte der Chalifen*, ii, 214 ff.

[6] Weil, ii, 261.

succession by divine right.[1] All this had occurred before any schools of theology existed.

The Motazilites, once started, divided gradually into a score of sects,[2] all more or less given to rationalising within the limits of monotheism.[3] The first stock were named *Kadarites*, because insisting on man's power (*Kadar*) over his acts.[4] Against them were promptly ranged the *jabarites*, who affirmed that man's will was wholly under divine constraint (*jabar*). Yet another sect, the *Sifatites*, opposed both of the others, standing for a literal interpretation of the Koran, which is in parts predestinationist, and in parts assumes free will; while the main body of orthodox, following the text, professed to respect as insoluble mystery the contradictions they found in it.[5]

It is to be noted that, while the heretics in time came under Greek and other foreign influences, their criticism of the Koran was at the outset entirely their own.[6] The Shîites, becoming broadly the party of the Persians, admitted in time Persian, Jewish, Gnostic, Manichean, and other dualistic doctrines, and generally tended to interpret the Koran allegorically.[7] A particular school of allegorists, the Bathenians, even tended to purify the idea of deity in an agnostic direction.[8] All of these would appear to have ranked generically as Motazilites; and the manifold play of heretical thought gradually forced a certain habit of reasoning on the orthodox,[9] who as usual found their advantage in the dissidences of the dissenters. On the other hand, the Motazilites found new resources in the study and translation of Greek

---

[1] G. Dugat, *Histoire des philosophes et des théologiens Mussulmans*, p. 44.
[2] Dugat, p. 55; Steiner, S. 4.
[3] "Motazilism represents in Islam a Protestantism of the shade of Schleiermacher" (Renan, *Averroès et l' Averroïsme*, 3e éd., p, 104). Cp. Syed Ameer Ali, *Crit. Exam. of Life of Mohammed*, pp. 300-8.
[4] Dugat, pp. 28, 44; Guyard, p. 36; Steiner, 24-5; Renan, *Averroès*, p. 101.
[5] Guyard, pp. 37-38; G. D. Osborn, *The Khalifs of Baghdad*, 1878, p. 134.
[6] Steiner, S. 16. Major Osborn (work cited, p. 136) attributes their rise to the influence of Eastern Christianity, but gives no proof.
[7] Guyard, p. 40.   [8] Dugat, p. 34.   [9] Steiner, S. 5.

works, scientific and philosophical.[1] They were thus the main factors, on the Arab side, in the culture-evolution which went on under the Abasside Khalifs (750-1258). Greek literature reached them mainly through the Syrian Christians, in whose hands it had been put by the Nestorians, driven out of their scientific school at Edessa and exiled by Leo the Isaurian (716-741) ;[2] possibly also in part through the philosophers who, on being exiled from Athens by Justinian, settled for a time in Persia.[3] The total result was that already in the ninth century, within two hundred years of the beginning of Mohammed's preaching, the Saracens in Persia had reached not only a remarkable height of material civilisation, their wealth exceeding that of Byzantium, but a considerable though quasi-secret measure of scientific knowledge and rational thought.[4]

Secresy was long imposed on the Motazilites by the orthodoxy of the Khalifs,[5] who as a rule atoned for many crimes and abundant breaches of the law of the Koran by a devout profession of faith. Freethinking, however, had its periods of political prosperity. The Khalif El-Mansour, though he played a very orthodox part,[6] favored the Motazilites (754-775), being generally a patron of the sciences ; and under him were made the

---

[1] Steiner, S. 5, 9, 88-9.
[2] Sedillot, Hist. des Arabes, p. 335 ; Prof. A. Müller, Der Islam (in Oncken's series) i, 470; Ueberweg, i, 402.
[3] Ueberweg, p. 403 ; Weil, Gesch. der Chalifen, ii, 281.
[4] For an orthodox account of the beginnings of freethinking (called Zendekism or atheism) see Weil, ii, 214. Cp. S. 261 ; also Tabari's Chronicle, Pt. v, c. 97 ; and Renan, Averroès, p. 103. Already, among the Ommayade Khalifs, Yezid III held the Motazilite tenet of freewill. Id. S. 260.
. [5] Steiner, S. 8. An association called "Brethren of Purity" or "Sincere Brethren" seemed to have latterly carried Motazilism far. They were in effect the encyclopedists of Arab science. Ueberweg, i, 411. See Dr. F. Dieterici, Die Naturanschauung und Naturphilosophie der Araber im roten Jahrhundert, aus den schriften der lautern Brüder, 1861, Vorrede, S. viii, and Flügel, as there cited. Flügel dates the writings of the Brethren about 970 ; but the association presumably existed earlier. Cp. Renan, Averroès, p. 104 ; and S. Lane-Poole's Studies in a Mosque, 1893, ch. 6, as to their performance.
[6] He made five pilgrimages to Mecca, and died on the last, thus attaining to sainthood.

first translations from the Greek.[1]   Despite his orthodoxy
he encouraged science ; and it was as insurgents and not
as unbelievers that he destroyed the sect of Rewandites,
(a branch of the anti-Moslem Ismailites) who are said to
have believed in metempsychosis.[2]   Partly on political
but partly also on religious grounds his successor El-
Mahdi made war on the Ismailites, whom he regarded as
Atheists, destroying their books and causing others to be
written against them.[3]   They were anti-Koranites; hardly
Atheists; but a kind of informal rationalism approaching
to Atheism, and involving unbelief in the Koran and
the Prophet, seems to have spread considerably, despite
the slaughter of many unbelievers by El-Mahdi.   Its source
seems to have been Persian aversion to the alien creed.[4]   The
great philosophic influence, again, was that of Aristotle ;
and though his abstract God-idea was nominally adhered
to, the scientific movement promoted above all things the
conception of a reign of law.[5]   El Hadi, the successor of
El Mahdi, persecuted much and killed many heretics ;
and Haroun Alraschid (Aaron the Orthodox) menaced
with death those who held the moderately rational tenet
that "the Koran was created",[6] as against the orthodox
dogma (on all fours with the Brahmanic doctrine concerning the Veda) that it was eternal in the heavens and
uncreated.

Haroun's crimes, however, consisted little in acts of
persecution.   The Persian Barmekides (the family of his
first Vizier, surnamed Barmek) were regarded as pro-
tectors of Motazilites ;[7] and one of the sons, Jaafer, was
even suspected of atheism, all three indeed being charged

[1] Weil, *Gesch. der Chalifen*, ii, 81 ; Dugat, pp. 59-61 ; A. Müller, *Der Islam*,
i, 470.   In Mansour's reign was born El-Allaf, " Sheikh of the Motazilites."
[2] Dugat, p. 62.
[3] Dugat, p. 71.
[4] *Id.* p. 72 ; Tabari's *Chronicle*, Pt. v, c. 97, Zotenberg's trans., 1874, iv,
447-453.   Tabari notes (p. 448) that all the Moslem theologians agree in
thinking *zendekism* much worse than any of the false religions, since it
rejects all and denies God as well as the Prophet.
[5] Cp. Steiner, S. 55 ff., 66 ff. ; Ueberweg, *Hist. of Philos.*, i, 405.
[6] Dugat, p. 76.
[7] Dugat, p. 79; Osborn, *Khalifs of Baghdad*, p. 195.

with it.[1] Their destruction, on other grounds, does not seem to have altered the conditions for the thinkers; but Haroun's incompetent son Emin was a devotee and persecutor. His abler brother and conqueror MAMOUN, on the other hand, directly favored the Motazilites, partly on political grounds, to strengthen himself with the Persian party, but also on the ground of conviction.[2] He even imprisoned some of the orthodox theologians who maintained that the Koran was not a created thing, though, like certain persecutors of other faiths, he had expressly declared himself in favor of persuasion as against coercion.[3] In one case he inflicted a cruel torture. Compared with others, certainly, he did not carry his coercion far, though, on being once publicly addressed as "Ameer of the Unbelievers", he caused the fanatic who said it to be put to death.[4] In private he was wont to conduct meetings for discussion, attended by believers and unbelievers of every shade, at which the only restriction was that the appeal must be to reason, and never to the Koran.[5] Concerning his personal bias, it is related that he had received from Kabul a book in old Persian, "The Eternal Reason," which taught that reason is the only basis for religion, and that revelation cannot serve as a standing ground.[6] The story is interesting, but enigmatic; the origin of the book being untraceable. The fact remains, however, that Mamoun was of all the Khalifs the greatest promoter of science[7] and culture; the chief encourager of the study and translation of Greek literature;[8] and, despite his

[1] Palmer, *Haroun Alraschid*, p. 82. They were really Theists.
[2] Weil, *Geschichte der Chalifen*, ii, 215, 261, 280; A. Müller, *Der Islam*, S. 514-5.
[3] Dugat, pp. 85-96.
[4] *Id.* p. 83.
[5] See extract by Major Osborn, *Khalifs*, p. 250.
[6] Osborn, *Khalifs*, p. 249.
[7] He it was who first caused to be measured a degree of the earth's surface. The attempt was duly denounced as atheistic by a leading theologian, Takyuddin. Montucla, *Hist. des Mathématiques*, éd. Lalande, i, 355, ff.; Draper, *Conflict of Religion and Science*, p. 109.
[8] A. Müller, *Der Islam*, i, 509 ff. Weil, *Gesch. der Chalifen*, ii, 280 ff.

coercion of the theologians on the dogma of the eternity of the Koran, tolerant enough to put a Christian at the head of a college at Damascus, declaring that he chose him not for his religion but for his science. In the same spirit he permitted the free circulation of the apologetic treatise of the Armenian Christian Al Kindy, in which Islam and the Koran are freely criticised. As a ruler, too, he ranks among the best of his race for clemency, justice, and decency of life, although orthodox imputations were cast on his subordinates. His successors Motasim and Wathik were of the same cast of opinion, the latter being, however, fanatical on behalf of his rationalistic view of the Koran as a created thing.[1]

A violent orthodox reaction set in under the worthless and Turk-ruled Khalif Motawakkel[2] (847-861), by whose time the Khalifate was in a state of political decadence, partly from the economic exhaustion following on its tyrannous and extortionate rule, partly from the divisive tendencies of its heterogeneous sections, partly from the corrupting tendency of all despotic power.[3] Despite the official restoration of orthodoxy, the private cultivation of science and philosophy proceeded for a time; the study and translation of Greek books continued;[4] and rationalism of a kind seems to have subsisted more or less secretly to the end. In the tenth century it is said to have reached even the unlearned. Faith in Mohammed's mission and law began again to shake; and the learned disregarded its prescriptions. Mystics professed to find the way to God without the Koran. Many decided that religion was useful for regulating the people, but was not for the wise. On the other side, however, the orthodox condemned all science as leading to unbelief,[5] and

---

[1] Dugat, pp. 105-111. Apart from this one issue, general tolerance seems to have prevailed. Osborn, *Khalifs*, p. 265.

[2] Dugat, p. 112; Steiner, S. 79.

[3] A good analysis is given by Dugat, pp. 337-348.

[4] The whole of Aristotle, except, apparently, the *Politics*, had been translated in the time of the philosopher Avicenna (fl. 1000).

[5] Steiner, *Die Mutaziliten*, S. 10-11, following Gazzali (Al-Gazel); Weil, *Gesch. der Chalifen*, iii, 72.

developed an elaborate and quasi-systematic theology. It was while the scientific encyclopedists of Bassorah were amassing the knowledge which, through the Moors, renewed thought in the West, that Al-Ashari built up the Kalâm or scholastic theology which thenceforth reigned in the Mohammedan East;[1] and the philosopher Al-Gazel, on his part, employed the ancient and modern device of turning a profession of philosophical scepticism to the account of orthodoxy.[2]

In the struggle between science and religion, in a politically decadent State, the latter inevitably secured the administrative power.[3] Under the Khalifs Motamid (d. 892) and Motadhed (d. 902), all science and phil-osophy were proscribed, and book-sellers were put upon their oath not to sell any but orthodox books.[4] Thus, though philosophy and science had secretly survived, when the political end came the popular faith was in much the same state as it had been under Haroun Alraschid. Under Islam as under all the faiths of the world, in the East as in the West, the mass of the people remained ignorant as well as poor ; and the learning and skill of the scholars served only to pass on the saved treasure of Greek thought and science to the new civil-isation of Europe. The fact that the age of military and political decadence was that of the widest diffusion of rationalism is naturally fastened on as giving the explana-tion of the decline ; but the inference is pure fallacy. The Bagdad Khalifate declined as the Christianised Roman Empire declined, from political and external causes; and the Turks who overthrew it proceeded to overthrow Christian Byzantium, where rationalism never reared its head.

[1] Guyard, pp. 41-42 ; Renan, *Averroès*, pp. 104-5. It was at first unfixed, but later definitely orthodox.
[2] Ueberweg, i, 405, 414 ; Steiner, S. 11.
[3] Hence, among other things, a check on the practice of anatomy, religious feeling being opposed to it under Islam as under Christianity. Dugat, pp. 62-3.
[4] Dugat, pp. 123-8.

The conventional view is thus set forth in a popular work
(*The Saracens*, by Arthur Gilman, 1887, p. 385):—"Unconsciously Mamun began a process by which that implicit faith
which had been at once the foundation and the inspiration of
Islam, which had nerved its warriors in their terrible warfare, and
had brought the nation out of its former obscurity to the
foremost position among the peoples of the world, was to be
taken from them." We have seen that this view is entirely
erroneous as regards the rise of the Saracen power; and it is
no less so as regards the decline. The Eastern Saracens had
been decisively defeated by the Byzantines in the very first
flush of their fanaticism and success; and the Western had
been routed by Charles Martel long before they had any
philosophy. There was no overthrow of faith among the
warriors of the Khalifate. The enlistment of Turkish mercenaries by Mamun and Motasim, by way of being independent of
the Persian and Arab factions in the army and the State,
introduced an element which, at first purely barbaric, became
as orthodox as the men of Haroun's day had been. Yet the
decadence, instead of being checked, was furthered. Nor
were the strifes set up by the rationalistic view of the Koran
nearly so destructive as the mere faction-fights and sectarian
insurrections which began with Motawakkel. The falling-
away of cities and provinces under the feeble Moktader (908-
932) had nothing whatever to do with opinions, but was strictly
analogous to the dissolution of the kingdom of Charlemagne
under his successors, through the rise of new provincial
energies; and the tyranny of the Turkish mercenaries was on
all fours with that of the Pretorians of the Roman Empire,
and with that of the Janissaries in later Turkey. The writer
under notice has actually recorded (p. 408) that the warlike
sect of Ismaïlitic Karmathians, who did more than any other
enemy to dismember the Khalifate, were unbelievers in the
Koran, deniers of revelation, and disregarders of prayer. The
later Khalifs, puppets in the hands of the Turks, were one and
all devout believers. On the other hand, fresh Moslem and
non-Moslem dynasties arose alternately as the conditions and
opportunities determined. Jenghiz Khan, who overran Asia,
was no Moslem; neither was Tamerlane; but new Moslem
conquerors did overrun India, as Pagan Alexander had done
in his day. Theological ideas counted for as little in one case
as in the other. Sultan Mahmoud of Ghazni (997-1030), who
reared a new empire on the basis of the province of Khorassan
and the kingdom of Bokhara, and who twelve times success-
fully invaded India, happened to be of Turkish stock; but he

is also recorded to have been in his youth a doubter of a future state, as well as of his personal legitimacy. His later parade of piety (as to which see Baron De Slane's tr. of Ibn Khallikan's *Biog. Dict.*, iii, 334) is thus a trifle suspect (*British India*, in Edin. Cab. Lib., 3rd ed. i, 189, following Ferishta); and his avarice seems to have animated him to the full as much as his faith, which was certainly not more devout than that of the Brahmans of Somnauth, whose hold he captured. During his reign, besides, unbelief was rife in his despite (Weil, *Geschichte der Chalifen*, iii, 72). The conventional theorem as to the political importance of faith, in short, will not bear investigation. Even Freeman here sets it aside (*Hist. and Conq. of the Saracens*, p. 124).

§ 4.

It is in the later and nominally decadent ages of the Bagdad Khalifate, when science and culture and even industry relatively prospered by reason of the personal impotence of the Khalifs, that we meet with the most pronounced and the most perspicacious of the Free-thinkers of Islam. In the years 970-1057 flourished at Bagdad the blind poet Aboul-Ala EL MARRI, who in his verse derided all religions as alike absurd, and yet was for some reason never persecuted. One of his sayings was that " The world holds two classes of men; intelligent men without religion, and religious men without intelligence ".[1] He may have escaped on the strength of a character for general eccentricity, for he was an ardent vegetarian and an opponent of all parentage, declaring that to bring a child into the world was to add to the sum of suffering.[2]

A century later still, and in another region, we come upon the (now) most famous of all Eastern Freethinkers, OMAR KHAYYAM. He belonged to Naishápúr in Khorassan, a province which had long been known for its rationalism,[3] and which had been part of the nucleus of the great Asiatic kingdom created by Sultan Mahmoud of Ghazni

---

[1] Dugat, p. 167; Weil, iii, 72.   [2] Dugat, pp. 164-168.
[3] Weil, *Geschichte der Chalifen*, ii, 215

at the beginning of the eleventh century, soon after the
rise of the Fatimite dynasty in Egypt. Under that
Sultan flourished Ferdusi (Firdausi), one of the chief
glories of Persian verse. After Mahmoud's death, his
realm and parts of the Khalifate in turn were overrun by
the Seljuk Turks under Togrul Beg; under whose grandson Malik it was that Omar Khayyám, astronomer and
poet, studied and sang in Khorassan. The Turk-
descended Shah favored science as strongly as any of
the Abassides; and when he decided to reform the
calendar, Omar was one of the eight experts he employed
to do it. Thus was set up for the East the Jaláli
calendar, which, as Gibbon has noted,[1] " surpasses the
Julian and approaches the accuracy of the Gregorian
style". Omar was in fact one of the ablest mathematicians of his age.[2]

Beyond all question, the poet-astronomer was un-
devout; and his astronomy doubtless helped to make him
so. His first English translators, reflecting the tone of
the first half of the century, have thought fit to moralise
censoriously over his attitude to life; and the first,
Professor Cowell, has austerely decided that Omar's
gaiety is " but a *risus sardonicus* of despair".[3] Even the
subtler Fitzgerald, who has so admirably rendered some
of the audacities which Cowell thought " better left in the
original Persian ", has the air of apologising for them
when he partly concurs in the same estimate. But
despair is not the name for the humorous melancholy
which Omar weaves around his thoughts on the riddle of
the universe. In epigrams which have never been
surpassed for their echoing depth, he disposes of the
theistic solution; whereafter, instead of offering another
shibboleth, he sings of wine and roses, of the joys of life
and of their speedy passage. It was his way of turning
into music the undertone of all mortality; and that it is

---

[1] *Decline and Fall*, c. 57. Bohn ed., vi, 382, and *note*.
[2] See the preface to Fitzgerald's translation of the *Rubáiyát*.
[3] Cited in introd. to Dole's variorum ed. of the Rubaiyat, 1896, i, p. xix.

now preferable, for any refined intelligence, to the affectation of zest for a "hereafter" on which no one wants to enter, would seem to be proved by the remarkable vogue he has secured in modern England, chiefly through the incomparable version of Fitzgerald. Much of the attraction, doubtless, is due to the canorous cadence and felicitous phrasing of those singularly fortunate stanzas ; but the thoughts of Omar remain their kernels : and whereas the counsel, " Gather ye roses while ye may," is common enough, it must be the weightier bearing of his deeper and more daring ideas that gives the quatrains their main hold to-day. Never popular in the Moslem world, he has had in ours an unparalleled welcome ; and it must be because from his scientific vantage ground in the East, in the age of the Norman Conquest, he had attained the vision and chimed with the mood of a later and larger age.

That Omar in his day and place was not alone in his mood, lies on the face of his verse. The allusions to the tavern, a thing suspect and illicit for Islam, show that he was in a society more Persian than Arab ; and doubtless Persian thought, always leaning to heresy, and charged with germs of scientific speculation from immemorial antiquity, prepared his rationalism ; though his monism excludes alike dualism and theism. " One for two I never did misread," is his summing up of his philosophy.[1] But the same formula would serve for the philosophy of the sect of Sufis, who in all ages seem to have included unbelievers as well as devoutly mystical pantheists. Founded, it is said, by a woman, Rabia, in the first century of the Hejra,[2] the sect really carries on a pre-Mohammedan mysticism, and may as well derive from Greece[3] as

---

[1] Fitzgerald's pref., 4th ed. p. xiii. Cp. quatrains cited in art. *Suftism*, in *Relig. Systems of the World*, 2nd ed. pp. 325-6.

[2] Guyard, as cited, p. 42. But cp. Ueberweg, i, 411.

[3] It is not impossible that the name may have come originally from the Greek *sophoi*, "the wise," though it is usually connected with *sufi* = the robe worn by the Sufite. There are other etymologies. Cp. Fraser, *Histor. and Descrip. Account of Persia*, 1834, p. 323, *note*; and art. *Suftism* in *Relig. Systems of the World*, 2d ed., p. 315 ; and Dugat, p. 326.

from Asia. Its original doctrine of divine love, as a reaction against Moslem austerity, gave it a fixed hold in Persia, and became the starting point of innumerable heterodox doctrines.[1] Under the Khalif Moktadir, a Persian Sufi is recorded to have been tortured and executed for teaching that every man is God.[2] In later ages, Sufiism became loosely associated with every species of independent thinking; and there is reason to suspect that the later poets SADI (fl. 13th c.) and HAFIZ[3] (fl. 14th c.) as well as hundreds of lesser status, held under the name of Sufiism views of life not far removed from those of Omar Khayyám; who, however, had bantered the Sufis so unmercifully that they are said to have dreaded and hated him.[4] In any case, Sufiism has included such divergent types as Al Gazel, the sceptical defender of the faith, devout pantheistic poets such as Jâmî,[5] and singers of love and wine such as Hafiz, whose extremely concrete imagery is certainly not as often allegorical as serious Sufis assert, though no doubt it is sometimes so.[6] It even became nominally associated with the destructive Ismaïlitism of the sect of the Assassins, whose founder, Hasan, had been the schoolfellow of Omar Khayyám.[7]

Of Sufiism as a whole it may be said that whether as inculcating quietism, or as widening the narrow theism of Islam into pantheism, or as sheltering an unaggressive rationalism, it has made for freedom and humanity in the Mohammedan world, lessening the evils of ignorance where it could not inspire progress.[8] On its more philosophic side, too, it connects with the long movement of speculation which, passing into European life through

---

[1] Cp. Renan, *Averroès*, p. 293, as to Sufi latitudinarianism.

[2] Guyard, p. 44; *Relig. Systems*, p. 319.

[3] Hafiz in his own day was reckoned impious by many. Cp. Malcolm, *Sketches of Persia*, 1827, ii, 100.

[4] Fitzgerald's pref., p. x.

[5] Whose *Salaman and Absal*, translated by Fitzgerald, is so little noticed in comparison with the Rubaiyat of Omar.

[6] E. C. Browne, in *Religious Systems*, as cited, p. 321; Dugat, p. 331.

[7] Fitzgerald's pref., following Mirkhond; Fraser, *Persia*, p. 329;

[8] Cp. Dugat, p. 336; Syed Ameer Ali, pp. 311-315.

the Western Saracens, revived Greek philosophic thought in Christendom after the night of the Middle Ages, at the same time that Saracen science passed on the more precious seeds of real knowledge to the new civilisation.

§ 5.

There is the less need to deal at any length in these pages with the professed philosophy of the Arabs, seeing that it was from first to last but little associated with any practical repudiation of dogma and superstition.[1] In the East, the rationalistic AL KINDI (fl. 850) seems to have been led to philosophise by the Motazilite problems; but his successors mostly set them aside, developing an abstract logic and philosophy on Greek bases, or studying science for its own sake, but as a rule professing a devout acceptance of the Koran.[2] Such was AVICENNA (Ibn Sina) in the East (d. 1037), though in comparison with his predecessor Alfarabi, who leant to Platonic mysticism, he is a rationalistic Aristotelian.[3] After Algazel (d. 1111), who attacked both of these somewhat in the spirit of Cicero's sceptical Cotta attacking the Stoics and the Epicureans,[4] uncritical orthodoxy prevailed in the Eastern schools; and it is in Moorish Spain that we are to look for the last efforts of Arab philosophy.

The course of culture-evolution there broadly corresponds with that of the Saracen civilisation in the East. In Spain the Moors came into contact with the Roman imperial polity, and at the same time with the different culture elements of Judaism and Christianity. To both of these faiths they gave complete toleration, and thus strengthened their own in a way that no other policy could have availed to do. Whatever was left of Græco-Roman art, handicraft, and science, saving the arts of portraiture, they encouraged; and whatever of agricultural science remained from Carthaginian times they

---

[1] Cp. Renan, *Averroès*, p. 101.
[3] Ueberweg, i, 412.
[2] Steiner, *Die Mutaziliten*, S. 6.
[4] Cp. Renan, *Averroès*, p. 97.

zealously adopted and improved. Like their fellow-
Moslems in the East, they further learned all the science
that the preserved literature of Greece could give them.
The result was that under energetic and enlightened
khalifs the Moorish civilisation became the centre of light
and knowledge as well as of material prosperity for
mediæval Europe. Whatever of science the world
possessed was to be found in their schools ; and thither
in the tenth, eleventh, and twelfth centuries, flocked
students from the Christian States of western and
northern Europe. It was in whole or in part from
Saracen hands that the modern world received astronomy,
chemistry, mathematics, medicine, botany, jurisprudence,
and philosophy. They were in fact the revivers of
civilisation after the age of barbarian Christianity.[1]

While the progressive period lasted, there was, of
course, an abundance of practical Freethought. But
after a marvellously rapid rise, the Moorish civilisation
was arrested and paralysed by the internal and the
external forces of anti-civilisation—religious fanaticism
within and Christian hostility without. Everywhere we
have seen culture-progress depending more or less clearly
on the failure to find solutions for political problems.
The most fatal defect of all Arab civilisation—a defect
involved in its first departure by way of conquest, and in
its constantly military basis—was the total failure to
substitute any measure of constitutional rule for despotism.
It was thus politically unprogressive, even while advancing
in other respects. But in other respects also it soon
reached the limits set by the conditions.

Whereas in Persia the Arabs overran an ancient
civilisation, containing many elements of rationalism
which acted upon their own creed, the Moors in Spain
found a population only slightly civilised, and predisposed
by its recent culture, as well as by its natural conditions,[2]

---

[1] Cp. Seignobos, *Hist. de la Civ.*, ii, 58 ; and *post*, ch. x.
[2] Cp. Buckle, *Introd. to Hist. of Civ. in England*, 3-vol. ed. i, 123-4.

to fanatical piety. Thus when, under their tolerant rule, Jews and Christians in large numbers embraced Islam, the new converts became the most fanatical of all.[1] All rationalism existed in their despite, and, abounding as they did, they tended to gain power whenever the Khalif was weak, and to rebel furiously when he was hostile. When, accordingly, the growing pressure of the feudal Christian power in Northern Spain at length became a menacing danger to the Moorish States, weakened by endless intestine strife, the one resource was to call in a new force of Moslem fanaticism in the shape of the Almoravide[2] Berbers, who, to the utmost of their power, put down everything scientific and rationalistic, and established a rigid Koranolatry. After a time they in turn, growing degenerate while remaining orthodox, were overrun by a new influx of conquering fanatics from Africa, the Almohades, who, failing to add political science to their faith, went down in the thirteenth century before the Christians in Spain, in a great battle in which their prince sat in their sight with the Koran in his hand.[3] Here there could be no pretence that "unbelief" wrought the downfall. The Jonah of Freethought, so to speak, had been thrown overboard; and the ship went down with the flag of faith flying at every masthead.[4]

It was in the last centuries of Moorish rule that there flourished the philosophers whose names connect it with the history of European thought, retaining thus a somewhat factitious distinction as compared with the men of science, many of them nameless, who developed and transmitted the sciences. The pantheistic AVEMPACE (Ibn Badja: d. 1138) was physician, astronomer, and mathematician, as well as metaphysician; as was ABUBACER (Abu Bekr, also known as Ibn Tophail:

---

[1] Lane-Poole, *The Moors in Spain*, p. 73.
[2] Properly Morabethin = men of God or of religion; otherwise known as "Marabouts".
[3] Sedillot, p. 298.
[4] Cp. Dozy, *Hist. des Musulmans d'Espagne*, iii, 248-286; Ueberweg, i, 415.

d. 1185), who regarded religious systems as "only a necessary means of discipline for the multitude",[1] and as being merely symbols of the higher truth reached by the philosopher. AVERROES, the most famous of all, because the most far-reaching in his influence on European thought, is pre-eminently the expounder of Aristotle, and as regards religion was more complaisant than Abubacer, pronouncing Mohammedanism the most perfect of all popular systems,[2] and preaching a patriotic conformity on that score to philosophic students. He expressly opposed, too, the scientific rationalism of the Motecallemîn, whom he likened to the Motazilites.[3] Even this, however, could not save him from proscription, at the hands of a Khalif who had long favored him, for the offence of cultivating Greek antiquity to the prejudice of Islam. All study of Greek philosophy was proscribed at the same time, and all books found on the subject were destroyed.[4] Disgraced and banished from court, Averroës died at Morocco in 1198, and soon afterwards the Moorish rule in Spain perished, in the odour of sanctity.[5]

§ 6.

Of later Freethought under Islam there is little to record; but the phenomenon has never disappeared. Motazilism is still heard of in Arabia itself.[6] In the Ottoman Empire, indeed, it is little in evidence; but in Persia—where the rise and the tragic end of the Bâb sect in our own age[7] is a further proof of heterogeneity—the ancient leaning to rationalism is still common. About 1830, a British traveller estimated that, assuming there

---

[1] Ueberweg, i, 415.
[2] Ueberweg, i, 416 ; Steiner, S. 6 ; Renan, *Averroès*, p. 162, ff.
[3] Renan, p. 106, *note*.
[4] Renan, *Averroès*, p. 5. Cp. *Avert.* p. iii.
[5] Cp. Ueberweg, i, 415-417.
[6] Dugat, p. 59. The Ameer Ali Syed, *Moulvi*, M.A., LL.B., whose *Critical Examination of the Life and Teachings of Mohammed* appeared in 1873, was a Motazilite of a moderate type.
[7] See the good account of this sect by E. C. Browne in *Religious Systems of the World.* Cp. Renan, *Les Apôtres*, pp. 378-381.

were between 200,000 and 300,000 Sufis in the country, those figures probably fell greatly short of the number "secretly inclined to infidelity ".[1] Whatever be the value of the figures, the statement is substantially confirmed by later observers.[2] Persian Freethought is, of course, the Freethought of ignorance, and seems to co-exist with astrological superstition[3]; but there is obviously needed only science, culture, and material development to produce, on such a basis, a renascence as remarkable as that of modern Japan.

In the British dominions, Mohammedans, though less ready than educated Hindus to accept new ideas, cannot escape the rationalising influence of European culture. Nor was it left to the British to introduce the rationalistic spirit in Moslem India. At the end of the sixteenth century, the eclectic Emperor Akbar,[4] himself a devout worshipper of the Sun,[5] is found tolerantly comparing all religions,[6] depreciating Islam,[7] and arriving at such general views on the equivalence of all creeds, and on the improbability of eternal punishment,[8] as pass for liberal among Christians in our own day. If such views could be generated by a comparison of the creeds of pre-British India, they must needs be encouraged now. The Mohammedan mass is of course still deeply fanatical, and habitually superstitious ; but not any more immovably so than the early Saracens. In the present century has arisen the fanatical Wahabi sect, which aims at a puritanic restoration of primeval Islam, freed from the accretions of later belief, such as saint-worship ; but the movement, though variously estimated, has had small success, and

---

[1] Fraser, *Persia*, p. 330. This writer (p. 329) describes Sufiism as "the superstition of the freethinker", and as "often assumed as a cloak to cover entire infidelity".

[2] *E.g.* Dr. Wills, *The Land of the Lion and the Sun*, ed. 1891, p. 339.

[3] Fraser, *Persia*, p. 331 ; Malcolm, *Sketches of Persia*, ii, 108.

[4] See the documents reproduced by Max Müller, *Introd. to the Science of Religion*, ed. 1882, App. 1.

[5] *Id.*, pp. 214, 216.

[6] *Id.*, pp. 210, 217, 224, 225. [7] *Id.*, pp. 224, 226. [8] *Id.*, pp. 226, 229.

seems destined to extinction.[1]   Of the traditional seventy-
three sects in Islam, only four to-day count as orthodox.[2]

It may be worth while in conclusion to note that the
comparative prosperity or progressiveness of Islam as a
proselytising and civilising force in Africa—a phenomenon
regarded even by some Christians with satisfaction, and
by some with alarm[3]—is not properly a religious phenomenon at all.   Moslem civilisation suits with negro life
in Africa in virtue not of the teaching of the Koran, but
of the comparative nearness of the Arab to the barbaric
life.   He interbreeds with the natives, fraternises with
them (when not engaged in kidnapping them), and so
stimulates their civilisation ; where the European colonist,
looking down on them as an inferior species, isolates,
depresses and degrades them.   It is thus conceivable
that there is a future for Islam at the level of a low
civilisation ; but the Arab and Turkish races out of
Africa are rather the more likely to concur in the
rationalistic movement of the higher civilisation.

---

[1] Guyard, p. 45 ; Steiner, S. 5, *note*. Cp. Spencer, *Study of Sociology,*
c. xii, p. 292 ; Bosworth Smith, *Mohammed and Mohammedanism*, 2d ed.,
pp. 315-319.

[2] Derenbourg, p. 72 ; Steiner, S. 1.

[3] Cp. Bosworth Smith, *Mohammed and Mohammedanism*, Lectures I and
IV ; Canon Isaac Taylor, address to Church Congress at Wolverhampton,
1887, and letters to *Times*, Oct. and Nov., 1887.

CHAPTER IX.

CHRISTENDOM IN THE MIDDLE AGES.

IT would be an error, in view of the biological generalisation proceeded on in this enquiry, to suppose that even in the Dark Ages, so called, the spirit of critical reason was wholly absent from the life of Christendom. It had simply grown very rare, and was the more discountenanced where it strove to speak. But the most systematic suppression of heresies could not secure that no private heresy should remain. Apart, too, from such elementary rationalism as was involved in semi-Pelagianism,[1] critical heresy chronically arose even in the Byzantine provinces, which by the curtailment of the Empire had been left the most homogeneous and therefore the most manageable of the Christian States. It is necessary to note those survivals of partial freethinking, when we would trace the rise of modern thought.

§ 1.

In the early ages of heresy-smashing, apart from the wider movements, single teachers here and there stood for a measure of reason as against the fast-multiplying insanities of faith. Thus the Italian monk JOVINIAN, (end of 4th c.) fought against the creed of celibacy and asceticism, and was duly denounced, vituperated, ecclesiastically condemned, and banished, penal laws being at the same time passed against those who adhered to him.[2] Contemporary with him was the Eastern AERIUS, who advocated priestly equality as against episcopacy, and objected to prayers for the dead, to fasts, and to the too

[1] According to which God predestinated good, but merely foreknew evil.
[2] Mosheim, *E. H.*, Cent. IV, Pt. II, c. iii, § 22 ; Gieseler, § 106, ii, 75.

significant practice of slaying a lamb at the Easter festival.[1] In this case matters went the length of schism. With less of practical effect, in the next century, VIGILANTIUS of Aquitaine made a more general resistance to a more manifold superstition, condemning and ridiculing the veneration of the tombs and bones of martyrs, pilgrimages to shrines, the miracle stories therewith connected, and the practices of fasting, celibacy, and the monastic life. He, too, was promptly put down, largely by the efforts of his former friend Jerome, the most voluble and the most scurrilous pietist of his age, who had also denounced the doctrine of Jovinian.[2] For centuries no such appeal was heard in the West; the next ferment of a rationalistic sort being the new controversy over image-worship raised in Byzantium.

§ 2.

It was probably from some indirect influence of the new anti-idolatrous religion of Islam that in the eighth century the soldier-emperor, Leo the Isaurian, known as the Iconoclast, derived his aversion to the image-worship[3] which had long been as general in the Christian world as ever under polytheism. Save on this one point, however, he was an orthodox Christian and Trinitarian, and his long effort to put down images and pictures was in itself rather fanatical[4] than rationalistic, though a measure of freethinking was developed among the religious party he created.[5] Of this spirit, as well as of the aversion to

---

[1] Gieseler, § 106, vol. ii, p. 74; Mosheim, Cent. IV, Pt. II, c. iii, § 21; and Schlegel's note in Reid's ed., p. 152.

[2] Milman, *Hist. of Chr.*, B. iii, c. 11, (ii, 268-270); Mosheim, Cent. V Pt. II, c. iii, § 14; Gilly, *Vigilantius and his Times*, 1844, pp. 8, 389 ff., 470 ff. As to Jerome's persecuting ferocity, see also Gieseler, ii, 65, *note*. For a Catholic polemic on Jerome's side, see Amedée Thierry, *Saint Jérome*, 2e édit., pp. 141, 363-6.

[3] For Leo's contacts with the Saracens see Finlay, *Hist. of Greece*, ed. Tozer, ii, 14-20, 24, 31-2, 34-5, 37, etc., and compare p. 218.

[4] As to his hostility to letters, see Gibbon, ch. 53. Bohn, ed. vi, 228. Of course the other side were not any more liberal. Cp. Finlay; ii, 222.

[5] Gieseler, ii, 202. Per. III, Div. I, Pt. i, § 1. In the next century, this was said to have gone in some churches to the point of rejection of Christ. *Id.*, p. 207, note 28.

image-worship,[1] something must have survived the official restoration of idolatry ; but the traces are few. In the ninth century, when Saracen rivalry had stung the Byzantines into some partial revival of culture and science,[2] the all-learned PHOTIUS, who reluctantly accepted ecclesiastical office, earned a dangerous repute for freethinking by declaring from the pulpit that earthquakes were produced by earthly causes and not by divine wrath.[3] But though the reigning emperor, Michael the Drunkard, was something of a freethinker, and could even with impunity burlesque the religious processions of the clergy,[4] the orthodox populace joining in the laugh, there was no such culture at Constantinople as could develop a sober rationalism, or sustain it against the clergy if it showed its head.

§ 3.

It was in a sect whose doctrine at one point coincided with iconoclasm that there were preserved such rude seeds of oriental rationalism as could survive the rule of the Byzantine emperors, and carry the stimulus of heresy to the west. The rise of the Paulicians in Armenia dates from the seventh century, and was nominally by way of setting up a creed on the lines of Paul as against the paganised system of the church. Their original tenets seem to have been anti-Manichean, anti-Gnostic (though partly Marcionite), opposed to the worship of images and relics, to sacraments, to the adoration of the Virgin, of saints, and of angels, and to the acceptance of the Old Testament ; and in an age in which the reading of the Sacred Books had already come to be regarded as a

---

[1] *Id.*, pp. 205, 207 ; Finlay, ii, 195.
[2] On their connection at this time with the culture-movement of the Khalifate of Mamoun, see Finlay, ii, 224-5 ; Gibbon, ch. 53, ed. cited, vi, 228-9.
[3] Finlay, ii, 181, *note.* Cp. Mosheim, Cent. IX, Pt. II, c. iii, § 7 ; and Gibbon, ch. 53, ed. cited, vi, 229. Finlay declares (p. 222) that no Greek of the intellectual calibre of Photius, John the Grammarian, and Leo the Mathematician, has since appeared.
[4] Finlay, ii, 174-5, 180.

privilege of monks and priests, they insisted on reading the New Testament for themselves.[1] In course of time they acquired some Manichean and Gnostic characteristics[2]; and in the ninth century, when they had become a powerful and militant sect, often at war with the empire, they were marked by their refusal to make any difference between priests and laymen. Anti-ecclesiasticism was thus a main feature of the whole movement. The first iconoclastic emperor, who agreed with them on the subject of images, had nevertheless persecuted them by way of avoiding the stigma of their other heresies.[3] They were thus driven over to the Saracens, whose advance-guard they became as against the Christian State; but the iconoclast Constantine Copronymus sympathetically[4] transplanted many of them to Constantinople and Thrace, thus introducing their doctrine into Europe. The Empress Theodora (841-855), who restored image-worship,[5] sought to exterminate those left in Armenia, slaying, it is said, a hundred thousand. The remnant were thus driven wholly into the arms of the Saracens, and did the empire desperate mischief during many generations.

Meantime those planted in Thrace, in concert with the main body, carried propaganda into Bulgaria, and these again were further reinforced by refugees from Armenia in the ninth century, and in the tenth by a

---

[1] Gibbon, ch. 54; Mosheim, Cent. IX, Pt. II, ch. v; Gieseler, Per. III, Div. I, Pt. i, § 3; G. S. Faber, *The Ancient Vallenses and Waldenses*, 1838, pp. 32-60. Some fresh light is thrown on the Paulician doctrines by the discovery of the old Armenian book *The Key of Truth*, edited and translated by F. C. Conybeare, Oxford, 1898. It belonged to the ancient Armenian sect of Thonraki. For a criticism of Mr. Conybeare's theories see the *Church Quarterly Review*, Jan., 1899, Art. V.

[2] Gieseler; Per. III, §§ 45, 46, vol. ii, pp. 489, 492. The sect of Euchites, also anti-priestly, seem to have joined them. Faber denies any Manichean element.

[3] Gibbon, as cited, vi, 242.

[4] Gibbon, vi, 245, and note; Finlay, ii, 60.

[5] Despite the express decision, the use of statues proper ($\dot{a}\gamma\dot{a}\lambda\mu\alpha\tau\alpha$) gradually disappeared from the Greek church, the disuse finally creating a strong antipathy, while pictures and *ikons* remained in reverence (Tozer's note to Finlay, ii, 165).

fresh colony transplanted from Armenia by the emperor
John Zimisces, who valued them as a bulwark against the
barbarous Slavs.[1] Fresh persecution under Alexius I at
the end of the eleventh century failed to suppress them;
and imperial extortion constantly drove to their side
numbers of fresh adherents,[2] while the Bulgarians for
similar reasons tended in mass to adopt their creed as
against that of Constantinople. Thus it came about
that from Bulgaria there passed into Western Europe,[3]
partly through the Slavonic sect called Bogomilians,[4]
partly by more general influences,[5] a contagion of democratic and anti-ecclesiastical heresy; so that the very
name Bulgar became the French bougre==heretic—and
worse.[6] It specified the most obvious source of the new
anti-Romanist heresies of the Albigenses, if not of the
Vaudois (Waldenses).

§ 4.

In the West, meanwhile, where the variety of social
elements was favorable to new life, heresy of a rationalistic kind was not wholly lacking. Though image-
worship finally triumphed there as in the East, it had
strong opponents, notably Claudius, bishop of Turin
(fl. 830), under the emperor Louis the Pious, son of
Charlemagne, and his contemporary Agobard, bishop of
Lyons.[7] It is a significant fact that both men were born
in Spain; and either to Saracen or to Jewish influence—
the latter being then strong in the Moorish and even in

---

[1] Gibbon, vi, 246; Finlay, iii, 64; Mosheim, Cent. X, Pt. II, ch. v.
[2] Finlay, iii, 66.
[3] Gibbon, as cited; Poole, Illustrations of the History of Medieval Thought,
pp. 91-96; Mosheim, Cent. XI, Pt. II, c. v.
[4] Finlay, iii, 67-68; Mosheim, Cent. XII, Pt. II, c. v, § 2.
[5] Gieseler, Per. III, Div. II, Pt. iii, § 46.
[6] Gibbon, vi, 249, note: Poole, p. 91, note; De Potter, L'Esprit de
L'Eglise, ed. 1821, vi, 16, note.
[7] For excellent accounts of both, see Mr. R. Lane Poole's Illustrations
of the History of Medieval Thought, 1884, pp, 28-50. As to Claudius, cp,
Monastier, Hist. of the Vaudois Church, Eng. tr., 1848, pp. 13-42, and Faber,
The Ancient Vallenses, B. iii, c. 4.

the Christian[1] world—may fairly be in part attributed
their marked bias against image-worship. Claudius was
slightly and Agobard well educated in Latin letters, so
that an early impression[2] would seem to have been at
work in both cases. However that may be, they stood
out as singularly rationalistic theologians in an age of
general ignorance and superstition. Claudius vehemently
resisted alike image-worship, saint-worship, and the
Papal claims, and is recorded to have termed a council
of bishops which condemned him " an assembly of
asses ".[3] Agobard, in turn, is quite extraordinary in the
thoroughness of his rejection of popular superstition,
being not only an iconoclast but an enemy to prayer for
change in the weather, to belief in incantations and the
power of evil spirits, to the ordeal by fire, to the wager
of battle,[4] and to the belief in the verbal inspiration of
the Sacred Books.

A grain of rationalism, as apart from professional
self-interest, may also have entered into the outcry made
at this period by the clergy against the rigidly pre-
destinarian doctrine of the monk Gottschalk.[5] His
enemy, Rabanus or Hrabanus (called "the Moor "),
seems again to represent some Saracen influence, inasmuch as he reproduced the scientific lore of Isidore of
Seville.[6] But the philosophic semi-rationalism of John
Scotus (d. 875), later known as Erigena (John the Scot—?
of Ireland[7]—the original " Scots " being Irish) seems to be
traceable to the Greek studies which had been cherished
in Christianised Ireland while the rest of Western

---

[1] See Mr. Poole's *Illustrations*, pp. 46-48, for an account of the
privileges then accorded to Jews.
[2] This is not incompatible with their having opposed both Saracens
(Claudius in actual war) and Jews, as Christian bishops.
[3] Poole, *Illustrations*, p. 37
[4] This when the church found its account in adopting all such usages.
Lea, *Superstition and Force*, pp. 242, 280, etc.
[5] Poole, pp. 50-52.
[6] Noack, *Philosophie-Geschichtliches Lexikon*, s. v. Rabanus. As to the
doubtful works in which Rabanus coincides with Scotus Erigena, cp.
Poole, p. 336; Noack, as cited; Ueberweg, i, 367-8.
[7] Ueberweg, i, 359. But cp. Poole, pp. 55-56, *note*.

Europe lost them, and represents at once the imperfect beginning of the relatively rationalistic philosophy of Nominalism,[1] and the first western revival of the philosophy of Plato and Aristotle, howbeit by way of accommodation to the doctrine of the Church.[2]   Called in by the abbot Hincmar, himself a normally superstitious believer,[3] to answer Gottschalk,[4] Scotus Erigena in turn was accused of heresy, as he well might be on many points. His doctrine that the Deity could not cause evil was, in particular, Platonic, and goes back in a direct line to the Gnostics ;, but he must be credited with some original thought.[5]

From this point onward, the movement of new ideas may for a time be conveniently traced on two general lines, one that of the philosophic discussion in the schools, reinforced later by Saracen influences, the other that of partially rationalistic and democratic heresy among the common people, by way first of contagion from the East.   The latter was on the whole as influential for sane thought as the former, apart from such scholarly freethinking as that of Berengar of Tours and Roscelin. Berengar (fl. 1050) was led by moral reflection to doubt the priestly miracle of the Eucharist,[6] and thence " to open the whole question of the meaning of authority ", to which, however, he had outwardly to succumb.   His stimulus seems to have counted for much ; though not till Zwingli was his doctrine widely professed.   Roscelin (fl. 1090), on the other hand, was led by his logical and Nominalistic training to dispute the dogma of the Trinity,.

---

[1] Ueberweg, pp. 366, 371 ; Poole, pp. 99, 101, 336.
[2] Ueberweg, pp. 356-365.   That there was, however, an Irish scholasticism as early as the eighth century is shown by Mosheim, Cent. VIII, Pt. II., c. iii, § 6, note 3.
[3] Lea, as cited, p. 280.
[4] As to the cruel punishment of Gottschalk by Hincmar, see Hampden, Bampton Lectures on *The Scholastic Philosophy*, 3rd. ed, p. 418.
[5] Poole, pp. 64, 76.
[6] Poole, 103.   He later argued his case on grounds supplied by John Scotus.   As to his forced prevarications, see Mosheim, Cent. XI, Pt. II, ch. iii, §§ 13-18.   Earlier still than John the Scot, Ratramnus, or Bertram (fl. 850), had suggested a semi-rational view of the Eucharist.

but got no further in philosophy than tritheism,[1] and
seems to have treated the question as one of dialectics
rather than of faith.   The popular heresies bit rather
deeper into practical life.

It is doubtless true of the Paulicians that "there was no
principle of development in their creed : it reflected no genuine
freedom of thought " (Poole, *Illustrations*, p. 95) ; but the same
thing might be—and has been—said of scholasticism itself.
It may indeed be urged that " the contest between Ratramn
and Pashasc on the doctrine of the Eucharist ; of Lanfranc
with Berengar on the same subject ; of Anselm with Roscelin
on the nature of Universals; the complaints of Bernard
against the dialectical theology of Abelard ; are all illustrations
of the collision between Reason and Authority . . . . varied
forms of rationalism—the pure exertions of the mind within
itself . . . . against the constringent force of the Spiritual
government " (Hampden, *The Scholastic Philos.*, 3d ed., p. 37) ;
but none of the scholastics ever professed to set Authority
aside.   None dared.   Scotus Erigena indeed affirmed the
identity of true religion with true philosophy, without pro-
fessing·to subordinate the latter; but the most eminent of the
later scholastics affirmed such a subordination.   "The
vassalage of philosophy consisted in the fact that an im-
passable limit was fixed for the freedom of philosophising in
the dogmas of the Church" (Ueberweg, i, 357); and some of the
chief dogmas were not allowed to be philosophically discussed ;
though " with its territory thus limited, philosophy was indeed
allowed by theology a freedom which was rarely and only by
exception infringed upon " (*Ib.*).   In course of time, the further
narrowing of the field forced a reaction on the part of the
Aristotelian scholastics against orthodoxy ; and some, "notably
Pomponatius and his followers, came secretly to favor a
direction of thought hostile to the dogmatic supra-naturalism
of the Church " (*Ib.*).   But this progress is hardly to be credited
to the thought of their predecessors.   The popular heresy
might have had similar results in an atmosphere of education;
and in its beginnings it was the hardier movement.

§ 5.

The first Western traces of the imported Paulician
heresy are about the year 1000, when a rustic of Châlons
is heard of as destroying a cross and a religious picture,

[1] Or ditheism.   Poole, pp. 103-4, and *note* ; cp. p. 99.

and asserting that the prophets are not wholly to be believed.[1] From this time forward, the world having begun to breathe again after the passing of the year 1000 without any sign of the Day of Judgment, heresy begins to multiply. In the year 1022 (sometimes put as 1017) we hear of a secret society of so-called Manicheans at Orleans, ten canons of one church being members.[2] An Italian woman was said to be the founder, and all were burned alive on their refusal to recant. According to the records, they denied all miracles, including the Virgin Birth and the Resurrection; rejected Baptism and the miracle of the Eucharist; and affirmed the eternity of matter and the non-creation of the world. They were also accused, like the first Christians, of promiscuous nocturnal orgies and of eating sacrificed infants; but unless such charges are to be held valid in the other case, they cannot be here.[3] The stories told of the Manichean community who lived in the castle of Montforte, near Turin, a few years later, and who were likewise burned alive, are similarly mixed with fable.[4]

A less savage treatment may have made possible the alleged success of Gerhard, bishop of Cambray and Arras, in reconciling to the church at Arras, in 1025 or 1030, a number of laymen, also said to have been taught by an Italian, who as a body rejected all external worship— setting aside baptism and the sacraments, penance and images, funeral rites, holy oil, church bells, altars and even churches—and denied the necessity of an order of priests.[5] None of the Protestants of a later age were so thorough-going; but the fact that the sect stood to the old Marcionite veto on marriage and the sexual instinct, gives to their propaganda its own cast of

---

[1] Mosheim, Cent. X, Pt. II, ch. v, § 3; Poole, *Illustrations*, p. 91.

[2] Mosheim, Cent. XI, Pt. II, ch. v, § 3; De Potter, *L'Esprit de l'Eglise*, vi, 18-19; Poole, pp. 96-98; Lea, *History of the Inquisition*, i, 108; Gieseler, Per. III, Div. II, § 46,

[3] Cp. Murdock's note on Mosheim, Reid's ed., p. 386; Monastier, *Hist. of the Vaudois Church*, p. 33.

[4] De Potter, pp. 20-21; Gieseler, as cited, p. 497.

[5] Mosheim, as last cited, § 4; Gieseler, ii, 496 (§ 46).

fanaticism. This last tenet it seemingly was that gave
the Paulicians their common Greek name of *cathari*,[1]
"the pure," corrupted in Italian to *gazzari*, whence
presumably the German word for heretic, *ketzer*.[2] Such a
doctrine had the double misfortune that if acted on it
left the sect without the normal recruitment of members'
children, while if departed from it brought on them the
stigma of wanton hypocrisy; and as a matter of fact
every movement of the kind, ancient and modern, seems
to have contained within it the two extremes of asceticism
and license, the former generating the latter.

It could hardly, however, have been the ascetic
doctrine that won for the new heresy its vogue in
medieval Europe; nor is it likely that the majority of
the heretics even professed it.[3] If, on the other hand,
we ask how it was that in an age of dense superstition so
many uneducated people were found to reject so promptly
the most sacrosanct doctrines of the Church, it seems
hardly less difficult to account for the phenomenon on
the bare ground of their common - sense. Critical
common-sense there must have been, to allow of it at all;
but it is reasonable to suppose that then, as clearly
happened later at the Reformation, common-sense had a
powerful stimulus in pecuniary interest.

We have considered the rise of Christianity without
resort to that factor for any part of the explanation,
beyond noting it in the case of the rise of the Christian
priesthood; because the economic principle in history is
still so little recognised that to suggest it, however
guardedly, in connection with the rise of a religion,
especially of the Christian, is to give an opening for
misrepresentation that is sure to be taken. It is, how-

---

[1] Mosheim, Cent. XI, Pt. II, ch. v, § 2 and Murdock's notes; Cent. XII,
Pt. II, ch. v, §§ 4, 5.
[2] These etymologies are disputed. Cp. Murdock's note to Mosheim,
Reid's ed., p. 385, and Gieseler, ii, 486. The *Chazari*, a Slavic (?) people,
partly Christian and partly Moslem in the 9th century (Gieseler, as cited),
may have given the name of *Gazzari*, as *Bulgar* gave *Bougre*.
[3] Cp. Mosheim, Cent. XII, Pt. II, ch. v, § 6.

ever, the historic fact that as soon as Christianity had become the religion of the State, not only were the revenues of the temples confiscated as we have seen, but a number of Christians took to the business of plundering pagans in the name of the laws forbidding sacrifice, and confiscating the property of the temples. Libanius in his *Oration for the Temples*[1] (390), addressed to Theodosius, circumstantially avers that the bands of monks and others who went about demolishing and plundering temples were also wont to rob the peasants, adding :

"They also seize the lands of some, saying, it is sacred; and many are deprived of their paternal inheritance upon a false pretence. Thus those men thrive upon other people's ruin who say 'they worship God with fasting'. And if they who are wronged come to the pastor in the city . . . he commends (the robbers) and rejects the others. . . . . Moreover, if they hear of any land which has anything that can be plundered, they cry presently, 'Such an one sacrificeth, and does abominable things, and a troop ought to be sent against him . And presently the self-styled reformers (σωφρονισται) are there. . . . . Some of these . . . deny their proceedings. . . . Others glory and boast and tell their exploits. . . . . But they say, ' We have only punished those who sacrifice, and thereby transgress the law, which [forbids sacrifice'. O emperor, when they say this, they lie . . . . Can it be thought that they who are not able to bear the sight of a collector's cloak, should despise the power of your government ? . . . . I appeal to the guardians of the law " [to confirm the denial].[2]

The whole testimony is explicit and weighty,[3] and, being corroborated by Ammianus Marcellinus, is accepted by clerical historians.[4] Ammianus declares that some of the courtiers of the Christian emperors before Julian were " glutted with the spoils of the temples".[5]

With this evidence as to Christian practice in the

---

[1] See it translated in full by Lardner, in his *Testimonies of Ancient Heathen*, ch. 49. *Works*, ed. 1835, vol. viii.

[2] Lardner, as cited, pp. 25-27.

[3] As to the high character of Libanius, who used his influence to succour his Christian friends in the reign of Julian, see Lardner, pp. 15-17.

[4] Milman, *Hist. of Christianity*, B. iii, c. 6: vol. ii, p. 131. See the passage there cited from the *Funeral Oration* of Libanius *on Julian*, as to Christians building houses with temple stones; also the further passages pp. 129, 161, 212 of Mr. King's trans. of the Oration in his *Julian the Emperor* (Bohn Lib.).

[5] Ammianus, xxii, 4.

fourth century on the one hand, and the later evidence as
to the Reformation on the other, we are entitled to infer
some play of financial motive in the Middle Ages. And
whereas it is intelligible that such rapacity as Libanius
describes should promote a heresy which rejected alike
religious ceremonial and the claims of the priest, it is
further reasonable to surmise that resentment of priestly
rapacity and luxury helped men to similar heresy in
Western Europe when the doctrine reached them. If
any centuries are to be singled out as those of maximum
profligacy and extortion among the clergy, they are the
ninth and the three following.[1] It had been part of the
policy of Charlemagne everywhere to strengthen the
hands of the clergy by way of checking the power of the
nobles[2]; and in the disorder after his death the conflicting
forces were in semi-anarchic competition. The feudal
habit of appointing younger sons and underlings to
livings wherever possible; the disorders and strifes of the
papacy ; and the frequent practice of dispossessing priests
to reward retainers, thereby driving the dispossessed to
plunder on their own account, must together have created
a state of things almost past exaggeration. Thus orthodoxy and heterodoxy alike had strong economic motives;
and in these may be placed a main part of the explanation
of the gross savagery of persecution now normal in the
Church. Such a heresy, for instance, as that of Gottschalk, by denying to the priest all power of affecting
the predestined course of things here or hereafter, im-
peached the very existence of the whole hierarchy, and
was resented accordingly. The same principle entered

---

[1] Cp. Gieseler, Per. III, §§ 24, 34 ; Mosheim, Cent. IX, Pt. II, c. ii,
§§ 1-4 ; with his and Murdock's refs. ; Cent. X, Pt. II, c. ii, §§ 1, 2;
Cent. XI, Pt. II, c. ii, § 1 ; c. iii, §§ 1-3 : Cent. XII, Pt. II, c. ii, § 1;
Cent. XIII, Pt. II, c. ii, §§ 1-7. The authorities are often eminent churchmen, as Agobard, Ratherius, Bernard, and Gregory IX. The common
expectation, in the tenth century, that the world would end in the year
1000, led to an enormous bestowal of landed and other property on the
clergy. See Mosheim, Cent. X, Pt. II,.c. iii, § 3. Against this proceeding
the next age naturally reacted.
[2] See Mosheim, Cent. VIII. Pt. II, c. ii, § 5, note 2.

.nto the controversies over the Eucharist. Still more would the clergy resent the new Manichean heresy, of which every element, from the Euchite tenet of the necessity of personal prayer and mortification as against the innate demon, to the rejection of all the rites of normal worship and all the pretensions of priests, was radically hostile to the entire organisation of the Church. When the heretics in due course developed a priestly system of their own,[1] the hostility was only the more embittered.

Persecution soon took the dimensions of massacre. Bishop Wazon of Lüttich (d. 1048) in vain protested against the universal practice of putting the heretics to death.[2] Manicheans found in 1052 at Goslar, in Germany, were hanged,[3] a precedent being thus established in the day of small things. The occurrence of the first and second crusades, the work respectively of Peter the Hermit and St. Bernard, created a period of new fanaticism, somewhat unfavorable to heresy; but even in that period the new sects were at work,[4] and in the twelfth century, when crusading had become a mere feudal conspiracy of conquest and plunder,[5] heresy reappeared, to be duly met by slaughter. A perfect ferment of anti-clerical heresy had arisen in Italy, France, and Flanders. Peter de Brueys (burned in 1130), opposing infant baptism, the use of churches, holy crosses, prayers for the dead (a great source of clerical income), and the doctrine of the Real Presence in the Eucharist, set up the sect of Petrobrussians. The monk Henry (died in prison, 1148) took a similar line, directly denouncing the clergy in Switzerland and France; as did Tanquelin in Flanders (killed by a priest, 1125); though in his case there seems to have been as much of religious

---

[1] Mosheim, Cent. XII, Pt. II, ch. v, § 6.
[2] Gieseler, Per. III, § 46, *end.*
[3] Monastier, *Hist, of the Vaudois Ch.*, p. 32.
[4] Cp. Heeren, *Essai sur l'influence des Croisades*, 1808, p. 172.
[5] Sir G. Cox, *The Crusades.* p. 111.

hallucination as of the contrary. A peasant, Eudo of Stella (died in prison), is said to have half-revolutionised Brittany with his anti-ecclesiastical preaching.[1] The more famous monk Arnold of Brescia (strangled or crucified in 1155), a pupil of Abailard, simplified his plan of reform into a proposal that the whole wealth of the Church, from the Pope to the monks, should be transferred to the civil power, leaving churchmen to lead a spiritual life on voluntary offerings.[2] Among the other heresies of the time Arianism revived; on the other hand a wandering sect of anarchists, called the Caputiati, wore on their caps a leaden image of the Virgin; while the Apostolici, advocates of a return to primitive simplicity and to chastity, reproduced what they supposed to be the morals of the early Church, including the profession of ascetic cohabitation.[3] These called themselves the "chaste brethren and sisters"; and in this period of new departures probably originated the "Brethren of the Free Spirit", (*fratres liberi spiritus*)[4] who in the next and the fourteenth century are found widespread in Northern Europe,[5] and whose name is the forecast of that of the *libertini* of the Reformation period. In Italy, during the period of the Renaissance, all alike were commonly called *paterini*, a word of no clear meaning.[6]

The original *cathari*, scattered between Constantinople and Lombardy, are reckoned to have numbered in all, in the twelfth century, some 4,000 persons.[7] Though soon hardly distinguishable from the other anti-clerical sects, they figure freely in the rolls of persecution. About 1170 four *cathari* from Flanders are burned alive at Cologne;

---

[1] Mosheim, Cent. XII, Pt. II, ch. v, §§ 7-9, and varior. notes: Monastier, pp. 38-41, 43²47; Milman, *Hist. of Latin Chr.*, v, 384-390.
[2] Mosheim, as last cited, § 10; Monastier, p. 49.
[3] Mosheim, as last cited, §§ 14-16.
[4] Mosheim, Cent. XI, Pt. II, c. v, § 3; Cent. XIII, Pt. II, ch. v, § 9.
[5] As to their rise cp. Gieseler, Per. III, Div. iii, § 90 (American ed. 1865, ii, 590, *note*).
[6] Mosheim, Cent. XI, Pt. II, c. ii, § 13, and note; Milman, *Latin Christianity*, v, 401. On the sects in general see De Potter, vi, 217-310.
[7] Murdock's note to Mosheim, p. 426; Monastier, pp. 106-7.

and others (called *boni homines*) at Toulouse; in France
and England laws are passed excommunicating them;
at an œcumenical council at Rome in 1179, a sweeping
canon was drawn up for the same purpose; and within
the next twenty years the Pope and the Emperor
successively continued the attack.[1] Beheading, hanging,
burning, confiscation of property and burning of houses
were the normal methods. Soon the Church saw fit to
take more systematic measures against a spread of heresy
which threatened to reduce it to poverty. In the middle
of the twelfth century, the new ideas were preached so
near Rome as Orvieto.[2] In the latter part of the century
a foremost place was taken by the sect of Waldenses, or
Vaudois (otherwise the Poor Men of Lyons), which
—whether deriving from ancient dissent surviving in the
Vaux or Valleys of Piedmont,[3] or taking its name and
character from the teaching of the Lyons merchant,
Peter Waldus, or an earlier Peter of Vaux or Valdis[4]—
conforms substantially to the general heretical tendencies
of that age, in that it rejected the Papal authority,
stipulated for poverty on the part of priests and denied
their special status, opposed prayers for the dead, and
preached peace and non-resistance. Manicheans and
non-Manichean Albigenses and Waldenses were on all
fours for the Church, as opponents of its claims. A first
attempt made by Pope Innocent III to force the people
of Orvieto to take an oath of fidelity, in the year 1199,
ended in the killing of his representative by the people.[5]
The Papacy accordingly laid plans to destroy the enemy
at its centre of propagation.

[1] De Potter, vi, 23.
[2] *Id.*, p. 26.
[3] Cp. Mosheim, Cent. XII, P. II, c. v, § 11, and notes in Reid's ed.;
Monastier, *Hist. of the Vaudois Church*, Eng. tr., 1848, pp. 12-29; Faber,
The Ancient Vallenses and Albigenses, pp. 28, 284, etc. As Vigilantius took
refuge in the Cottian Alps, his doctrine may have survived there, as argued
by Monastier (p. 10) and Faber (p. 290). The influence of Claudius of
Turin, as they further contend, might also come into play. On the whole
subject see Gieseler, Per. III, Div. iii, § 88.
[4] Cp. Mosheim with Faber, B. III, cc. 3, 8, and Monastier, pp. 53-82.
[5] De Potter, vi, 28.

§ 6.

In Provence and Languedoc, the scene of the first great Papal crusade against anti-clerical heresy, there were represented all the then existing forces of popular Freethought; and the motives of the crusade were equally typical of the cause of authority.

1. In addition to the Paulician and other movements of religious rationalism above noted, the Languedoc region was a centre of semi-popular literary culture, which was to no small extent anti-clerical, and by consequence somewhat anti-religious. The Latin-speaking jongleurs or minstrels, known as Goliards,[1] possessing as they did a clerical culture, were by their way of life committed to a joyous rather than an ascetic philosophy; and though given to blending the language of devotion with that of the drinking-table, very much after the fashion of Hafiz, they were capable of burlesquing the mass, the creed, hymns to the Virgin, the Lord's Prayer, confessions, and parts of the Gospels.[2] Denounced by some of the stricter clergy, they were protected by others. They were in fact the minstrels of the free-living churchmen.[3]

2. A kindred spirit is seen in much of the verse alike of the northern Trouvères and the southern Troubadours. A modern Catholic historian of mediæval literature complains that their compositions " abound with the severest ridicule of such persons and of such things as, in the temper of the age, were highly estimated and most generally revered," and notes that in consequence they were ranked by the devout as " lewd and impious libertines ".[4] In particular they satirised the practice of

[1] Bartoli, *Storia della Letteratura Italiana*, 1878, p. 262, *note*, also his *I Precursori del Rinascimento*, 1877, p. 37. In this section and in the next chapter I am indebted for various clues to the Rev. John Owen's *Skeptics of the Italian Rénaissance*. As to the Goliards generally, see that work, pp. 38-45; Bartoli, *Storia*, cap. viii; and Gebhart, *Les Origines de la Renaissanse en Italie*, 1879, pp. 125-6.
[2] Bartoli, *Storia*, pp. 271-9. Cp. Schlegel's note to Mosheim, Reid's ed., p. 332, following Ratherius; Gebhart, as cited.
[3] Owen, as cited, pp. 43, 45; Bartoli, *Storia*, i, 293.
[4] Rev. Joseph Berington, *Literary History of the Middle Ages*, ed. 1846, p. 229. Cp. Owen, p. 43.

excommunication and the use made by the Church of Hell and Purgatory as sources of revenue.[1] Their anti-clerical poetry having been as far as possible destroyed by the Inquisition, its character has to be partly inferred from the remains of the northern trouvères,—*e.g.*, Ruteboeuf and Raoul de Houdan, of whom the former wrote a *Voye de Paradis*, in which Sloth is a canon and Pride a bishop, both on their way to heaven; while Raoul has a *Songe d'enfer* in which Hell is treated in a spirit of the most audacious burlesque.[2] The Provençal literature, further, was much influenced by the culture of the Saracens,[3] who held Sicily and Calabria in the ninth and tenth centuries, and had held part of Languedoc itself for a few years in the eighth. On the passing of the duchy of Pro-vence to Raymond Berenger, Count of Barcelona, at the end of the eleventh century, not only were the half-Saracenised Catalans mixed with the Provençals, but Raymond and his successors freely introduced the arts and science of the Saracens into their dominion.[4] In the Norman kingdom of Sicily, too, the Saracen influence was great even before the time of Frederic II; and thence it reached through Italy to Provence,[5] carrying with it everywhere, by way of poetry, an element of anti-clerical and even anti-Christian rationalism.[6] And though this spirit was not that of the *cathari* and Waldenses, yet the fact that the latter strongly condemned the Crusades[7] was a point in common between them and the sympathisers with Saracen culture. And as the tolerant Saracen schools of Spain were in that age resorted to by the youth of all the countries of Western Europe for scientific

---

[1] Owen, p. 43; Bartoli, *Storia*, p. 295, as to the French *fabliaux*.

[2] Labitte, *La divine comédie avant Dante*, in Charpentier ed. of Dante, pp. 133-4

[3] Sismondi, *Literature of Southern Europe*, Eng. tr., i, 74-95.

[4] Sismondi, as cited, p. 76.

[5] Zeller, *Histoire d'Italie*, 1853, p. 152.

[6] "The Troubadours in truth were freethinkers" (Owen, *Italian Skeptics*, p. 48).

[7] Heeren, *Essai sur l'influence des Croisades*, 1808, p. 174, *note*; Owen, *Italian Skeptics*, p. 44, *note*.

teaching[1]—all the latest medical and most other scientific
knowledge being in their hands—the influence of such
culture must have been peculiarly strong in Provence.[2]

3. The medieval mystery-plays and moralities, already
common in Provence, mixed at times with the normal
irreverence of illiterate faith[3] a vein of surprisingly pronounced skeptical criticism,[4] which at the least was a
stimulus to critical thought among the auditors, even if
they were supposed to take it as merely dramatic. Inasmuch as the drama was hereditarily Pagan, and had been
continually denounced and ostracised by Fathers and
Councils,[5] it would be natural that its practitioners, even
when in the service of the Church, should be unbelievers.

4. The philosophy and science of both the Arabs and
the Spanish Jews were specially cultivated in the Provence
territory. The college of Montpellier practised on Arab
lines medicine, botany, and mathematics; and the Jews,
who had been driven from Spain by the Almohades, had
flourishing schools at Narbonne, Beziers, Nîmes, and
Carcassonne, as well as Montpellier, and spread alike the
philosophy of Averroës and the semi-rational theology of
Maimonides.[6]

For the rest, every one of the new literary influences
that were assailing the Church would tend to flourish in
such a civilisation as that of Languedoc, which had been
peaceful and prosperous for over two hundred years. Its
probable lack of military strength may have been one of
the inducements to Innocent III, a zealous assertor of

---

[1] Sismondi, as cited, p. 82; Owen, pp. 66, 68; Mosheim, Cent. XI,
Pt. II, ch. i, § 4; XII, Pt. II, ch. i, § 9, and Reid's note to § 8; Hampden,
Bampton Lectures, p. 446. The familiar record that Gerbert, afterwards
Pope Sylvester II, studied in Spain among the Arabs (Ueberweg, i, 369),
has of late years been called in question (Ueberweg, p. 430; Poole,
Illustrations, p. 88); but its very currency depended on the commonness of
such a proceeding in his age.

[2] Sismondi, p. 83.

[3] Cp. G. H. Lewes, *The Spanish Drama*, 1846, pp. 11-14; Littré, *Etudes
sur les barbares et le moyen age*, 3e édit. p. 356.

[4] See the passages cited by Mr. Owen, p. 58.

[5] Cp. Bartoli, *Storia*, pp. 200-2.

[6] Gebhart, *Les Origines de la Renaissance*, pp. 4, 17, Renan, *Averroès et
l'Averroïsme*, pp. 145, 183, 185.

the Papal power,[1] to attack it in preference to other and remote centres of enmity. In the first year of his pontificate, 1198, he commenced an Inquisition[2] in the doomed region; and in the year 1207, when as much persecution had been accomplished as the lax faith of the nobility and many of the bishops would consent to, the scheme of a crusade against the dominions of Raymond Count of Toulouse was conceived. The alternate weakness and obstinacy of Raymond, and the fresh provocation given by the murder of the arrogant papal legate, permitted the success of the scheme in such hands. The crusade was planned exactly on the conditions of those against the Saracens—the heretics at home being declared far worse than they.[3] The crusaders were freed from payment of interest on their debts, exempted from the jurisdiction of all law courts, and absolved from all their sins past or future.[4] To earn this reward they were to give only forty days' service—a trifle in comparison with the hardships of the crusades to Palestine. " Never therefore had the cross been taken up with a more unanimous consent."[5] Bishops and nobles in Burgundy and France, the English Simon de Montfort, the Abbot of Citeaux, and the Bernardine monks throughout Europe, combined in the cause. The result was such a campaign of crime and massacre as European history cannot match.[6] Despite the abject submission of the Count of Toulouse and the efforts of his nephew the Count of Albi to make

---

[1] As to this Pope's character compare Sismondi, *Hist. of the Crusades against the Albigenses* (Eng. tr. from vols. vi and vii of his *Histoire des Français*) p. 10 ; Hallam, *Europe during the Middle Ages*, 11th ed., ii, 198; Mosheim, Cent. XIII, Pt. II, c. ii, §§ 6-8.

[2] As to previous acts of inquisition and persecution by Pope Alexander III, see Llorente, *Hist. Crit. de l'Inquisition en Espagne*, French trans., 2e édit., i, 27-30. Cp. Gieseler, Per. III, Div. iii, § 89 (Amer. ed. ii, 564).

[3] Sismondi, *Crusades against the Albigenses*, p. 21.

[4] On the history of indulgences, see Lea, *History of the Inquisition*, i, 41-47. For later developments cp. his *Studies in Church History*, 1869, p. 450 ; Vieusseux, *History of Switzerland*, 1840, pp. 121, 125.

[5] Sismondi, *Crusades*, p. 23.

[6] For a modern Catholic defence of the whole proceedings, see the Comte de Montalembert's *Histoire de Sainte Elisabeth de Hongrie*, 13e édit., intr., pp. 35-40.

terms, village after village was fired, all heretics caught
were burned, and on the capture of the city and castle of
Carcassone every man, woman, and child within the walls
was slaughtered, many of them in the churches, whither
they had run for refuge. The legate, Arnold, abbot of
Citeaux, being asked at an early stage how the heretics
were to be distinguished from the faithful, gave the never-
to-be-forgotten answer, " Kill all, God will know his
own ".[1]   Seven thousand dead bodies were counted in the
great church of St. Mary Magdalene.   The legate
in writing estimated the total quarry at 15,000 ; others
put the number at sixty thousand.[2]   Systematic treachery,
authorised and prescribed by the Pope,[3] completed the
success of the undertaking. The Church had succeeded,
in the name of religion, in bringing half of Europe to the
attainment of the ideal height of wickedness, in that it
had learned to make evil its good ; and the Papacy had
on the whole come nearer to destroying the moral sense
of all Christendom[4] than any conceivable combination of
other causes could ever have done in any age.

The first crusade was followed by others, in which
Simon de Montfort reached the maximum of massacre,
varying his procedure by tearing out eyes and cutting off
noses when he was not hanging victims by dozens or
burning them by scores or putting them to the sword by
hundreds[5] (all being done "with the utmost joy ") ;[6]
though the " White Company" organised by the Bishop
of Toulouse[7] maintained a close rivalry.   The Church's

---

[1] Sismondi, *Crusades*, p. 35, and refs.
[2] *Id.*, p. 37, and refs.
[3] *Id.*, pp. 21, 41.   Cp. p. 85 as to later treachery towards Saracens ;
and p. 123 as to the deeds of the Bishop of Toulouse.   See again pp. 140-2
as to the massacre of Marmande.
[4] As to the international character of the crusade, see Sismondi,
Crusades, p. 53.   It was the Pope, finally, who first faltered, when " the
whole of Christendom demanded the renewal of those scenes of massacre "
(*Id.*, p. 95).   The bishops assembled in council at Lavaur, in 1213,
demanded the extermination of the entire populaton of Toulouse.   On the
crusade in general, cp. Lea, *History of the Inquisition*, B. i, c. 4 ; Gieseler,
Per. III, Div. iii, § 89.
[5] Sismondi, p. 62, ff.   [6] Pp. 77, 78.   [7] Pp. 74, 75.

great difficulty was that as soon as an army had bought its plenary indulgence for all possible sin by forty days' service it disbanded. Nevertheless, "the greater part of the population of the countries where heresy had prevailed was exterminated".[1] Organised Christianity had contrived to murder the civilisation of Provence and Languedoc while the fanatics of Islam in their comparatively bloodless manner were doing as much for that of Moorish Spain. It was owing to no lack of the principle of evil in the Christian system, but simply to the much greater and more uncontrollable diversity of the political elements of Christendom, that the whole culture and intelligence of Europe did not undergo the same fate. The dissensions and mutual injuries of the crusaders ultimately defeated their ideal;[2] after Simon de Montfort had died in the odour of sanctity[3] the crusade of Louis VIII of France in 1226 seems to have been essentially one of conquest, there being practically no heretics left; and the disasters of the expedition, crowned by the king's death, took away the old prestige of the movement. Meanwhile, the heresy of the Albigenses, and kindred ideas, had been effectually driven into other parts of Europe;[4] and about 1231 we find Gregory IX burning a multitude of them at the gates of the church of Santa Maria Majora in Rome,[5] and compassing their slaughter in France and Germany.[6] The political heterogeneity of Europe, happily, made heresy indestructible.

---

[1] P. 87. "The worship of the reformed Albigenses had everywhere ceased" (p. 115). Cp. p. 116 as to the completeness of the final massacres. It is estimated (Monastier, p. 115, following De la Mothe-Langon) that a million Albigenses were slain in the first half of the thirteenth century. The figures are of course speculative.

[2] *Id.*, pp. 115, 117.   [3] P. 133.   [4] *Id.*, pp. 235-9.

[5] *Id.*, p. 236; Llorente, as cited, i, 60-64.

[6] Matthew Paris records that in 1249 four hundred and forty-three heretics were burned in Saxony and Pomerania. Previously multitudes had been burned by the inquisitor Conrad, who was himself finally murdered in revenge. He was the confessor of Saint Elizabeth of Hungary, and he taught her among other things, "Be merciful to your neighbor," and "Do to others whatsoever you would that they should do to you". See his praises recorded by Montalembert, as cited, vol. i, ch. 10. Cp. Gieseler, Per. III, Div. iii, § 89 (ii, 567).

§ 7.

Despite the premium put by the Church on devotion
to its cause and doctrine, and despite its success in
strangling specific forms of heresy, hostility to its own
pretensions germinated everywhere,[1] especially in the
countries most alien to Italy in language and civilisation.
Its own economic conditions, constantly turning its priesthood, despite all precautions, into a moneyed and wealth-
seeking class, ensured it a perpetuity of ill-will and
denunciation. The popular literature which now began
to grow throughout Christendom with the spread of
political order was everywhere turned to the account of
anti-clerical satire; and only the defect of real knowledge
secured by the Church's own policy prevented such
hostility from developing into rational unbelief.

It is somewhat of a straining of the facts to say of the
humorous tale of *Reynard the Fox*, so widely popular in the
thirteenth century, that it is essentially anti-clerical to the
extent that " Reynard is laic; Isengrim [the wolf] is clerical "
(Bartoli, *Storia della Letteratura Italiana*, i, 307; cp. Owen,
Skeptics of the Italian Renaissance, p. 44). The *Reynard* epic, in
origin a simple humorous animal-story, had various later
forms. Some of these, as the Latin poem, and especially the
version attributed to Peter of St. Cloud, were markedly anti-
clerical, the latter exhibiting a spirit of all-round profanity
hardly compatible with belief (cp. Gervinus, *Geschichte der
deutschen Dichtung*, 5te Ausg. i, 227-8; Gebhart, *Les Origines de
la Renais. en Italie*, 1879, p. 39); but the version current in the
Netherlands, which was later rendered into English prose by
Caxton, is of a very different character (Gervinus, S. 229, ff.).
In Caxton's version it is impossible to regard Reynard as laic
and Isengrim as clerical; though in the Latin and other
versions the wolf figures as monk or abbot. (See also the
various shorter satires published by Grimm in his *Reinhart
Fuchs*, 1834.) Sometimes the authorship is itself clerical, one
party or order satirising another; sometimes the spirit is
religious, sometimes markedly irreverent. (Gervinus, S.
214-221.) The anti-clerical tendency was strongest in France,
where in the thirteenth century lay scholarship stood highest.

---

[1] Hallam, *Middle Ages*, 11th ed., ii, 218; Lea, *History of the Inquisition*, i,
5-34; Gieseler, § 90 (ii, 572).

In the reign of Philippe le Bel (end of 13th c.) was composed the poem *Fauvel*, by François de Rues, which is a direct attack on pope and clergy (Saintsbury, *Short Hist. of French Lit.*, 1882, p. 57). But the remark that the *Roman de la Rose* is a "popular satire on the beliefs of Romanism" (Owen, p. 44) can hardly be taken without qualification. The *Roman* is rather an intellectual expression of the literary reaction against asceticism (cp. Bartoli, p. 319, quoting Lenient) which had been spontaneously begun by the Goliards and Troubadours. At the same time this lengthy poem, one of the most popular books in Europe for two hundred years, does stand for the new secular spirit alike in "its ingrained religion and its nascent freethought" (Saintsbury, p. 87); and with the *Reynard* epic it may be taken as representing the beginning of "a whole revolution, the resurgence and affirmation of the laity, the new force which is to transform the world, against the Church" (Bartoli, *Storia*, i, 308; Cp. Demogeot, *Hist. de la litt. Fr.*, 5e éd., pp. 130-1, 157; Lanson, pp. 132-6). The semi-irreligious cynicism of Jean de Meung's part of the work (*Cp.* the pseudo-Chaucerian English version, Bell's ed. of Chaucer, 1878, passage in vol. iv, p. 230) and the frequent flings at the clergy, were sufficient to draw upon it the anger of the church (Sismondi, *Lit. of Southern Europe*, i, 216).

For lack of other culture than Biblical, the popular heresy tended to run into mysticisms which were only so far more rational than the dogmas and rites of the Church that they stood for some actual reflection. The sect of the Brethren of the Free Spirit, however (apparently that known in France by the names of *Turlupins* and *Beguins*, and in Germany and Belgium as *Beguttae* or *Beghards*[1]), developed a pantheism which suggests some contact with the philosophical thought[2] then being introduced from Saracen Spain. As usual, the profession of spiritual freedom carried with it a measure of antinomianism, thus strengthening the hands of the Church against it. The Brethren, however, had a sacred book of their own, *The Nine Rocks*, and in virtue of their doctrine of individual

---

[1] Mosheim, Cent XIII, Pt. II, c. ii, §§ 40-43, and notes; c, v, § 9. Various other names were given.

[2] Gieseler (Per. III, Div. iii, § 90; Amer. ed. 1865, ii, 590) holds that the Brethren derived their doctrine from that of Amalrich of Bena (see below, p. 222).

inspiration and sanctification[1] were persistent and dangerous enemies to the priesthood. Concurrently, at the beginning of the century, the *Eternal Gospel* of the Abbot Joachim, of Flora in Calabria, expressed a spirit of innovation[2] and revolt that seemed to promise the utter disruption of the Church. Adopted by the "Spiritual" section of the Franciscans, it brought heresy within the organisation itself, as did the movement of the ultra-Franciscan *Fraticelli*, who had their *Gospel of the Holy Spirit*, composed by John of Parma.[3] The old cohesive and political force of the central system, nevertheless, and the natural strifes of the new movements, whether within or without[4] the Church, sufficed to bring about their absorption or their destruction. It needed a special concurrence of economic, political, and culture forces to disrupt the fabric of the Papacy.

The Church, too, spontaneously evolved measures of protection calculated to bring some of the main forces of disaffection round to its own side. The great orders of Mendicant Friars, the special feature of thirteenth century Christianity, realised the impulse of conscientious believers to disarm criticism of priestly avarice and worldliness by creating a priesthood of poverty. Nothing availed more to restore and preserve the Church's prestige. Yet the descent of the new orders to the economic level of the old was only a question of time. The corporate life carried with it the power to amass wealth by donations or bequests; and the party within any Order willing to amass, soon overbore those who refused. The *Humiliati*, founded before the thirteenth century, had to be suppressed by the Pope in the sixteenth, for sheer corruption of morals. The Franciscans, vowed to poverty, soon obeyed

---

[1] A full account of their tenets is given by Mosheim, Cent. XIII, Pt. II, c. v, §§ 9-11, and notes.

[2] It asserted a new dispensation, that of the Holy Spirit, superseding the Christian. The *Introduction* to the book, produced about the middle of the century by the Franciscan Gerhard, made St. Francis the angel of Rev. xiv, 6; and the ministers of the new order were to be his friars. Mosheim, Cent. XIII, Pt. II, c. ii, §§ 33-36 and notes. Cp. Lea, *History of the Inquisition*, iii, 19-24.

[3] Ueberweg, i, 431; Mosheim, Cent. XIII, Pt. II, c. ii, §§ 39, 40.

[4] As to the external movements connected with Joachim's *Gospel*, see Mosheim, sect. last cited, c. v, §§ 13-15. They were put down by sheer bloodshed. Cp. Ueberweg, i, 431; Lea, *Hist. of Inq.*, pp. 25-6, 86.

the economic law ; and when the Spiritual section resisted the
demoralisation, the other had the support of the Popes against
them.   Thus even in the thirteenth century they were
attacked by the Sorbonne doctor, William of St. Amour, in a
book on *The Perils of the Latter Times* (praised in the *Roman de la
Rose*, Eng. ed. cited, p. 228) ; and in England in the fourteenth
century we find Wiclif assailing the begging friars as the
earlier satirists had assailed the abbots and monks.   The
worst of the trouble for the Church was that the mendicants
were detested by bishops and the regular priests, whose
credit they undermined, and whose revenues they intercepted.
That the Franciscans and Dominicans remained socially
powerful till the Reformation was due to the energy developed
by their corporate organisation and the measure of education
they soon secured on their own behalf.   (Cp. Mosheim,
Cent. XIII, Pt. II, c. ii, §§ 18-40 ; Hallam, *Europe in the Middle
Ages*, ch. vii, pt. 2 (11th ed., ii, 305 ff.) ; Gebhart, *Les Origines
de la Renaissance*, p. 42 ; Berington, *Lit. Hist. of the Middle Ages*,
p. 244 ; Lea, *Hist. of Inq.*, B. iii, c. 1.)   The special work of the
Dominicans was the establishment everywhere of the Inquisition
(Mosheim, as last cited, c. v, §§ 3-6, and notes ; Llorente,
Hist. Crit. de l'Inquis. en Espagne, as cited, i, 49-55, 68, etc.).

§ 8.

The indestructibility of Freethought, meanwhile, was
being proved in the philosophic schools.   Already in the
ninth century we have seen Scotus Erigena putting the
faith in jeopardy by his philosophic defence of it.   In the
eleventh century, the simple fact of the production of a
new argument for the existence of God by Anselm, archbishop of Canterbury, is a proof that, apart from the
published disputes, a measure of doubt had arisen in the
schools.

It is urged (Poole, *Illustr. of the Hist. of Medieval Thought*,
pp. 104-5) that though the argumentation of Anselm seems
alien to the thought of his time, there is no proof that the
idea of proving the existence of God was in any way pressed
on him from the outside.   It is, however, inconceivable that
such an argument should be framed if no one had raised a
doubt.   And as a matter of fact the question *was* discussed in
the schools, Anselm's treatise being a reproduction of his
teaching.   The monks of Bec, where he taught, urged him to

write a treatise wherein nothing should be proved by mere authority, but all by necessity of reason or evidence of truth, and with an eye to objections of all sorts (*Præfatio in Monologium*).   It is further on record that in the twelfth century, John of Salisbury put in his list of "things about which a wise man may doubt, so . . . . that the doubt extend not to the multitude," some "things which are reverently to be enquired about God himself" (Poole, p. 223).   Further, the nature of part of Anselm's argument, and the very able but friendly reply of Gaunilo (a Count of Montigni, who entered a convent near Tours, 1044-1083) shows that the subject wa within the range of private discussion.   Anselm substantially follows St. Augustine (Ueberweg, i, 381) ; and men cannot have read the ancient books which so often spoke of atheism without confronting the atheistic idea.   It is not to be supposed that Gaunilo was an unbeliever; but his argumentation is that of a man who had pondered the problem.   (See it in Ueberweg, i, 384-5 ; cp. Ch. de Rémusat, *Saint Anselme*, 1853, pp. 61-2 ; Dean Church, *Saint Anselm*, ed. 1888, pp. 86-7).   As to previous uses of Anselm's argument cp. Poole, *Illustrations*, p. 338, ff.

Despite the ostensibly rationalistic nature of his argument, however, Anselm stipulated for absolute sub-mission of the intellect to the creed of the Church ;[1] so that the original sub-title of his Proslogium, *Fides quaerens intellectum,* in no way admits rational tests.   In the next century ABAILARD takes up the more advanced position that reason must prepare the way for faith, since otherwise faith has no certitude.[2]   He, however, was in the main dependent on the authority either of Aristotle[3] or of the Scriptures, though he partly sets aside that of the Fathers.[4]   When St. Bernard accused him of Arianism and of heathenism he was expressing personal ill-will rather than criticising.   Abailard himself complained that many heresies were current in his time ;[5] and as a matter of fact "more intrepid views than his were promulgated without risk by a multitude of less conspicuous masters".[6]

---

[1] Ueberweg,.i, 379-380.   [2] Ueberweg, i. 387
[3] See cit. from the *Dialectic* in Ueberweg, i, 391.
[4] Ueberweg, i, 394-5.
[5] Hampden, Bampton Lectures, pp. 420-1.
[6] 1 cole, p. 175.

For instance, Bernard Sylvester (of Chartres) in his cosmology, treated theological considerations with open disrespect[1]; and William of Conches, who held a similar tone on physics,[2] taught, until threatened with punishment, that the Holy Ghost and the universal Soul were convertible terms.[3] If, as is said, Abailard wrote that "a doctrine is believed not because God has said it but because we are convinced by reason that it is so",[4] he went as far on one line as any theologian of his time ; but his main service to freethought seems to have lain in the great stimulus he gave to the practice of reasoning on all topics. His enemy, St. Bernard, on the contrary, gave an "immense impulse to the growth of a genuinely superstitious spirit among the Latin clergy".[5]

The worse side of scholasticism at all times was that it was more often than not a mere logical expatiation *in vacuo*; this for sheer lack of real knowledge. John of Salisbury probably did not do injustice to the habit of verbiage it developed.[6] With him begins some measure of a new life, introduced into philosophy through the communication of Aristotle to the western world by the Saracens, largely through the mediation of the Jews.[7] The latter, in their free life under the earlier Moorish toleration, had developed something in the nature of a school of philosophy, in which the Judaic Platonism set up by Philo of Alexandria in the first century was blended with the Aristotelianism of the Arabs. As early as the eighth and ninth centuries, anti-Talmudic (the Karaites) and pro-Talmudic parties professed alike to appeal to reason;[8] and in the twelfth century the mere production

---

[1] *Id.* pp. 117-123, 169.   [2] Ueberweg, i, 398.
[3] Poole, p. 173.   [4] *Id.* p. 153.
[5] *Id.* p. 161. Contrast the singularly laudatory account of St. Bernard given by two contemporary Positivists, Mr. Cotter Morrison in his *Life and Times of St. Bernard;* and Mr. F. Harrison in his essay on that work in his *Choice of Books.*
[6] Cp. Poole, pp. 220-2, and the extracts of Hampden, pp. 438-443.
[7] Ueberweg, i, 419, 430 ; Hampden, p. 443, ff. John of Salisbury tells of having heard many discourse on physics *aliter quam fides habeat.* Hampden, p. 443. Cp. Renan, *Averroès,* Pt. ii, c. i, p. 173.
[8] Ueberweg, i, 418.

of the *Guide of the Doubting* by the celebrated Moses
Maimonides tells of a good deal of practical rationalism,
of which, however, there is no direct literary result, save
of a theosophic kind.   The doctrine which makes Aristotle
a practical support to rationalism, and which was adopted
by the Motazilites of Islam—the eternity of matter—was
rejected by Maimonides, on Biblical grounds; though his
attempts to rationalise Biblical doctrine made him odious
to the orthodox Jews, some of whom, in France, did not
scruple to call in the aid of the Christian inquisition
against his partisans.[1]

The habit of debating for debating's sake made it
possible that in the schools the new influence of Aristotle
and Averroës should go far without seriously affecting
doctrine, belief, or life.[2] Some teachers, as Amalrich of
Bena (end of 12th c.) and his pupil David of Dinant,
under the Arabic influence, taught a pantheism akin to
that noted as flourishing among the Brethren of the Free
Spirit;[3] and this seems likewise to have been the creed
of many of the Franciscan *Fraticelli*. But the Church
promptly put a veto on the study of Aristotle and his
commentators at Paris, interdicting first the *Physics* and
soon after the *Metaphysics*;[4] and this held until 1237.
From the time of the adoption of Aristotle by the Church,
and his establishment on a canonical footing in the
theological system of Thomas Aquinas (1225-74), scholasticism counts for little in the liberation of European life
from either dogma or superstition.[5] The practically
progressive forces are to be looked for outside.   In the
thirteenth century in England we find the Franciscan
friars in the school of Robert Grosstête at Oxford discussing the question " Whether there be a God?"[6] but

[1] Ueberweg, i, 428.
[2] The description by Mr. Lecky (*Rationalism in Europe*, ed. 1887, i, 48)
of Averroïsm and the Arab philosophy in general as a " stern and uncompromising infidelity" is hopelessly astray.
[3] Ueberweg, i, 388, 431.
[4] Poole, p. 225; Ueberweg, i, 431.
[5] Cp. Gebhart, *Les Origines de la Renaissance*, pp. 29-44.
[6] Berington, *Lit. Hist. of the Middle Ages*, p. 245.

such a dispute was an academic exercise like another ; and in any case the authorities could be trusted to see that it came to nothing.

We shall perhaps best understand the inner life of the schools in the Middle Ages by likening it to that of the universities of our own day, where there is unquestionably much unbelief among teachers and taught, but where the economic and other pressure of the institution suffices to preserve an outward acquiescence. In the Middle Ages it was much less possible than in our day for the unbeliever to strike out a free course of life and doctrine for himself. If then to-day the scholarly class is in large measure tied to institutions and conformities, much more so was it then. The cloister was almost the sole haven of refuge for studious spirits, and to enjoy the haven they had to accept the discipline and the profession of faith. We may conclude, accordingly, that such works as Abailard's *Sic et Non*, setting forth opposed views of so many problems, stood for and made for a great deal of quiet scepticism ; that the remarkable request of the monks of Bec for a ratiocinative teaching, which should meet even extravagant objections, covered a good deal of resigned unfaith ; and that in the Franciscan schools at Oxford the disputants were not all at heart orthodox.[1] But the unspoken and unwritten word died, the *litera scripta* being solely those of faith, and liberation had to come from without. Even when a bold saying won general currency—as that of King Alfonso the Wise of Castile (1223-1284), that " if he had been of God's council when he made the world he could have advised him better ", it did but crystallise scepticism in a jest, and supply the enemy with a text against impiety.

---

[1] Cp. Lange, i, 218, as to the phrases of the Paris scholastics in the 13th c.: "Nothing more can be known because of the science of theology." " The Christian religion prevents us from learning anything more."

CHAPTER X.

FREETHOUGHT IN THE RENAISSANCE.

WHAT is called the Renaissance was, broadly speaking, an evolution of the culture forces seen at work in the later "Middle Ages", reinforced by the recovery of classic literature. Renascent Italy is, after ancient Greece, the great historical illustration of the sociological law that the higher civilisations arise through the passing-on of seeds of culture from older to newer societies, under conditions that specially foster them and give them freer growth. The straitened and archaic Byzantine art, unprogressive in the hidebound life of the Eastern Empire, developed in the free and striving Italian communities till it paralleled the sculpture of ancient Greece; and it is to be said for the Church that, however she might stifle rational thought, she elicited the arts of painting and architecture (statuary being tabooed as too much associated with Pagan worships), even as Greek religion had promoted architecture and sculpture. In virtue, however, of the tendency of the arts to keep religion anthropomorphic where deeper culture is lacking, popular belief in Renaissance Italy was substantially on a par with that of polytheistic Greece.

Before the general recovery of ancient literature, the main motives to rationalism, apart from the tendency of the Aristotelian philosophy to set up doubts about creation and Providence and a future state, were (1) the spectacle of the competing creed of Islam,[1] made known to the Italians first by intercourse with the Moors, later by the Crusades; and further and more fully by the Saracenised culture of Sicily and commercial intercourse with the

[1] Cp. Renan, *Averroès*, pp. 280-2, 295.

(224)

East; (2) the spectacle of the strife of creeds within[1] Christendom; and (3) the spectacle of the worldliness and moral insincerity of the bulk of the clergy. The first clear traces of rational unbelief appear in the thirteenth century when the Emperor Frederic II had the repute of being an infidel[2] in the double sense of being semi-Moslem[3] and semi-atheist. He was in reality superstitious enough; he worshipped relics; and he was nearly as merciless as the Popes to rebellious heretics and Manicheans; but he is recorded to have ridiculed the doctrine of the Virgin Birth, the viaticum, and other dogmas, "as being repugnant to reason and to nature";[4] and his general hostility to the Pope would tend to make him a bad Churchman. Of his son Manfred it is recorded that he was a thorough Epicurean, believing neither in God nor the saints.[5] But positive unbelief in a future state, mockery of the Christian religion, and even denial of Deity—usually in private, and never in writing—are frequently complained of by the clerical writers of the time in France and Italy.[6]

The commonest form of rationalistic heresy seems to have been unbelief in immortality. Thus Dante in the *Inferno* estimates that among the heretics there are more than a thousand followers of Epicurus, "who make the soul die with the body,"[7] specifying among them the

---

[1] Cp. Burckhardt, *Civilisation of the Renaissance in Italy*, Eng. tr. ed. 1892, pp. 490, 492.

[2] He was currently believed to have written a treatise dealing with Moses, Jesus, and Mohammed as *The Three Impostors*. The story is certainly a myth; and probably no such book existed in his century. Cp. Maclaine's note to Mosheim, Cent. XIII, Pt. I, *end;* Renan, *Averroès*, pp. 280-1, 295.

[3] The Moslems were inclined to regard him as of their creed "because educated in Sicily". Cantù, *Gli Eretici d'Italia*, i, 66.

[4] Cantù, *Gli Eretici d'Italia*, i, 65-66; Renan, *Averroès*, pp. 287-291, 296.

[5] G. Villani, *Istorie fiorentine*, vi, 46.

[6] Mosheim, Cent. XIII, Pt. I, c. ii, § 2, citing in particular Moneta's *Summa contra Catharos et Valdenses*, lib. cc. 4, 11, 15; Tempier (bishop of Paris), *Indiculum Errorum* (1272) in the *Bibliotheca Patrum Maxima*, t. xxv; Bulæus, *Hist. Acad. Paris*, iii, 433. Cp. Renan, *Averroès*, pp. 230-1, citing William of Auvergne, and pp. 283, 285; Ozanam, *Dante*, pp. 47, 48; Gebhart, *Les Origines de la Renaissance en Italie*, pp. 79-81; Lange, i, 218.

[7] *Inferno*, Canto x, 14-15, 118.

Emperor Frederic II, a cardinal,[1] the Ghibelline noble
Farinata degli Uberti, and the Guelph Cavalcante Caval-
canti.[2]   He was thinking, as usual, of the men of his own
age ; but the world of Dante is so distinctly that of the
Middle Ages that there is ground for the inference that
this particular heresy had existed in previous centuries,[3]
having indeed probably never disappeared from Italy.
Other passages in his works[4] show, in any case, that it
was much discussed in his time ; and it is noteworthy
that, so far as open avowal went, Italian freethought had
got no further two hundred years later.[5]   Dante's own
poetic genius, indeed, did much to arrest intellectual
evolution in Italy on the side of belief.   Before his time,
as we have seen, the trouvères of northern France and the
Goliards of the south had handled hell in a spirit of
burlesque ; and his own teacher, Brunetto Latini, had
framed a poetic allegory, *Il Tesoretto*, in which Nature
figures as the universal power, behind which the God-idea
disappeared.[6]   But Dante's tremendous vision effaced all
others of the kind ; and his intellectual predominance in
virtue of mere imaginative art is at once the great characteristic and the great anomaly of the Renaissance.
Happily the profound malignity of his pietism was in large
part superseded by a sunnier spirit ; but his personality

---

[1] Ottavio Ubaldini, d. 1273, of whom the commentators tell that he
said that if there were such a thing as a soul he had lost his for the cause
of the Ghibellines.

[2] As to whom see Renan, *Averroès*, p. 285, *note;* Gebhart, *Renaissance*,
p. 81. His son, also mentioned by Dante, was reputed an atheist
(*Decamerone*, vi, 9).   But see Owen, *Skeptics of the Ital. Renais.*, p. 138, *note*.

[3] The chronicler Giovanni Villani (iv, 29) actually records that among
many other heretics in 1115 and 1117 were some "of the sect of the
Epicureans.", who "with armed hand defended the said heresy" against
the orthodox.   Cp. Ozanam, *Dante*, 2e édit., pp. 47-48 to supposed secret
anti-Christian societies.

[4] In the *Convito*, ii, 9, he writes that "amongst all the bestialities, that
is the most foolish, the most vile, the most damnable, which believes no
other life to be after this life".   Another passage (iv, 5) heaps curses on the
"most foolish and vile beasts . . . who presume to speak against our
Faith."

[5] "Le 16e siècle n'a eu aucune mauvaise pensée que le 13e n'ait eue
avant lui" (Renan, *Averroès*, p. 231).

[6] Cp. Labitte, *La Divine Comédie avant Dante*, as cited, p. 139.

and his poetry helped to hold the balance of authority on
the side of faith.[1] Within a few years of his death there
was burned (1327) one of the most daring heretics of the
early Renaissance, CECCO D'ASCOLI, a professor of
philosophy and astrology at Bologna, who, combining
anti-Christian opinion with the universal belief in astrology,
declared that Jesus lived as a sluggard (come un poltrone)
with his disciples, and died on the cross, under the compulsion of his star.[2] Such audacity was not often repeated.

As against Dante, the great literary influence for
tolerance and liberalism if not rationalism of thought was
BOCCACCIO (1313—1375), whose Decameron[3] reflects every
aspect of the Renaissance — its levity, its license, its
humor, its bantering anti-clericalism, its incipient
tolerance, its irreverence, its partial freethinking, as well
as its exuberance in the joy of living. The most significant
part of its contents, in the present connection, is the
famous story of The Three Rings,[4] embodied later by
Lessing in his Nathan the Wise as an apologue of tolerance.
Such a story, introduced with whatever parade of orthodox
faith, could not but make for rational scepticism, sum-
marising as it does the whole effect of the inevitable
comparison of the rival creeds made by the men of Italy
and those of the East in their intercourse. The story
itself, centring on Saladin, is of Eastern origin[5] and so tells
of even more freethinking than meets the eye in the
history of Islam.[6] Current in Italy before Boccaccio, it

[1] As to an element of doubt, even in Dante, concerning Divine government, see Burckhardt, p. 497. But the attempt made by some critics to
show that the " sins " to which Dante confessed had been intellectual—i.e.,
heresies—falls to the ground. See Döllinger, Studies in European History,
Eng. tr. 1890, pp. 87-90.
[2] G. Villani, x, 39. It is to be noted that the horoscope of Jesus was
cast by several professed believers, as Albertus Magnus and Pierre d'Ailli,
Cardinal and Bishop of Cambrai, as well as by Cardan. See Bayle, art.
CARDAN, note Q.
[3] Cp. Owen, pp. 128, 135-142; Hallam, Lit. Hist., i, 141-2.
[4] Decam. Gior. i, nov. 3.
[5] Dr. Marcus Landau, Die Quellen des Dekameron, 2te Aufl. 1884, S. 182.
[6] The story is recorded to have been current among the Motecallemin
—a party kindred to the Motazilites—in Bagdad. Renan, Averroès, p. 294,
citing Dozy. Renan thinks it may have been of Jewish origin. Id., note.

had been improved from one Italian hand to another;[1] and the main credit for its full development is Boccaccio's.[2] The Church speedily scented the hostility in Boccaccio's book, first denouncing it, then seeking to expurgate all the anti-clerical passages;[3] and the personal pressure brought to bear upon him had the effect of dispiriting and puritanising him ; so that the *Decameron* finally wrought its effect in its author's despite.[4]

Side by side with Boccaccio, his friend PETRARCH (1304—1374), who with him completes the great literary trio of the early Italian Renaissance, belongs to Freethought in that he too, with less aggressiveness but also without recoil, stood for independent culture and rational habit of mind as against the dogmatics and tyrannies of the Church.[5] He was in the main a practical humanist, out of sympathy with the verbalising scholastic philosophy of his time, and disposed to find his intellectual guide in the sceptical yet conservative Cicero. The scholastics had become as fanatical for Aristotle or Averroës as the churchmen were for their dogmas; and Petrarch made for mental freedom by resisting all dogmatisms alike.[6] The general liberality of his attitude has earned him the titles of "the first modern man"[7] and "the founder of

---

[1] It is found some time before Boccaccio in the *Cento Novelle antiche* (No. 72 or 73) in a simpler form ; but Landau (S. 183) thinks Boccaccio's immediate source was the version of Busone da Gubbio (b. 1280) who had improved on the version in the *Cento Novelle*, while Boccaccio in turn improved on him by treating the Jew more tolerantly.   Bartoli (*I Precursori del Boccaccio*, 1876, pp. 26-28) disputes any immediate debt to Busone ; as does Mr. Owen, *Skeptics of the Italian Renaissance*, p. 29, *note*.

[2] Burckhardt (*Renaissance in Italy*, p. 493, *note*) points out that Boccaccio is the first to name the Christian religion, his Italian predecessors avoiding the idea ; and that in one Eastern version the story is used polemically against the Christians.

[3] Owen, p. 142, and refs.

[4] *Id.* pp. 143-5.   He was even so far terrorised by a monk's menaces as to propose to give up his classical studies ; and would have done so but for Petrarch's persuasion.   Petrarch's letter (*Epist. Senil*, i, 5) is translated (Lett. xii) by M. Develay, *Lettres de Pétrarque à Boccace.*

[5] As to his anti-clericalism, cp. Gebhart, *Origines de la Renaissance*, p. 71, and ref. ;   Owen, p. 113.

[6] See the exposition of Mr. Owen, pp. 109-128, and refs. on p. 113.

[7] Renan, *Averroès*, p. 328.

modern criticism"[1]—both somewhat high-pitched.[2]   He
represented in reality the balancing and clarifying influence
of the revived classic culture on the fanaticisms developed
in the Middle Ages ; and when he argued for the rule of
reason in all things[3] it was not that he was a deeply
searching rationalist, but that he was spontaneously averse
to all the extremes of thought around him, and was
concerned to discredit them.   For himself, having little
speculative power, he was disposed to fall back on a
simple and tolerant Christianity.   His judgment, like his
literary art, was clear and restrained; opening no new
vistas, but bringing a steady and placid light to bear on
its chosen sphere.

From this time forward till the Catholic reaction after
the Reformation, a large measure of rationalistic and
anti-clerical thought is a constant feature in Italian life.
It was so ingrained that the Church had on the whole to
leave it alone.   From Pope to monk, the mass of the
clergy had forfeited respect ; and gibes at their expense
were household words,[4] and the basis of popular songs.
The popular poetic literature, with certain precautions,
carried the anti-clerical spirit as far as to parade a
humorous non-literary scepticism, putting in the mouths
of the questionable characters in its romances all manner
of anti-religious opinions which it would be unsafe to print
as one's own, but which in this way reached appreciative

---

[1] Mézières, *Pétrarque*, 1868, p. 362.
[2] It is to be noted that in his opposition to the scholastics he had predecessors.   Cp. Gebhart, *Origines de la Renaissance en Italie*, p. 65 ; and ref.
to John of Salisbury above, p. 221.
[3] Owen, p. 113.   It is to be remembered that Dante also (*Convito*, ii, 8,
9 ; iii, 14 ; iv, 7) exalts Reason ; but he uses the word in the old sense of
mere mentality—the thinking as distinguished from the sensuous element
in man ; and he was fierce against all resort to reason as against faith.
Petrarch was of course much more of a rationalist.   As to his philosophic
scepticism, see Owen, p. 120.   He drew the line only at doubting those
things " in which doubt is sacrilege ".   Nevertheless he grounded his belief
in immortality not on the Christian creed but on the arguments of the
Pagans (Burckhardt, p. 546).
[4] Cp. Gebhart, *Renaissance en Italie*, pp. 72-3 ; Burckhardt, pp. 458-465 ;
Lea, *History of the Inquisition*, i, 5-34.   " The authors of the most scandalous
satires were themselves mostly monks or beneficed priests." (Burckhardt, p. 465.)

readers who were more or less in sympathy with the author's sentiments and stratagems. The *Morgante Maggiòre* of PULCI (1488) is the great type of such early Voltairean humor :[1] it revives the spirit of the Goliards, and passes unscathed in the new Renaissance world, where the earlier Provençal impiety had gone the way of the Inquisition bonfire, books and men alike. Beneath its mockery there is a constant play of rational thought, and every phase of contemporary culture is glanced at in the spirit of always unembittered humor which makes Pulci "the most loveable among the great poets of the Renaissance ".[2] As he had specially satirised the clergy and ecclesiastical miracles, his body was refused burial in consecrated ground ; but the general temper was such as to save him from clerical enmity up to that point.

Shortly after his death, too, we find a freethinking physician at Bologna, Gabriele de Salò, protected by his patrons against the wrath of the Inquisition, although he " was in the habit of maintaining that Christ was not God, but son of Joseph and Mary . . . .; that by his cunning he had deceived the world ; that he may have died on the cross on account of crimes which he had committed,"[3] and so forth. This was in 1497. Nineteen years before, Galeotto Marcio had come near being burned for writing that any man who lived uprightly according to his own conscience would go to heaven, whatever his faith ; and it needed the Pope, Sixtus IV, his former pupil, to save him from the Inquisition.[4] Others, who went further, ran similar risks ; and in 1500 Giorgio da Novara was burned at Bologna, presumptively for denying the divinity of Jesus.[5] A bishop of Aranda, however, is said to have done the same with impunity, in the same year.[6] Humorous blasphemy generally seems

---

[1] See it well analysed by Mr. Owen, pp. 147-160. It is noteworthy that Pulci is found affirming the doctrine of an Antipodes with absolute openness, and with impunity, over a hundred years before Galileo.

[2] Owen, p. 160. So also Leigh Hunt, and the editor of the *Parnaso Italiano*, there cited.

[3] Burckhardt, p. 502.   [4] *Id.*, p. 500.   [5] *Id.*, p. 502.   [6] *Id.*, p. 503, *note.*

to have fared better than serious unbelief; so that there was doubtless much more of the latter than was avowed.

One of the great literary figures of the later Renaissance, MACHIAVELLI (1469—1527) is the standing proof of the divorce of the higher intelligence of Italy from the faith as well as the cause of the Church before the Reformation. To him the Church was the supreme evil in Italian politics,[1] the " stone in the wound "; and in a famous passage he gives his opinion that "our religion having shown us the truth and the true way, makes us esteem less political honor (*l'onore del mondo*) "; and that whereas the Pagan religion canonised only men crowned with public honor, as generals and statesmen, " our religion has glorified rather the humble and contemplative men than the active," placing the highest good in humility and abjection, teaching rather to suffer than to do, and so making the world debile and ready to be a prey to scoundrels.[2] The passage which follows, putting the blame on men for thus misreading their religion, is a fair sample of the grave mockery with which the men of that age veiled their unfaith.[3] Machiavelli was reputed in his own world an atheist; and he certainly was no religionist. He indeed never avows atheism, but neither did any other writer of the epoch[4]; and the whole tenor of his writings is that of a man who had at least put aside the belief in a prayer-answering Deity.[5] Guicciardini, his contemporary, who in comparison was unblamed for irreligion, though an even warmer hater of the Papacy, has left in writing the most explicit avowals of incredulity as to the current conceptions of the supernatural, and declares concerning miracles that as they occur in every religion they prove

---

[1] *Discorsi sopra Tito Livio*, 1, 12.
[2] *Discorsi sopra Tito Livio*, ii, 2.
[3] For another point of view, see Owen, as cited, p. 167.
[4] Burckhardt, pp. 499-500. Cp. Owen, pp. 165-168.
[5] Mr. Owen's characterisation of Machiavelli's *Asino d'oro* as a " satire on the Freethought of his age " (p. 177) will not stand investigation. See his own note, p. 178.

none.[1] At the same time he professes firm faith in
Christianity[2] ; and others who would not have joined him
there were often as inconsistent in the ready belief they gave
to magic and astrology. The time was after all one of artistic
splendor and scientific and critical ignorance;[3] and its Freethought had the inevitable defects that ignorance entails.

Of the literary freethinking of the age, the most
famous representative is POMPONAZZI (1462—1525), for
whom it has been claimed that he "really initiated
the philosophy of the Italian Renaissance".[4] The
Renaissance, however, was in reality as good as over when
Pomponazzi's treatise on the Immortality of the Soul
appeared : and that topic was the commonest in the
schools and controversies of that day.[5] What is remarkable in his case is not his elaborate denial of immortality,
which we have seen to be common in Dante's time, but
his contention that ethics could do very well without
the belief[6]—a thing that it still took some courage to
affirm, though the spectacle of the life of the faithful might
have been supposed sufficient to win it a ready hearing.
Presumably his rationalism, which made him challenge
the then canonical authority of Aristotle, went further
than his avowed doubts as to a future state ; since his
profession of obedience to the Church's teaching, and
his reiteration of the old academic doctrine of twofold
truth—one truth for science and philosophy and another
for theology[7]—are as dubious as any in philosophic

---

[1] Burckhardt, p. 464 ; Owen, p. 180, and refs..
[2] Owen, p. 181. Compare the whole account of Guicciardini's rather
confused opinions.
[3] Despite the fact that Italy had most of what scientific knowledge
existed. Burckhardt, p. 292.
[4] F. Fiorentino, *Pietro Pomponazzi*, 1868, p. 30.
[5] Owen, pp. 197-8, and refs. Cp. Renan, *Averroès*, pp. 353-362.
[6] Cp. Owen, pp. 201, 218 ; Lange, i, 220-225.
[7] This principle had been affirmed by so high an orthodox authority as
Albertus Magnus. Cp. Owen, pp. 211-212, *note*. While thus officially
recognised, it was of course denounced by the devout when they saw how
it availed to save heretics from harm. Mr. Owen has well-pointed out
(p. 238) the inconsistency of the believers who maintain that faith is
independent of reason, and yet denounce as blasphemous the profession to
believe by faith what is not intelligible by philosophy.

history.[1] Of him more justly than of Petrarch might it
be said that he is the father of modern criticism, since he
anticipates the treatment given to Biblical miracles
by the rationalising German theologians of last century,[2]
He, too, was a fixed enemy of the clergy; and it was not
for lack of will that they failed to destroy him.

Whether his metaphysic on the subject of the immortality of the soul had much effect on popular thought
may be doubted. What the Renaissance most needed
both in its philosophic and its practical thought was a
scientific foundation; and science, from first to last, was
more hindered than helped by the environment. In the
thirteenth and fourteenth centuries, charges of necro-
mancy against physicians and experimenters were
frequently joined with imputations of heresy, and on
such charges not a few were burned.[3] The economic
conditions, too, were all unfavorable to solid research.[4]
Medicine was nearly as dogmatic as theology. Even
philosophy was in large part shouldered aside by the
financial motives which led men to study law in preference[5]; and when the revival of ancient literature gained
ground it absorbed energy to the detriment of scientific
study,[6] the wealthy amateurs being ready to pay high
prices for manuscripts of classics, and for classical
teaching; but not for patient investigation of natural
fact. The humanists, so-called, were often forces of
enlightenment and reform; witness such a type as the
high-minded POMPONIUS LAETUS,[7] one of the many
" pagan " scholars of the later Renaissance; but the
discipline of mere classical culture was insufficient to
make them, as a body, qualified leaders either of thought
or action,[8] in such a society as that of decaying Italy.

[1] Owen, p. 209, note.   [2] Id., p. 210.   [3] Burckhardt, p. 291.
[4] When Galileo in the sixteenth century was made Professor of Mathematics at Pisa, his salary was only 60 scudi, when the Professor of Medicine
got 2,000. (Karl von Gebler, Galileo Galilei, Eng. tr. 1879, p. 9.)
[5] Gebhart, pp. 59-63 ; Burckhardt, p. 211.
[6] Cp. Burckhardt, p. 291.
[7] Burckhardt, pp. 279-280.
[8] Id. Part iii, c. 11.

Only after the fall of Italian liberties, the decay of the Church's wealth and power, the loss of commerce, and the consequent decline of the arts, did men turn to truly scientific pursuits.   From Italy, indeed, after the Reformation, came the new stimulus to Freethought which affected all the higher civilisation of northern Europe.   But the failure to solve the political problem, a failure which led to the Spanish tyranny, meant the establishment of bad conditions for the intellectual as for the social life; and an arrest of Freethought in Italy was a necessary accompaniment of the arrest of the higher literature.   What remained was the afterglow of a great and energetic period rather than a spirit of enquiry.

§ 2.

Inasmuch as the direct process of the Renaissance was continuous only in Italy, it is properly to Italian history that the name applies.   A similar process of course occurred later in France and in England, and in a sense in Germany; but the great intellectual revivals in these countries were tardy results of Italian influence. There is indeed no more remarkable figure in the Middle Ages than ROGER BACON (? 1214—1294) the English Franciscan friar, schooled at Paris.   For heresies which we cannot now trace, he underwent two long imprisonments at the hands of his superiors, the first lasting ten years. His works remain to show the scientific reach of which his age was capable, when helped by the lore of the Arabs; but in the England of that day his ideals of research were as unattainable as his wrath against clerical obstruction was powerless.[1]   The English Renaissance properly sets-in in the sixteenth century, when the glory of that of Italy is passing away.   In the fourteenth century, indeed, a remarkable new life is seen arising in England in the poetry of Chaucer, from contact with the literature of Italy and

---

[1] See the careful notice by Professor Adamson in *Dict of Nat. Biog.*

France; but while Chaucer reflects the spontaneous medieval hostility to the self-seeking and fraudulent clergy, he shows no trace of the Renaissance spirit of unbelief; and after his day there is social retrogression and literary relapse in England for two centuries. That there was some practical rationalism in his day, however, we gather from the *Vision of Piers Ploughman*, by the contemporary poet Langland (fl. 1360-90), where there is a vivid account of the habit among anti-clerical laymen of arguing against the doctrine of original sin and the entailment of Adam's offence on the whole human race.[1] Langland's reply is mere angry dogmatism. There flourished, further, a remarkable amount of heresy of the species seen in Provence and Northern Italy in the eleventh and twelfth centuries, such sectaries being known in England under the generic name of "Lollards", derived from the Flemish, in which it seems to have signified singers of hymns.[2] Lollards or "Beghards", starting from the southern point of propagation, spread all over civilised Northern Europe, meeting everywhere persecution alike from the regular priests and the mendicant monks; and in England as elsewhere their anti-clericalism and their heresy were correlative. In the formal Lollard petition to Parliament in 1395, however, there is evident an amount of innovating opinion which implies more than the mere stimulus of financial pressure. Not only the Papal authority, monasteries, clerical celibacy, nuns' vows, transubstantiation, exorcisms, bought blessings, pilgrimages, prayers for the dead, offerings to images, confessions and absolutions, but war and capital punishment and "unnecessary trades", such as those of goldsmiths and armorers, are condemned by those early Utopists.[3] In what proportion they really thought out

---

[1] *Vision of Piers Ploughman*, vv. 5809, ff.   Wright's ed., *Lib. of Old Authors*, pp. 179-180.

[2] Mosheim, *E. H.*, Cent. XIV, Pt. II, c. ii, § 36 and *note*.   Cp. Green *Short History of the English People*, ch. v, sect. 3, ed. 1881, p. 235.

[3] Cp. Green, ch. v, sect. 5, p. 253 ; Massingberd, *The English Reformation*, 4th ed., p. 171.

the issues they dealt with we can hardly ascertain ; but a chronicler of Wiclif's time, living at Leicester, testifies that you could not meet two men in the street but one was a Lollard.[1] The movement substantially came to nothing, suffering murderous persecution in the person of Oldcastle (Lord Cobham) and others, and disappearing in the fifteenth century in the ruin of the civil wars ; but apart from Chaucer's poetry it is more significant of Renaissance influences in England than almost any other phenomenon down to the reign of Henry VIII.

In the powerful Wiclif, again, we see rather a superior mind of the Middle Ages, scholastically nourished, than a man of the Renaissance. It is still doubtful whence he derived his marked protestantism as to Romish dogmas ; but it would seem that he too must have been reached by the older Paulician or other southern heresy.[2] In any case, his practical and moral resentment of ecclesiastical abuses was the mainspring of his doctrine ; and his heresies as to transubstantiation and other articles of faith can be seen to connect with his anti-priestly attitude. He, however, was morally disinterested as compared with the would-be plunderers who formed the bulk of the anti-Church party of John of Gaunt ; and his failure to effect any reformation was due to the fact that on one hand there was not intelligence enough in the nation to respond to his doctrinal common-sense, while on the other he could not so separate ecclesiastical from feudal tyranny and extortion as to set up a political movement which should strike at clerical evils without inciting some to impeach the nobility who held the

[1] Cited by Lechler, *John Wycliffe and his English Precursors*. Eng. tr., 1-vol. ed., p. 440.
[2] Cp. Prof. Montagu Burrows, *Wiclif's Place in History*, ed. 1884, p. 49. As early as 1286 a form of heresy approaching the Albigensian and the Waldensian is found in the province of Canterbury, certain persons there maintaining that Christians were not bound by the authority of the Pope and the Fathers, but solely by that of the Bible and " necessary reason ". See Wilkins' *Concilia*, ii, 124.

balance of political power.[1] The revolt led by John Ball
in 1381, though in no way promoted by Wiclif,[2] showed
that the country people suffered as much from lay as
from clerical oppression.

The time, in short, was one of extreme ferment, and
not only were there other reformers who went much
farther than Wiclif in the matter of social reconstruction,[3]
but we know from his writings that there were heretics
who carried their criticism as far as to challenge the
authority and credibility of the Scriptures. Against these
accusatores and *inimici Scripturae* he repeatedly speaks in
his treatise *De veritate Scripturae Sacrae*,[4] which is thus
one of the very earliest works in defence of Christianity
against modern criticism.[5] His position, however, is
wholly medieval. The infinite superiority of Christ to all
other men, and Christ's virtual authorship of the entire
Scriptures, are his premises — a way of begging the
question so simple-minded that it is clear the other side
was not heard in reply, though these arguments had
formed part of his theological lectures,[6] and so presupposed a real opposition. Wiclif was in short a typical
Protestant in his unquestioning acceptance of the Bible
as a supernatural authority; and when his demand for
the publication of the Bible in English was met by
"worldly clerks" with the cry that it would "set
Christians in debate, and subjects to rebel against their
sovereigns," he could only protest that they "openly

---

[1] Charged with setting vassals against tyrant lords, he was forced to plead
that he taught the reverse, though he justified the withholding of tithes
from bad curates. See the passages cited in Lewis's *Life of Wiclif*, ed.
1820, pp. 224-5. Cp. Burrows, as cited, p. 19; Le Bas, *Life of Wiclif*,
1832, p. 357-9.

[2] See Lechler's *John Wycliffe and his English Precursors*, pp. 371-6.

[3] Cp. Green, *Short History*, ch. v, sect. 4.

[4] Lechler, as cited, p. 236. This treatise forms the sixth book of
Wiclif's theological *Summa*.

[5] Baxter, in the address *To the doubting and unbelieving readers*, prefixed to
his *Reasons of the Christian Religion*, 1667, names Savonarola, Campanella,
Ficinus, Vives, Mornay, Grotius, Cameron, and Micraelius, as defenders
of the faith, but no writer of the fourteenth century.

[6] Lechler, p. 236.

slander God, the author of peace, and his holy law".[1]
Later English history proved that the worldly clerks were
perfectly right, and Wiclif the erring optimist of faith.
For the rest, his essentially dogmatic view of religion did
nothing to counteract the spirit of persecution ; and
the passing of the Statute for the Burning of Heretics in
1401, with the ready consent of both Houses of Parliament, constituted the due dogmatic answer to dogmatic
criticism.   Yet within three years the Commons were
proposing to confiscate the revenues of the higher clergy :
so far was anti-clericalism from implying heterodoxy.

Of a very different type from Wiclif is the remarkable
personality of the Welshman REGINALD PECOCK (1395 ?—
1460 ?), who seems divided from Wiclif by a whole era of
intellectual development, though born within about ten
years of his death.   It is a singular fact that the most
genuinely rationalistic mind among the serious writers of
the fifteenth century should be an English bishop.   It
was as the rational and temperate defender of the Church
against the attacks of the Lollards in general that he
formulated the principle of natural reason as against
Scripturalism.   This attitude it is that makes his treatise,
the *Repressor of overmuch Banning of the Clergy*, the most
modern of theoretic English books before Bacon.   In a
series of serenely argued points he urges his thesis that
the Bible is not the basis of the moral law, but merely
an illustration thereof, and that the natural reason is
obviously presupposed in the bulk of its teaching.   It is
the position of Hooker, anticipated by a hundred years ;
and this in an age of such intellectual backwardness
and literary decadence that the earlier man must be
pronounced by far the more remarkable figure.   In such
a case the full influence of the Renaissance seems to be
at work ; though in the obscurity of the records we can
do no more than conjecture that the new contacts with
French culture between the invasion of France by

---

[1] Lechler, p. 213.

Henry V in 1415 and the expulsion of the English in
1451 may have introduced forces of thought unknown or
little known before. If indeed there were English opponents of Scripture in Wiclif's day, the idea must have
ripened somewhat in Pecock's. Whether, however, the
victories of Jeanne D'Arc made some unbelievers as well
as many dastards among the English, is a problem that
does not seem to have been investigated.

Pecock's reply to the Lollards creates the curious
situation of a churchman rebutting heretics by being
more profoundly heretical than they.[1] In his system, the
Scriptures " reveal " only supernatural. truths not otherwise attainable, a way of safeguarding dogma not likely
to reassure believers. There is reason, indeed, to suspect
that Pecock held no dogma with much zeal; and when in
his well-named treatise (now lost), *The Provoker*, he
denied the authenticity of the Apostles' Creed, " he
alienated every section of theological opinion in England".[2] He was in short far too intelligent for his age;
and the reward of his effort to reason down the menacing
Lollards and rebut Wiclif,[3] was his formal disgrace and
virtual imprisonment. In that age of brutal strife, when
" neither the Church nor the opponents of the Church
had any longer a sway over men's hearts ",[4] he figures
beside the mindless prelates and their lay peers somewhat
as does More later beside Henry VIII, as Reason *versus*
the Beast; and it was illustrative of his entire lack of

---

[1] A German ecclesiastical historian of last century (Werner, *Kirchen-
geschichte des 18ten Jahrhunderts*, 1756, cited by Lechler), calls Pecock the first
English Deist. See a general view of his opinions in Lewis' *Life of Dr.
Reynold Pecock* (rep. 1820) ch. v. The heresies charged on him are given on
p. 160; also in the R. T. S. *Writings and Examinations*, 1831, pp. 200-1.

[2] Miss A. M. Cooke, art. REGINALD PECOCK in *Dict. of Nat. Biog.*
This valuable notice is the best short account of Pecock. It is character
istic of the restricted fashion in which history is still treated that neither
in the *Student's History* of Prof. Gardiner nor in the *Short History* of Green
is any mention made of Pecock.

[3] He repels, *e.g.*, Wiclif's argument that a priest's misconduct sufficed
to destroy his right to his endowments. *Repressor*, Babington's ed. in
Rolls Series, 1860, ii, 413.

[4] Gardiner, *Student's History*, p. 330. Cp. Green, ch. vi, Sec. i, 2, pp.
267, 275; Stubb's, *Const. Hist.*, iii, 631-3.

fanaticism that he made the demanded recantations, and went his way in silence to solitude and death. The ruling powers disposed of Lollardism in their own way ; and in the Wars of the Roses every species of heretical thought seems to disappear.

§ 3.

As regards France, the record of intellectual history between the thirteenth and the sixteenth centuries is hardly less scanty than as regards England. In the twelfth and thirteenth centuries the intellectual life of the French philosophic schools was more vigorous and expansive than that of any other country ; so that, looking further to the Provencal literature and to the French beginnings of Gothic architecture, France might even be said to lead the Renaissance. In the latter part of the thirteenth century, too, rationalism at the Paris university seems to have been frequently carried in private to a rejection of all the dogmas peculiar to Christianity.[1] From about the middle of the fourteenth century, however, there is a relative arrest of French progress for some two centuries.[2] Three main forces served to check intellectual advance : the loss of the communal liberties which had been established in France between the eleventh and thirteenth centuries ;[3] the repressive power of the Church ; and the devotion of the national energies to war. Drained off chronically by the Eastern crusades, French energy was kept running in anti-intellectual channels by the crusades against the Albigenses, the many wars of the unification of France, the wars with the

---

[1] Ueberweg, i, 471,   Cp. p. 460, on Simon of Tournay ; Lange, i, 218.
[2] Gebhart,·Orig. de la Renais. en Italie, pp. 2, 19, 24-29, 32-35, 41 50 ; Le Clerc and Renan, Hist. Litt. de la France au XIVe Siècle, i, 4 ; ii, 123 ; Littré, Etudes sur les barbares et le moyen age, 3e edit., pp. 424-9.   It is noteworthy that French culture affected the very vocabulary of Dante, as it did that of his teacher, Brunetto Latini.   Cp. Littré, Etudes, as cited, pp. 399-400. The influence of French literature is further seen in Boccaccio, and in Italian literature in general from the thirteenth to the fifteenth century. Gebhart, pp. 209-221.
[3] Gebhart, pp. 35-41.

Flemings and the English, the ruinous English invasion under Edward III, and the still more destructive invasion under Henry V; so that in the fifteenth century France was hardly more civilised than England. It is from the French invasion of Italy under Charles VIII, that the real renascence in France broadly dates. Earlier impulses had likewise come from Italy: Lanfranc, Anselm, Peter Lombard, Thomas Aquinas, and others of lesser note,[1] had gone from Italy to teach in France or England; but it needed the full contact of Italian civilisation to raise monarchic France to the stage of general and independent intellectual life.

During the period in question, there had been established the following universities :—Paris, 1200 ; Toulouse, 1220; Montpellier, 1289; Avignon, 1303 ; Orléans, 1312 ; Cahors, 1332; Angers, 1337; Orange, 1367; Dôle, 1422 ; Poitiers, 1431; Caen, 1436; Valence, 1454; Nantes, 1460; Bourges, 1463; Bordeaux, 1472 (Desmaze, *L'Université de Paris*, 1876, p. 2. Other dates for some of these are given on p. 31). But the militarit conditions prevented any sufficient development of such opportunities. In the fourteenth century, says Littré (*Etudes sur les barbares et le moyen age*, p. 419) "the university of Paris . . . . was more powerful than at any other epoch. . . . Never did she exercise such a power over men's minds." But he also decides that in that epoch the first florescence of French literature withered away (p. 387). The long location of the anti-Papacy at Avignon (1305-1376) doubtless counted for something in French culture (V. Le Clerc, *Hist. Litt. de la France au XIVe siècle*, i, 37 ; Gebhart, pp. 221-6) but the devastation wrought by the English invasion was sufficient to countervail that and more. See the account of it by Petrarch (letter of the year 1360) cited by Littré, *Etudes*, pp. 416-7 ; and by Hallam, *Middle Ages*, i, 59, *note*. Cp. Michelet, *Hist. de France*, liv. vi, ch. 3. As to the consequences of the English invasion of the fifteenth century see Martin, *Hist. de France*, 4e édit. vi, 132-133; Sismondi, *Hist. des Français*, 183, i, xii, 582; Hallam, *Middle Ages*, i, 83-87.

In northern France of the fourteenth century, as in Provence, and Italy, and England, there was a manifold

[1] Gebhart, p. 54.

stir of innovation and heresy : there as elsewhere the insubordinate Franciscans with their *Eternal Gospel*, the *Paterini*, the *Beghards*, fought their way against the Dominican Inquisition. But the Inquisitors burned books as well as men ; and much anti-ecclesiastical poetry, some dating even from the Carlovingian era, shared the fate of many copies of the Talmud, translations of the Bible, and, *a fortiori*, every species of heretical writing. In effect, the Inquisition for the time " extinguished freethought "[1] in France. As in England, the ferment of heresy was mixed with one of democracy ; and in the French popular poetry of the time. there are direct parallels to the contemporary English couplet, " When Adam delved and Eve span, Where was then the gentleman ? "[2]   Such a spirit could no more prosper in feudal France than in feudal England ; and when France emerged from her struggle with the English, to be effectively solidified by Louis XI, there was in her life little of the spirit of free enquiry. It has been noted that whereas the chronicler Joinville, in the thirteenth century, is full of religious feeling, Froissart in the fourteenth, priest as he is, exhibits hardly any ; and again Comines, in the fifteenth, reverts to the orthodoxy of the twelfth and thirteenth.[3]   The middle period was one of indifference, following on the killing out of heresy :[4] the fifteenth century is a resumption of the Middle Ages, and Comines has the medieval cast of mind,[5] although of a superior order.   There seems to be no community of thought between him and his younger Italian contemporaries, Machiavelli and Guicciardini ; though

---

[1] Littré, as cited, pp. 411-413.
[2] Le Clerc, as cited, p. 259 ; Gebhart, pp. 48-9.
[3] Sir James F. Stephen, *Horae Sabbaticæ*, 1892, i, 42.
[4] The Italians said of the French Pope Clement VI (1342-52) that he had small religion.   M. Villani, *Cronica*, iii, 43 (ed. 1554).
[5] Cp. Dr. T. Arnold, *Lectures on Modern History*, 4th ed. pp. 111-118 ; Buckle, 3-vol. ed., i, 326-7 ; Sir J. F. Stephen, *Horae Sabbaticæ*, i, 121. "It is hardly too much to say that Comines's whole mind was haunted at all times and at every point by a belief in an invisible and immensely powerful and artful man whom he called God." (Stephen, as cited).

"even while Comines was writing, there were un-equivocal symptoms of a great and decisive change".[1]

The special development in France of the spirit of "chivalry" had joined the normal uncivilising influence of militarism with that of clericalism; the various Knightly Orders, as well as knighthood pure and simple, being all under ecclesiastical sanctions, and more or less strictly vowed to "defend the church";[2] while supremely incompetent to form an intelligent opinion. It is the more remarkable that in the case of one of the crusading Orders, heresy of the most blasphemous kind was finally charged against the entire organisation, and that it was on that ground annihilated. It remains incredible, however, that the Order of the Templars can have systematically practised the extravagances or held the tenets laid to their charge. They had of course abused their power and departed from their principles like every other religious Order enabled to amass wealth; and the hostility they aroused is perfectly intelligible from what is known of the arrogance of its members and the general ruffianism of the Crusaders. Their wealth alone goes far to explain the success of their enemies against them; for though the numbers of the Order were much smaller than tradition gives out, its possessions were considerable. These were the true ground of the French king's attack. But that its members were as a rule either *Cathari* or anti-Christians, either disguised Moslems or Deists, or that they practised obscenity by rule, there is no reason to believe. What seems to have happened was a resort by some unbelieving members to more or less gross burlesque of the mysteries of initiation—a phenomenon paralleled in ancient Greece and in the modern Catholic world, and which stood rather for hardy irreligion than for any reasoned heresy whatever.

---

[1] Buckle, i, 329.
[2] Buckle, ii, 133; Hallam, *Middle Ages*, iii, 395-6.   Religious ceremonies were attached to the initiation of knights in the 13th century.   Seignobos, *Hist. de la Civilisation*, ii, 15.

The long-continued dispute as to the guilt of the Knights Templars is still chronically reopened. Hallam, after long hesitation, came finally to believe them guilty, partly on the strength of the admissions made by Michelet in defending them (*Europe in the Middle Ages*, 11th ed. i, 138-142—note of 1848). He attaches, however, a surprising weight to the obviously weak "architectural evidence" cited by Hammer-Purgstall. The excellent summing-up of Mr. H. C. Lea (*History of the Inquisition*, New York ed. 1888-90, B. iii, c. 5, pp. 263-276) perhaps gives too little weight to the mass of curious confirmatory evidence cited by writers on the other side (*e.g.* F. Nicolai, *Versuch über die Beschuldigungen welche dem Tempelherrenorden gemacht worden*, 1782); but his conclusion as to the falsity of the charges against the Order as a whole seems irresistible. The solution that offensive practices occurred irregularly (Lea, pp. 276-7) is pointed to even by the earlier hostile writers (Nicolai, S. 17). That there was no Catharism in the Order seems certain (Lea, p. 249). The suggestion that the offensive and burlesque practices were due to the lower grade of "serving brethren", who were contemned by the higher, seems however without firm foundation. The courage for such freaks, and the disposition to commit them, were rather more likely to arise among the crusaders of the upper class, who could come in contact with Moslem-Christian unbelief through those of Sicily.

For the further theory that the "Freemasons" (at that period really cosmopolitan guilds of masons) were already given to freethinking, there is again no evidence. That they at times deliberately introduced obscene symbols into church architecture is no proof that they were collectively unbelievers in the Church's doctrines ; though it is likely enough that some of them were. Obscenity is the expression not of an intellectual but of a physical and unreasoning bias, and can perfectly well concur with religious feeling. The fact that the medieval masons did not confine obscene symbols to the churches they built for the Templars (Hallam, as cited, pp. 140-1) should serve to discredit alike the theory that the Templars were systematically anti-Christian, and the theory that the Freemasons were so. That for centuries the builders of the Christian churches throughout Europe formed an anti-Christian organisation, is a grotesque hypothesis. It could well be that there survived among the freemasons various Gnostic ideas ; since the architectural art itself came in a direct line from antiquity. Such heresy, too, might conceivably be winked at by the Church, which depended so much on the heretics' services. But their obscenities were the mere expression of the animal imagination and normal salacity of all ages. Only in modern times, and that only in Catholic countries, has the derivative organisation of Freemasonry been identified with freethought propaganda. In England in the seventeenth century the Freemasonic clubs—no longer connected with any trade—were thoroughly royalist and orthodox (Nicolai, S. 196-8).

§ 4.

Some remarkable intellectual phenomena, however, do connect with the French university life of the first half of the fourteenth century. WILLIAM OF OCCAM (d. 1347), the English Franciscan, who taught at Paris, is on the whole the most rationalistic of medieval philosophers. Though a pupil of the Realist Duns Scotus, he became the renewer of Nominalism ; and his anticlerical bias was such that he had to fly from France to Bavaria for protection. To the same refuge fled Marsiglio of Padua, author (with John of Jandun) of the *Defensor Pacis* (1324), "the greatest and most original political treatise of the Middle Ages,"[1] in which it is taught that, though monarchy may be expedient, the sovereignty of the State rests with the people ; and the hereditary principle is flatly rejected ; while it is insisted that the Church properly consists of all Christians, and that the clergy's authority is restricted to spiritual affairs and moral suasion.[2] Of all medieval writers on politics, he is the most modern. Only less original is Occam, who at Paris came much under Marsiglio's influence. His philosophic doctrines apparently derive from PIERRE AUREOL (Petrus Aureolus, d. 1321), who with remarkable clearness and emphasis rejected both Realism and the doctrine that what the mind perceives are not realities but *formæ speculares*. Pierre it was who enounced the Law of Parsimony in philosophy and science—that causes are not to be multiplied beyond mental necessity—which is specially associated with the

[1] Poole, *Illustrations*, p. 265.
[2] *Id.*, pp. 266-276.

name of Occam. Both anticipated modern criticism alike of the Platonic and the Aristotelian philosophy; and Occam in particular drew so decided a line between the province of reason and that of faith, that there can be little doubt on which side his allegiance lay. Whereas Duns Scotus had reduced the number of matters of faith held by Thomas Aquinas to be demonstrable by reason, Occam denied that there was any such. He granted that on rational grounds the existence of a God was probable, but denied that it was strictly demonstrable, and rejected the ontological argument of Anselm. As to matters of faith he significantly observed that the will to believe the indemonstrable is meritorious.[1]

Contemporary with Occam was Durand de St. Pourçain, who became a bishop (d. 1332), and, after ranking as of the school of Thomas Aquinas, rejected and opposed its doctrine. With all this heresy in the air, the principle of " double truth ", originally put in currency by Averroism, came to be held in France as in Italy, in a sense which implied the consciousness that theological truth is not truth at all.[2] Occam's pupil, Buridan, rector of the University of Paris (fl. 1340), substantially avoided theology, and dealt with moral and intellectual problems on their own merits.[3] It is recorded by Albert of Saxony, who studied at Paris in the first half of the century, that one of his teachers held by the theory of the motion of the earth.[4] Even a defender of Church doctrines, Pierre d'Ailly, accepted Occam's view of Theism.[5] On the other hand, the Spanish physician Raymund of Sebonde,[6] who taught philosophy at Toulouse, undertook (about 1335) to establish Christianity on a rational foundation[7] in his

---

[1] Ueberweg, i, 460-4; cp. Poole, *Illustrations*, pp. 275-281.

[2] Cp. Ueberweg, p. 464. Mr. Poole's judgment (p. 280) that Occam " starts from the point of view of a theologian ", hardly does justice to his attitude towards theology. Occam had indeed to profess acceptance of theology; but he could not well have made less account of its claims.

[3] Ueberweg, pp. 465-6.		[4] *Id.* p. 466.		[5] *Id. ib.*

[6] This name has many forms; and it is contended that Sabieudè is the correct one. See Owen; *Evenings with the Skeptics*, 1881, ii, 423.

[7] Cp. Hallam, *Introd. to Lit. of Europe*, ed. 1872, i, 142-4.

Theologia Naturalis, made famous later by Montaigne. But Raymund set up no school of thought, and the intellectual Nominalists were followed, in the evil times after the invasion of Edward III, by minds of a different order,[1] seeking in mysticism and quietism a solace for the ills of life; while for the nation at large there was little intellectual life worthy of the name. The remarkable case of Nicolaus of Autricuria, who in 1348 was forced to recant his teaching of the atomistic doctrine,[2] illustrates at once the persistence of the spirit of reason in times of darkness and the impossibility of its triumphing in the wrong conditions.

§ 5.

The life of the rest of Europe in the early Renaissance period has little special significance in the history of Freethought. The poetry of the German Minnesingers, a development from that of the Troubadours, developed the same anti-clerical features[3]; and the story of *Reynard the Fox* was turned to anti-ecclesiastical purpose in Germany as in France. Material prosperity rather than culture, however, was the main feature of German progress in the Middle Ages; architecture being the only art greatly developed. Heresy of the anti-ecclesiastical order indeed abounded; and was duly persecuted; but the higher freethinking developments were in the theosophic rather than the rationalistic direction. The principal German figure of the period is Master Eckhart (d. 1329), who, finding religious beliefs excluded from the sphere of reason by the freer philosophy of his day, undertook to show that they were all matters of reason. He was, in fact, a mystically reasoning preacher; and he taught in the interests of popular religion. Naturally, as he philo-

---

[1] It is true that Occam had, broadly speaking, "an unbroken line of successors" down to the Reformation (Poole, p. 281); but in France they in no sense dominated thought in the period after him.

[2] Lange, *Hist. of Materialism*, i, 225-6.

[3] Gervinus, *Gesch. der deutschen Dichtung*, 5te Ausg. i, 489-499. Even in the period before the Minnesingers, the clerical poetry had its anti-clerical side. *Id*. S. 194.

sophised on old bases, he did not really subject his beliefs
to any sceptical scrutiny; but took them for granted and
proceeded speculatively upon them. This sufficed to
bring him before the Inquisition at Cologne, where he
recanted conditionally on an appeal to the Pope. Dying
soon after, he escaped the Papal bull condemning twenty-
eight of his doctrines. His school later divided into a
heretical and a Church party, of which the former, called
the "false free spirits", seems to have either joined or
resembled the antinomian Brethren of the Free Spirit,
then numerous in Germany. The other section became
known as the "Friends of God". Through Tauler and
others, Eckhart's pietistic doctrine gave a lead to later
Protestant evangelicalism; but the system as a whole can
never have been held by any popular body.[1]

> Dr. Lasson pronounces (Ueberweg, i, 483) that the type of
> Eckhart's character and teaching "was derived from the
> innermost essence of the German national character". At the
> same time he admits that all the offshoots of the school
> departed more or less widely from Eckhart's type, that is, from
> the innermost essence of their own national character. It
> would be as plausible to say that the later mysticism of
> Fénelon derived from the innermost essence of the French
> character. The *Imitatio Christi* has been similarly described
> as expressing the German character, on the assumption that it
> was written by Thomas à Kempis. Many have held that the
> author was the Frenchman Gerson (Hallam, *Introd. to Lit. of
> Europe*, ed. 1872, i, 139-140). It was in all probability, as was
> held by Suarez, the work of several hands, one a monk of the
> twelfth century, another a monk of the thirteenth, and the
> third a theologian of the fifteenth; neither Gerson nor Thomas
> a Kempis being concerned (Le Clerc, *Hist. Litt. du XIVe
> Siècle*, 2e édit., pp. 384-5).

In the Netherlands and other parts of western
Europe, including even Spain, the popular anti-ecclesiastical heresy of the thirteenth century spread in various
degrees; but there is no outstanding trace of literate or

---

[1] For a very full account of Eckhart's teaching, see Dr. A. Lasson's
monograph (§ 106) in Ueberweg's *Hist. of Philos.*, i, 467-484. Cp. Lea,
Hist. of the Inquisition, ii, 354-9, 362-9, as to the sects.

properly rationalistic freethinking.   Lack of leisured
culture in the Low Countries, and the terrorism of the
Inquisition in Spain, would sufficiently account for the
absence of avowed unbelief, though everywhere, probably,
some was set up by the contact of travellers with the
culture of Italy.   That was the chief source of practical
criticism of Christian dogmas ; and the extent to which a
unitarian theism was now connected with the acceptance
of the philosophy of Averroës[1] is a ground for crediting
much of such freethinking to the Arab stimulus ; though
it was by reason rather of the heresy of Italian Averroists
than of any active teaching of Averroës himself that he
came to figure as Antichrist for the faithful.[2]   Petrarch in
his letters speaks of much downright hostility to the
Christian system on the part of Averroists[3] ; and the
association of Averroism with the great medical school
of Padua[4] must have promoted practical scepticism among
physicians.   Being formally restricted to the schools,
however, it tended there to undergo the usual scholastic
petrifaction ; and the common-sense Deism it encouraged
outside had to subsist without literary discipline.   In this
form it probably reached many lands, without openly
affecting culture or life ; since Averroism itself was professed generally in the Carmelite order, who claimed for
it orthodoxy.[5]

---

[1] It was identified with the heresy of Amalrich of Bena and David of
Dinant. Renan, *Averroès*, pp. 222-3. Cp. pp. 286-300.

[2] *Id.*, pp. 301-315.   [3] *Id.*, pp. 333-7.   [4] *Id.*, pp. 326-7.

[5] *Id.*, pp. 318-320.   Two Englishmen, the Carmelite John of Bacon-
thorpe (d. 1346) and Walter Burleigh, were among the orthodox Averroists ;
the latter figuring as a Realist against William of Occam.   Roger Bacon,
on the other hand, seems to have drawn from Averroes some of his inspiration to research (*Id.*, p. 263).

CHAPTER XI.

THE REFORMATION.

§ I.

IN a very broad and general sense, the ecclesiastical revolution known as the Reformation was a phenomenon of Freethought. It was, however, much more akin to a revolt against a hereditary king than to the process of self-examination and logical scrutiny by which men pass from belief to disbelief in a theory of things, a dogma, or a document. This becomes the more clear when we note that the Reformation was only the culmination or explosion of certain social and political forces seen at work throughout Christendom for centuries before. In point of mere doctrine, the Protestants of the sixteenth century had been preceded and even distanced by heretics of the eleventh, and by teachers of the ninth. The absurdity of relic-worship, the folly of pilgrimages and fastings, the falsehood of the doctrine of transubstantiation, the heresy of prayers to the saints, the unscripturalness of the hierarchy—these and a dozen other points of protest had been raised by Paulicians, by *paterini*, by *beghards*, by Lollards, long before the time of Luther. As regards his nearer predecessors, indeed, this is now a matter of accepted Protestant history. What is not properly realised is that the conditions which wrought political success where before there had been political failure were strictly political conditions; and that to these, and not to supposed differences in national character, is due the geographical course of the Reformation.

We have seen that the spirit of reform was strong in Italy three hundred years before Luther ; that some of the strongest movements within the Church were strictly

(250)

reformatory, and originally disinterested in a high degree. In less religious forms the same spirit abounded throughout the Renaissance; and at the end of the fifteenth century Savonarola was preaching reform religiously enough at Florence. His death, however, was substantially due to the perception that ecclesiastical reform, as conducted by him, was a socio-political process, whence the reformer was a socio-political disturber.[1] Intellectually he was no innovator: on the contrary he was a hater of literary enlightenment; and he was as ready to burn astrologers as his enemies were to burn him.[2] That he failed in his crusade, and that Luther succeeded in his, was due to no difference between Italian and German character, but to the vast difference in the political potentialities of the two cases. The fall of public liberty in Florence, which must have been preceded as it was accompanied by a relative decline in popular culture,[3] and which led to the failure of Savonarola, may be in a sense attributed to Italian character; but that character was itself the product of peculiar social and political conditions.

In England, again, the so-called Reformation was purely a political process; which at the outset had no doctrinal principle behind it. Lollardism, once numerically powerful, had come to nothing; and even the designs of Parliament on the revenues of the Church had failed through the alliance knit between Church and crown in the periods when the latter needed backing. At the accession of Henry VIII, England was more orthodox than any of the other leading States of Northern Europe.[4]

---

[1] He actually sent organised bodies of boys, latterly accompanied by bodies of adults, to force their way into private houses and confiscate things thought suitable for the reformatory bonfire. Burckhardt, p. 477; Perrens, *Jérome Savonarole*, 2e édit., pp. 140-1 The things burned included pictures and busts of inestimable artistic value, and manuscripts of exquisite beauty. Perrens, p. 229. Savonarola, too, actually proposed to put obstinate gamblers to the torture. *Id.*, p. 132.

[2] Burckhardt, pp. 476-7.

[3] As to the education of the Florentine common people in the fourteenth century, cp. Burckhardt, pp. 203-4.

[4] Cp. Froude, *History of England*, ed. 1872, i, 173; Burnet, *Hist. of the Reformation*, Nares' ed., i, 17-18. Henry "cherished churchmen more than any king in England had ever done".

The personal need of the despotic king for a divorce which the Pope dared not give him was the first *vera causa*, leading to the rejection of the Papal authority. On this the plunder of the monasteries followed, as a forced measure of finance,[1] of precaution against Papal influence, and for the creation of a body of new interests vitally hostile to a Papal restoration. The king and the people were alike Romanists in doctrine ; and on the accession of Queen Mary the nation gladly reverted to Romish usages, though the spoil-holders would not surrender a yard of Church lands. Protestantism was only slowly built up by the new clerical and heretical propaganda, and by the state of hostility set up between England and the Catholic Powers. It was the episode of the Spanish Armada that, by identifying Catholicism with the cause of the great national enemy, made the people grow definitely anti-Catholic. Even in Shakspere's dramas, the old state of things is seen not yet vitally changed. In Scotland, though there the priesthood had fewer friends than almost anywhere else, the act of Reformation was one of pure and simple plunder of Church property by the needy nobility, in conscious imitation of the policy of Henry VIII, at the time when the throne was vacant; and there too Protestant doctrine was only gradually established by the new race of preachers, trained in the school of Calvin. In Ireland, on the other hand, Protestantism became identified with the cause of the oppressor, just as for England Romanism was the cause of the enemy-in-chief. Race and national character had nothing whatever to do with the course of events, and doctrinal enlightenment had just a little.[2] In the words of a distinguished clerical historian : " no truth is more certain than this, that the real motives of religious action do not work on men in masses; and that the enthusiasm which creates Crusaders, Inquisitors, Hussites, Puritans, is not the result of con-

---

[1] Cp. Burnet, as cited, pref. p. xl, and p. 3.
[2] The subject is treated at some length in *The Dynamics of Religion*, by " M. W. Wiseman " (J. M. R.), 1897, pp. 3-46.

viction, but of passion provoked by oppression or resistance, maintained by self-will, or stimulated by the mere
desire of victory ".[1] To this it need only be added that
the anti-Papal movement succeeded where the balance of
political forces could be turned against the clerical interest,
and failed where the latter predominated.

Prof. Gebhart (Orig. de la Renais. en Italie, p. 68) writes that
" Italy has known no great national heresies : one sees there
no uprising of minds which resembles the profound popular
movements provoked by Waldo, Wiclif, John Huss or Luther ".
The decisive answer to this is soon given by the author himself
(p. 74) :—" If the Order of Franciscans has had in the peninsula
an astonishing popularity ; if it has, so to speak, formed a
Church within the Church, it is that it responded to the
profound aspirations of an entire people ". (Cp. p. 77.) Yet
again, after telling how the Franciscan heresy of the Eternal
Gospel so long prevailed, M. Gebhart speaks (p. 78) of the Italians
as a people whom " formal heresy has never seduced ". These
inconsistencies derive from the old fallacy of attributing the
course of the Reformation to national character. The simple
truth is that in Italy reform could not for a moment be dreamt of
save as within the Church. It was a relatively easy matter in
Germany and England to renounce the Pope's control and
make the churches national or autonomous. To attempt that
in Italy would have meant creating a state of permanent and
insoluble strife. Apart from that, the Italians were as much
bent on Reformation as any other people in mass ; there was a
strong " Protestant " movement among them in the time of
Luther (see McCrie's Reformation in Italy) ; and the earlier
Franciscan movement was obviously more disinterested than
either the later German or the English, in both of which
plunder was the inducement to the leading adherents, as it
was also in Switzerland. There the wholesale bestowal of
church livings on Italians was the strongest motive to ecclesiastical revolution ; and in Zurich, the first canton which
adopted the Reformation, the process was made easy by the
State guaranteeing posts and pensions for life to the whole
twenty-four canons of the chapter. (Vieusseux, History of
Switzerland, 1840, pp. 120, 128 ; cp. Zschokke, Schweizerland's
Geschichte, 9te Ausg. c. 32.) The Protestants had further the
support of the unbelieving soldiery, made anti-religious in the

[1] Bishop Stubbs, Const. Hist. of England, 3d. ed., iii, 638. Cp. Bishop
Creighton, The Age of Elizabeth, p. 6 ; Hallam, Lit. Hist., i, 366

Italian wars, who rejoiced in the process of priest-baiting and
plunder (Vieusseux, p. 130). That the Reformation was a
product of "Teutonic conscience" is an inveterate fallacy.
The country in which Protestantism was most intellectually
disinterested and most morally active was France. "The main
battle of erudition and doctrine against the Catholic Church,"
justly contends M. Guizot, "was sustained by the French
reformers: it was in France and Holland, and always in
French, that most of the philosophic, historical, and polemic
works on that side were written; neither Germany nor England,
certainly, employed in the cause at that epoch more intelligence
and science." (*Hist. de la Civ. en France*, 13e édit., i, 18). Nor
was there in France any such license on the Protestant side as
arose in Germany, though the French Protestants were as
violently intolerant as any. Their ultimate decline, after long
and desperate wars ending in a political compromise, was due
to the play of socio-economic causes under the wise and
tolerant administration of Richelieu. The French character
had proved as unsubduable in Protestantism as any other; and
the generation which in large part gradually reverted to Protestantism did but show that it had learned the lesson of the
strifes which had followed on the Reformation—that Protestantism was no solution of either the moral or the intellectual
problems of religion and politics.

§ 2.

In the circumstances, the Reformation could thus
stand for only the minimum of freethought needed to
secure political action. Coming as it did within one or
two generations of the invention of printing, it stood not
for new ideas but for the spread of old. That invention
had for a time positively checked the production of new
books, the multiplication of the old having for the time
turned attention to the past;[1] and the diffusion of the
Bible in particular determined the mental attitude of the
movement in mass. The thinking of its most disinterested
promoters began and ended in Bibliolatry: Luther and
Calvin alike did but set up an infallible book and a local
tyranny against an infallible Pope and a tyranny centring

[1] Bishop Stubbs, *Const. Hist. of England*, iii, 627. The bishop, however, holds that in the time of Lollard prosperity the ability to read was
widely diffused in England (p. 628).

at Rome. Neither dreamt of toleration ; and Calvin, the
more competent mind of the two, did but weld the
detached irrationalities of the current theology into a
system which insulted reason and stultified the morality
in the name of which he ruled Geneva with a rod of iron.[1]
It is remarkable that both men reverted to the narrowest
orthodoxies of the early Church, in defiance of whatever
spirit of reasonable enquiry had been on the side of their
movement. After once breaking away from Rome, they
become typical Anti-Freethinkers. The more rational
Zwingli, who tried to put an intelligible aspect on one or
two of the mysteries of the faith, was scouted by both,
as they scouted each other.

Luther, though he would probably have been ready
enough to punish Copernicus[2] as a heretic, was saved the
evil chance which befel Calvin, of being put in a place of
authority where he could commit judicial murder. Such
an act it is that most directly connects Calvin's name
with the history of Freethought. Servetus was a reformer
who went further than the others, grounding his rejection
of the doctrine of the Trinity on the Bible itself, somewhat in the modern Unitarian manner, but with the
difference that he accepted a modal Trinity—or three
God aspects—while rejecting that of three persons.[3] The
whole Protestant world was of one opinion in desiring to
suppress his anti-Trinitarian books ; Luther calling the
first horribly wicked; Melanchthon writing to the Venetian
Senate to warn them against letting it be sold.[4] It is
significant of the random character of Protestant as of
Catholic thought that Servetus, like Melanchthon, was a
convinced believer in astrology,[5] while Luther on Biblical

---

[1] Cp. Willis, *Servetus and Calvin*, 1877, B. ii, ch. 1 ; Audin, *Histoire de
Calvin*, éd. abrég. ch. xxiv-xxvii ; and art. *Mr. Morley on Machiavelli*, in
University Magazine, Sept. 1897.

[2] See his derision of Copernicus, on Scriptural grounds, in the *Table-
Talk*, c. 69, *Of Astronomy and Astrology*. The passage is deliberately
omitted from the English translation in the Bohn Library, p. 341 ; and
the whole chapter is dropped from the German abridgement published by
Reclam.

[3] Willis, *Servetus and Calvin*, 1877, pp. 50, 61, 309, etc.

[4] *Id.*, pp. 44, 49.   [5] *Id.*, p. 117.

grounds rejected astrology and the Copernican astronomy
alike, and held devoutly by the belief in witchcraft.
The superiority of Servetus consists in his real scientific
work—he having in part given out the true doctrine
of the circulation of the blood—and his objection to all
persecution of heresy.[1]

Calvin's guilt in the matter begins with his devices to
have Servetus seized by the Catholic authorities at
Lyons[2]—to set misbelievers, as he regarded them, to slay
the misbeliever—and his use of Servetus' confidential
letters against him.[3] The later trial at Geneva is a classic
document in the records of the cruelties committed in
honour of chimeras : and Calvin's part is the sufficient
proof that the Protestant could hold his own with the
Catholic Inquisitor in the spirit of hate.[4] All the
Protestant leaders, broadly speaking, grew more intolerant as they grew in years—a fair test as between the
spirit of dogma and the spirit of freethought. Calvin had
begun by pleading for tolerance and clemency ; Luther
came to be capable of hounding on the German nobility
against the unhappy peasants ; Melanchthon, tolerant in
his earlier days, applauded the burning of Servetus ;[5] Beza
laboriously defended the act. Erasmus stood for tolerance ;
and Luther accordingly called him godless, an enemy
of true religion, a slanderer of Christ, a Lucian, an
Epicurean, and the vilest miscreant that ever disgraced
the earth.[6]

The burning of Servetus in 1553, however, marked a
turning point in Protestant history on the Continent.
He was not the first victim ; but he was nearly the last.
In 1550 Calvin had secured the execution of JACQUES

---

[1] *Id.*, p. 53.   [2] *Id.*, ch. xix.   [3] *Id.*, ch. xx. Cp. pp. 457, 503.
[4] Ten years after the death of Servetus, Calvin calls him a " dog and
wicked scoundrel " (Willis, p. 530) ; and in his Commentary on Genesis
(i, 3 ; ed. 1838, p. 9) he says of him : "*Latrat hic obscoenus canis.*" And
Servetus had asked *his* pardon at the end.
[5] Willis, pp. 47, 511.
[6] *Table Talk*, c. 43.   Cp. Michelet's *Life of Luther*, Eng. tr 1846
pp. 195-6 ; and Hallam, *Lit. Hist. of Europe*, i, 360-5.

GRUET, of the "Libertine" faction in Geneva, who on being arrested for issuing placards against the clerical junto in power, was found to have among his papers some revealing his disbelief in the Christian religion.[1] On the strength of this and other cases the *Libertines* have been sometimes supposed to be generally unbelievers; but there is no more evidence for this than for the general ascription to them of licentious conduct. The presumption is that they included the more honest and courageous men of liberal and tolerant tendencies. The really antinomian *Libertini* of the period were, as before noted,[2] the sect so called, otherwise known as Spirituals, who held a species of pantheism, and who seem to have been a branch of the Brethren of the Free Spirit. These Calvin denounced in his manner; but in 1544 he had forced into exile Sebastian Castalio, master of the public school at Geneva, for simply rejecting his doctrine of absolute predestination;.and in 1551 he had caused to be imprisoned a physician and ex-Carmelite monk, Jerome Bolsec, for publicly denying the same dogma, whereupon Bolsec returned to Catholicism.[3] The later treatment of Bernardino Ochino, who had turned Protestant after being vicar-general of the Capuchin order, shows the slackening of ferocity after the end of Servetus. Ochino ventured to suggest certain relaxations of the law of monogamy—a point on which some Lutherans went much further than he—and was further heretical about the Trinity. He was in consequence expelled with his family from the canton of Zurich, at the age of seventy-six. Finding Switzerland wholly inhospitable, and being excluded by the Catholics from Poland, where he had sought to join the Socinians, he went to die in Moravia.[4] This was no worse treatment than Lutherans[5] and Calvinists normally meted out to each other. Finally, when the Italian Valentinus Gentilis,

---

[1] Audin, *Histoire de Calvin,* as cited, pp. 279-287.   [2] Above, p 1.
[3] Mosheim, Cent. XIV, Sect. III, Pt. ii, c. ii, §§ 38-41; Audin, *Histoire de Calvin,* ch. xxix, xxx.
[4] McCrie, *Hist. of the Ref. in Italy,* 1827, pp. 391-6; Audin, ch. xxxv.
[5] Cp. Pusey, *Histor. Eng. into Ger. Rationalism,* 1828, p. 14, ff.

the anti-Trinitarian, variously described as Tritheist, Deist, and Arian, uttered his heresies at Geneva, he was allowed to go thence with his life, but was duly burned at Berne, in 1566.[1]

The Protestant Bibliolatry, in short, was as truly the practical negation of freethought and tolerance as was Catholicism itself; and it was only their general remoteness from each other that kept the different reformed communities from absolute war. As it was, they had their full share in the responsibility for the desperate civil wars which so long convulsed France, and for those which ultimately reduced Germany to the verge of destruction, arresting her civilisation for a hundred years.

§ 3.

Freethought gained as little in England as elsewhere in the process of substituting local tyranny for that of Rome. Under Henry, anti-Romanist heretics were put to death on the old Romanist principles. Under the Protectorate which followed, such new heresy as there was stood equally with orthodoxy on Biblical grounds; and the punishment was the same.[2] The Elizabethan Archbishops and the Puritans were equally intolerant; and the idea of free enquiry was undreamt of. The Reformation in fact had over-clouded with fanaticism what new light of Freethought had been glimmering before; turning into Bibliolators those who had rationally doubted some of the Catholic mysteries, and forcing back into Catholic bigotry those more refined spirits who, like Sir Thomas More, were really in advance of their age intellectually and morally, and desired a transmutation of the old system rather than its overthrow. Nothing so essentially rational as the *Utopia* appeared again in

---

[1] Mosheim, Cent. XVI, Sec. iii, Pt. ii, c. iv, § 6; Audin, pp. 394-9; Aretius, *Short Hist. of Val. Gentilis*, Eng. tr. 1696.

[2] In 1532 was burnt James Bainham, who not only rejected the specially Catholic dogmas, but affirmed the possible salvation of unbelievers.

English literature for a century : it is indeed, in some respects, a lead to social science in our own day.

It is in the wake of the overthrow, in the second generation, that a real Freethought begins to be heard of in England ; and this clearly comes by way of new continental and literary contact, which would have occurred in at least as great a degree under Catholicism, save in so far as unbelief was facilitated by the state of indifference which among the upper classes was the natural sequel of the policy of plunder and the oscillation between Protestant and Catholic forms. And it was finally in this negative way only that Protestantism furthered Freethought anywhere. In Bohemia, where in the fifteenth century the movement of Huss led to an actual political outbreak, the practical sequel was mere furious civil war and exacerbated fanaticism. Led up to by the rather more radical teaching of Wiclif, many of whose works had been carried to Bohemia, the Protestantism of Huss and Jerome of Prague in turn stimulated the later movement of Luther ; but it did no more. Huss and Jerome were nationalists of a narrow type, and were the means of making the university of Prague a merely Bohemian instead of a universal German one.[1] The Hussite war which followed on their deaths was one of the most ferocious in modern history, and the Hussite sect known as Taborites were fanatics of the wildest type.[2]

In Germany, Protestantism failed alike as a moral and as an intellectual reform. The lack of any general moral motive in the ecclesiastical revolution is sufficiently proved by the general dissolution of conduct which, on the express admission of Luther, followed upon it. This was quite apart from the special disorders of the Anabaptist movement, which, on the other hand, contained elements of moral and religious rationalism, as against Bibliolatry, that have been little recognised.[3] The test of the new

---

[1] K. von Raumer, *Contrib. to the Hist. of the German Universities*, New York, 1859, p. 19.

[2] Mosheim, Cent. XV, Pt. II, c iii, §§ 3-7.

[3] See Beard, Hibbert Lect. on *The Reformation*, pp. 189-190, 196.

regimen lay, if anywhere, in the University of Wittenberg; and there matters were no better than anywhere else. German university life in general went from bad to worse till a new life began slowly to germinate after the Thirty Years' War[2]; and the germs came mainly from the neighbouring nations.

Hardly more fortunate was the course of things intellectual after the Reformation in the Netherlands, where by the fifteenth century remarkable progress had been made alike in science and the arts, and where Erasmus acquired his culture and did his service to culture's cause. The fact that Protestantism had to fight for its life against Philip was of course not the fault of Protestantism; and to that ruinous struggle is to be attributed the arrest of the civilisation of Flanders. But it lay in the nature of the Protestant impulse that it should turn all intellectual life for generations into vain controversy. The struggle between reform and Popery was followed by the struggle between Calvinism and Arminianism; and the second was no less bitter if less bloody than the first,[3] the religious strife passing into civil feud. Grotius, the most distinguished Dutch scholar and the chief apologist of Christianity in his day, had to seek refuge, on his escape from prison, in Catholic France, whose king granted him a pension. The circumstance which in Holland chiefly favored freethought, the freedom of the press, was, like the great florescence of the arts in the seventeenth century, a result of the whole social and political conditions, not of any Protestant belief in free discussion. That there were freethinkers in Holland in and before Grotius' time is implied in the pains he took to defend Christianity; but that they existed in despite of the ruling Protestantism is proved by the fact that they did not venture to publish their opinions. In the end, Grotius and Casaubon alike recoiled from the narrow Protestantism around them,

---

[1] K. von Raumer, as cited, pp. 32-37.
[2] *Id.*, pp. 42-52; Pusey, as cited, p. 112.
[3] Cp. T. C. Grattan, *The Netherlands*, 1830, pp. 231-243.

which had wholly failed to realise their hopes.[1] Just
before the Protestant period (1511) HERMAN VAN
RYSTWICH was burnt alive at the Hague for persisting
(after imprisonment and recantation), in denying hell and
the immortality of the soul, and for affirming the eternity
of matter.   Such views were no safer under the Protestant
regimen.

Of Dirk (or Theodore) KOORNHERT (1522-1590) it is
recorded that he agreed with neither Protestant nor
Catholic, but wrote strongly against persecution in reply
to Beza and Calvin, and opposed the dogma of predestination, giving a lead to Arminius.   He made the
interesting proposal that the clergy should not be allowed
to utter anything save the actual words of the Scriptures ;
and that all works of theology should be sequestrated.
For these and other heteroclite suggestions he was expelled
from Delft by the magistrates.[2]   It may be inferred what
would have been the fate of any rationalist who went
further.   A History of the Netherlands, by Liewe van
Aitzema, a nobleman of Friesland, was suppressed between
1621 and 1628 on the score of his or its atheism.   The
charge of atheism was brought against the *Excercitationes
Philosophicae* of Gorlæus, published in 1620 ; but the book
being posthumous, conclusions could not be tried.   In the
generation after Grotius, one Koerbagh, a doctor, for
publishing (1668) a dictionary of definitions containing
advanced ideas, had to fly from Amsterdam.   At Culenberg
he translated a Unitarian work and began another, but
was betrayed, tried for blasphemy and sentenced to ten
years' imprisonment, to be followed by ten years' banish-
ment.   He compromised by dying in prison within the
year.   Even as late as 1678, Hadrian Beverland, nephew
of Isaac Vossius, was imprisoned and struck off the rolls
of Leyden University for his *Peccatum Originale*, in which
he speculated oddly as to the nature of the sin of Adam
and Eve.   The book was publicly burned.

[1] Hallam, *Lit. Hist. of Europe*, ii, 406-416.
[2] Bayle, *Dictionnaire*, s.v. KOORNHERT.   Cp. Pünjer, p. 269.

CHAPTER XII.

§ 1.

THE negative bearing of the Reformation on Freethought is made clear by the historic fact that the new currents of thought which broadly mark the beginning of the "modern spirit" arose outside of its sphere. It is to Italy, where the political and social conditions always tended to frustrate the Inquisition, that we trace the rise alike of modern Deism, modern Unitarianism, modern Pantheism, modern physics, and the tendency to rational Atheism. The first mention of Deism noted by Bayle is in the epistle dedicatory to the second and expanded edition of the *Instruction Chrétienne* of the Swiss Protestant Viret (1563), where professed Deists are spoken of as a new species bearing a new name. On the admission of Viret, who was the friend and bitter disciple of Calvin, they rejected all revealed religion, but called themselves Deists by way of repudiating Atheism ; some having a belief in immortality, some rejecting it. In the theological manner he goes on to call them all execrable Atheists, and to say that he has added to his treatise on their account an exposition of natural religion grounded on the " Book of Nature " ; stultifying himself by going on to say that he has also dealt with the professed Atheists.[1] Of the Deists he admits that among them were men of the highest repute for science and learning. Thus within ten years of the burning of Servetus we find privately avowed Deism and Atheism in the area of French-speaking Protestantism.

---

[1] Bayle, *Dictionnaire*, art. VIRET, note D.

Doubtless the spectacle of Protestant feuds would go far to foster such unbelief; but though Martin Cellarius avowed Unitarianism in 1522, having been converted by German Anabaptists, thereafter there is reason to look to Italy as the source of the propaganda.   Thence came the two Sozzini, the founders of Socinianism, of whom Laelio, the uncle of Faustus, travelled much in northern Europe (including England) between 1546 and 1552.[1] Before Socinianism had taken form, it was led up to in the writings of the ex-monk Bernardo Ochino (1487-1564), who combined mystical and Unitarian tendencies with a leaning to polygamy and freedom of divorce.[2] His influence was considerable among the Swiss Protestants, though they expelled him for his heresies.   It was about the year 1563, again, that Roger Ascham wrote his *Scholemaster*, wherein are angrily described, as a species new in England, men who " where they dare", scorn both Protestant and Papist, rejecting scripture, and counting the Christian mysteries as fables.   He describes them as " $\ddot{\alpha}\theta\epsilon o\iota$ in doctrine"; adding, " this last word is no more unknowne now to plaine Englishe men than the Person was unknown somtyme in England, untill some Englishe man took peines to fetch that develish opinion out of Italie ".[3]   The whole tendency he connects in a general way with the issue of many new translations from the Italian, mentioning in particular Petrarch and Boccaccio.   Alongside of the old unbelief in Italy there now sprang up a crop of religious Unitarianism.   Giorgio Biandrata (b. 1515 ; assass. in Poland, 1591) was seized by the Inquisition at Pavia for such opinion.   In 1562, Giulio Guirlando of Treviso, and in 1566 Francesco Saga of Rovigo, were burned at Venice for anti-Trinitarianism. Giacomo Aconzio, who dedicated his *Stratagems of Satan*

---

[1] Calvin, scenting his heresy, menaced him in 1552.   Bayle, art. MARIANUS SOCIN, the first, note B.

[2] Cp. Bayle, art. OCHIN ; Miss M. E. Lowndes, *Michel de Montaigne*, p. 266; Owen, *Skeptics of the French Renaissance*, p. 588.

[3] *The Scholemaster*. Arber's reprint, p. 82.

(1565) to Queen Elizabeth, was a decided latitudinarian ;[1] and Aonio Paleario, poet and professor of rhetoric at Milan, hanged in 1570 (in his seventieth year) for denouncing the Inquisition, seems to have been no less so.

It is remarkable that all this occurs in the period of the Catholic Reaction, the Council of Trent, and the subjection of Italy. It would seem that in the compulsory peace which had now fallen on Italian life, men's thoughts turned more than ever to mental problems, as had happened in Greece after the rise of Alexander's empire. The authority of the Church was outwardly supreme; the Jesuits had already begun to do great things for education ;[2] the Inquisition was everywhere in Italy; Pius V and the hierarchy everywhere sought to enforce decorum in life ; the " pagan " academies were dissolved ; and classic culture rapidly decayed with the arts, while clerical learning flourished,[3] and a new religious music began with Palestrina. Nevertheless, whatever outward restoration of religion took place, and despite commercial decadence and misrule, freethought privately held its ground ; and under an exterior conformity has prevailed more or less among the educated classes down to our own time, when it may be said to be normal. Open heresy was crushed by Pius V ; the Protestant Carnesecchi was burnt ; but under a forced dissimulation the deeper unbelief was ineradicable ; and in that age (1548) was born Giordano Bruno, one of the types of modern freethought.

§ 2.

In the other countries influenced by Italian culture in the sixteenth century the rationalist spirit had various fortune. The true renascence of letters in France had begun before and gone on during the Reformation period ; and all along it showed a tincture of freethought. Along-

---

[1] Art. ACONTIUS, in *Dict. of Nat. Biog.* Cp. Tayler, *Retrospect of the Religious Life of England*, 2nd ed., pp. 205-6.
[2] Bacon, *Advancement of Learning*, B. i (Bohn ed. p. 38).
[3] Cp. Zeller, *Hist. de l'Italie*, pp. 400-412 ; Green, *Short Hist.*, ch. viii, § 2.

side of Luther, we have the enormous raillery of RABELAIS, who, whatever be the truth as to his personal beliefs, was visibly the most unclerical of priests, and counted wholly for audacity and intellectual adventure. So careful was he to elude the bigots that it remains impossible to say with confidence whether or not he believed in a future state.[1] In his concern to keep himself safe with the Sorbonne he made a rather unworthy attack (1542) on his former friend ETIENNE DOLET for the mere oversight of reprinting one of his books without deleting passages which Rabelais had expunged;[2] but no expurgation could make his *évangile*, as he called it, a Christian treatise, or keep for him an orthodox reputation. Dolet was at least no more of an unbeliever than he; but where Rabelais could with impunity convey vast inuendos by way of jests about the people of *Ruach* (the Spirit), who lived solely on wind,[3] and narratives about the *Papefigues* and *Papimanes*,[4] Dolet was done to death in priestly revenge[5] for his youthful attack on the religion of inquisitorial Toulouse, where gross pagan superstition and gross orthodoxy went hand in hand.[6] Of the freethought of such an age there could be no adequate record. Its tempestuous energy, however, implies not a little of private unbelief; and there are some memorable traces.

The most articulate French freethinker of that age, though even he had to wear the veil of allegory, is BONAVENTURE DES PERIERS, author of the *Cymbalum Mundi* (1537). Early associated with Calvin and Olivetan in revising the French translation of the Bible by Le Fèvre d'Etaples (rev. 1535), Bonaventure turned away from the Protestant movement, as did Rabelais and

---

[1] Prof. Stapfer, *Rabelais, sa personne, son génie, son œuvre*, 1889, pp. 365-8. Cp. the *Notice* of Bibliophile Jacob, ed. 1841 of Rabelais, pp. lvii-lviii.

[2] R. Christie, *Etienne Dolet*, pp. 369-372. This point and the persistent Catholic calumnies against Dolet, are examined by the author in art. "The Truth about Etienne Dolet", in *National Reformer*, June 2 and 9, 1889.

[3] Liv. iv, ch. 43.

[4] Liv. iv, ch. 45-48.

[5] Cp. author's art. above cited.

[6] Christie, *Etienne Dolet*, pp. 105-6.

Dolet, caring as little for the new presbyter as for the old priest; and all three were duly accused by Calvin of atheism and *libertinage*.[1] In the same year Bonaventure published his much-praised *Commentarii linguae latinae ;* and within two years he had produced his satire, *Cymbalum Mundi*,[2] wherein, by way of Pagan dialogues, are allegorically ridiculed the Christian scheme, its miracles, Bible contradictions, and the spirit of persecution, then in full fire in France against the Protestants. The allegory is not always clear to modern eyes ; but there was no question then about its general bearing ; and Bonaventure, though groom of the chamber (after Clement Marot) to Marguerite of Navarre, had to fly for his life as Marot did before him. From that time he disappears, probably dying, whether or not by suicide is doubtful, before 1544, when his miscellaneous works were published. The age was too inclement for such literature ; and it was much that it spared Gringoire (d. 1544), who, without touching doctrine, satirised in his verse both priests and Protestants. Other men had worse fates; for instance, Louis de Berquin, the friend of Erasmus, burnt for his anti-clericalism at Paris in 1529; and Jean de la Garde, bookseller, who met the same fate in 1537 for selling four " blasphemous " tractates, which were burned with him.

Among the eminent ones then surmised to lean to rationalism was the sister of King Francis, Marguerite of Navarre, whom we have noted as a protectress of the pantheistic *Libertini*, denounced by Calvin. She is held to have been substantially sceptical until her forty-fifth year ;[3] though her final religiousness seems also beyond

---

[1] *Notice* of Bonaventure des Periers, by Bibliophile Jacob, in 1841 ed. of *Cymbalum Mundi*, etc.

[2] For a solution of the enigma of the title, see the *Clef* of Eloi Johanneau, in ed. cited, p. 83.   The book is dedicated by *Thomas Du Clevier à son ami Pierre Tyrocan*, which is found to be, with one letter altered, an anagram for *Thomas Incrédule à son ami Pierre Croyant*, " Unbelieving Thomas to his friend Believing Peter."   *Clef* cited. pp. 80-85.

[3] Ch. Nodier, quoted by Bibliophile Jacob in ed. of *Cymbalum Mundi*, as cited, p. xviii.

doubt.[1] In her youth she bravely protected the Protestants from the first persecution of 1523 onwards ; and the strongly Protestant drift of her *Miroir de l'âme pécheresse* exasperated the Catholic theologians ; but after the Protestant violences of 1546 she seems to have sided with her brother against the Reform.[2] The strange taste of the *Heptaméron,* of which again her authorship seems certain,[3] constitutes a moral paradox not to be solved save by recognising in her a woman of genius, whose alternate mysticism and bohemianism expressed a very ancient duality in human nature.

A similar mixture will explain the intellectual life of the poet Ronsard. A persecutor of the Huguenots,[4] he was denounced as an Atheist by two of their ministers ; [5] and the pagan fashion in which he handled Christian things scandalised his own side. But though the spirit of the French Renaissance, so eagerly expressed in the *Défense et Illustration de la langue françoise* of Joachim du Bellay (1549), is at its outset as emancipated as that of the Italian, we find Ronsard in his latter years edifying the pious.[6] Any ripe and consistent rationalism, indeed, was then impossible. One of the most powerful minds of the age was BODIN (1530-96) whose *République* is perhaps the most scientific treatise on government between Aristotle and our own age, and whose *Colloquium Heptaplomeres*[7] is reputed no less original an outline of a Naturalist[8] philosophy. He was repeatedly and emphatically accused of unbelief by friends and foes ; [9] and his rationalism on some heads is beyond doubt ; yet he not only held

---

[1] Cp. Brantome, *Des dames illustres.* Œuvres, ed. 1838, ii, 186.

[2] Bayle, *Dictionnaire,* art. MARGUERITE DE NAVARRE (the first), notes F and G.

[3] Bayle, note N. But cp. Nodier, as cited.

[4] Bayle, art. RONSARD, note D

[5] Garasse, *La Doctrine Curieuse des Beaux Esprits de ce Temps,* 1623, pp. 126-7. Ronsard replied to the charge in his poem *Des misères du temps.*

[6] Bayle, art. RONSARD, note O.

[7] MS. 1588. First printed in 1857 by L. Noack.

[8] As before noted, he seems to have coined the word. Cp. Lechler, *Geschichte des englischen Deismus,* S. 31, 455, *notes.*

[9] Bayle, art. BODIN, note O.

by the belief in witchcraft, but wrote a furious treatise in support of it.[1] But he also stood for religious toleration : the new principle that was to change the face of intellectual life. A few liberal Catholics shared it with him to some extent[2] long before St. Bartholomew's Day; eminent among them being L'Hopital,[3] whose humanity, tolerance, and concern for practical morality and the reform of the Church brought upon him the charge of Atheism. He was, however, a believing Catholic.[4] Deprived of power, his edict of tolerance repealed, he saw the long and ferocious struggle of Catholics and Huguenots renewed, and crowned by the massacre of St. Bartholomew's Day (1572). Broken-hearted, and haunted by that monstrous memory, he died six months later.

A generation of insane civil war for religion's sake must have gone far to build up unbelief; and already in 1564 we find an *Atheomachie* published by one De Bourgeville; but the Massacre must have consummated the work. In 1581 appears another *Atheomachie, ou réfutation des erreurs et impietés des Athéistes, Libertins, etc.*, issued at Geneva, but bearing much on French life. In the greatest French writer of that age, a professed Catholic, but averse alike to Catholic and to Protestant bigotry, the shock can be seen disintegrating once for all the spirit of faith. MONTAIGNE typifies the pure scepticism produced in an unscientific age by the practical demonstration that religion can avail immeasurably more for evil than for good.[5] A few years before the Massacre he had translated

[1] Cp. Lecky, *Rationalism in Europe*, ed. 1887, i, 66, 87-91. In the *République*, too, he has a chapter on astrology.

[2] Cp Villemain, *Vie de L'Hopital*, in *Études de l'histoire moderne*, 1846, pp. 363-8, 428.

[3] Buckle (3-vol. ed. ii, 10) errs in representing L'Hopital as the only statesman of the time who dreamt of toleration. It is to be noted on the other hand that the Huguenots themselves protested against any toleration of Atheists or Anabaptists; and even the reputed freethinker Gabriel Naudé, writing in 1639, defended the massacre on political grounds (Owen, *Skeptics of the French Renaissance*, p. 470, *note*).

[4] Villemain, p. 429.

[5] "Our religion," he writes, " is made to extirpate vices : it protects, nourishes, and incites them " (*Essais*, B. ii, c. 12 : ed. Firmin-Didot, ii, 464). " There is no enmity so extreme as the Christian "

for his dying father [1] the old *Theologia Naturalis* of Raymond of Sebonde; and we know from the later *Apology* in the Essays that freethinking contemporaries declared the argument of Raymond to be wholly insufficient.[2] It is clear from the same essay that Montaigne felt as much; though the gist of his polemic is a vehement attack upon all forms of confident opinion, religious and anti-religious alike. " In replying to arguments of so opposite a tenor, Montaigne leaves Christianity, as well as Raimond Sebonde, without a leg to stand upon. He demolishes the arguments of Sebonde with the rest of human presumption, and allows Christianity, neither held by faith nor provable by reason, to fall between the two stools." [3] It was the Massacre that above all made Montaigne recoil from public life [4] : it must have affected likewise his working philosophy.

That philosophy was not, indeed, an original construction; he found it to his hand partly in the Deism of his favorite Seneca ; partly in the *Hypotyposes* of Sextus Empiricus, of which the Latin translation is known to have been among his books; from which he took several of the mottoes inscribed on his library ceiling,[5] and from which he frequently quotes towards the end of his *Apology*. The body of ideas compacted on these bases cannot be called a system; it was not in Montaigne's nature to frame a logical scheme of thought ; and he was far from being the philosophic sceptic he set out to be [6] by way of confounding at once the bigots and the Atheists. But on

---

[1] Mr. Owen was mistaken (*Skeptics of the French Renaissance*, 1893, p. 414) in supposing that Montaigne spent several years over this translation. It was done rapidly. Cp. Miss M. E. Lowndes' excellent monograph, *Michel de Montaigne*, 1898, pp. 103, 106.

[2] Ed. Firmin-Didot, ii, 469.

[3] Miss Lowndes, as cited, p. 145.

[4] Cp. the *Essais*, B. iii, c. 1 (Ed. Firmin-Didot, ii, 208). Mr. Owen gives a somewhat misleading idea of the passage (*French Skeptics*, p. 486).

[5] Miss Lowndes, *Michel de Montaigne*, p. 131. Cp. Mr. Owen, *Skeptics of the French Renaissance*, p. 444.

[6] He was consistent enough to doubt the new cosmology of Copernicus (*Essais*, as cited, i, 615) ; but he was a keen and convinced critic of the prevailing abuses in law and education. Mr. Owen's discussion of his opinions is illuminating.

the other hand his whole habit of mind is perfectly fatal
to orthodox religion; and it is clear that despite his pro-
fessions of conformity he did not hold the ordinary Christian beliefs.[1] Above all, he rejected the great superstition
of the age, the belief in witchcraft. His function in literature was thus to set up a certain mental atmosphere;[2]
and this the extraordinary vitality of his utterance enabled
him to do to an incalculable extent. He had the gift to
disarm or at least to baffle[3] hostility, to charm kings,
to stand free between warring factions. No book ever
written conveys more absolutely the sensation of a living
voice; and after three hundred years he has as friendly
an audience as ever.

The momentum of such an influence is seen in the
work of CHARRON (1541-1603), Montaigne's friend and
disciple. The *Essais* had first appeared in 1580; the
expanded and revised issue in 1588; and in 1601 there
appeared Charron's *De la Sagesse*, which gives methodic
form and as far as was permissible a direct application to
Montaigne's naturalistic principles. Charron's is a curious
case of mental evolution. First a lawyer, then a priest,
he became a highly successful popular preacher and
champion of the Catholic League; and as such was
favored by the notorious Marguerite (the second[4]) of
Navarre. Becoming the friend of Montaigne in 1586, he
shows already in 1593, in his *Three Truths*, the influence of
the essayist's scepticism,[5] though Charron's book was
expressly framed to refute, first, the Atheists; second, the

---

[1] Cp. the clerical protests of Sterling (*Lond. and Westm. Review*, July,
1838, p. 346) and Dean Church (*Oxford Essays*, p. 279).

[2] Cp. citations in Buckle, 3-vol. ed. ii, 18, note 42; and Lecky, *Rationalism*,
i, 92-5.

[3] Mr. Owen notes (*French Skeptics*, p. 446) that though the Papal curia
requested him to alter certain passages in the Essays, "it cannot be shown
that he erased or modified a single one of the points". Sainte Beuve,
however, has noted many safeguarding clauses added to the later versions
of the essay on Prayers (i, 56).

[4] Not, as Mr. Owen states (*French Skeptics*, p. 569), the sister of Francis I,
who died when Charron was eight years old, but the daughter of Henri II,
and first wife of Henri of Navarre, afterwards Henri IV.

[5] Cp. Sainte-Beuve, as cited by Owen, p. 571, *note*, and Owen's own
words, pp. 572

pagans, Jews, Mahommedans; and third, the Christian
heretics and schismatics. The *Wisdom*, published only
eight years later, is a work of a very different cast, proving
a mental change. Even in the first work, " the growing
teeth of the sceptic are discernible beneath the well-worn
stumps of the believer ";[1] but the second almost testifies
to a new birth. Professedly orthodox, it was yet recognised at once by the devout as a " seminary of impiety ",[2]
and brought on its author a persecution that lasted till his
sudden death from apoplexy, which his critics pronounced
to be a divine dispensation. In the second and re-
arranged edition, published a year after his death, there
are some modifications ; but they are so far from essential[3]
that Buckle found the book as it stands a kind of pioneer
manual of rationalism.[4] Its way of putting all religions
on one level, as being alike grounded on bad evidence
and held on prejudice, is only the formal statement of an
old idea, found, like so many others of Charron's, in
Montaigne ; but the didactic purpose and method turn
the sceptic's shrug into a resolute propaganda. So with
the formal and earnest insistence that true morality cannot
be built on religious hopes and fears,—a principle which
Charron was the first to bring directly home to the modern
intelligence,[5] as he did the principle of development in
religious systems.[6] Attempting as it does to construct a
systematic practical philosophy of life, it puts aside so
positively the claims of the theologians,[7] and so emphatically subordinates religion to the rule of natural reason,[8]

---

[1] Owen, p. 571. Cp. pp. 573, 574.
[2] Bayle, art. CHARRON. "A brutal atheism " is the account of Charron's
doctrine given by the Jesuit Garasse.
[3] Mr. Owen (p. 570) comes to this conclusion after carefully collating
the editions. Cp. p. 587, *note.* The whole of the alterations, including
those proposed by President Jeannin, will be found set forth in the edition
of 1607, and the reprints of that.
[4] "The first . . . attempt made in a modern language to construct a
system of morals without the aid of theology" (*Introd. to Hist. of Civ. in
England*, 3-vol. ed. ii, 19).
[5] Cp. Owen, pp. 580-5.
[6] Buckle, ii, 21.
[7] *E.g.*, the preface to the first edition, *ad init.*
[8] *E.g.* Liv. ii, ch. 28 of revised ed. (ed. 1609, p. 399).

that it constitutes a virtual revolution in public doctrine for Christendom. As Montaigne is the true beginner of modern literature, so is Charron the beginner of modern secular teaching. He is a Naturalist, professing theism.

It was only powerful protection that could save such a book from proscription ; but Charron and his book had the support at once of Henri IV and the President Jeannin—the former a proved indifferentist to religious forms ; the latter the author of the remark that a peace with two religions was better than a war which had none. After the assassination of the king in 1610, the last of the bloody deeds which had kept France on the rack of uncertainty in religion's name for three generations, the spirit of rationalism naturally did not wane. In the Paris of the early seventeenth century, doubtless, the new emancipation came to be associated, as "libertinism", with license as well as with freethinking. In the nature of the case there could be no serious and free literary discussion of the new problems either of life or belief, save in so far as they had been handled by Montaigne and Charron ; and inasmuch as the accounts preserved of the freethought of the age are almost invariably those of its worst enemies, it is chiefly their side of the case that has been presented. Thus in 1623 the Jesuit Father François Garasse published a thick quarto of over a thousand pages entitled *La Doctrine Curieuse des Beaux Esprits de ce temps, ou prétendu tels*, in which he assails the " libertins" of the day with an infuriated industry. The eight books into which he divides his treatise proceed upon eight alleged maxims of the freethinkers, which run as follows :—

I. There are very few good wits [*bons Esprits*] in the world ; and the fools, that is to say, the common run of men, are not capable of our doctrine ; therefore it will not do to speak freely, but in secret, and among trusting and cabalistic souls.

II. Good wits [*beaux Esprits*] believe in God only by way of form, and as a matter of public policy (*par Maxime d'Etat*).

III. A *bel Esprit* is free in his belief, and is not readily to be taken in by the quantity of nonsense that is propounded to the simple populace.

IV. All things are conducted and governed by Destiny, which is irrevocable, infallible, immovable, necessary, eternal and inevitable to all men whomsoever.

V. It is true that the book called the Bible, or the Holy Scripture, is a good book (*un gentil livre*), and contains a lot of good things; but that a *bon esprit* should be obliged to believe under pain of damnation all that is therein, down to the tail of Tobit's dog, does not follow.

VI. There is no other divinity or sovereign power in the world but NATURE, which must be satisfied in all things, without refusing anything to our body or senses that they desire of us in the exercise of their natural powers and faculties.

VII. Supposing there be a God, as it is decorous to admit, so as not to be always at odds with the superstitious, it does not follow that there are creatures which are purely intellectual and separated from matter. All that is in Nature is composite, and therefore there are neither angels nor devils in the world, and it is not certain that the soul of man is immortal.

VIII. It is true that to live happily it is necessary to extinguish and drown all scruples; but all the same it does not do to appear impious and abandoned, for fear of offending the simple or losing the support of the superstitious.

This is obviously neither candid nor competent writing; and as it happens there remains proof in the case of the life of LA MOTHE LE VAYER, that "earnest free-thought in the beginning of the seventeenth century afforded a *point d'appui* for serious-minded men, which neither the corrupt Romanism nor the narrow Protestantism of the period could furnish".[1] Garasse's own doctrine was that "the true liberty of the mind consists in a simple and docile (*sage*) belief in all that the Church propounds, indifferently and without distinction".[2] The later social history of Catholic France is the sufficient comment on the efficacy of such teaching to regulate life. In any case, the new ideas steadily gained ground; and on the heels of the treatise of Garasse appeared that of Marin Mersenne, *L'impieté des Déistes, Athées et Libertins de ce temps combattue, avec la refutation des opinions de Charron, de Cardan, de Jordan Brun, et des quatraines du Déiste* (1624). Such were the signs of the times when Pascal was in his cradle.

[1] Owen, *French Skeptics*, p. 659. Cp. Lecky, *Rationalism*, i, 97, citing Maury, as to the resistance of *libertins* to the superstition about witchcraft.
[2] *La Doctrine des Beaux Esprits*, as cited, p. 208. This is one of the passages which fully explain the opinion of the orthodox of that age that Garasse "helped rather than hindered Atheism" (Reimmann, *Hist. Atheismi*, 1725, p. 408).

§ 3.

While France was thus passing from general fanaticism to a large measure of freethought, England was passing by a less tempestuous path to a less advanced stage of opinion. The comparative bloodlessness of the strife between Protestant and Catholic under Mary and Elizabeth, the treatment of the Jesuit propaganda under the latter queen as a political rather than a doctrinal question, prevented any such vehemence of recoil from religious ideals as took place in France. Unbelief, as we have seen, there certainly was ; and it is recorded that Walter, Earl of Essex, on his deathbed at Dublin in 1576, murmured that among his countrymen neither Popery nor Protestantism prevailed : "there was nothing but infidelity, infidelity, infidelity; atheism, atheism ; no religion, no religion[1]." But seventeen years later, and over thirty years after the outburst of Ascham before cited, we find only a sporadic and secret unbelief, going in fear of its life. Open rationalism could go no further than such a protest against superstition as Reginald Scot's *Discoverie of Witchcraft* (1584), which, however, is a sufficiently remarkable expression of reason in an age in which a Bodin held angrily by the superstition.[2] Elizabeth was herself substantially irreligious,[3] and preferred to keep the clergy few in number and subordinate in influence[4]; but her Ministers regarded the Church as part of the State system, and punished all open heresy in the manner of the Inquisition. One Matthew Hamond, a ploughwright, was burned at Norwich in 1579 for declaring the New Testament "a fable, Christ a mere sinful man, erected into an abominable idol, the Holy Ghost a nonentity, and the sacraments useless "[5]; one Peter Cole,

---

[1] Froude, *History of England*, ed. 1875, xi, 199, citing *MSS. Ireland.*

[2] Lecky, *Rationalism*, i, 103-4. Scot's book had practically no influence in his own day.

[3] " No woman ever lived who was so totally destitute of the sentiment of religion " (Green, *Short History*, c. vii, Sec. 3, p. 369).

[4] Soame, *Elizabethan Religious History*, 1839, p. 225.

[5] Soame, as cited, p. 234.

an Ipswich tanner, was burned in 1587 (again at
Norwich) for similar doctrine ; and Francis Kett, a young
clergyman, ex-fellow of Corpus Christi College, Cambridge, was burnt at the same place in 1589 for heresy of
the Unitarian order.   Hamond and Cole seem, however, to have been religious men,[1] and Kett a devout
mystic, with ideas of a Second Advent[2]. All founded on the
Bible.

In 1593, finally, we find atheism charged against two
famous men, CHRISTOPHER MARLOWE and Sir WALTER
RALEIGH, of whom the former is documentarily connected
with Kett, and Raleigh in turn with Marlowe.   An official
document[3], preserved by some chance, reveals that
Marlowe was given to singularly audacious derision of
the received beliefs ; and so explicit is the evidence that
it is almost certain he would have been executed for
blasphemy had he not been privately killed (1593) while
the proceedings were pending.   The " atheism " imputed
to him is not made out in any detail ; but many of the
other utterances are notably in keeping with Marlowe's
daring temper ; and they amount to unbelief of the most
stringent kind.

Concerning Raleigh, again, there is no shadow of
proof of atheism ; but it is matter of literary history that
he, like Montaigne, had been influenced by the *Hypotyposes*
of Sextus Empiricus[4]; his short essay *The Sceptick* being a
naïf exposition of the thesis that " the sceptick doth neither
affirm neither deny any position ; but doubteth of it, and
applyeth his Reason against that which is affirmed, or
denied, to justifie his non-consenting ".[5]   But the essay
itself proceeds upon a set of wildly false propositions in

[1] Art. MATTHEW HAMOND, in *Dict. of Nat. Biog.*
[2] Art. FRANCIS KETT, in *Dict. of Nat. Biog.*
[3] MS. Harl. 6853, fol. 320.   It is given in full in the appendix to the
first issue of the selected plays of Marlowe in the Mermaid Series, edited
by Mr. Havelock Ellis; and, with omissions, in the editions of Cunning-
ham, Dyce, and Bullen.
[4] Translated into Latin by Henri Etienne in 1562.
[5] *Remains of Sir Walter Raleigh*, ed. 1657, p. 123.

natural history, concerning which the adventurous reasoner has no doubts whatever; and altogether we may be sure that his artificial scepticism did not carry him far. The evidence goes to show only that he was ready to read a Unitarian essay, supposed to be Kett's; and that he had intercourse with Marlowe and others, in particular his secretary, HARRIOTT or HERIOTS, known to be free-thinkers. A prosecution begun against him on this score, at the time of the enquiry concerning Marlowe (when Raleigh was in disgrace with the Queen), came to nothing. It had been led up to by a Catholic pamphlet, which affirmed that his private group was known as " Sir Walter Rawley's school of Atheisme ", and that therein " both Moyses and our Savior, the Old and the New Testaments, are jested at, and the scholars taught among other things to spell God backwards ".[1] This seems to have been idle gossip, though it tells of unbelief somewhere; and Raleigh's own writings always indicate belief in the Bible[2]; though his dying speech and epitaph are noticeably deistic. That he was a deist, given to free discussion, seems the probable truth.[3]

The latest documentary evidence as to the case of Marlowe is produced by Mr. F. C. Boas in his article " New Light on Marlowe and Kyd " in the *Fortnightly Review*, February, 1899. In addition to the formerly known data as to Marlowe's " atheism ", it is now established that Thomas Kyd, his fellow-dramatist, was arrested on the same charge, and that there was found among his papers one containing " vile hereticall con-ceiptes denyinge the divinity of Jhesus Christe our Saviour ". This Kyd declared he had had from Marlowe, denying all sympathy with its views. The paper however proves to be a vehement Unitarian argument on Scriptural grounds, and is more likely to have been written by Francis Kett than by Marlowe. In the MSS. now brought to light, one Cholmeley, who " confessed that he was persuaded by Marlowe's reasons

---

[1] Art. RALEGH, in *Dict. of Nat. Biog.*, xlvii, 192.   [2] *Id.*, pp. 200-1.
[3] It is asserted by Francis Osborn, who had known Raleigh, that he got his title of *Atheist* from Queen Elizabeth. See the preface (*Author to Reader*) to Osborn's *Miscellany of Sundry Essays*, etc., in 7th ed. of his *Works*, 1673. As to atheism at Elizabeth's court, see Tayler, *Retrospect of Relig. Life of England*, 2nd ed., p. 198, and ref.

to become an Athieste ", is represented by a spy as speaking
" all evil of the Counsell, saying that they are all Athiestes
and Machiavillians, especially my Lord Admirall ". The same
"Atheist ", who imputes atheism to others as a vice, is described
as regretting he had not killed the Lord Treasurer, " sayenge
that he could never have done God better service ".

For the rest, the same spy tells that Cholmeley believed
Marlowe was " able to shewe more sound reasons for Atheisme
than any devine in Englande is able to geve to prove devinitie,
and that Marloe told him that he hath read the Atheist lecture
to Sir Walter Raleigh and others ". On the last point there is
no further evidence, save that Sir Walter, with his dependant
Harriott and Mr. Carewe Rawley, were on March 21, 1593-4,
charged upon sworn testimonies with holding "impious opinions
concerning God and Providence ". Harriott had published
in 1588 a work on his travels in Virginia, at the close of which
is a passage in the devoutest vein telling of his missionary
labors (quoted by Mr. Boas, art. cited, p. 225). Yet by
1592 he had, with his master, a reputation for] Atheism ; and
that it was not wholly on the strength of his great scientific
knowledge is suggested by the statement of Anthony Wood that
he " made a philosophical theology, wherein he cast off the
Old Testament ". Of this no trace remains; but it is established
that he was a highly accomplished mathematician, much
admired by Kepler; and that he " applied the telescope to
celestial purposes almost simultaneously with Galileo " (art.
HARRIOTT in *Dict. of Nat. Biog.*).

But there remains the great illustration of the rationalistic spirit of the English literary renascence of the sixteenth century—the drama of SHAKSPERE. Of that it
may confidently be said that every attempt to find for it a
religious foundation has failed.[1] A clerical historian sums
up concerning Shakspere that " the religious phrases which
are thinly scattered over his work are little more than
expressions of a distant and imaginative reverence. And
on the deeper grounds of religious faith his silence is
significant. . . . The riddle of life and death . . . he
leaves . . . a riddle to the last, without heeding the common theological solutions around him."[2] There is good

[1] Some typical attempts of the kind are discussed in the author's two
lectures on *The Religion of Shakspere*, 1887 (South Place Institute).

[2] Green, *Short History*, ch. vii, sec. vii, *end*.

reason to think that he was much influenced by Montaigne's Essays, read by him in Florio's translation, which was issued when he was recasting the old *Hamlet;* and his whole treatment of life in the great tragedies and serious comedies produced by him from that time forward is even more definitely untheological than Montaigne's own doctrine.[1]

A serious misconception has been set up as to Shakspere's cast of mind by the persistence of editors in including among his works plays which are certainly not his, as the *Henry VI* group, and in particular the First Part. It is on the assumption that that play is Shakspere's work that Mr. Lecky (*Rationalism in Europe,* ed. 1887, i, 105-6) speaks of "that melancholy picture of Joan of Arc which is, perhaps, the darkest blot upon his genius". Now, whatever passages Shakspere may have contributed to the Second and Third Parts, it is certain that he has barely a scene in the First, and that there is not a line from his hand in the La Pucelle scenes. Most students will probably agree that Dr. Furnivall has even gone too far in saying that "the only part of it to be put down to Shakspere is the Temple Garden scene of the red and white roses" (Introd. to *Leopold* Shakspere, p. xxxviii); so little is there to suggest even the juvenile Shakspere there. But that any critical and qualified reader can still hold him to have written the rest of the play is to me inconceivable. The whole work would be a "blot on his genius" in respect of its literary worthlessness. The doubt was raised long before Mr. Lecky wrote, and was made good more than twenty years ago. When Mr. Lecky further proceeds, with reference to the witches in *Macbeth,* to say (*id., note*) that it is "probable that Shakspere . . . . believed with an unfaltering faith in the reality of witchcraft," he strangely misreads that play. Nothing is clearer than that it grounds Macbeth's action from the first in Macbeth's own character and his wife's, employing the witch machinery (already used by Middleton) to meet the popular taste, but never once making them really causal forces. An "unfaltering" believer in witchcraft who wrote for the stage would surely have turned it to serious account in other tragedies. This Shakspere never does. On Mr. Lecky's view, he is to be held as having believed in the fairy magic of the *Midsummer Night's Dream* and the *Tempest.* But who for a moment

---

[1] Cp. the author's *Montaigne and Shakspere,* 1897, pp. 136-155.

supposes him to have held any such belief? It is probable that the entire undertaking of *Macbeth* (1605?) and later of the *Tempest* (1610?) was due to a wish on the part of the theatre management to please King James (acc. 1603), whose belief in witchcraft and magic was notorious. Even the use of the Ghost in *Hamlet* is an old stage expedient, common to the pre-Shaksperean play and to others of Kyd's. Shakspere significantly altered the dying words of Hamlet from the "heaven receive my soul" of the old version to "the rest is silence". The bequest of his soul to the Deity in his will is merely the regulation testamentary formula of the time. In his sonnets, which hint his personal cast if anything does, there is no trace of religious creed.

Nor is Shakspere in this aspect abnormal among his colleagues. To say nothing of the weak Greene, who had professed a loose Atheism, and published his deathbed repentance in *A Groatsworth of Wit*, the bulk of his dramatic rivals are similarly unconcerned with religion. Hence, in fact, the bitter hostility of the Puritans to the stage. Some of the Elizabethans do indeed take up matters of creed in their plays; for instance, Peele, whose *David and Bethsabe* (1599) is the first regular drama on a Biblical subject, mishandles Mohammedanism in his *Battle of Alcazar*; and it is clearly Fletcher's hand that penned the part of *Henry VIII* in which occurs the Protestant tag "In her [Elizabeth's] days ... God shall be truly known".[1] But the prevailing color of the whole drama of the Shaksperean period is pre-Puritan and semi-Pagan; and the theological spirit of the next generation, intensified by King James, was recognised by cultured foreigners like Casaubon and Grotius as a change for the worse.[2]

Not that rationalism became extinct. The "Italianate" incredulity as to a future state, which Sir John Davies had sought to repel by his poem *Nosce Teipsum* (1599) can hardly have been overthrown even by that remarkable production; and there were other forms of doubt. Careful as was Bacon to distinguish between religion and philo-

[1] As to the expert analysis of this play, which shows it to be in large part Fletcher's, see Furnivall, as cited, pp. xciii-xcvi.
[2] Hallam, *Lit. Hist. of Europe*, ed. 1872, ii, 371, 376, and notes.

sophy—as to which he fully adopts the equivoque of a
" twofold truth "[1]—he could not divest his work of a
rationalistic influence, or escape the charge of atheism.[2]
Practically he wrote as a Deist, and by putting aside
" final causes " he made his deism tolerably impersonal.[3]
On the other hand, the critical spirit was secretly at
work on the text of the Scriptures. Bishop Fotherby's
posthumous folio *Atheomastix*, published in 1622, affirms
that as a result of constant disputing "the Scriptures (with many) have lost their authority, and are
thought onely fit for the ignorant, and idiote ".[4] There
was thus already a basis for the Deistic propaganda which
began immediately afterwards, in Latin, with the first
work of Lord Herbert of Cherbury. But for more than a
generation there was no propaganda in English ; and
save for the remarkable outbreak of manifold free speech
at the time of the Civil War, to be considered later, there
was no overt expression of freethought on religion among
the mass of the people. The authority of the now
dominating Church on the one hand, and on the other
the new spirit of Bibliolatry among the lay population,
whose chief culture was Bible-reading and sermon-hearing,
overlaid what rationalism there was.

§ 4.

Of Freethought in the rest of Europe, there is little
chronicle for a hundred and fifty years after the to
Reformation. The epoch-making work of COPERNICUS,
published in 1543, had little or no immediate effect in Ger-

---

[1] See the *Advancement of Learning*, B. i ; B. ii, c. 11 ; B. iv, c. 3 ; B. ix ;
Novum Organum, B. i, *passim* (Bohn ed. pp. 31, 68, 173, 368-374, 392,
400-2, etc.).
[2] Cp. Francis Osborn's pref. (*Author to Reader*) to his *Miscellany* in *Works*,
as cited.
[3] Lechler (*Gesch. des englischen Deismus*, S. 23-25) notes that Bacon
involuntarily made for Deism.· Dean Church (*Bacon*, in " Men of Letters ''
series, pp. 174, 205) insists that Bacon held by revelation and immortality
but the whole tendency of his writings is to put these beliefs aside.
[4] *Atheomastix*, 1622, preface.

many, where physical and verbal strifes had begun with
the ecclesiastical revolution, and were to continue to
waste the nation's energy for a century. The Peasants'
Revolt had been crushed by massacre in 1525, a hundred
thousand men being destroyed.[1] Another multitude of
Anabaptists perished in 1535, their leaders dying by
public torture. In 1546, all attempts at ecclesiastical
reconciliation having failed, the emperor, Charles V, in
whom Melanchthon had seen a model monarch,[2] decided
to put down the Protestant heresy by war. Luther had
just died, ill at ease for his cause. Civil war now raged
till the peace of Augsburg in 1555; whereafter Charles
abdicated in favor of his son Philip. Here were in part
the conditions which in France and elsewhere had been
followed by a growth of rational unbelief. But in Germany the balance of forces amounted only to a deadlock
between the ecclesiastical parties. Protestantism on the
intellectual side, as already noted, had sunk into a bitter
and barren polemic[3] among the reformers themselves;
and many who had joined the movement reverted to
Catholicism.[4] Melanchthon died in 1560, glad to be " set
free from the monstrous and implacable hatreds of the theologians ". Meanwhile the teaching and preaching Jesuits
were zealously at work, turning the dissensions of the
enemy to account, and contrasting its schism upon
schism with the unity of the Church. But Protestantism
was well welded to the financial interest of the many
princes and others who had acquired the Church lands
confiscated at the Reformation ; since a return to
Catholicism would mean the surrender of these.[5] Thus
there wrought on the one side the organised spirit of
anti-heresy and on the other the organised spirit of
Bibliolatry, neither gaining ground; and between the

---

[1] Kohlrausch, *Hist. of Germany*, Eng. tr. p. 377.
[2] *Id.*, p. 385.
[3] Cp. Gardiner, *The Thirty Years' War*, 8th ed., pp. 12-13 ; Kohlrausch,
p. 438 ; Pusey, *Histor. Enq. into German Rationalism*, pp. 9-25.
[4] Kohlrausch, p. 439.
[5] Cp. Gardiner, *Thirty Years' War*, pp. 16, 18, 21 ; Kohlrausch, p. 370.

two, intellectual life was paralysed. Protestantism saw
no way of advance ; and the prevailing temper began to
be that of the Dark Ages, expectant of the end of the
world.[1] Superstition abounded, especially the belief in
witchcraft, now acted on with frightful cruelty throughout
the whole Christian world[2]; and in the nature of the
case Catholicism counted for nothing on the opposite
side.   The only element of rationalism that one historian of
culture can detect, is the tendency of the German moralists
of the time to turn the Devil into an abstraction by
identifying him with the different aspects of human folly
and vice[3]!   There was, as a matter of fact, a somewhat
higher manifestation of the spirit of reason, in the shape
of John Wier's treatise on witchcraft, a work[4] which,
though fully adhering to the belief in the devil and
things demoniac, argued against the notion that witches
were conscious workers of evil.   Wier was a physician
and saw the problem partly as one in pathology.   Other
laymen, and even priests, had reacted more strongly
against the prevailing insanity ; but it had the authority
of Luther on its side, and the protests counted for little.
At length, after a generation of gloomy suspense, came
the explosion of the hostile ecclesiastical interests, and
the long-drawn horror of the Thirty Years' War, which
left Germany mangled, devastated, drained of blood and
treasure, decivilised, and well-nigh destitute of the
machinery of culture.   What intellectual life was left
had been affected in the usual way by the spectacle of
evil wrought for religion ; and in 1662 there duly
appeared at Erfurt a *Preservatio wider die Pest des heutigen
Atheisten*, by one Theophilus Grosgebauer, to be followed
within the next fifteen years by six other treatises of the

---

[1] Freytag, *Bilder aus der deutschen Vergangenheit*, Bd. II, Abth. II, 1883
S. 381 ; Bd. III, *ad init*.
[2] Cp. Lecky, *Rationalism in Europe*, small ed. i, 53-83.
[3] Freytag, *Bilder*, Bd. II, Abth. II, S. 378.
[4] *De Praestigiis Daemonum*, 1563.   See it described by Lecky, *Rationalism*
i, 85-7 ; Hallam, *Lit. Hist.*, ii, 76.

same order.[1] This polemic activity was specially forced on by a positive and aggressive development of Atheism such as no other country had yet seen. A wandering scholar, MATTHIAS KNUTZEN (b. 1645) who had studied philosophy at Königsberg, went about teaching, as far as can be gathered, a hardy Religion of Humanity, rejecting alike immortality, God and Devil, churches and priests, and insisting that conscience could perfectly well take the place of the Bible as a guide to conduct. His followers, as holding by conscience, were called *Gewissener;* and it is said that at Jena alone, about 1674, there were seven hundred of them.[2] Yet he and the whole movement passed rapidly out of sight—hardly by reason of the orthodox refutations, however. Germany was in no state to sustain such a party; and even the manifold argumentation of Leibnitz at the end of the century was addressed rather to the rest of Europe than to his own countrymen, who paid him small heed. Not till the eighteenth century could Germany come abreast of European culture.

It was the fate of Spain, meanwhile, to illustrate once for all the power of a dogmatic religious system to extirpate the spirit of reason from an entire nation for a whole era. There and there only was the Inquisition all-powerful; and it wrought for the evisceration of the intellectual and material life of Spain with a demented zeal to which there is no parallel in later history. In the reign of Ferdinand and Isabella, after several random massacres and much persecution, the unconverted Jews of Spain were in 1489 penned into Ghettos, and were in 1492 expelled bodily from the country, so far as Church and State could compass their plans. By this measure, at

---

[1] J. Müller, *Atheismus devictus* (in German), 1672, Hamburg. J. Lassen, *Arcana-Politico-Atheistica* (in German), 1672 ; *Besiegte Atheisterey*, 1673. Val. Greissing, *Corona Transylvani*, Exerc. 2, de Atheismo, contra Cartesium et Math. Knutzen, Wittemberg, 1677. Tobias Wagner, *Examen . . . . atheismi speculativi*, Tübingen, 1677. Rudrauf, *Theol. Giessensis Dissertatio de Atheismo*, 1677. In 1689 there appears yet another polemic, the *Narrischer Atheist* of Th. Undereyck (Bremen).

[2] Cp. Trinius, *Freydenker Lexicon*, s.v. KNUTZEN ; Pünjer, i, 437-8.

least 160,000 subjects [1] of more than average value were lost to the State. Portugal and other Christian countries took the same cruel step a few years later; but Spain carried the policy much further. From the year of its establishment, the Inquisition was hotly at work destroying heresy of every kind; and the renowned Torquemada, the confessor of Isabella, is credited with having burnt over ten thousand persons in his eighteen years of office as Grand Inquisitor. Close upon a hundred thousand more were terrified into submission; and a further six thousand burned in effigy in their absenee or after death.[2] The destruction of books was proportionally thorough [3]; and when Lutheran Protestantism arose, it was persistently killed out; thousands leaving the country in view of the hoplessness of the cause.[4] At this rate, every vestige of independent thought must soon have disappeared from any nation in the world. If she is to be judged by the number of her slain and exiled heretics, Spain must have been nearly as fecund in reformative and innovating thought as any state in northern Europe; but the fatal conjunction of the royal and the clerical authority sufficed to denude her of every variety of the freethinking species.[5]

A century after the expulsion of the Jews came the turn of the Moors, whose last hold in Spain, Granada, had been overthrown in 1492. Within a generation they had been deprived of all exterior practice of their religion [6]; but that did not suffice; and the Inquisition never left them alone. Harried, persecuted, compulsorily baptised, deprived of their Arabic books, they repeatedly revolted, only to be beaten down. At length, in the opening years

---

[1] The number has been put as high as 800,000. Cp. E. La Rigaudière, *Hist. des Perséc. Relig. en Espagne*, 1860, pp. 112-114; Prescott, *Hist. of Ferdinand and Isabella*, Kirk's ed., 1889, p. 323.

[2] Llorente, *Hist. Crit. de l'Inquis. en Espagne*, ed. 1818, i, 280. As to Llorente's other estimates, which are of doubtful value, cp. Prescott's note, ed. cited, p. 746.

[3] Llorente, i, 281.

[4] McCrie, *Reformation in Spain*, ch. viii.

[5] Cp. La Rigaudière, pp. 309-314; Buckle, ii, 478-597.

[6] Buckle, ii, 484, and references.

of the seventeenth century, under Philip III, on the score that the great Armada had failed because heretics were tolerated at home, it was decided to expel the whole race ; and now a million Moriscoes, among the most industrious inhabitants of Spain, were driven the way of the Jews. It is needless here to recall the ruinous effect upon the material life of Spain[1] : the aspect of the matter which specially concerns us is the consummation of the policy of killing out all intellectual variation. The Moriscoes may have counted for little in positive culture ; but they were one of the last and most important factors of variation in the country ; and when Spain was thus successively denuded of precisely the most original and energetic types among the Jewish, the Spanish, and the Moorish stocks, her mental ruin was complete.

To modern Freethought, accordingly, she has till our own age contributed practically nothing. The brilliant dramatic literature of the reigns of the four Philips, which influenced the rising drama alike of France and England, is notably unintellectual[2], dealing endlessly in plot and adventure, but yielding no great study of character, and certainly doing nothing to further ethics. Calderon was a thorough fanatic, and became a priest[3] ; Lope de Vega found solace under bereavement in the duties of an Inquisitor. The humorous and kindly spirit of Cervantes, so incongruously neighboured, must have counted for much in keeping life sweet in Spain in the succeeding centuries of bigotry and ignorance. But from the seventeenth century till the other day the brains were out, in the sense that genius was lacking ; though last century, under the Bourbons, French enlightenment set up a new life until reaction set in with the French Revolution.[4]

---

[1] Cp. Buckle, ii, 497-9; La Rigaudière, pp. 220-6.
[2] Cp. Lewes, *Spanish Drama*, passim.
[3] " He inspires me only with horror for the faith which he professes. No one ever so far disfigured Christianity, no one ever assigned to it passions so ferocious, or morals so corrupt " (Sismondi, *Lit. of South of Europe*, Bohn tr. ii, 379).
[4] Cp. Buckle, ii, 521-571.

Then came the opportunity of the party of superstition, never really superseded. Nor is the work of the age of devout destruction yet undone.

§ 5.

It remains to trace briefly the movement of scientific and speculative thought which constituted the transition between the Scholastic and the modern philosophy. It may be compendiously noted under the names of Copernicus, Bruno, Vanini, Sanchez, Galileo, Ramus, Gassendi, Bacon and Descartes.

The great performance of COPERNICUS, given to the world with an editor's treacherous preface as he lay on his deathbed in 1543, did not become a general possession for nearly a hundred years.[1] One of the first to bring the new cosmological conception to bear on philosophic thought was GIORDANO BRUNO (1548—1600), whose life and death of lonely chivalry have won him his place as the typical martyr of modern Freethought.[2] He may be conceived as a blending of the pantheistic and naturalistic lore of ancient Greece[3] with the spirit of modern science (itself a revival of the Greek) as it first takes firm form in Copernicus, whose doctrine Bruno promptly and

---

[1] The doctrine of the earth's two-fold motion had actually been taught in the fifteenth century by Nicholas of Cusa (1401-64), who, instead of being prosecuted, was made a cardinal, so little was the question then considered (Ueberweg, ii, 23-24). Only slowly did the work even of Copernicus make its impression. Mr. Green (*Short History*, ed. 1881, p. 297) makes first the blunder of stating that it influenced thought in the *fifteenth* century, and then the further mistake of saying that it was brought home to the general intelligence by Galileo and Kepler in the later years of the *sixteenth* century (*Id.*, p. 412). Galileo's European notoriety dates from 1616; his *Dialogues of the Two Systems of the World* appeared only in 1632; and his *Dialogues of the New Sciences* in 1638. Kepler's indecisive *Mysterium Cosmographicum* appeared only in 1597; his treatise on the motions of the planet Mars not till 1609.

[2] A good study of Bruno—preferable to Mrs. Frith's *Life*—is supplied by Mr. Owen, in his *Skeptics of the Italian Renaissance*. For a hostile view see Hallam, *Lit. of Europe*, as cited, ii, 105-111. The biography of M. Bartholmèss, *Jordano Bruno*, 1846, is extremely full and sympathetic, but loose as to dates and translations. For other authorities see Mr. Owen's list.

[3] Cp. Bartholmèss, i, 49-53; Lange, *Hist. of Materialism*, Eng. tr. i, 232.

ardently embraced.[1] Of all men of his time he had perhaps the least affinity with the Christian creed, which was repellent to him alike in the Catholic and the Protestant versions. A philosophic poet rather than a philosopher or man of science, he yet set abroad for the modern world that conception of the physical infinity of the universe which, once psychologically assimilated, makes an end of the medieval theory of things. On this head he was eagerly affirmative ; and the merely Pyrrhonic sceptics he assailed as he did the "asinine" orthodox,[2] though he insisted on doubt as the beginning of wisdom. Fate placed him as a boy among the Dominicans, punningly named the "hounds of the Lord " (domini canes) for their work as the corps of the Inquisition ; and in his thirteen years of cloister life he was twice arraigned for heresy. Quite early he seems to have become Unitarian.[3] A well-grounded fear made him at length take to flight ; and he wandered eagerly through Europe, teaching and writing wherever he lingered, till at last the "hounds", always on the scent, caught their prey. Between 1583 and 1585 he was in England, where he met Sidney and Spenser; and debated at Oxford, maintaining the Copernican theory against the Ptolemaic. His picture of "Oxford ignorance, and English ill-manners"[4] is not lenient; and there is no reason to suppose that his doctrine was then assimilated by many.[5] Teaching successively as he did, however, at Toulouse, Paris, Oxford, and Wittemberg, he sowed the seeds of his thought all over Europe, and his numerous books had an increasing number of readers.

Nothing was more natural that, when in 1592 he ventured within the sphere of the Inquisition at Venice, he should be seized, albeit by treachery. Charged on the

---

[1] Owen, as cited, p. 249; Ueberweg, ii, 27 ; Pünjer, i, 93-101.
[2] Owen, pp. 296, 299.
[3] Owen, p. 265.
[4] Owen, p. 275 ; Cp. Bartholmèss, Jordano Bruno, i, 136-8.
[5] Cp. Hallam, Lit. of Europe, ii, 111, note. As to Bruno's supposed influence on Bacon and Shakspere, cp. Bartholmèss, i, 134-5; Mrs. Frith's Life, pp. 104-8; and the author's Montaigne and Shakspere, pp. 82-7.

traitor's testimony with many blasphemies, he warmly
denied them all, but stood to his published writings,[1] and
professed in the usual manner to believe in conformity
with the Church's teachings, whatever he might write on
philosophy. It is impossible to trust the Inquisition
records as to his words of self-humiliation;[2] though on
the other hand no blame can rationally attach to anyone
who, in his place, should try to deceive such enemies,
morally on a level with hostile savages seeking one's life.
It is certain that the Inquisitors frequently wrung recantations by torture.[3]

What is historically certain is that Bruno was not
released, but sent on to Rome, and was kept there in
prison for seven years. He was not the sort of heretic
likely to be released. Certainly not an Atheist (he called
himself in his book-titles *Philotheus;* and his quasi-pan-
theism always lapses into theistic modes), he yet was from
first to last essentially though not professedly anti-Christian in his view of the universe. If the Church had cause
to fear any philosophic teaching, it was his. He had,
moreover, finally refused to make any fresh recantation;
and the only detailed document extant concerning his
final trial describes him as saying to his judges: "With
more fear, perchance, do you pass sentence on me than I
receive it". According to all accessible records, he was
burned alive at Rome in February, 1600, in the Field of
Flowers, near where his statue now stands.

An attempt has been made by Professor Desdouits in a
pamphlet (*La Légende Tragique de Jordano Bruno :* Paris, 1885),
to show that there is no evidence that Bruno was burned; and
an anonymous writer in the *Scottish Review* (October, 1888,
Art. II); rabidly hostile to Bruno, has maintained the same
proposition. Doubt on the subject dates from Bayle. Its main
ground is the fewness of the documentary records, of which,

---

[1] See the document in Mrs. Frith's *Life,* pp. 270-279.
[2] See Owen, pp. 285-6; Mrs. Frith, pp. 282-3.
[3] The controversy as to whether Galileo was tortured leaves it clear
that torture was common. See Dr. Parchappe, *Galilée, sa vie,* etc., 1866,
Ptie. ii, ch. 7.

further, the genuineness is now called in question. But no good reason is shown for doubting them. They are three in number. 1. The Latin letter of Gaspar Schopp (Scioppius), dated 17 February, 1600, is an eye-witness' account of the sentencing and burning of Bruno at that date. (See it in full, in the original Latin, in App. V to Mrs. Frith's *Life of Bruno*.) It was not printed till 1621, but the grounds urged for its rejection are totally inadequate, and involve assumptions, which are themselves entirely unproved, as to what Scoppius was likely to do. Finally, no intelligible reason is suggested for the forging of such a document. The remarks of Professor Des-douits on this head have no force whatever. The writer in the *Scottish Review* (p. 263, and *note*) suggests as "at least as possible an hypothesis as any other, that he [Bruno] was the author of the forged accounts of his own death". Such are the conceptions offered as substitutes for the existing view. 2. There are preserved two extracts from a Roman newsletter (*Avvisa*) of the time; one, dated February 12, 1600, commenting on the case; the other, dated February 19, relating the execution on the 17th. (See both in *S. R.*, pp. 264-5.) Against these testimonies the sole plea is that they misstate Bruno's opinions and the duration of his imprisonment! The writer in the *Scottish Review* makes the suicidal suggestion that, inasmuch as the errors as to dates occur in Schopp's letter, "the so-called Schopp was fabricated from these notices, or they from Schopp"—thus admitting that one ranked as a historical document. 3. There has been found, by a Catholic investigator, a double entry in the books of the Lay Brotherhood of *San Giovanni Decollato*, whose function was to minister to prisoners under capital sentence, giving a circumstantial account of Bruno's execution. (See it in *S. R.*, pp. 266, 269, 270.) In this case, the main entry being dated "1600. Thursday. February 16," the anonymous writer argues that "the whole thing resolves itself into a make-up", because February 16 was the Wednesday. The entry refers to the procedure of the Wednesday night and the Thursday morning; and such an error could easily occur in any case. Whatever may be one day proved, the cavils thus far count for nothing. All the while, the records as to Bruno remain in the hands of the Catholic authorities; but despite the discredit constantly cast on the Church on the score of Bruno's execution, they offer no official denial of the common statement; while they do officially admit (*S. R.*, p. 252) that on February 8 Bruno was sentenced as an "obstinate heretic", and "given over to the Secular Court". On the other hand, the episode is well

vouched; and the argument from the silence of ambassadors'
letters is so far void. No pretence is made of tracing Bruno
anywhere after February, 1600.

Bruno has been zealously blackened by Catholic
writers for the obscenity of some of his writing and the
alleged freedom of his life—piquant charges, when we
remember the life of the Papal Italy in which he was
born. LUCILIO VANINI (otherwise Julius Caesar Vanini)
the next martyr of Freethought, is open to the more
relevant charges of an inordinate vanity and some
duplicity. Figuring as a Carmelite friar, which he was
not, he came to England (1612) and professed to abjure
Catholicism,[1] gaining however nothing by the step. His
treatise *Amphitheatrum Æternæ Providentiæ* (Lyons, 1615)
is professedly directed against "Atheists, Epicureans,
Peripatetics, and Stoics," and is ostensibly quite orthodox.[2] The later *Dialogues*, while discussing many
questions of creed and science in a free fashion, no less
profess orthodoxy; and while one passage is pantheistic,[3]
they also denounce atheism, and profess faith in immortality.[4] Other passages imply doubt;[5] but it is to be
remembered that the Dialogues were penned not by
Vanini but by his disciples at Paris, he only tardily giving
his consent to their publication.[6] And whereas one
passage does avow that the author in his *Amphitheatre*
had said many things he did not believe, the context
clearly suggests that the reference was not to the main
argument but to some of its dubious facts.[7] In any case,
Vanini cannot be shown to be an Atheist; and the
attacks upon him as an immoral writer are not any better
supported.[8] The publication of the work was in fact

---

[1] Owen, *Skeptics of the Italian Renaissance*, p. 357.
[2] See it analysed by Owen, pp. 361-8.
[3] See Rousselot's French trans., 1842, p. 227.
[4] *Id.*, pp. 219-221.   [5] *E.g.* pp. 347-8.
[6] Owen, pp. 369 370. It is thus possible that the passages on the score
of which Vanini is charged with wild conceit were not written by him at all.
[7] Cp. the passages cited by Hallam, *Lit. Hist.* ii, 461, with Mr. Owen's
defence, p. 368, *note*.
[8] See Mr. Owen's vindication, pp. 371-4.

formally authorised by the Sorbonne, and it does not even appear that when he was charged with Atheism and blasphemy at Toulouse that work was at all founded on.[1] The charges rested on the testimony of a treacherous associate as to his private conversation; and if true, it only amounted to proving his pantheism, expressed in his use of the word Nature. At his trial he expressly avowed and argued for theism. Yet he was convicted[2] and burned alive (February 9, 1619) on the day of his sentence. Drawn on a hurdle, in his shirt, with a placard on his shoulders inscribed " Atheist and Blasphemer of the Name of God", he went to his death with a high heart, rejoicing, as he cried in Italian, to die like a philosopher.[3] A Catholic historian,[4] who was present, says he hardly declared that "Jesus facing death sweated with fear: I die undaunted". But before burning him they tore out his tongue by the roots; and the Christian historian is humorous over the victim's long cry of agony.[5] No martyr ever faced death with a more dauntless courage than this

> "Lonely antagonist of Destiny
> That went down scornful before many spears;"[6]

and if the man had all the faults falsely imputed to him[7] his death might shame his accusers.

Contemporary with Bruno and Vanini was SANCHEZ, a physician of Portuguese-Jewish descent, settled as a Professor at Toulouse, who contrived to publish a treatise (written 1576; printed 1581) affirming "That Nothing is Known" (*Quod Nihil Scitur*) without suffering any

---

[1] Owen, p. 395.

[2] Personal enmity on the part of the prosecuting official was commonly held to explain the trial. Owen, p. 393.

[3] *Mercure Français*, 1619, tom. v, p. 64.

[4] Gramond (Barthélemi de Grammont), *Historia Galliæ ab excessu Henri IV*, 1643, p. 209.

[5] *Id.*, p. 210. Of Vanini, as of Bruno, it is recorded that at the stake he repelled the proffered crucifix. Mr. Owen and other writers, who justly remark that he well might, overlook the once received belief that it was the official practice, with obstinate heretics, to proffer a *red-hot* crucifix, so that the victim should be sure to spurn it with open anger.

[6] Stephen Phillips, *Marpessa*.

[7] Cp. Owen, pp. 389, 391, as to the worst calumnies. It is significant that Vanini was tried *solely* for blasphemy and atheism.

molestation.   It is a formal putting of the Pyrrhonist
scepticism of Montaigne, which is thus seen to have been
to some extent current before he wrote ; but there is no
sign that Sanchez' formal statement had any philosophic
influence.   His most important aspect is as a thinker on
natural science; and here he is really corrective and
constructive rather than Pyrrhonist; his poem on the
comet of 1577 being one of the earliest rational utterances on the subject in the Christian period.[1]

But it is with GALILEO that the practical application
of the Copernican theory to life begins.   The fashion in
which Galileo's sidereal discoveries were met is typical
of the whole history of freethought : the clergy pointed
to the story of Joshua stopping the sun and moon; the
schoolmen insisted that there was no authority in
Aristotle for the new assertions, and refused to look
through the telescope[2] : with such minds the man of
science had to argue,[3] and in deference to such he had to
affect to doubt his own demonstrations.[4]   The Catholic
Reaction had built up as complete a spirit of hostility to
free science in the Church as existed among the
Protestants.   Condemned for heresy but not punished
in 1616,[5] he lived under the menace of the Jesuists until
1632, when he was again sent to Rome, tried, and sentenced to formal imprisonment (1633) for teaching the
" absurd" and " false doctrine " of the motion of the
earth and the non-motion of the sun from east to west.
In both cases the Popes, while agreeing to the verdict,
abstained from officially ratifying it,[6] so that in proceeding
to force Galileo to abjure his doctrine, the Inquisition
technically exceeded its powers—a circumstance in which
some Catholics appear to find comfort.[7]   The stories of

---

[1] Cp. Owen, *Skeptics of the French Renaissance*, pp. 631-6—a fairer and
more careful estimate than that of Hallam, *Lit. Hist. of Europe*, ii, 111-113.
[2] Karl von Gebler, *Galileo Galilei and the Roman Curia*, Eng. tr. 1879, p. 25.
[3] *Id.*, p. 54 and *passim*.   [4] *Id.*, p. 129, etc.   [5] *Id.*, p. 88.
[6] *Id.*, p. 239.
[7] *Id.*, p. 241.   For an exposure of the many perversions of the facts as
to Galileo by Catholic writers, see Parchappe, *Galilée, sa vie*, etc., 2e Partie.

his being tortured and blinded, and saying "still it moves", are myths.[1] The broken-spirited old man was in no mood so to speak : he was, moreover, in all respects save his science, an orthodox Catholic[2] : and as such not likely to defy the Church to its face. Yet he speedily got his condemned Dialogues published in Latin by the Elzevirs ; soon they appeared in English ; and in 1638 appeared his new " Dialogues of the New Sciences", the "foundation of mechanical physics ". Thenceforth he suffered no outward constraint, dying, after five years of blindness, in 1642, the year of Newton's birth. Not till 1757 did the Papacy permit other books teaching his system ; not until 1820 was permission given to treat it as true ; and not until 1835 was it withdrawn from the *Index Expurgatorius*.[3]

While modern science was thus being placed on its special basis, a continuous resistance was being made in the schools to the dogmatism which made the mutilated lore of Aristotle the sum of human wisdom. Like the ecclesiastical revolution, this had been protracted through centuries. Often in the Italian Renaissance—*e.g.*, in the case of the Greek Platonist Gemistos Plethon at Florence in the fifteenth century[4]—had the Aristotelianism of the schools been impugned ; sometimes in the spirit of religious orthodoxy,[5] sometimes not ; and in the sixteenth century the attacks became numerous and vehement.

---

[1] Gebler, pp. 249-263. The "e pur si muove" story is first heard of in 1774. As to the torture, it is to be remembered that Galileo recanted under *threat* of it. Cp. Prof. Lodge, *Pioneers of Science*, 1893, pp. 128-131.
[2] Gebler, p. 281.   [3] *Id.*, pp. 312-315.
[4] Gemistos appears to have been non-Christian in his Platonism. Burckhardt, pp. 524, 541, *notes*. As he came from Constantinople, his case affords a presumption that there were other Pagan freethinkers there in the Middle Ages.
[5] Ueberweg, ii, 12. Several leading Aristotelians in the sixteenth century were accused of atheism (Hallam, *Lit. Hist.* ii, 101-2), the old charge against the Peripatetic school. Hallam (p. 102) complains that CESALPINI of Pisa " substitutes the barren unity of pantheism for religion". Cp. Ueberweg, ii, 14. An Averroïst on some points, he believed in separate immortality. CREMONINI of Padua was one of the reputed atheists. Yet he is one of those said to have refused to look through a telescope (Lange *Hist. of Materialism*, i, 220).

Luther was a furious anti-Aristotelian.[1] Telesio influenced
Bruno in that direction.[2] Ludovicus Vives urged progress
beyond Aristotle in the spirit of naturalist science.[3] But
the typical anti-Aristotelian of the century was RAMUS
(Pierre de la Ramée, 1515-72), whose long and strenuous
battle against the ruling school at Paris brought him to
his death in the Massacre of St. Bartholomew.[4] There
was thus no special originality in the anti-scholastic
attitude of BACON,[5] whose name is in modern times
chiefly associated with the recoil from the verbalist to the
rational method in philosophy and science. As we have
seen, though presumably a Deist, he held by the compromise of "two-fold truth"; in science he confidently
rejected the doctrine of Copernicus;[6] and despite some
striking anticipations of the scientific thought of the
present century, he laid down a nearly useless method for
discovering truth.[7] There has consequently been much
dispute as to whether he in any way promoted the
scientific movement.[8] The truth seems to be that he did
notably influence some men towards rational science—in
particular Boyle[9]—and that, despite his fallacies, by his
thousand scattered sagacities he did more than any other
writer of his time to make popular the new spirit.[10] It
seems to have been the praise of his work from the
Continent[11] that first overbore the English disposition to
denounce him as an Atheist.

[1] Ueberweg, ii, 17.
[2] Bartholmèss, *Jordano Bruno*, i, 49.
[3] Lange, *Hist. of Materialism*, i, 228.
[4] Mr. Owen has a good account of him in his *French Skeptics*.
[5] In the *Advancement of Learning*, B. i (Bohn ed., p. 43) he notes how,
long before his time, the new learning had discredited the schoolmen.
[6] *Advancement*, B. iv, c. i, p. 151.   Whewell (*Hist. of Induct. Sciences*,
3d. ed., i, 296, 388) ignores this passage in discussing Bacon's view.
[7] Cp. Ellis, Gen. Pref. to his and Spedding's ed. of Bacon's *Works*, i, 38.
[8] Cp. Dean Church, *Bacon*, pp. 186-201 ; Lange, *Hist. of Materialism*, i,
236-7, and cit. from Liebig ; Brewster's *Life of Newton*, 1855, ii, 400-4 ;
Draper, *Intel. Development of Europe*, ed. 1875, ii, 258-260; Prof. Lodge,
Pioneers of Science, pp. 145-151 ; T. Martin, *Character of Bacon*, pp. 210-238.
[9] Martin, as cited, pp. 216, 227.
[10] Cp. Martin, pp. 222-3 ; Church, pp. 201-4.
[11] Osborn, as before cited, *re* Raleigh.   Martin, p. 230, citing Rawley's
Life of Bacon ; Lange, i, 238, *note*.

Like fallacies to Bacon's may be found in DESCARTES; but he in turn unquestionably laid a good part of the foundation of modern materialist philosophy and science,[1] GASSENDI largely aiding. All through his life Descartes anxiously sought to propitiate the Church;[2] Gassendi was a priest; and both were unmenaced in France under Richelieu and Mazarin; but the unusual rationalism of Descartes' method, avowedly aiming at the uprooting of all his own prejudices[3] as a first step to truth, could not escape the hostile attention of the Protestant theologians of Holland, where Descartes passed so many years of his life; and despite his constant theism he had at length to withdraw.[4] France was for the time, in fact, the most freethinking part of Europe;[5] and Descartes, though not so unsparing with his prejudices as he set out to be, was the greatest innovator in philosophy that had arisen in the Christian era. He made real scientific discoveries where Bacon only schemed an impossible road to them; and though his timorous conformities deprive him of any heroic status, it is perhaps not too much to pronounce him "the great reformer and liberator of the European intellect".[6] From Descartes, then, as regards philosophy, more than from any professed thinker of his day; but also from the other thinkers we have noted, and from the practical free-thinking of the more open-minded in general, derives the great rationalistic movement which, taking clear literary form first in the seventeenth century, has with some fluctuations broadened and deepened down to our own day.

---

[1] Buckle, ii, 77-85. Cp. Lange, i, 248, *note.*
[2] Cp. Lange, i, 248-9, *note;* Bartholmèss, *Jordano Bruno*, i, 354-5; Memoir in Garnier ed. of *Œuvres Choisies*, p. v, also pp. 6, 17, 19, 21.
[3] *Discours de la Méthode*, Pts. i, ii, iii, iv (*Œuvres Choisies*, pp. 8, 10, 11, 22, 24); *Meditation I* (*id.* pp. 73-74).
[4] Full details in Kuno Fischer's *Descartes and his School*, Eng. tr. 1890 B. i, ch. 6.
[5] Cp. Buckle, ii, 97.
[6] Buckle, ii, 82.

CHAPTER XIII.

THE ENGLISH DEISTIC MOVEMENT.

§ I.

THE propagandist literature of Deism begins with an English diplomatist, Lord HERBERT of Cherbury, the friend of Bacon, who stood in the full stream of the current freethought of England and France[1] in the first quarter of the seventeenth century. We have seen the state of upper-class and middle-class opinion in France about 1624. It was in Paris in that year that he published his *De Veritate*, after acting for many years as the English ambassador at the French court. Hitherto Deism had been represented by published answers to unpublished arguments: henceforth there slowly grows up a Deistic literature. Herbert was a powerful and audacious nobleman, with a weak king ; and he could venture on a publication which would have cost an ordinary man dear. Yet even he saw fit to publish in Latin ; and he avowed hesitations. His argument[2] is, in brief, that no professed revelation can have a decisive claim to rational acceptance; that none escapes sectarian dispute in its own field ; that as each one misses most of the human race none seems to be divine ; and that human reason can do for morals all that any one of them does. The negative generalities of Montaigne here pass into a positive anti-Christian argument ; for Herbert goes on to pronounce the doctrine of forgiveness for faith immoral. Like all pioneers, Herbert

---

[1] Jenkin Thomasius in his *Historia Atheismi* (1709) joins Herbert with Bodin as having five points in common with him.
[2] For a good analysis see Pünjer, *Hist. of the Christ. Philos. of Religion*, Eng. tr. 1887, pp. 292-9; also Noack, *Die Freidenker in der Religion*, Bern, 1853, i, 17-40; Lechler, *Geschichte des englischen Deismus*, S. 36-54.

falls into some inconsistency on his own part; the most flagrant being his claim to have had a sign from heaven— that is, a revelation—encouraging him to publish his book[1]. But his criticism is none the less telling and persuasive so far as it goes, and remains valid to this day. Nor do his later and posthumous works[2] add to it in essentials.

The next great freethinking figure in England is HOBBES (1588—1679), the most important thinker of his age, after Descartes, and hardly less influential. But the purpose of Hobbes being always substantially political and regulative, his unfaith in the current religion is only incidentally revealed in the writings in which he seeks to show the need for keeping it under monarchic control.[3] Hobbes is in fact the anti-Presbyterian or anti-Puritan philosopher; and to discredit anarchic religion in the eyes of the majority he is obliged to speak as a judicial church- man. Yet nothing is more certain than that he was no orthodox Christian; and even his professed Theism resolves itself somewhat easily into virtual agnosticism on logical pressure. Of atheism he was repeatedly accused[4] by both royalists and rebels; and his answer was forensic rather than fervent, alike as to his scripturalism, his Christianity, and his impersonal conception of Deity[5]. He expressly contends, it is true, for the principle of a Providence; but it is hard to believe that he laid any store by prayer, public or private; and it would appear that whatever thoughtful atheism there was in England in the latter part of the century, looked to him as its

---

[1] See his *Autobiography*, Murray's reprint, p. 93.

[2] *De causis errorum* (1645); *De religione laici; De religione gentilium* (1663) The two former are short appendices to the *De Veritate*.

[3] It is to be remembered that the doctrine of the supremacy of the civil power in religious matters (Erastianism) was maintained by some of the ablest men on the Parliamentary side, in particular, Selden.

[4] Reviving as he did the ancient rationalistic doctrine of the eternity of the world *(De Corpore*, Pt. II, c. viii, § 20), he gave a clear footing for Atheism as against the Judæo-Christian view.

[5] Cp. his letter to an opponent, *Considerations upon the Reputation, etc., of Thomas Hobbes*, 1680, with cc. xi and xii of *Leviathan*, and *De Corpore Politico*, Pt. ii, c. 6.

philosopher[1], in so far as it did not derive from Spinoza.
Nor could the Naturalist school desire a better scientific
definition of religion than Hobbes gave them : " Fear of
power invisible, feigned by the mind or imagined from
tales publicly allowed, RELIGION ; *not allowed,* SUPERSTI-
TION.[2]"   With him too begins the public criticism of the
Bible on literary or documentary grounds[3] ; though, as
we have seen, this had already gone far in private[4] ; and
he gave a new lead, partly as against Descartes, to a
materialistic philosophy[5].   He was, in fact, in a special
and peculiar degree for his age, a Freethinker ; and so
deep was his intellectual hostility to the clergy of all
species that he could not forego enraging those of his
own political side by his sarcasms[6].   Here he is in marked
contrast with Descartes, who dissembled his opinion about
Copernicus and Galileo for peace' sake[7] ; and was always
the close friend of the orthodox champion Mersenne down
to his death.   With the partial exception of the more
refined and graceful Pecock, Hobbes has of all English
thinkers down to his period the clearest and hardest head
for all purposes of reasoning ; and against the theologians
of his time his argumentation is as a two-edged sword.
That such a man should have been resolutely on the side
of the king in the Civil War is one of the proofs of the
essential fanaticism and arbitrariness of the orthodox
Puritans, who plotted more harm to the heresies they
disliked than was ever wreaked on themselves.   Hobbes
came near enough being clerically ostracised among the
Royalists ; but among the Puritans he would have stood a
fair chance of execution.   His hostility to such fanaticism
shaped his whole literary career, which began in 1628
with a translation of Thucydides, undertaken by way of

[1] Cp. Bentley's letter to Bernard, 1692, cited in the author's *Dynamics of
Religion*, pp. 82-3.
[2] *Leviathan*, Pt. i, c. 6.   Morley's ed. p. 34.
[3] *Leviathan*, Pt. iii, c. 33.
[4] Above, p. 280.
[5] On this see Lange, *Hist. of Materialism*, Sec. iii, c. ii.
[6] E.g., *Leviathan*, Pt. iv, c. 47.
[7] Kuno Fischer, *Descartes and his School*, pp. 232-5.

showing the dangers of democracy. Next came the *De Cive* (Paris, 1642), written when he was already an elderly man; and thenceforth the Civil War tinges his whole temper.

§ 2.

When we turn from the higher literary propaganda to the verbal and other transitory debates of the period of the Rebellion, we realise how much partial rationalism had hitherto subsisted without notice. In that immense ferment some very advanced opinions, such as quasi-Anarchism in politics[1] and anti-Scripturalism in religion, were more or less directly professed. In 1645-6 the authorities of the City of London, alarmed at the unheard-of amount of discussion, petitioned Parliament to put down all private meetings[2]; and a solemn fast was proclaimed on the score of the increase of heresies and blasphemies. Notable among the new parties were the Levellers, who insisted that the State should leave religion entirely alone, tolerating all creeds, including even atheism. The presbyterian Thomas Edwards, writing about the same time, speaks of " monsters " unheard-of theretofore, " now common among us—as denying the Scriptures, pleading for a toleration of all religions and worships, yea, for blasphemy, and denying there is a God "[3]. Among the 180 sects named by him[4] there were " Libertines ", " Antiscripturists," " Sceptics and Questionists,"[5] who held nothing save the doctrine of free speech and liberty of conscience;[6] as well as

[1] Cp. Overton's pamphlet *An Arrow against all Tyrants and Tyranny* (1646) cited in the *History of Passive Obedience since the Reformation*, 1689, i, 59; Part II of Thomas Edwards' *Gangræna*, 1646, p. 179; and Part III, pp. 14-17.
[2] *Lords Journals*, Jan. 16, 1645-6; cp. Gardiner, *Hist. of the Civil War*, ed. 1893, iii, 11.
[3] *Gangræna*, 1645 (or 1646), ep. ded. (p. 5). Cp. *Second Part of Gangræna*, 1646, pp. 178-9, and Bailie's *Letters*, ed. 1841, ii, 234-7; iii, 393.
[4] *Gangræna*, pp. 18-36.
[5] *Id.*, p. 15. As to other sects mentioned by him, cp. Tayler, p. 194.
[6] On the intense aversion of most of the Presbyterians to toleration, see Tayler, *Retrospect of Relig. Life of Eng.*, p. 136. They insisted, rightly enough, that the principle was never recognised in the Bible.

Socinians, Arians, and Anti-trinitarians ; and he speaks
of serious men who had not only abandoned their religious
beliefs but sought to persuade others to do the same.[1]
Under the rule of Cromwell, tolerant as he was of
Christian sectarianism, and even of Unitarianism as
represented by Biddle, the more advanced heresies would
get small liberty. It was only privately that such men as
Henry Marten and Thomas Chaloner, the regicides, could
avow themselves to be of " the natural religion ".[2]

But between the advance in speculation forced on by
the disputes themselves, and the usual revolt against the
theological spirit after a long and ferocious display of it,
there arose even under the Commonwealth a new temper
of secularity. On the one hand the temperamental
distaste for theology took form in the private associations
for scientific research which were the antecedents of the
Royal Society. On the other hand the spirit of religious
doubt spread widely in the middle and upper classes. A
work entitled *Dispute betwixt an Atheist and a Christian*
(1646), shows the existence not indeed of Atheists but of
Deists, though the Deist in the dialogue is a Fleming.
The discourse on Atheism in the posthumous works of
John Smith of Cambridge (d. 1652) is entirely retro-
spective ; but soon another note is sounded. As
early as 1652 the prolific Walter Charleton, who had
been physician to the king, issued a book entitled
The Darkness of Atheism expelled by the light of Nature,
wherein he asserted that England " hath of late produced and doth . . . . foster more swarms of
Atheisticall monsters . . . . then any *Age*, then any
Nation hath been infested withall ". In the following
year, Henry More, the Cambridge Platonist, published
his *Antidote against Atheism*, which assumes that the
atheistic way of thinking had lately become rather

---

[1] Cp. citations in Buckle, i, 347.
[2] Cp. Carlyle's *Cromwell*, iii, 194 ; and articles in *Nat. Dict. of Biog.*
Vaughan (*Hist. of England*, 1840, ii, 477, *note*) speaks of Walwyn and Overton
as " among the freethinkers of the times of the Commonwealth " They
were, however, Biblicists, not unbelievers.

fashionable. In 1654, again, there is noted[1] a treatise in Latin, *Atheismus Vapulans*, by William Towers, whose contents can in part be inferred from its title.[2] After the Restoration, naturally, all the new tendencies were greatly reinforced,[3] alike by the attitude of the king and his companions, all influenced by French culture, and by the general reaction against Puritanism. Whatever ways of thought had been characteristic of the Puritans were now in more or less complete disfavor; the belief in witchcraft was scouted as much on this ground as on any other[4]; and the Deistic doctrines found a ready audience among royalists[5] whose enemies had been above all things Bibliolators.

We gather this, however, still from the apologetic treatises; not from new Deistic literature; for Herbert was thus far the only professed Deistic writer in the field, and Hobbes the only other of similar influence. Baxter, writing in 1655 on *The Unreasonableness of Infidelity*, handles chiefly Anabaptists; but in his *Reasons of the Christian Religion*, issued in 1667, he thinks fit to prove the existence of God and a future state, and the truth and the supernatural character of the Christian religion. Any Deist or Atheist who took the trouble to read through it would have been rewarded by the discovery that the learned author has annihilated his own case. In his first part he affirms : " If there were no life of Retribution after this, Obedience to God would be finally men's loss and ruine : But Obedience to God shall not be finally men's loss and ruine : Ergo, there is another life.[6] " In the second part he writes that "Man's personal interest is an unfit rule and measure of God's goodness";[7]

---

[1] Fabricius, *Delectus Argumentorum et Syllabus Scriptorum*, 1725, p. 341.
[2] No copy in British Museum.
[3] Cp. Glanvil, pref. *Address* to his *Scepsis Scientifica*, Owen's ed., 1885, pp. lv-lvii ; and Henry More's *Divine Dialogues*, Dial. i, c. 32.
[4] Cp. Lecky, *Rationalism*, i, 109.
[5] There is evidence that Charles II was himself at heart a Deist. See Burnet's *History of his Own Time*, ed. 1838, pp. 61, 175, and notes.
[6] Work cited, ed. 1667, p. 136. The proposition is reiterated.
[7] *Id.*, p. 388.

and, going on to meet the new argument against Christianity based on the inference that an infinity of stars are inhabited, he writes :—

" Ask any man who knoweth these things whether all this earth be any more in comparison of the whole creation, than one Prison is to a Kingdom or Empire, or the paring of one nail . . . . in comparison of the whole body. And if God should cast off *all this earth*, and use *all the sinners* in it as they deserve, it is no more sign of a want of benignity or mercy in him than it is for a King to cast *one subject* of a *million* into a jail . . . . or than it is to *pare a man's nails*, or cut off a wart, or a hair, or to pull out a rotten aking tooth." [1]

Thus the second part absolutely destroys one of the fundamental positions of the first. No semblance of levity on the part of the freethinkers could compare with the profound intellectual insincerity of such a propaganda as this ; and Deism and Atheism continued to gain ground. A " Person of Honour " [2] produced in 1669 an essay on *The Unreasonableness of Atheism made Manifest*, which, without supplying any valid arguments, gives some explanation of the growth of unbelief in terms of the political and other antecedents [3]. Baxter in 1671 [4] complains that " infidels are grown so numerous and so audacious, and look so big and talk so loud " ; and still the process continues. In 1672 appeared *The Atheist Silenced*, by one J. M. ; in 1677 Bishop Stillingfleet's *Letter to a Deist ;* and in 1678 the massive work of Cudworth on *The True Intellectual System of the Universe,* attacking Atheism (not Deism) on philosophic lines which sadly compromised the learned author. [5] All the while, the censorship of the press, which was one of the means by which the clerical party under Charles combated heresy, prevented any new and outspoken writing on the Deistic side. The *Humane Reason* (1674) of Martin Clifford, a scholarly man-about-town who was made

---

[1] *Id.*, pp. 388-9.
[2] Said to be Sir Charles Wolseley.
[3] Cp. *Dynamics of Religion*, pp. 86-7, 89-90.
[4] Replying to Herbert's *De Veritate*, which he seems not to have read before.
[5] Cp *Dynamics of Religion*, pp. 87, 94-98, 111, 112.

Master of the Charterhouse, was guarded enough to allow of his putting his name to the second edition. But the tendency of such claims was obvious enough to inspire Boyle's *Discourse of Things above Reason* (1681), an attempt which anticipates Berkeley's argument against free-thinking mathematicians.[1]

At length, during an accidental lapse of the press laws, the Deist CHARLES BLOUNT[2] produced his *Anima Mundi* (1679), in which there is set forth a measure of cautious unbelief: following it up (1680) by his much more pronounced essay, *Great is Diana of the Ephesians*, a keen attack on the principle of revelation and clericalism in general, and his translation of Philostratus' *Life of Apollonius of Tyana*, so annotated as to be an ingenious counter-blast to the Christian claims. The book was condemned to be burnt; and only the influence of Blount's family[3], probably, prevented his being prosecuted. The propaganda, however, was resumed by Blount and his friends in small tracts, and after his suicide[4] in 1692 these were collected as the *Oracles of Reason* (1693), his collected works (without the *Apollonius*) appearing in 1695. By this time the political tension of the Revolution of 1688 was over : the Boyle Lecture had been established for the confutation of unbelievers ; and henceforth it rains refutations. A partial list will suffice to show the rate of increase of the ferment from 1692 onwards :—

1683. Dr. Rust, *Discourse on the Use of Reason in . . . Religion, against Enthusiasts and Deists.*

[1] Work cited, pp. 10, 14, 30, 55.
Concerning whom see Macaulay's *History*, ch. xix, ed. 1877, ii, 411-412—a grossly prejudiced account. Blount is there spoken of as "one of the most unscrupulous plagiaries that ever lived" and as having "stolen" from Milton, because he issued a pamphlet "By Philopatris", largely made up from the *Areopagitica*. Compare Macaulay's treatment of Locke, who adopted Dudley North's currency scheme (ch. xxi, vol. ii, p. 547).
[3] As to these, see the *Dict. of Nat. Biog.* The statements of Anthony à Wood as to the writings of Blount's father, relied on in the author's *Dynamics of Religion*, appear to be erroneous.
[4] All that is known of this tragedy is that Blount loved his deceased wife's sister and wished to marry her ; but she held it unlawful, and he was in despair. An overstrung nervous system may be diagnosed from much of his writing.

1685. *The Atheist Unmask'd.* By a Person of Honour.
1692. Bentley's *Sermons on Atheism.* (First Boyle Lecture.)
1693. *A Conference between an Atheist and his Friend.*
1694. J. Goodman, *A Winter Evening Conference between Neighbours.*
1694. Bishop Kidder, *A Demonstration of the Messias.* (Boyle Lect.).
1695. John Edwards, D.D., *Some Thoughts concerning the Several Causes and occasions of Atheism.*
1695. John Locke, *The Reasonableness of Christianity.*
1696. *An Account of the Growth of Deism in England.*
1696. *Reflections on a Pamphlet, etc.* (the last named).
1696. Sir Charles Wolseley, *The Unreasonableness of Atheism Demonstrated.* (Reprint.)
1696. Dr. Nichols' *Conference with a Theist.* Pt. I. (Answer to Blount).
1697. Stephen Nye, *A Discourse concerning Natural and Revealed Religion.*
1697. Bishop Gastrell, *The Certainty and Necessity of Religion.* (Boyle Lect.).
1697. H. Prideaux, *Discourse vindicating Christianity,* etc.
1697. C. Leslie, *A Short and Easy Method with the Deists.*
1698. Dr. J. Harris, *A Refutation of Atheistical Objections.* (Boyle Lect.)
1699. J. Bradley, *An Impartial View of the Truth of Christianity.* (Answer to Blount.)
1700. Bishop Bradford. *The Credibility of the Christian Revelation.* (Boyle Lect.)
1701. W. Scot, *Discourses concerning the wisdom and goodness of God.*
1702. *A Confutation of Atheism.*
1702. Dr. Stanhope, *The Truth and Excellency of the Christian Religion.* (Boyle Lect.)
1704. *An Antidote of Atheism* (? Reprint of More).
1705. Ed. Pelling, *Discourse concerning the existence of God.*
1705. Dr. Samuel Clarke, *A Demonstration of the Being and Attributes of God,* etc. (Boyle Lect.)
1706. *A Preservative against Atheism and Infidelity.*
1707. Dr. John Hancock, *Arguments to prove the Being of a God.* (Boyle Lect.)

Still there was no new deistic literature. Blount's famous stratagem[1] had led to the dropping of the official censorship of the press (1695 : last Act, 1693) ; but the new Blasphemy Law of 1696 served sufficiently to terrorise writers and printers for the time being. Free-thinking ideas were still mainly for private circulation. The anonymous pamphlet entitled *The Natural History of Superstition,* by the Deist John Trenchard, M.P. (1709), does not venture on overt heresy.

---

[1] Macaulay, as cited.

§ 3.

Alongside of the more popular and native influences, there were at work others, foreign and more academic; and even in professedly orthodox writers there are signs of the influence of Deistic thought. Thus even Sir Thomas Browne's *Religio Medici* (written about 1634; published 1642) has been repeatedly characterised[1] as tending to promote Deism by its tone and method; and his later treatise on *Vulgar Errors* (1645) shows much of the practical play of the new scepticism. Again, a clergyman, Joseph Glanvill, is found publishing a treatise on *The Vanity of Dogmatizing* (1661: amended in 1665 under the title *Scepsis Scientifica*), wherein, with careful reservation of religion, the spirit of critical science is applied to the ordinary processes of opinion with much energy,[2] and the "mechanical philosophy" of Descartes is embraced with zeal. At the university of Cambridge, the Cartesian philosophy was already naturalised[3]; and the influence of Glanvill, who was an active member of the Royal Society, must have carried it further. The remarkable treatise of the great anatomist Glisson, *De natura substantiæ energetica* (1672), suggests the influence of either Descartes or Gassendi.

It is stated by Mr. Leslie Stephen (*English Thought in the Eighteenth Century*, 2nd ed., i, 32) that in England the philosophy of Descartes made no distinguished disciples; and that John Norris "seems to be the only exception to the general indifference". This overlooks Glanvill, who constantly cites and applauds Descartes (*Scepsis Scientifica*, Owen's ed., pp. 20, 28, 30, 38, 43, 46, 64, 70, etc.). In Henry More's *Divine Dialogues*, again, (1668) one of the disputants is made to speak (*Dial.* i, c. 24) of "that admired wit Descartes". More had been one of the admirers in his youth; but changed his view; and his *Enchiridion Metaphysicum* (1671) is an attack on the Cartesian system as tending to atheism. The continual criticisms of Descartes on the same score throughout Cudworth's *True*

---

[1] Trinius, *Freydenker-Lexicon*, 1759, S. 120 : Pünjer, i, 291, 300-1.
[2] Glanvill, however, held stoutly by the belief in witchcraft.
[3] Owen, pref. to ed. of *Scepsis Scientifica*, p. ix.

Intellectual System, further, imply anything but "general indifference". See again Clarke's Answer to Butler's Fifth Letter (1718) as to the "universal prevalence" of Descartes' notions in natural philosophy. Cp. Berkeley, *Siris*, § 331. Of Berkeley himself, Prof. Adamson writes (*Encyc. Brit.*, iii, 589) that "Descartes and Locke .... are his real masters in speculation". The Cartesian view of the eternity and infinity of matter had further become an accepted ground for "philosophical atheists" in England before the end of the century (Molyneux, in *Familiar Letters of Locke and his Friends*, 1708, p. 46). As to the many writers who charged Descartes with promoting Atheism, see Mosheim's notes in Harrison's ed. of Cudworth's *Intellectual System*, i, 275-6.

At the same time there was growing up not a little Socinian Unitarianism. Church measures had been taken against the importation of Socinian books as early as 1640.[1] The famous Lord Falkland, slain in the Civil War, is supposed to have leant to that opinion[2]; and Chillingworth, whose *Religion of Protestants* (1637) was already a remarkable application of rational tests to ecclesiastical questions in defiance of patristic authority,[3] seems in his old age to have turned Socinian.[4] Violent attacks on the Trinity are noted among the heresies of 1646.[5] Colonel John Fry, one of the regicides, pronounced the doctrine of the Trinity "chaffie and absurd", in a book which was condemned to be burnt. In 1652 the Parliament ordered the destruction of a certain Socinian Catechism; and by 1655 the heresy seems to have become common.[6] It is now certain that Milton was substantially a Unitarian;[7] and that Locke and Newton were at heart no less so.[8] Rationalism of this tint, in fact, seems to have spread in all directions.

---

[1] Two men, Legate and Wightman, for avowing Socinian views, were burnt in 1612. Cp. J. J. Tayler, *Retrospect of the Religious Life of England*, Martineau's ed., pp. 219-220.
[2] *Id.*, p. 204.   [3] Cp. Buckle, ii, 347-351.
[4] Tayler, *Retrospect*, pp. 204-5.   [5] *Gangræna*, Pt. i, p. 38.
[6] Tayler, p. 221. As to Biddle, the chief propagandist of the sect, see pp. 221 4.
[7] Macaulay, *Essay on Milton*.
[8] Cp *Dynamics of Religion*, ch. 5.

William Penn, the Quaker, held a Unitarian attitude ;[1] and in the Church itself, sad confusion arose on the attempt being made to define the orthodox view[2] in opposition to a widely-circulated anti-Trinitarian treatise.[3] Archbishop Tillotson (d. 1694) was often accused of Socinianism; and in the next generation was smilingly spoken of by Anthony Collins as a leading Freethinker. The so-called Latitudinarians,[4] all the while aiming as they did at a non-dogmatic Christianity, served as a connecting medium for the different forms of liberal thought ; and a new element of critical disintegration was introduced by a speculative treatment of the Creation story in the *Archæologia* (1692) of Dr. T. Burnet, a professedly orthodox scholar. Its ideas were partly popularised through Blount's *Oracles of Reason*. Much more remarkable, but outside of popular discussion, were the *Evangelium medici* (1697) of Dr. B. CONNOR, wherein the Gospel miracles were explained away, on lines later associated with German rationalism, as natural phenomena; and the curious treatise of John Craig, *Theologiæ christianæ principia mathematica* (1699), wherein it is argued that all evidence grows progressively less valid in course of time; and that accordingly the Christian religion will cease to be believed about the year 3144, when probably will occur the Second Coming. Connor, when attacked, protested his orthodoxy ; Craig held successively two prebends of the Church of England ;[5] and both died unmolested, probably because they had the prudence to write in Latin.

§ 4.

There was thus an abundant soil already prepared for critical Deism when the posthumously collected works of Blount (1695) were followed by JOHN TOLAND'S

[1] Tayler, *Retrospect*, p. 226.
[2] Tayler, p. 227; *Dynamics*, pp. 113-115.
[3] This was by William Freeke, who was prosecuted and fined £500 The book was burnt by the common hangman (1693).
[4] As to whom see Tayler, ch. v, Sec. 4.
[5] See arts. in *Dict. of Nat. Biog.*

Christianity not Mysterious in 1696. This adroit treatise professedly founded on Locke's anonymous *Reasonableness of Christianity*, its young author being on terms of acquaintance with the philosopher.[1] Toland, however, lacked alike the timidity and the prudence which so safely guided Locke in his latter years; and though his argument was only a logical and outspoken extension of Locke's position, to the end of showing that there was nothing supernatural in Christianity of Locke's type, it separated him from "respectable" society in England and Ireland for the rest of his life. The book was "presented" by the Grand Juries of Middlesex and Dublin;[2] half-a-dozen answers appeared immediately; and when in 1698 he produced another, entitled *Amyntor*, showing the infirm foundation of the Christian canon, there was again a speedy crop of replies. Despite the oversights inevitable to such pioneer work, it opens the era of documentary criticism of the New Testament; and in some of his later freethinking books, as the *Nazarenus* (1718), and the *Pantheisticon* (1720), he continues to show himself in advance of his time in "opening new windows" for his mind[3]; the latter work representing in particular the influence of Spinoza. He lacked, however, the strength of character that in his day was peculiarly needed to sustain a freethinker. Much of his later life was spent abroad; and his *Letters to Serena* show him permitted to discourse to the Queen of Prussia; but his life was largely passed in poverty, cheerfully endured, with chronic help from well-to-do sympathisers.

A certain amount of evasion was forced upon Toland by the Blasphemy Law of 1695; inferentially, however, he was a thorough Deist; and the discussion over his books showed that views essentially deistic were held

---

[1] Cp. *Dynamics of Religion*, p. 129.

[2] As late as 1701, a vote for its prosecution was passed in the Lower House of Convocation. Farrar, *Crit. Hist. of Freethought*, p. 180.

[3] No credit for this is given in Mr. Leslie Stephen's notice of Toland in *English Thought in the Eighteenth Century*, i, 101-112. Compare the estimate of Lange, *History of Materialism*, i, 324-330.

even among his antagonists. One, an Irish bishop, got into trouble by setting forth a view of Deity which squared with that of Hobbes.[1] The whole of our present subject, indeed, is much complicated by the distribution of heretical views among the nominally orthodox, and of orthodox views among heretics.[2] Thus the school of Cudworth, zealous against Atheism, was less truly theistic than that of Blount[3] who, following Hobbes, pointed out that to deny to God a continual personal and providential control of human affairs was to hold to Atheism under the name of Theism.[4] Over the same crux, in Ireland, Bishop Browne and Bishop Berkeley accused each other of promoting Atheism; and Archbishop King was embroiled in the dispute.[5] Locke's ideal of a practical and undogmatic Christianity, again, was practically that of Hobbes[6] and of the Rev. Arthur Bury, whose *Naked Gospel* (1690) was burned as heretical. On the other hand, the theistic Descartes had laid down a "mechanical" theory of the universe which perfectly comported with Atheism, and partly promoted that way of thinking; and the Church included Cartesians and Cudworthians, Socinians and Deists. Each group, further, had inner differences as to free-will[7] and Providence; and the theistic schools of Newton, Clarke, and Leibnitz rejected each other's philosophies as well as that of Descartes. It can hardly be doubted that if educated England could have been

---

[1] Cp. Mr. Stephen, as cited, p. 115.

[2] "The Christianity of many writers consisted simply in expressing deist opinions in the old-fashioned phraseology" (Stephen, i, 91).

[3] Cp. Pünjer, *Christ. Philos. of Religion,* pp. 289-290; and *Dynamics of Religion,* pp. 94-98. Mr. Morley's reference to "the godless Deism of the English school" (*Voltaire,* 4th ed., p. 69) is a serious misrepresentation of the case.

[4] Macaulay's description of Blount as an atheist is thus doubly dishonest.

[5] Stephen, *English Thought,* i, 114-118.

[6] Cp. *Dynamics of Religion,* p. 122.

[7] Mr. Stephen (i, 33) makes the surprising statement that a "dogmatic assertion of Free-will became a mark of the whole deist and semi-deist school". On the contrary, Hobbes and Anthony Collins wrote with uncommon power against the conception of Free-Will; and had many disciples on that head.

polled in 1710, under no restraints from economic, social, and legal pressure, some form of rationalism inconsistent with Christianity would have been found to be fully as common as orthodoxy. It was, in fact, the various pressures under notice that determined the outward fortunes of belief and unbelief, and have substantially determined them since. When the devout Whiston was deposed from his professorship for his Arianism, and the unbelieving Saunderson was put in his place, the lesson was learned that outward conformity was the sufficient way to income.[1]

Hard as it was, however, to kick against the pricks of law and prejudice, it is clear that many in the upper and middle classes privately did so. The clerical and the new popular literature of the time prove this abundantly. In the *Tatler* and its successors,[2] the decorous Addison and the indecorous Steele, neither of them a competent thinker, frigidly or furiously asperse the new tribe of Freethinkers; the evangelically pious Berkeley and the extremely unevangelical Swift rival each other in the malice of their attacks on those who rejected their creed. Berkeley, a man of philosophic genius but intense prepossessions, maintained Christianity on grounds which are the negation of philosophy.[3] Swift, the genius of neurotic misanthropy, fought venomously for the creed of salvation. And still the Deists multiplied. In the Earl of SHAFTESBURY[4] they had a satirist with a finer and keener weapon than was wielded by either Steele or Addison, and a much better temper than was owned by Swift or Berkeley. He did not venture to parade his

---

[1] Cp. the pamphlet by "A Presbyter of the Church of England", attributed to Bishop Hare, cited in *Dynamics of Religion*, pp. 177-8.

[2] *Tatler*, Nos. 12, 111, 135; *Spectator*, Nos. 234, 381, 389, 599; *Guardian*, Nos. 3, 9, 27, 35, 39, 55, 62, 70, 77, 83, 88, 126, 130, 169. Most of the *Guardian* papers cited are by Berkeley. They are extremely virulent; but Steele's run them hard.

[3] *Analyst*, Queries 60 and 62: *Defence of Freethinking in Mathematics*, §§ 5, 6, 50. Cp. *Dynamics of Religion*, pp. 141-2.

[4] The essays in the *Characteristics* appeared between 1708 and 1711, being collected in the latter year, at Shaftesbury's death.

unbelief: to do so was positively dangerous; but his thrusts at faith left little doubt as to his theory.

§ 5.

Deism had been thus made in a manner fashionable when, in 1713, ANTHONY COLLINS began a new controversial era by his *Discourse of Freethinking*. He had previously published an *Essay Concerning the Use of Reason* (1707); carried on a discussion with Clarke on the question of the immateriality of the soul; and issued treatises entitled *Priestcraft in Perfection* (1709, dealing with the history of the Thirty-nine Articles) and *A Vindication of the Divine Attributes* (1710), exposing the Hobbesian Theism of Archbishop King on lines followed twenty years later by Berkeley in his *Minute Philosopher*. But none of these works aroused such a tumult as the *Discourse of Freethinking*. To the reader of to-day, it is no very aggressive performance: the writer was a man of imperturbable amenity and genuine kindliness of nature; and his style is the completest possible contrast to that of the furious replies it elicited. It was to Collins that Locke wrote, in 1703: " Believe it, my good friend, to love truth for truth's sake is the principal part of human perfection in this world, and the seed-plot of all other virtues ; and if I mistake not, you have as much of it as I ever met with in anybody ". The *Discourse* does no discredit to this uncommon encomium, being a plea for the conditions under which alone truth can be prosperously studied, and the habits of mind which alone can attain it. Of the many replies, the most notorious is that of Bentley writing as *Phileleutherus Lipsiensis*, a performance which, on the strength of its author's reputation for scholarship, has been uncritically applauded by not a few professed critics. It is in reality pre-eminent only for insolence and bad faith, the latter quality being sometimes complicated by lapses of scholarship hardly credible on its author's part.[1] It was Bentley's cue to represent

[1] See the details in *Dynamics of Religion*, ch. vii.

Collins as an Atheist, though he was a very pronounced
Deist; and in the first uproar Collins had to fly to Holland
to avoid arrest. But Deism was too general to permit
of such a representative being exiled; and he returned to
study quietly, leaving Bentley's vituperation and pre-
varication unanswered, with the other attacks made upon
him. In 1715 he published his brief but masterly
Inquiry concerning Human Liberty—anonymous like all
his works—which remains unsurpassed in its essentials
as a statement of the case for Determinism.

Not till 1723 did he publish his next work, *A Discourse
of the Grounds and Reasons of the Christian Religion*, a
weighty attack on the argument from prophecy, to which
the replies numbered thirty-five; on which followed in
1727 his *Scheme of Literal Prophecy Considered*, a reply to
criticisms. The movement was now in full flood, the
acute Mandeville having issued in 1720 his *Free Thoughts
on Religion*, and in 1723 a freshly expanded edition of his
Fable of the Bees; while the half-deranged ex-clergyman,
THOMAS WOOLSTON, contributed in 1726-28 his rather
ribald *Discourses on Miracles*, of which Voltaire, who was in
England in 1728, tells that thirty thousand copies were
sold, while sixty pamphlets were written in opposition.
With MATTHEW TINDAL'S *Christianity as old as Creation*
(1730) the excitement seems to have reached high-water
mark, that work eliciting over a hundred-and-fifty replies.
Tindal, like Collins, wrote anonymously, and so escaped
prosecution, dying in 1733, when the second part of his
book, left ready for publication, was deliberately destroyed
by Bishop Gibson, into whose hands it came. Woolston,
who put his name to his books, paid the penalty of
imprisonment for the rest of his life (d. 1733), being
unable to pay a fine of £100. The punishment was the
measure of the anger felt at the continuous advance of
deistic opinions. Berkeley, in 1721, had complained
bitterly[1] of the general indifference to religion, which his

---

[1] *Essay towards preventing the Ruin of Great Britain.*

writings had done nothing to alter; and in 1736 he angrily demanded that blasphemy should be punished like high treason.[1]

In point of fact there was little overt Atheism, whether by reason of the special odium attaching to that way of thinking, or of a real production of theistic belief by the concurrence of the deistic propaganda on this head with that of the clergy, themselves in so many cases Deists.[2] Collins observed that nobody had doubted the existence of God until the Boyle lecturers began to prove it; but though they probably promoted Deism, and roused much discussion on the theistic issue, the stress of the apologetic literature passed from the theme of Atheism to that of Deism. There was, in fact, an arrest of the higher philosophic thought under the stress of the concrete disputes over ethics, miracles, prophecy, and politics; and a habit of taking Deity for granted became normal, with the result that when the weak point was pressed upon by Law and Butler there was a sense of blankness on both sides. But among men theistically inclined, the argument of Tindal against revelationism was extremely telling, and it had more literary impressiveness than any writing on the orthodox side before Butler. By this time the philosophic influence of Spinoza had spread among the studious class, greatly reinforcing the Deistic movement; so that in 1732 Berkeley, who ranked him among "weak and wicked writers", described him as "the great leader of our modern infidels ".[3] Among the Deists of the upper

---

[1] *Id.* Cp. *Discourse to Magistrates.* Berkeley's account of a blasphemous secret society calling themselves "blasters" remains unsupported.

[2] Complaint to this effect was made by orthodox writers. *E.g.*, the Scotch Professor Halyburton complains that in many sermons in his day "Heathen Morality has been substituted in the room of *Gospel Holiness.* And Ethicks by some have been preached instead of the *Gospel* of Christ." *Natural Religion Insufficient* (Edinburgh), 1714, p. 25. Cp. pp. 23, 26-27, 59, etc.

[3] *Minute Philosopher,* § 29. Mr. Stephen's opinion (i, 33) that "few of the deists, probably," read Spinoza, is thus outweighed. Cp. Halyburton, *Natural Religion Insufficient,* Edinburgh, 1714, p. 31, as to the "great vogue amongst our young Gentry and Students" of Hobbes, Spinoza, and others.

classes was the young William Pitt, afterwards Lord Chatham, if, as has been alleged, it was he who in 1733, two years before he entered Parliament, contributed to the *London Journal* a " Letter on Superstition ", the work of a pronounced freethinker.[1] On the other hand such Deistic writing as that of THOMAS CHUBB, an energetic tallow-chandler of Salisbury (d. 1747), brought an ethical " Christian rationalism" within the range of the unscholarly many; while THOMAS MORGAN (d. 1741), a physician, began to sketch a rationalistic theory of Christian origins, besides putting the critical case with new completeness. The main line of Deistic propaganda, as apart from the essays and treatises of Hume and the posthumous works of Bolingbroke, ends with DODWELL's ironical essay, *Christianity not Founded on Argument* (1743), of which the thesis might have been seriously supported by reference to the intellectual history of the preceding thirty years, wherein much argument had certainly failed to establish the reigning creed or to discredit the unbelievers.

> Currency has been given to a misconception of intellectual history by the authoritative statement that in the deistic con-troversy " all that was intellectually venerable in England " appeared " on the side of Christianity " (Stephen, *English Thought in the Eighteenth Century*, i, 86). In the first place, all the writing on the other side was done under peril of Blasphemy Laws, and under menace of all the calumny and ostracism that in Christian society follow on advanced heresy; while the orthodox side could draw on the entire clerical profession, over ten thousand strong, and trained for and pledged to defence of the faith. Yet when all is said, the ordinary list of Deists amply suffices to disprove Mr. Stephen's phrase. His " intellectually venerable " list runs : Bentley, Locke, Berkeley, Clarke, Butler, Waterland, Warburton, Sherlock, Gibson, Conybeare, Smalbroke, Leslie, Law, Leland, Lardner, Foster, Doddridge, Lyttelton, Barrington, Addison, Pope, Swift. He might have added Newton and Boyle. Sykes,[2] Balguy, Stebbing,

---

[1] The question remains obscure. Cp. the Letter cited, reprinted at end of Carver's 1830 ed. of Paine's Works (New York) ; F. Thackeray's *Life of Chatham*, ii, 405 ; and Chatham's " scalping-knife " speech.

[2] Really an abler man than half of the others in Mr. Stephen's list.

and a " host of others " he declares to be " now for the most
part as much forgotten as their victims " ; Young and Black-
more he admits to be in similar case. All told, the list includes
only three or four men of any permanent interest as thinkers,
apart from Newton ; and only three or four more important as
writers. To speak of Waterland,[1] Warburton,[2] Smalbroke,[3]
Sherlock, Leslie, and half-a-dozen more as " intellectually
venerable " seems grotesque : even Bentley is a strange subject
for veneration.

On the other hand the list of " the despised Deists ", who
" make but a poor show when compared with this imposing
list ", runs thus :— Herbert, Hobbes, Blount, Halley (well
known to be an unbeliever, though he did not write on the
subject), Toland, Shaftesbury, Collins, Mandeville, Tindal,
Chubb, Morgan, Dodwell, Middleton, Hume, Bolingbroke,
Gibbon. It would be interesting to know on what principles
this group is excluded from the intellectual veneration so
liberally allotted to the other. It is nothing to the purpose
that Shaftesbury and Mandeville wrote " covertly " and " indirectly ". The law and the conditions compelled them to do
so. It is still more beside the case to say that " Hume can
scarcely be reckoned among the deists. He is already [when ?]
emerging into a higher atmosphere." ·Hume wrote emphatically as a Deist ; and only in his posthumous Dialogues did he
pass on to the atheistic position. At no time, moreover, was
he " on the side of Christianity ". On the other hand, Locke
and Clarke and Pope were clearly " emerging into a higher
atmosphere " than Christianity ; since Locke is commonly
reckoned by the culture-historians, and even by Mr. Stephen,
as making for Deism ; Pope was the pupil of Bolingbroke, and
wrote as such ; and Clarke was shunned as an Arian. Newton,
again, was a Unitarian, and Leibnitz accused his system of
making for irreligion. It would be interesting to know,
further, who are the " forgotten victims " of Balguy and the
rest. The main line of Deists is pretty well remembered.
And if we pair off Hume against Berkeley, Hobbes against
Locke, Middleton (as historical critic) against Bentley, Shaftesbury against Addison, Mandeville against Swift, Bolingbroke
against Butler, Collins against Clarke, Herbert against Lyttel-
ton, Tindal against Waterland, and Gibbon against—shall we

---

[1] Whose doctrine Mr. Stephen elsewhere (p. 258) pronounces a " brutal
theology which gloried in trampling on the best instincts of its opponents ",
and a " most unlovely product of eighteenth-century speculation ".
[2] Of Warburton Mr. Stephen writes elsewhere (p. 353) that " this
colossus was built up of rubbish ". See p. 352 for samples.
[3] As to whose " senile incompetence " see same vol., p. 234.

say ?—Warburton, it hardly appears that the overplus of merit goes so overwhelmingly as Mr. Stephen alleges, even if we leave Newton, with brain unhinged, standing against Halley. The statement that the deists " are but a ragged regiment " and that " in speculative ability most of them were children by the side of their ablest antagonists", is simply unintelligible unless the names of all the ablest deists are left out. Locke, be it remembered, did not live to meet the main deistic attack on Christianity; and Mr. Stephen admits the weakness of his pro-Christian performance.

The bases of Mr. Stephen's verdict may be tested by his remarks that " Collins, a *respectable country gentleman*, showed considerable acuteness; Toland, *a poor denizen of Grub Street*, and Tindal, a Fellow of All Souls, made a *certain* display of learning, and succeeded in planting some effective arguments ". To write thus is surely to concede too much to the standards of the religious press. Elsewhere (pp. 217-227) Mr. Stephen admits that Collins had the best of the argument against his " venerable " opponents on Prophecy; and Professor Huxley credits him with equal success in the argument with Clarke. The work of Collins on *Human Liberty*, praised by a whole series of students and experts, is philosophically as durable as any portion of Locke, whose chosen friend and trustee he was, and who did not live to meet his anti-Biblical arguments; Tindal, who had also won Locke's high praise by his political essays, profoundly influenced such a student as Laukhard (Lechler, S. 451); and Toland, whom even Mr. Farrar (Bampton Lectures, p. 179) admitted to possess " much originality and learning ", has struck Lange as a notable thinker, though he *was* a poor man. Leibnitz, who answered him, praises his acuteness, as does Pusey, who further admits the uncommon ability of Morgan and Collins (*Historical Enquiry into German Rationalism*, 1828, p. 126). It is time that the conventional English standards in these matters should be rectified.

§ 6.

It is commonly assumed that after Chubb and Morgan the Deistic movement in England " decayed ", or " passed into scepticism " with Hume ; and that the decay was mainly owing to the persuasive effect of Bishop Butler's *Analogy* (1736).[1] This appears to be a complete misconception, arising out of the habit of looking to the

---

[1] Sir James Stephen, *Horæ Sabbaticæ*, ii, 281 ; Lechler, S. 451.

succession of books without considering the accompanying social conditions. Butler's book had very little influence till long after his death[1]; being indeed very ill-fitted to turn contemporary deists to Christianity. Its main argument being that Natural Religion is open to the same objections as Revealed, on the score of the inconsistency of Nature with Divine Benevolence, and that we must be guided in opinion as in conduct by Probability, a Mohammedan could as well use the theorem for the Koran as could a Christian for the Bible; and the argument against the Justice of Nature tended logically to Atheism. But the deists had left to them the resource of our modern theists—that of surmising a Beneficence above human comprehension; and it is clear that if Butler made any converts they must have been of a very unenthusiastic kind. On the other hand, even deists who were affected by the plea that the Bible need not be more consistent and satisfactory than Nature, could find refuge in Unitarianism, a creed which, as industriously propounded by Priestley[2] in the latter half of the century, made a numerical progress out of all proportion to that of orthodoxy. The argument of William Law,[3] again, which insisted on the irreconcilability of the course of things with human reason, and called for an abject submission to revelation, could only appeal to minds already thus prostrate. Both his and Butler's methods, in fact, prepared the way for HUME.

Yet it is not to be supposed that Hume's philosophy, in so far as it was strictly sceptical—that is, suspensory —drew away Deists from their former attitude of confidence to one of absolute doubt. Nor did Hume ever aim at such a result. What he did was to countermine the mines of Berkeley and others, who, finding their supra-rational dogmas set aside by rationalism, deistic

---

[1] Cp. *Dynamics of Religion*, ch. viii.

[2] In criticising whom, Mr. Stephen barely notices his scientific work, but dwells much on his religious fallacies, a course which would make short work of the fame of Newton.

[3] See it set forth by Mr. Stephen, i, 158-163.

or atheistic, sought to discredit at once deistic and atheistic philosophies based on study of the external world, and to establish their creed anew on the basis of their subjective consciousness. As against that method, Hume showed the futility of all apriorism alike; but, knowing that mere scepticism is practically null in life, he counted on leaving the ground cleared for experiential rationalism.

And he did, in so far as he was read. His essay, *Of Miracles* (with the rest of the *Inquiries* of 1748-51, which recast his early *Treatise of Human Nature*, 1739), posits a principle valid against all supernaturalism whatever; while his *Natural History of Religion* (1757) though affirming Deism, rejected the theory of a primordial monotheism, and laid the basis of the science of Comparative Hierology.[1] Finally, his posthumous *Dialogues Concerning Natural Religion* (1779) admit, though indirectly, the untenableness of Deism, and fall back decisively upon the atheistic or agnostic position. Like Descartes, he lacked the heroic fibre; but like him he recast philosophy for modern Europe; and its subsequent course is but a development of or a reaction against his work. It is remarkable that this development of opinion took place in that part of the British Islands where religious fanaticism had gone furthest, and speech and thought were socially least free. Freethought in Scotland before the latter part of the eighteenth century existed only as a thing furtive and accursed. Even in 1697 the clergy had actually succeeded in getting a lad of eighteen, Thomas Aikenhead, hanged for professing Deism in general, and in particular for calling the Old Testament " Ezra's Fables ", and denying the divinity of Jesus, though he broke down and pleaded

---

[1] The general reader should take note that in A. Murray's issue of Hume's Essays (now or lately published by Ward, Lock and Co.), which omits altogether the essays on Miracles and a Future State, the *Natural History of Religion* is much mutilated, though the book professes to be a verbatim reprint.

penitence.[1] At this date the clergy were hounding on the Privy Council to new activity in trying witches; and all works of supposed heretical tendency imported from England were confiscated in the Edinburgh shops, among them being Thomas Burnet's *Sacred Theory of the Earth.*[2] Scottish intellectual development had in fact been arrested by the Reformation, so that save for Napier's *Logarithms* (1614) and such a political treatise as Rutherford's *Lex Rex* (1644), the nation of Dunbar and Lyndsay produced for two centuries no secular literature of the least value, and not even a theology of any enduring interest. Deism, accordingly, seems in the latter part of the seventeenth and the early part of the eighteenth century to have made fully as much progress in Scotland as in England[3]; and the bigoted clergy could offer little intellectual resistance. The very aridity of the Presbyterian life[4] intensified the recoil among the educated classes to philosophical and historical interests, leading to the performances of Hume, Smith, Robertson, Ferguson and yet others, all rationalists in method and sociologists in their interests.

While, however, this interest in ideas grew up in Scotland, so recently hide-bound in theology, there went

[1] Macaulay, *History*, ch. xxii; student's ed. ii, 620-1; Burton, *History of Scotland*, viii, 76-77. Aikenhead seems to have been a boy of unusual capacity, even by the bullying account of Macaulay. See his arguments on the bases of ethics, set forth in his "dying speech", as cited by Halyburton, *Natural Religion Insufficient*, 1714, pp. 119-123, 131.

[2] Macaulay, as cited.

[3] See in the posthumous work of Professor Halyburton of St. Andrews, *Natural Religion Insufficient*, Edinburgh, 1714, Epist. of Recom.; pref., pp. 25, 27, and pp. 8, 15, 19, 23, 31, etc. Halyburton's treatise is interesting as showing the psychological state of argumentative Scotch orthodoxy in his day. He professes to repel the Deistical argument throughout by reason; he follows Huet and concurs with Berkeley in contending that mathematics involve anti-rational assumptions; and he takes entire satisfaction in the execution of the lad Aikenhead for Deism. Yet in a second treatise, *An Essay Concerning the Nature of Faith*, he contends, as against Locke and the "Rationalists", that the power to believe in the word of God is "expressly deny'd to man in his natural estate" and is a supernatural gift. Thus the Calvinists, like Baxter, were at bottom absolutely insincere in their profession to act upon reason, while insolently charging insincerity on others.

[4] This all the while was rent by barren theological controversy. See *A Sober Enquiry into the Grounds of the Present Differences in the Church of Scotland*, 1723.

on in England a contrary diversion of interest from ideas as such to political and mercantile interests. At the same time, the pillory and the jail were used against any new deistic writers who spoke out plainly. JACOB ILIVE, for denying in a pamphlet (1753) the truth of revelation, was pilloried thrice, and sent to hard labor for three years; and Peter Annet, aged 70, and of unbalanced mind, was pilloried twice and set to a year's hard labor for ridiculing the Pentateuch. That there should be a dearth of new deistic treatises under these circumstances was not surprising. Yet other freethinking treatises did appear at intervals [1]; and in 1756 the Arian Bishop Clayton proposed in the Irish House of Lords to drop the Nicene and Athanasian creeds. He in turn was about to be prosecuted for the heresies of his *Vindication of the Old and New Testaments* (1757) when he died. There was at the same time, however, a change in the prevailing mental life. The middle and latter part of the eighteenth century is the period of the rise of (1) the new machine industries, and (2) the new imperialistic policy of Chatham.[2] Both alike withdrew men from problems of mere belief, whether theo-

---

[1] The following (save Evanson) are overlooked in Mr. Stephen's survey:—
1736. Henry Coventry. *Philemon to Hydaspes* (on False Religion).
1739—1746. Parvish, Samuel. *An Inquiry into the Jewish and Christian Revelation.*
1746. *Essay on Natural Religion.* Attributed to Dryden.
1746. *Deism fairly stated and fully vindicated*, etc. Anon.
1749. Cooper, J. G. *Life of Socrates.*
1750. Dove, John. *A Creed founded on Truth and Common Sense.*
1765. Dudgeon, W. *Philosophical Works.* Privately printed—? at Edinburgh.
1768. *The Pillars of Priestcraft and orthodoxy shaken.* Four vols. of free-
(1st ed.   thinking pamphlets, collected (and some written) by Thomas
1752).   Gordon, formerly secretary to Trenchard. Edited by R. Barron.
1772. Evanson, E. *The Doctrines of a Trinity and the Incarnation.*
1777.   „   „   *Letter to Bishop Hurd.*
1781. Nicholson, W. *The Doubts of the Infidels.* Re-published by Carlile.
1782. Turner, W. *Ans. to Dr. Priestley's Letters to a Philosophical Unbeliever.*
1785. Toulmin, Dr. Joshua.* *The Antiquity and Duration of the World.*
1789.   „   „   *The Eternity of the Universe.*
1789. Cooper, Dr. T. *Tracts, Ethical, Theological and Political.*
1792. Evanson, E. *The Dissonance of the Four Evangelists.*
1795. O'Keefe, Dr. J. A. *On the Progress of the Human Understanding.*
1797. Davies, J. C. *The Scripturian's Creed.* Prosecuted and imprisoned.
[2] Cp. *Dynamics of Religion*, pp. 175-6.
* Unitarian, biographer of Socinus. Much molested in 1791.

logical or scientific. That the reaction was not one of mere fatigue over Deism is proved by the flagrant decadence of mathematical and astronomical science after Newton, the primacy in these branches being transferred to France.[1] It was a general diversion of energy, analogous to what had previously taken place in France in the reign of Louis XIV. As the poet Gray, himself orthodox, put the case in 1754, "the mode of freethinking has given place to the mode of not thinking at all".[2] In Hume's opinion the general pitch of national intelligence south of the Tweed was lowered. This state of things of course was favorable to religious revival; but what took place was rather a new growth of emotional pietism in the new industrial masses (the population being now on a rapid increase), under the ministry of the Wesleys and Whitfield, and a further growth of similar religion in the new provincial middle-class that grew up on the industrial basis. The universities all the while were at the lowest ebb of culture, but officially rabid against philosophic freethinking.[3] Instead of being destroyed by the clerical defence, the Deistic movement had really penetrated the Church, which was become as rationalistic in its methods as its function would permit, aud the educated classes, which had arrived at a state of compromise. In short, the Deistic movement had done what it lay in it to do. The old evangelical or pietistic view of life was discredited among instructed people, and in this sense it was Christianity that had "decayed".

The next intellectual step in natural course would have been a revision of the deistic assumptions, in so far, that is, as certain positive assumptions were common to the Deists. But, as we have seen, certain fresh issues were raised as among the Deists themselves. In addition to those above noted, there was the profoundly important

---

[1] Brewster, *Memoirs of Newton*, 1855, vol. i, ch. xiii.

[2] Letter xxxi, in Mason's *Memoir*.

[3] Compare the verdicts of Gibbon in his *Autobiography*; and of Adam Smith, *Wealth of Nations*, B. v, ch. i, art. 2; and see the memoirs of Smith in 1831 ed. and McCulloch's ed., and Rae's *Life of Adam Smith*, 1895, p. 24.

one as to ethics. Shaftesbury, who rejected the religious basis, held a creed of optimism ; and this optimism was assailed by Mandeville, who in consequence was opposed as warmly by the deist Hutcheson and others as by Law and Berkeley.   To grapple with this problem, and with the underlying cosmic problem, there was needed at least as much general mental activity as went to the antecedent discussion ; and in the terms of the case the activity of the nation was otherwise directed, and was further affected by persecuting laws.   The negative process, the impeach-ment of Christian supernaturalism, had been accomplished so far as the current arguments went.   Toland. and Collins had fought the battle of free discussion, forcing ratiocination on the Church ; Collins had shaken the creed of prophecy; Shaftesbury had impugned the religious conception of morals ; and Mandeville had done so more profoundly, laying the foundations of scientific utilitarianism.[1]   Woolston, following up Collins, had shaken the faith in New Testament miracles ; and Hume had laid down the philosophic principle which rebuts all attempts to prove miracles as such.[2]   Tindal had clinched the case for "natural" theism as against revelationism ; and the later Deists, notably Morgan, had to some extent combined these results.[3]   This literature was generally distributed ; and so far the case had been thrashed out.

For the rest, though the due philosophic progress was arrested, deistic opinion was far from dying out.[4]   It simply remained in the background of current discussion, the more concrete interests and the new imaginative

[1] Cp. essay on *The Fable of the Bees* in the author's *Essays towards a Critical Method*, 1889.

[2] As against the objections of Mr. Lang, see the author's art. in *Reformer*, Jan. and Feb., 1899.

[3] Cp. the summary of Farrar, *Critical History of Freethought*, 1862, pp. 177-8, which is founded on that of Pusey's early *Historical Enquiry* con-cerning the causes of German Rationalism, pp. 124, 126.

[4] The German Dr. G. W. Alberti, writing in 1752 (*Briefe betreffende. . . Religion . . . . in Gross - Brittanien*, Hannover, S. 440) cites the *British Magazine* as stating in 1749 that half the educated people in England were then Deists ; and he, after full enquiry, agrees.

literature occupying the foreground. The literary status of Deism after 1750 was really higher than ever. It was now represented by Hume ; by ADAM SMITH (*Moral Sentiments*, 1759); by the scholarship of CONYERS MIDDLETON, whose *Letter from Rome* (1729) and *Free Inquiry* into the miracles of post-apostolic Christianity (1749) laid fresh basis for the comparative method, and certainly made for unbelief[1]; by the posthumous works (1754) of BOLING-BROKE, who, though more of a debater than a thinker, debated with masterly power, in a style unmatched for harmony and energetic grace, which had already won him a great literary prestige ;[2] and last but not least, by the new writings of VOLTAIRE, who had assimilated the whole propaganda of English Deism, and gave it out anew with a wit and brilliancy hitherto unknown in argumentative and critical literature. The freethinking of the third quarter of the century, though kept secondary to more pressing questions, was thus at least as deeply rooted and as convinced as that of the first quarter.

On this state of things supervened the massive performance of the greatest historical writer England had yet produced. GIBBON, educated not by Oxford but by the recent scholarly literature of France, had as a mere boy seen, on reading Bossuet, the theoretic weakness of Protestantism, and had straightway professed Romanism. Shaken as to that by a skilled Swiss Protestant, he speedily became a rationalist pure and simple, with as little of the dregs of Deism in him as any writer of his age ; and his great work begins or rather signalises (since Hume and Robertson preceded him) a new era of historical writing, not merely by its sociological treatment of the rise of Christianity, but by its absolutely anti-theological handling of all things.

---

[1] See Mr. Stephen's account, i, 253-272, and *Dynamics of Religion*, p. 179, as to Middleton's work and his treatment at the hands of the theologians.

[2] His influence, commonly belittled, was probably much greater than writers like Johnson would admit ; and it went deep. Voltaire tells (*Dieu et les Hommes*, ch. 39) that he had known some young pupils of Bolingbroke who altogether denied the historic actuality of the Gospel Jesus.

In a world which was eagerly reading Gibbon[1] and Voltaire, there was a peculiar absurdity in Burke's famous question (17   ) as to "Who now reads Bolingbroke" and the rest of the older Deists. The fashionable world was actually reading Bolingbroke even then[2]; and the work of the older Deists was being done with new incisiveness and massiveness by their successors.[3] Beside Burke in Parliament was the Prime Minister, WILLIAM PITT the younger, a high agnostic Deist. One of the most popular writers of the day was ERASMUS DARWIN, a Deist, whose *Zoonomia* (1794) brought on him the charge of atheism. Even in rural Scotland, the vogue of the poetry of BURNS, who was substantially a Deist, told of germinal doubt. A seeming justice was given to Burke's phrase by the undoubted reaction which took place immediately afterwards. In the vast panic which followed on the French Revolution, the multitude of mediocre minds in the middle and upper classes, formerly deistic or indifferent, took fright at unbelief as something now visibly connected with democracy and regicide; and orthodoxy became fashionable on political grounds just as scepticism had become fashionable at the Restoration. Class interest and political prejudice wrought in both cases alike; only in opposite directions. Democracy was no longer Bibliolatrous, so aristocracy was fain to become so. But even in the height of the revolutionary tumult, and while Burke was blustering about the disappearance of unbelief, THOMAS PAINE was laying deep and wide the English foundations of a new democratic Freethought; and the upper-class reaction in

---

[1] Cp. Bishop Watson's *Apology for Christianity* (1776) as to the vogue of unbelief at that date. (*Two Apologies*, ed. 1806, p. 121. Cp. pp. 179, 399.)

[2] See Hannah More's letter of April, 1777, in her *Life*, abridged 16mo. ed., p. 36.

[3] The essays of Hume, including the *Dialogues concerning Natural Religion* (1779) were now circulated in repeated editions. Mr. Rae, in his valuable *Life of Adam Smith*, p. 311, cites a German observer, Wendeborn, as writing in 1785 that the *Dialogues*, though a good deal discussed in Germany, had made no sensation in England, and were at that date entirely forgotten. But a second edition had been called for in 1779, and they were added to a fresh edition of the essays in 1788.

the nature of the case was doomed to impermanency, though it was to arrest English intellectual progress for over a generation. The French Revolution had re-introduced Freethought as a vital issue, even in causing it to be banned as a danger.[1]

Whether or not the elder Pitt was a Deist, the younger gave very plain signs of being at least no more. Mr. Gladstone (*Studies subsidiary to the Works of Bishop Butler*, ed. 1896, pp. 30-33) has sought to discredit the recorded testimony of Wilberforce (*Life of Wilberforce*, 1838, i, 98) that Pitt told him "Bishop Butler's work raised in his mind more doubts than it had answered". Mr. Gladstone points to another passage in Wilberforce's diary which states that Pitt "commended Butler's *Analogy*" (*Life*, i, 90). But the context shows that Pitt had commended the book for the express purpose of turning Wilberforce's mind from its evangelical bias. Wilberforce was never a Deist, and the purpose accordingly could not have been to make him orthodox. The two testimonies are thus perfectly consistent; especially when we note the further statement credibly reported to have been made by Wilberforce (*Life*, i, 95), that Pitt later "*tried to reason me out of my convictions*". We have further the emphatic declaration of Pitt's niece, Lady Hester Stanhope, that he "never went to church in his life . . . never even talked about religion" (*Memoirs of Lady Hester Stanhope*, 1845, iii, 166-7). This was said in emphatic denial of the genuineness of the unctuous death-bed speech put in Pitt's mouth by Gifford. Lady Hester's high veracity is accredited by her physician (*Travels of Lady Hester Stanhope*, 1846, i, pref. p. 11). No such character can be given to the conventional English biography of the period.

---

[1] That Freethought at the end of the century was rather driven inwards and downwards than expelled is made clear by the multitude of fresh treatises on Christian evidences. Growing numerous after 1790, they positively swarm for a generation after Paley (1794). Cp. *Essays on the Evidence and Influence of Christianity*, Bath, 1790, pref.; Andrew Fuller, *The Gospel its own Witness*, 1799, pref. and concluding address to Deists; Watson's sermon of 1795, in *Two Apologies*, ed. 1806, p. 399; Priestley's *Memoirs* (written in 1795), 1806, pp. 127-8; Wilberforce's *Practical View*, 1797, *passim* (*e.g.* pp. 366-9, 8th ed. 1841); Rev. D. Simpson, *A Plea for Religion . . . addressed to the Disciples of Thomas Paine*, 1797. The latter writer states (2d. ed., p. 126) that "infidelity is at this moment running like wildfire among the common people"; and Fuller (2d ed. p. 128) speaks of the *Monthly Magazine* as "pretty evidently devoted to the cause of infidelity".

CHAPTER XIV.

EUROPEAN FREETHOUGHT, FROM DESCARTES TO THE
FRENCH REVOLUTION.

§ I. *France and Holland.*

1. We have seen France, in the first quarter of the seventeenth century, pervaded in its upper classes by a Freethought partly born of the knowledge that religion counted for little but harm in public affairs, partly the result of such argumentation as had been thrown out by Montaigne and codified by Charron. That it was not the freethinking of mere idle men of the world is clear when we note the names and writings of LA MOTHE LE VAYER, GUI PATIN, and GABRIEL NAUDE, all scholars, all heretics of the sceptical and rationalistic order. The first, one of the early members of the new Academy founded by Richelieu, is an interesting figure[1] in the history of culture, being a skeptic of the school of Sextus Empiricus, but practically a great friend of tolerance. Standing in favor with Richelieu, he wrote at that statesman's suggestion a treatise *On the Virtue of the Heathen*, justifying toleration by Pagan example — a course which raises the question whether Richelieu himself was not strongly touched by the rationalism of his age. Le Vayer's *Dialogues of Orasius Tubero* (1633) is philosophically his most important work; but its Pyrrhonism was not calculated to affect greatly the current thought of his day; and he ranked rather as a man of all-round learning[2] than as a polemist, being

---

[1] See the notices of him in Owen's *Skeptics of the French Renaissance;* and in Sainte Beuve, *Port Royal,* iii, 180, etc.

[2] "On le régarde comme le Plutarque de notre siècle" (Perrault, *Les Hommes Illustres du XVIIe Siècle,* éd. 1701, ii, 131).

reputed " a little contradictory, but in no way bigoted or obstinate, all opinions being to him nearly indifferent, excepting those of which faith does not permit us to doubt ".[1]

2. Between this negative development of the doctrine of Montaigne and the vogue of upper-class Deism, the philosophy of Descartes, with its careful profession of submission to the Church, had an easy reception; and on the appearance of the *Discours de la Méthode* (1637) it speedily affected the whole thought of France, the women of the leisured class, now much given to literature, being among its students.[2] From the first, the Jansenists, who were the most serious religious thinkers of the time, accepted the Cartesian system as in the main soundly Christian; and its founder's authority had some such influence in keeping up the prestige of orthodoxy as had that of Locke later in England. ' Boileau is named among those whom he so influenced.[3] But a merely external influence of this kind could not counteract the whole social and intellectual tendency towards a secular view of life, a tendency revealed on the one hand by the series of treatises from eminent Churchmen, defending the faith against unpublished attacks, and on the other hand by the prevailing tone in *belles lettres*. Malherbe, the literary dictator of the first part of the century, had died in 1628 with the character of a scoffer; and the fashion lasted till the latter half of the reign of Louis XIV. The case of the poet Théophile de Viau, who about 1623 suffered persecution on a charge of impiety,[4] appears to be the only one of the kind for over a generation. It was in 1665, some years after the death of Mazarin, who had maintained Richelieu's policy of tolerance, that Claude Petit was burnt at Paris for "impious pieces"; and even

---

[1] *Id.*, p. 232.
[2] Lanson, *Hist. de la litt. française*, 5e édit. p. 396; Brunetière, *Etudes Critiques*, 3e série, p. 2; Buckle, ii, 95.
[3] Lanson, p. 397.
[4] See Condorcet, *Vie de Voltaire*, ch. i, and note 1. The charge seems to have been false.

then there was no general reversion to orthodoxy, the upper-class tone remaining, as in the age of Richelieu and Mazarin, unbelieving. When Corneille had introduced a touch of Christian zeal into his *Polyeucte* (1643) he had given general offence to the dilettants of both sexes.[1] MOLIERE, again, the genius of character comedy, was unquestionably an unbeliever, as was his brilliant predecessor CYRANO DE BERGERAC.[2]

3. Even in the apologetic reasoning of the greatest French prose writer of that age, Pascal, we have the most pregnant testimony to the prevalence of unbelief; for not only were the fragments preserved as *Pensées* (1670) part of a planned defence of religion against contemporary rationalism,[3] but they themselves show their author profoundly unable to believe, save by a desperate abnegation of reason. The case of Pascal is that of Berkeley with a difference : the latter suffered from hypochondria, but reacted with nervous energy ; Pascal, a physical degenerate, prematurely profound, was prematurely old ; and his pietism in its final form is the expression of the physical collapse.[4] The man who advised doubters to make a habit of causing masses to be said and practising religious habits, on the score that *cela vous fera croire et vous abêtira*—" that will make you believe and will stupefy you "[5]—was a pathological case ; and though the whole Jansenist movement stood for a reaction against freethinking, it may be

---

[1] Guizot, *Corneille et son temps*, ed. 1880, p. 200. The circle of the Hôtel Rambouillet were especially hostile. Cp. Palissot's note to *Polyeucte*, end.

[2] Cp. Lanson, p. 520 ; Fournier, *Etudes sur Molière*, 1885, pp. 122-3 ; Soury, *Brév. de l'hist. du matér.*, p. 384 ; pref. by " Jacob " to ed. of Cyrano.

[3] It is to be remembered that the work as published contained matter not Pascal's. Cp. Brunetière, *Etudes*, iii, 46-47 ; and the editions of the *Pensées* by Faugère and Havet.

[4] This is disputed by M. Lanson, an always weighty authority. He writes (p. 464) that Pascal was "neither mad nor ill" when he gave himself up wholly to religion. But Pascal had *chronically* suffered from intense pains in the head from his eighteenth year ; and M. Lanson admits (p. 451) that the *Pensées* were written in intervals of acute suffering. Cp. Pascal's *Prière pour demander à Dieu le bon usage des maladies ;* and Owen, *French Skeptics*, pp. 746, 784.

[5] *Pensées*, ed. Faugère, ii, 168-9. The "abêtira " comes from Montaigne.

doubted whether the *Pensées* did not generally act as a solvent rather than as a sustainer of religious beliefs.[1] The same question arises concerning the *Lettres Provinciales* (1656). It is strange that those who charge upon the satire of the later philosophers the downfall of Catholicism in France should not realise the plain tendency of these brilliant satires to discredit the entire authority of the Church, and further, by their own dogmatic weaknesses, to put all dogma alike under suspicion.[2] It was in fact the eternal strifes of the religious factions that more than any other single cause fostered unbelief[3]; and Pascal's writings only deepened the trouble. Even Bossuet, in his *History of the Variations of the Protestant Churches,* did but throw a new light on the hollowness of the grounds of religion; and for thoughtful readers gave a lead rather to atheism than to Catholicism. The converts it would make to the Catholic Church would be precisely those whose adherence was of least value, since they had not even the temperamental basis which, rather than argument, kept Bossuet a believer, and were but Catholics for lack of courage to put all religion aside. A similar fatality attended the labors of the learned Huet, bishop of Avranches, whose *Demonstratio Evangelica* (1679) is remarkable as anticipating Berkeley in the argument from the arbitrariness of mathematical assumptions. He, too, by that and by his later works, made for sheer philosophical scepticism,[4] always a dangerous basis for orthodoxy.[5]

4. Meanwhile a new rationalising influence was at work in the doctrine of GASSENDI, who, living his life as a Canon of the Church, reverted in his doctrine to the philosophy of Epicurus, alike in physics and ethics.

---

[1] Thus Mr. Owen treats him as a sceptic, which philosophically he was.

[2] Cp. the *Eloge de Pascal* by Bordas Demoulin in Didot ed. of the *Lettres,* 1854, pp. xxii-xxiii, and cit. from Sainte-Beuve.

[3] Cp. Voltaire's letter of 1768, cited by Mr. Morley, *Voltaire,* 4th ed , p. 159.

[4] Cp. Owen, *French Skeptics,* pp. 762-3, 767.

[5] This was expressly urged against Huet by Arnauld. See the *Notice* in Jourdain's ed. of the *Logique de Port Royal,* 1854, p. xi.

Professing like Descartes a strict submission to the Church, he yet set forth a theory of things which had in all ages been recognised as fundamentally irreconcilable with the Christian creed; and his substantial exemption from penalties is one of the proofs of the permeation of the Church at the time by the new spirit. The correspondent of Galileo and Kepler, he was the friend of La Mothe le Vayer and Naudé; and Gui Patin was his physician and intimate.[1] Strong as a physicist and astronomer where Descartes was weak, he divides with him the credit of practically renewing natural philosophy; Newton following Gassendi rather than Descartes.[2] Indeed Gassendi's youthful attack on the Aristotelian physics (1624) makes him the predecessor of Descartes; and he expressly opposed his contemporary on points of physics and metaphysics on which he thought him chimerical, and so promoted unbelief where Descartes made for orthodoxy.[3] Yet the works of Descartes were placed on the *Index Librorum Prohibitorum*, and later even vetoed at Paris university, and those of Gassendi were not.[4] Himself one of the most abstemious of men,[5] like his master Epicurus (of whom he wrote a Life), he attracted disciples of another temperamental cast as well as many of his own; and as usual his system is associated with the former, who are duly vilified on the orthodox side, although certainly no worse than the average adherents of that.

5. Of the new Epicureans, the most famous in his day was SAINT-EVREMOND,[6] who, exiled from France for

---

[1] For a good account of Gassendi and his group (founded on Lange, Sec. iii, ch. 1) see Soury, *Bréviaire de l'hist. de matérialisme*, Pt. iii, ch. 2.

[2] Voltaire, *Eléments de philos. de Newton*, ch. ii; Lange, i, 267, and *note*, and p. 269.

[3] Bayle, art. POMPONACE, Notes F and G. The complaint was made by Arnauld, who with the rest of the Jansenists was substantially a Cartesian.

[4] Apparently just because the Jansenists adopted Descartes and opposed Gassendi. But Gassendi is extremely guarded in all his statements.

[5] See Soury, pp. 397-8, as to a water-drinking " debauch " of Gassendi and his friends.

[6] B. 1613; d. 1703. A man who lived to ninety can have been no great debauchee.

his politics, maintained both in London and in Paris, by his writings, a leadership in polite letters. In England he greatly influenced young men like Bolingbroke; and a translation (attributed to Dryden) of one of his writings seems to have given Bishop Butler the provocation to the first and weakest chapter of his *Analogy*.[1] REGNARD, the dramatist, had a similar private repute as an "Epicurean". And even among the nominally orthodox writers of the time in France a subtle scepticism touches nearly all opinion. FONTENELLE (1657-1757), whose *Conversations on the plurality of Worlds* (1686) popularised for the elegant world the new cosmology, cannot but have undermined dogmatic faith in some directions; above all by his graceful and skilful *Histoire des Oracles* (also 1686), where "the argumentation passes beyond the thesis advanced. All that he says of oracles could be said of miracles."[2] The Jesuits found the book essentially "impious"; and a French culture-historian sees in it "the first attack which directs the scientific spirit against the foundations of Christianity. All the purely philosophic arguments with which religion has been assailed are in principle in the work of Fontenelle."[3] Living to his hundredth year, he could join hands with the Freethought of Gassendi and Voltaire, Descartes and Diderot.

6. Yet another new departure was made in the France of Louis XIV by the scholarly performance of RICHARD SIMON (1638—1712), who was as regards the Scriptural texts what Spencer of Cambridge was as regards the culture-history of the Hebrews, the founder of modern methodical criticism. The congregation of the Oratory, where he laid the foundations of his learning, was so little inclined to his critical views that he decided to leave it, and though persuaded to stay, and to become

---

[1] *Dynamics of Religion,* p. 172.
[2] Lanson, *Hist. de la litt. Française*, p. 627.
[3] *Id. ib.* Cp. Demogeot, p. 468. Fontenelle was also credited with a heretical letter on the doctrine of Resurrection, an essay on the Infinite, and a *Traité sur la Liberté*, all pointing to unbelief. As the *Histoire des Oracles* was itself anonymous, the question remains open.

for a time a professor of philosophy at Julli, he at length broke with the Order. Then, from his native town of Dieppe, came his strenuous series of critical works, *L'histoire critique du vieux Testament* (1678), which among other things decisively impugned the Mosaic authorship of the Pentateuch ; the *Histoire critique du texte du Nouveau Testament* (Rotterdam, 1689) ; numerous other volumes of critical studies on texts, versions, and commentators ; and finally a French translation of the New Testament with notes. His *Bibliothèque Critique* (4 vols. under the name of Saint-Jarre) was suppressed by an order in council ; the translation was condemned by Bossuet and the Archbishop of Paris ; and the two first-named works were suppressed by the Parliament of Paris and attacked by a host of orthodox scholars ; but they were translated promptly into Latin and English ; and they gave a new breadth of footing to the deistic argument, though Simon always wrote as an avowed believer. Before Simon, the Protestant Peyrere, the friend of La Mothe le Vayer and Gassendi, had fired a somewhat wild shot at the Pentateuch in his *Systema Theologica ex Præ-adamitarum Hypothesi* (1654), for which he was imprisoned at Brussels, with the result that he recanted and joined the Church of Rome. But Simon laid a scholarly foundation where Peyrere framed a guess, and had a corresponding influence.

7. Such an evolution could not occur in France without affecting the neighbouring civilisation of Holland. We have seen Dutch life at the beginning of the seventeenth century full of Protestant fanaticism and sectarian strife ; and in the time of Descartes these elements, especially on the Calvinist side, were strong enough virtually to drive him out of Holland (1647) after nineteen years' residence.[1] He had, however, made disciples ; and his doctrine bore fruit, finding doubtless some old soil ready. At Amsterdam the young SPINOZA (1632—1677) was first led to rationalise by his friend and teacher, Van den Ende, a scientific materialist, hostile to all

---

[1] Kuno Fischer, *Descartes and his School*, pp. 254-268.

religion[1]; and it was while under that influence that he was excommunicated by his father's synagogue. Becoming deeply influenced later by Descartes, partly also by Bacon[2] and further by Hobbes,[3] Spinoza produced a philosophic system which thenceforth affected all European thought. The *Tractatus Theologico-Politicus* (1670) was promptly condemned by a clerical synod, along with Hobbes's *Leviathan*, which it followed in the matter of criticism of the scriptural text. Deism and Atheism could alike found on its pantheistic positions, and did, in the ensuing generations. Its effect in Holland was at least as great as elsewhere; and there seems to have gone on from this time a rapid modification of the old orthodoxy. Frans Cuper, who in 1676 published an *Arcana Atheismi Revelata* professedly refuting Spinoza, was charged with writing in bad faith and with being on Spinoza's side. The appearance in 1678 of a Dutch treatise ".against all sorts of Atheists "[4]; and in 1681, at Amsterdam, of an attack in French on Spinoza's Scriptural criticism,[5] points to a movement outside of the clerical and scholarly class. Already in 1685, Locke's friend Le Clerc had taken up the position of Hobbes and Spinoza and Simon on the Pentateuch in his · *Sentimens de quelques théologiens de Hollande*. In the time of the English Civil War, the fear of the opponents of the new multitude of sects was that England should become " another Amsterdam ".[6] This very multiplicity tended to promote doubt : and in 1713 we find Anthony Collins[7] pointing to Holland as a country where freedom to think has undermined superstition to a remarkable degree. During his stay, in the previous generation, Locke had found a measure of

---

[1] Martineau, *Study of Spinoza*, 1882, pp. 20-22 ; Coler, *Vie de Spinoza*, in Gfrörer's ed. of *Opera*, p. xxv; Willis, *Spinoza*, 1870, pp. 39, 79.

[2] Martineau, p. 46.   [3] *Id.*, p. 57.

[4] *Theologisch, Philosophisch, en Historisch process voor God, tegen allerley Atheisten.* By Francis Ridder, Rotterdam, 1678.

[5] *L'Impiété Convaincu*, par Pierre Yvon, Amsterdam, 1681.

[6] Edwards, *Gangræna*, as before cited.

[7] *Discourse of Freethinking*, p. 28.

liberal theology, in harmony with his own ; but in those days downright heresy was still dangerous. DEURHOFF (d. 1717), who translated Descartes and was accused of Spinozism, had at one time to fly Holland, though by his writings he founded a pantheistic sect known as Deur-hovians ; and BALTHASAR BEKKAR, persecuted first for Socinianism, incurred so much odium by publishing in 1691 a treatise denying the reality of witchcraft[1] that he had to give up his office as preacher.[2] In 1708 there was published at Amsterdam a more startling work, under the pseudonym of "Juan di Posos", wherein, by way of a relation of imaginary travels, something like atheism was said to be taught; but the pastor Leenhof had in 1703 been accused of Atheism for his treatise, *Heaven on Earth,* which was at most Spinozistic.[3] Even as late as 1714, a Spinozist shoemaker, BOOMS, was banished for his writings ; but henceforth liberal influences, largely traceable to the works of Bayle, begin to predominate.

8. No greater service was rendered in that age to the spread of rational views than that embodied in the great *Dictionnaire* of PIERRE BAYLE (1647-1706), who, born in France, but driven out by the revocation of the Edict of Nantes, spent the best part of his life and did his main work at Rotterdam. Persecuted there to the extent of having to give up his professorship, he yet produced a virtual encyclopedia for Freethinkers in his incomparable Dictionary, baffling hostility by the Pyrrhonian impartiality with which he handled all religious questions. He had read everything and followed every controversy ; and was thereby the better able to seem to have no convictions of his own. But even apart from the occasional defences of the character of Atheists dropped by him in the main body of the work and in the *Eclaircissements* in which he defended it, it is sufficiently

---

[1] *The Enchanted World,* translated into English in 1695.
[2] Art. in *Biographie Universelle.*
[3] Cp. Trinius, *Freydenker-Lexicon,* S. 336-7.

evident that he was an unbeliever. The only alternative
view is that he was strictly a sceptic, reaching no conclusions for himself; but this is excluded by the whole
management of his expositions.[1] His ostensible scepticism
was simply the tactic forced on him by his conditions;
and it was the positive unbelievers who specially delighted
in his volumes. He laid down no doctrines, but he
illuminated all; and his air of repudiating such views as
Spinoza's had the effect rather of forcing Spinozists to
leave neutral ground than of rehabilitating orthodoxy.
Welcomed by students everywhere, he must have made
powerfully for tolerance and rationalism in his adopted
country, which after his time became a centre of culture
for the States of northern Europe rather than a source of
original works. Holland in the eighteenth century was
receptive alike of French and English thought and
literature, especially the former; and besides reprinting
many of the French Deists' works and translating some
of the English, the Dutch cities harbored such heretics
as the Italian Count PASSERANI, who, dying at Rotterdam in 1736, left a collection of deistic treatises of a
Voltairean cast to be posthumously published. The
deistic influence was strong throughout the century; and
in the latter half was represented by Dr. John BER-
KENHOUT, a Voltairean and cosmopolite, who produced a
biographical history of English literature. But the social
and political conditions were not favorable to such
general literary activity as prevailed in the larger States,
though good work was done in medicine and the natural
sciences. Not till the nineteenth century did Dutch
scholars again give an original lead to Europe in religious
thought.

9. Meantime, Spinoza had reinforced the critical
movement in France,[2] where the later policy of Louis XIV

---

[1] Cp. the essay on *The Scepticism of Bayle* in Sir J. F. Stephen's *Horæ
Sabbaticæ*, vol iii.

[2] The *Tractatus Theologico-Politicus* had been translated into French in
1678 by Saint-Glain, a Protestant, who gave it no fewer than three other
titles in succession, to evade prosecution.

sought as far as possible to extinguish freedom of thought. The crowning Catholic blunder and crime of the revocation of the Edict of Nantes, forcing out of France some eight hundred thousand industrious and educated inhabitants for the offence of Protestantism, wrought above all things for the ascendancy of rationalism. For a time there was a falling away in French intellectual prestige,[1] the result, not of the mere " protective spirit " in literature, but of the immense diversion of national energy under Louis XIV to militarism.[2] But during the period of exhaustion there was no real building up of belief. The king himself, so long morally discredited, could only discredit pietism by his adoption of it; the Jansenists and the Molinists fought incessantly; even on the side of authority there was dissension between Bossuet and Fénelon;[3] and the movement of mysticism associated with the latter came to nothing; though he had the rare credit of converting, albeit to a doubtful orthodoxy, the emotional young Scotch deist, Chevalier Ramsay.[4] When the old king died (1715) even the fashion of conformity passed away;[5] and France, left to recuperate in peace, was free to assimilate and apply the new lore of the English deists, the philosophies of the past century, and the treasure of knowledge amassed by Bayle.

10. With the ground thus prepared, Freethought was sure to progress fast and far in France after the age of Louis XIV; but it chanced that the lead fell into the hands of the most brilliant and fecund of all the writers of

---

[1] Cp. Huet, *Huetiana*, § 1.

[2] The question is discussed in the author's *Buckle and his Critics*, pp. 324-342. Buckle's view, however, was held by Huet, *Huetiana*, § 73.

[3] For a brief view of the facts, usually misconceived, see Lanson, pp. 610-611.

[4] Now remembered chiefly through the account of his intercourse with Fénelon (repr. in Didot ed. of Fénelon's misc. works), and Hume's long extract from his *Philosophical Principles of Natural and Revealed Religion* in the concluding note to the *Essays*. Cp. M. Matter, *Le Mysticisme en France au temps de Fénelon*, 1865, pp. 352-4.

[5] Cp. Condorcet, *Vie de Voltaire*, ch. i.

the century. VOLTAIRE[1] (1694-1778) was already something of a freethinker when a mere child. So common
was Deism already become in France at the end of the
seventeenth century that his godfather, an abbé, is said
to have taught him, at the age of three, a poem by
J. B. ROUSSEAU,[2] then privately circulated, in which Moses
in particular and religious revelations in general are
derided as fraudulent.[3] Knowing this poem by heart in
his childhood, the boy was well on the way to his life's
work. It is on record that many of his school-fellows
were, like himself, already deists, though his brother, a
juvenile Jansenist, made vows to propitiate the Deity on
the small unbeliever's behalf.[4] Voltaire was already a
distinguished young poet and dramatist when, in 1726,
after enduring the affronts of an assault by a nobleman's
lacqueys, and of imprisonment in the Bastile for seeking
revenge by duel, he came to England. Four years
previously, in the powerful poem, *For and Against*,[5] he
had put his early deistic conviction in a vehement
impeachment of the immoral creed of salvation and
damnation. Thus what he had to learn in England was
not Deism but the details of the Deist campaign against
revelationism ; and these he mastered. Not only was he
directly and powerfully influenced by Bolingbroke, who
became his intimate friend, but he read widely in the
philosophic, scientific, and deistic English literature of
the day, and went back to France, after three years' stay,
not only equipped for his battle with tyrannous religion,
but deeply impressed by the moral wholesomeness of

[1] Name assumed for literary purposes, and probably composed by
anagram from the real name AROUET, with "le jeune" (junior) added,
thus : A. R. O. V. E. T. L (e). I (eune).

[2] Not to be confounded with the greater and later Jean Jacques Rousseau.

[3] See the poem in note 4 to ch. ii of Condorcet's *Vie de Voltaire*.

[4] Condorcet, ch. ii. The free-hearted NINON DE L'ENCLOS, brightest
of old ladies, is to be numbered among the pre-Voltairean freethinkers,
and as leaving young Voltaire a legacy to buy books. She refused to "sell
her soul" by turning dévote on the invitation of her old friend Madame
de Maintenon. Madame du Deffand and Madame Geoffrin were among
the later freethinking *grandes dames* of the Voltairean period.

[5] *Pour et Contre, ou Epître à Uranie.*

free discussion.[1]   The rest of his long life was a sleepless and dexterous warfare, by all manner of literary stratagem,[2] facilitated by vast literary fame and ample acquired wealth, against what he called " the Infamous "—the Church and the Creed which he found still swift to slay for mere variation of belief, and slow to let any good thing be wrought for the bettering of men's lives. Of his prodigious literary performance it is probably safe to say that in respect of sheer influence on the general intelligence of the world it has never been equalled by any one man's writing ; and that whatever its measure of error and of personal misdirection, its broader influence was invariably for peace on earth, for tolerance among men, and for reason in all things. His faults were many, and some were serious ; but to no other man of his age can be attributed so much beneficent accomplishment. If in a literary way he hated his personal foes, much more did he hate cruelty and bigotry ; and it was his work more than any that made impossible a repetition in Europe of such clerical crimes as the hanging of the Protestant pastor, La Rochette ; the execution of the Protestant, Calas, on an unproved charge ; the torture of his widow and children ; the beheading of the lad La Barre for ill-proved blasphemy.[3] As against his many humanities, there is not to be charged on him one act of public malevolence. In his relations with his fickle admirer, FREDERICK THE GREAT, and with others of his fellow-thinkers, he and they painfully brought home to freethinkers the lesson that for them as for all men there is a personal art of life that has to be learned, over and above the rectification of opinion. But he and they wrought much towards that

---

[1] Mr. Morley (*Voltaire*, 4th ed., p. 40) speaks patriotically of the English people as having then won " a full liberty of thought and speech and person ". This ignores the case of Woolston, who died in prison for denying the Gospel miracles, in the year in which Voltaire left England. But discussion was nevertheless much more nearly free than in France.

[2] It has been counted that he used no fewer than a hundred and thirty different pseudonyms.

[3] See details in Mr. Morley's *Voltaire*, 4th ed., pp. 165-170 : 257-8.

liberation alike from unreason and from bondage that must precede any great improvement of human things. It is notable that most of the humanitarian ideas of the latter half of the century—the demand for the reform of criminal treatment, the denunciation of war and slavery, the insistence on good government and toleration of all creeds—are more definitely associated with the free-thinking than with any religious party, excepting perhaps the laudable but uninfluential sect of Quakers.

11. From Voltaire onwards, the rationalistic move-ment in eighteenth-century France so rapidly widens and deepens that it is impossible in the present survey to do more than note its main features. The number of ration-alistic writers, despite the Press laws which in that age inflicted the indignity of imprisonment on half the men of letters,[1] multiplied from decade to decade, especially after 1750; the audacious example of Voltaire, and the rising prestige of the *philosophes* in connection with the *Encyclo-pédie* (1751-72) giving new courage to writers and printers. In the earlier part of the century, freethought was disseminated largely by way of manuscripts[2] and reprints of foreign books in translation; but from the middle onwards, despite denunciations and prohibitions, new books multiply. The reputation of Voltaire has overshadowed even that of his leading contemporaries; and theirs and his have further obscured that of the lesser men; but a partial list of miscellaneous freethinking works by minor French writers during the century, up to the Revolution, will serve to show how general was the activity :—

1700. Gilbert (Claude). *Histoire de Calejava ou de l'isle des hommes raisonnables, avec le parallèle de leur Morale et du Christianisme.* (Dijon.) Sup-pressed : only one copy known to have escaped.

1704. *Dialogues de M. le Baron de la Houtan et d'un sauvage dans l'Amérique.* By Gueudeville, Amsterdam.

1710. Tissot de Patot. *Voyages et Avantures de Jaques Massé.* (Bourdeaux.)

1737. D'Argens, Marquis. *La Philosophie du Bon Sens.* (Berlin.)

1738. ————, *Lettres Juives*, 6 tom. (Berlin.)

1741. Deslandes, A. F. B. *Pygmalion, ou la Statue animée.* Condemned to be burnt at Dijon, 1742.

[1] Cp. Buckle, ii, 230-242.
[2] Cp. pref. (*La Vie de Salvian*) to Fr. trans. of Salvian, 1734, p. lxix.

1742. Deslandes, A. F. B. *Pygmalion.* (Dijon.) Book condemned to be burnt by Parliament of Dijon.
1743. *Nouvelles libertés de penser* (Amsterdam.)
1745. De la Serre (Lieut.). *Examen de la Religion.* Appeared under other titles. Condemned to be burnt by Parlt. of Paris.
1747. Deslandes, A. F. B. *De la Certitude des connaissances humaines.*
1748. Esteve, P. *L'Origine de l'Univers expliquée par un principe de matière.*
1751. Mirabaud, J. B. de. *Le Monde, son origine et son antiquité.*
1751. De Prades. *Sorbonne Thesis.* (Cp. Morley, *Diderot*, ch. v.)
1752. Maubert de Gouvest. *Lettres Iroquoises.*
1752. Genard, F. *L'Ecole de l'homme, ou Parallèle des Portraits du siècle et des tableaux de l'écriture sainte.* Author imprisoned.
1753. Baume-Desdossat, Canon of Avignon. *La Christiade.* Book suppressed. Author fined.
1754. Prémontval, A. I. le Guay de. *Le Diogène de d'Alembert, ou Pensées libres sur l'homme.* (Berlin.)
1754. Burigny, J. L. *Théologie payenne.*
1754. Beausobre, L. de (the Younger). *Pyrrhonisme du Sage.* (Berlin.) Burnt by Paris Parliament.
1755. *Les Trois Imposteurs.* Attributed to Boulainvilliers.
1755 *Analyse de Bayle.* Begun by Marsy, continued by Robinet.
1757. Prémontval. *Vues Philosophiques.* (Amsterdam.)
1762. Meister, J. H. *De l'origine des principes religieux.*
1765. Castillon, J. L. *Essai de philosophie morale.*
1766. Boulanger, N. A. *L'Antiquité dévoilée.* Recast by d'Holbach.
1766. De Prades. *Abrégé de l'histoire ecclésiastique de Fleury.* (Berlin.) Pref. by Frederick the Great.
1766. *L'Evangile de la Raison*, par M . . . . y, M.D. [ed. by Abbé Dulaurens.]
1766. Burigny, J. L. *Examen critique des Apologistes de la religion chrétienne.* Published by Naigeon under the name of Freret.
1767. Castillon, J. L. *Almanach Philosophique.*
1767. *Doutes sur la religion.* Attributed to Boulainvilliers and others.
1767. Dulaurens, Abbé H. J. *L'Antipapisme revélé.*
1768. D'Argens. *Œuvres complètes.* 24 tom. (Berlin.)
1768. Naigeon, J. A. *Le militaire philosophe.*
1768. Fréret, N. *Lettre de Thrasybule à Leucippe.*
1769-1780. *L'Evangile du jour.* 18 tom. Scores of pieces, chiefly by Voltaire, but with some by others.
1769. Castillon, J. L. *Histoire générale des dogmes et opinions philosophiques.*
1769. Isoard-Delisle (otherwise Delisle de Sales). *La Philosophie de la Nature.* Author imprisoned.
1770. *Recueil Philosophique.* Edited by Naigeon.

[In this year appeared the *Système de la Nature* of d'Holbach, which checked Deism, and turned discussion on Atheism. In 1776 appeared Condorcet's *Lettres d'un Théologue*, also atheistic.]

1773. Carra, J. L. *Système de la Raison, ou le prophète philosophe.*
1777. Carra, J. L. *Esprit de la morale et de la philosophie.*
1777. *Examen critique du nouveau Testament.*
Attrib. to J. B. de Mirabaud. Appd. in 1769 as *Reflexions impartiales sur l'evangile.*
1778. Barthez, P. J. *Nouveaux Eléments de la Science de l'Homme.*
1780. Duvernet, Abbé Th. J. *L'Intolérance religieuse.*
1781. Maréchal, Sylvain. *Le nouveau Lucrèce.*
1783. Brissot de Warville. *Lettres philosophiques sur S. Paul.*
1784. Doray de Longrais. *Faustin, ou le siècle philosophique.*
1784. Pougens, M. C. J. de. *Récréations de philosophie et de morale.*
1787. Pastoret, Marquis. *Zoroastre, Confucius, et Mahomet.*
1788. Meister, J. H. *De la Morale Naturelle.*

1788. Pastoret, Marquis. *Moïse considéré comme legislateur et comme moraliste.*
1788. Maréchal. *Almanach des honnêtes gens.*
1789. Duvernet, Abbé. *Les Dévotions de Madame de Betzamooth.*
1789. Cerutti (Jesuit Father). *Bréviaire Philosophique, ou Histoire du Judaisme, du Christianisme, et du Déisme.*
1791-93. Naigeon. *Dictionnaire de la philosophie ancienne et moderne.*

Though the bibliographers claim to have traced the authorship in most cases, such works were in the first instance nearly always published anonymously, as were those of Voltaire, d'Holbach and the leading freethinkers; and the clerical policy of suppression had the result of leaving them all unanswered when they nevertheless got into private circulation. It was impolitic that an official answer should appear to a book which was officially held not to exist ; so that the orthodox defence was mainly confined to the classic performances of Pascal, Bossuet, Huet, Fénelon, and some outsiders such as the exiled Protestant Abbadie, settled in Germany. These having been written to meet the mostly unpublished objections of previous generations, the Church through its chosen policy had the air of utter inability to confute the newer propaganda, though some apologetic treatises of fair power did appear, in particular those of the Abbé Bergier, which, however, all appear to date from 1770 onwards.[1] After the expulsion of the Jesuits (1762)[2] the Press grew practically more and more free ; and when, after the accession of Pope Clement XIV (1769), the freethinking books circulated with less and less restraint, Bergier opened fire on deism, and deists and clerics joined in answering the atheistic *Système de la Nature* of d'Holbach. But by this time the deistic books were legion, Voltaire's alone forming a small library ; and the political battle over the taxation of Church property had

---

[1] 1773, *La certitude des preuves du christianisme ; 1770, Apologie de la religion chrétienne; 1771, Le Déisme refuté par lui-même.* There were also two journals, Jesuit and Jansenist, which fought the *philosophes* (Lanson, p. 721); and sometimes even a manuscript was answered, *e.g.,* the *Réfutation du Celse moderne* of the Abbé Gautier (1752), a reply to Mirabaud's unpublished *Examen critique.*

[2] The Jesuits were expelled from Bohemia and Denmark in 1766 ; from Spain, Genoa, and Venice in 1767 ; and from Naples, Malta, and Parma in 1768. In 1773 the Society was suppressed by papal bull.

become the more pressing problem, especially seeing that the mass of the people remained conforming.

The English view that French orthodoxy made a "bad" defence to the Freethinking attack (Sir J. F. Stephen, *Horæ Sabbaticæ*, 2d. Ser. p. 281) proceeds on some misconception of the circumstances, which as we have seen were substantially different in the two countries. Could the English clergy have resorted to official suppression of deistic literature, they too would doubtless have done so. But the view that the English defence was relatively " good ", and that Butler's in particular was decisive, is also, as we have seen, fallacious. In Mr. Leslie Stephen's analysis, as apart from his preamble, the orthodox defence is exhibited as generally weak, and often absurd. In France, the defence began sooner and was more comprehensive and even more methodical. Pascal at least went deeper and Bossuet (in his *Discours sur l'Histoire Universelle*) more widely into certain inward and outward problems of the controversy than did any of the English apologists; Huet produced, in his *Demonstratio Evangelica*, one of the most methodical of all the defensive treatises of the time; and Fénelon, though his *Traité de l'Existence et des Attributs de Dieu* (1712) and *Lettres sur la Religion* (1716) are not very powerful processes of reasoning, contributed through his reproduced conversations (1710) with Ramsay a set of arguments at least as plausible as anything on the English side; and, what is more notable, marked by an amenity which no English apologist attained. The ground had been thus very fully covered by the defence in France before the main battle in England began; and when a new French campaign began with Voltaire, the defence against that incomparable attack, so far as the system allowed of any, was probably as good as it could have been made in England. The sceptical line of argument had been already employed by Huet and Pascal and Fénelon, with visibly small success; and Butler had no such effect in his day in England as to induce French Catholics to use him. (He does not appear to have been translated in French till 1821.) On the other hand, Voltaire circulated widely in England, and was no better answered there than in France. His attack was, in truth, at many points peculiarly baffling, were it only by its inimitable wit. The English replies to Spinoza, again, were as entirely inefficient or deficient as the French ; and the only intelligent English answers to Hume on Miracles (the replies on other issues were of no account) made use of the French investigations of the Jansenist miracles. Finally, though the deeper

reasonings of Diderot were over the heads alike of the French
and the English clergy, the *Système de la Nature* of d'Holbach
was met skilfully enough at many points by G. J. Holland
(1772) who, though not a Frenchman, wrote excellent French,
and supplied for French readers a very respectable rejoinder ;
whereas in England there was practically none. In this case,
of course, the defence was deistic; as was that of Voltaire,
who criticised d'Holbach as Bolingbroke attacked Spinoza and
Hobbes. But the *Examen du Matérialisme* of the Abbé Bergier
(1771), who was a member of the Academy of Sciences, was at
least as good as anything that could then have been done in
the Church of England. Broadly speaking, as we have said,
much more of French than of English intelligence had been
turned to the dispute in the third quarter of the century. In
England, political and industrial discussion relieved the
pressure on creed; in France, before the Revolution, the
whole habit of absolutism tended to restrict discussion to
questions of creed : and the attack would in any case have had
the best of it, because it embodied all the critical forces hitherto
available. The controversy thus went much further than the
pre-Humian issues raised in England ; and the English orthodoxy of the end of the century was, in comparison, intellectually
as weak as politically and socially it was strong.

Above the scattered band of minor combatants rise a
group of writers of special power, several of whom, without equalling Voltaire in ubiquity of influence, rivalled
him in intellectual energy and industry. The names of
DIDEROT, d'HOLBACH, D'ALEMBERT, HELVETIUS, and
CONDORCET are among the first in literary France of the
generation before the Revolution ; after them come
VOLNEY and DUPUIS ; and in touch with the whole
series stands the line of great mathematicians and
physicists (to which also belongs D'Alembert) LAPLACE,
LAGRANGE, LALANDE, DELAMBRE. When to these we
add the names of MONTESQUIEU, BUFFON, CHAMFORT,
VAUVENARGUES ; of the materialists LA METTRIE and
CABANIS ; of the philosophers CONDILLAC and DESTUTT
DE TRACY ; of the historian RAYNAL ; of the poet ANDRE
CHENIER ; of the politicians TURGOT, MIRABEAU, DAN-
TON, DESMOULINS, ROBESPIERRE — all deists or else
pantheists or atheists—it becomes clear that the intelli-

gence of France was predominantly rationalistic before
the Revolution.   No list of orthodox names remotely
comparable with these can be drawn from the literature
of France, or indeed of any other country of that time.
JEAN JACQUES ROUSSEAU (1712—1778), the one other
pre-eminent figure, though not an anti-Christian propagandist, is distinctly on the side of Deism.   In the
Contrat Social,[1] writing with express approbation of
Hobbes, he declares that " the Christian law is at bottom
more injurious than useful to the sound constitution of
the State " ; and even the famous *Confession of Faith of
a Savoyard Vicar* in the *Emile* is anti - revelationist,
and practically anti - clerical.   He was accordingly
anathematised ; and although his temperamental way
of regarding things has a clear affinity with some later
religious philosophy of a more systematic sort, he
undoubtedly made for Freethought as well as for the
revolutionary spirit in general.   Thus the cause of Christianity stood almost denuded of intellectually eminent
adherents in the France of 1789; for even among the
writers who had dealt with public questions without
discussing religion, or who had criticised Rousseau and
the *philosophes*—as the Abbés Mably, Morellet, Millot—
the tone was essentially rationalistic.

12. A certain broad development may be traced
throughout the century.   MONTESQUIEU, who in his
early *Persian Letters* (1721) had revealed himself as
" fundamentally irreligious ",[2] proceeded in his masterly
book on the *Greatness and Decadence of the Romans* (1734) and
his famous *Spirit of Laws* (1748) to treat the problems of
human history in an absolutely secular and scientific
spirit, making only a few such polite allusions to religion[3]
as were advisable in an age when all heretical works
were suppressible.   Even as it was, Jesuits and Jansenists
combined to attack the *Spirit of Laws*, which was

[1] Liv. iv, ch. 8.
[2] Lanson, p. 702.
[3] " Au point de vue religieux, Montesquieu tirait poliment son coup de
chapeau au christianisme."   Lanson, p. 714.

denounced at an assembly of the clergy, put on the
Roman Index, and prohibited by the censure until
Malesherbes came into office in 1750.[1] By this time the
attack of Voltaire and others had made aggressive unbelief familiar, the authorities zealously advertising him
by causing many of his freethinking books to be publicly
burnt by the hangman, and putting others under the
censure.[2] Voltaire's constant burden was that religion
was not only untrue but pernicious, and when he was not
showing this directly of Christianity, as in his poem
La Ligue (1723), he was saying it by implication in such
plays as *Zaïre* (1732) and *Mahomet* (1742), dealing with the
fanaticism of Islam; while in the *Essai sur les mœurs* (1756),
really a broad survey of general history, and in the
Siècle de Louis XIV, he applied the method of Montesquieu,
with direct and pungent criticism added. Later, he
added to his output direct criticisms of the Christian
books, as in the *Examen important de milord Bolingbroke*
(1767), and the *Recherches historiques sur le Christianisme*
(? 1769), continuing all his former lines of activity. Meanwhile, with the aid of his friend the MARCHIONESS DU
CHATELET, an accomplished mathematician, he had done
much to popularise the physics of Newton and discredit
the fallacies of the system of Descartes; all the while
preaching a Newtonian but rather agnostic Deism. This
is the purport of his *Philosophe Ignorant*, his longest
philosophical essay.[3] The destruction of Lisbon by the
earthquake of 1755 seems to have shaken him in his
deistic faith, since the upshot of his poem on that subject
is to leave the moral government of the universe an

---

[1] *Id.*, p. 714, *note*.

[2] The *Lettres Philosophiques* (otherwise the *Lettres anglaises*) were so
treated on their appearance in 1734, and the bookseller put in the Bastille;
the *Voix du Sage et du Peuple* was officially and clerically condemned in 1751;
the poem on *Natural Religion* was burned in 1758, and *Candide* in 1759; and
many of his minor pseudonymous performances had the same advertise-
ment. But even the *Henriade*, the *Charles XII*, and the first chapters of
the *Siècle de Louis XIV* were prohibited.

[3] M. Lanson seems to overlook it when he writes (p. 747) that "the
affirmation of God, the denial of Providence and miracles, is the whole
metaphysic of Voltaire".

absolute enigma; and in the later *Candide* (1759) he
attacks theistic optimism with his matchless ridicule.
But he never accepted the atheistic view : on the
contrary we find him arguing absurdly enough, in his
Homily on Atheism (1765), that atheism had been the
destruction of morality in Rome[1]; and the tale of *Jenni,
or, the Sage and the Atheist* (1775), is a polemic against the
atheism of d'Holbach.   By this time, the inconsistent
Deism of Voltaire's youth had itself been discredited
among the more thorough-going freethinkers; and for
years it had been said in society that Voltaire after all
" is a bigot : he is a Deist ! "[2]

13. Though it was Diderot and d'Holbach who more
than any other popular writers had thus carried forward
the process of criticism, the philosopher LA METTRIE
had given a powerful initial push in the same direction by
his materialistic philosophy; and others after him had
continued the impulse.   La Mettrie produced his *Natural
History of the Mind* in 1745; and in 1746 appeared the
Essay on the Origin of Human Knowledge of the Abbé
CONDILLAC, both essentially rationalistic and anti-theological works, though differing in their psychological
positions, Condillac being a non-materialist, though a
strong upholder of " sensism ".   The impulse towards
physical science was further reinforced by BUFFON, who
like the others was a freethinker, though like them he
avoided religious issues.   La Mettrie followed up his
system with the works *L'Homme Plante* and *L'Homme
Machine* (1748); and though he professed to think the
" balance of probability " was in favor of the existence of
a personal God,[3] his writings gave small support to the
hypothesis.   It is notable that he, the typical materialist
of his age, seems to have been one of its kindliest men, by

[1] Mr. Morley writes (p. 209) : " We do not know how far he ever
seriously approached the question . . . . whether a society can exist
without a religion ".   This overlooks the *Homélie sur l'Athéisme*, where it is
discussed seriously and explicitly.

[2] Horace Walpole, Letter to Gray, Nov. 19, 1765.

[3] Soury, *Breviaire de l'hist. du matérialisme*, p. 689.

the common consent of all who knew him.[1] Immediately
after him came MAUPERTUIS, now chiefly remembered
as one of the victims of the mockery of Voltaire, but
really an energetic man of science, who had preceded
Voltaire in setting up in France the Newtonian against the
Cartesian physics. In his *System of Nature* (not to be
confused with the later work of d'Holbach under the
same title) he in 1751 propounded a new version of the
hylozoisms of ancient Greece, and at the same time
anticipated some of the special philosophic positions of
Kant.[2] Next in the materialistic series came J. B.
ROBINET, whose *Nature* (1761) is a remarkable attempt
to reach a strictly naturalistic conception of things.[3] He
founds at once on Descartes and Leibnitz, but in his
*Philosophical Considerations on the natural gradation of
living forms* (1768) he definitely sets aside theism as
illusory, and puts ethics on a strictly scientific and
human footing,[4] extending the arguments of Hume and
Hutcheson somewhat on the lines of Mandeville. On
another line of reasoning a similar application of Mandeville's thesis had already been made by HELVETIUS in
his *Traité de l'Esprit*[5] (1758), a work which excited a
hostility now difficult to understand, but still reflected
in censures no less surprising.[6] Its faults are lack of

---

[1] Lange, *Hist. of Materialism*, ii, 78-80 ; Soury, pp. 663, 666-668 ; Voltaire,
Homélie sur l'athéisme, end. The conventional vilification of La Mettrie
(endorsed by Mr. Morley, *Voltaire*, p. 122) proceeds upon those of his
writings in which he discussed sexual questions with absolute scientific
freedom. He, however, insisted that his theoretic discussion had nothing
whatever to do with his practice ; and there is no evidence that he lived
otherwise than as nine men out of ten did in his age, and ours.

[2] Soury, p. 579. The later speculations of Maupertuis by their extravagance discredited the earlier.

[3] Lange, ii, 27, 29 ; Soury, pp. 603-644.

[4] Soury, pp. 594-600 ; Lange, ii, 27.

[5] This may best be translated *Treatise on Intelligence*.

[6] One of the worst misrepresentations in theological literature is the
account of Helvetius by the late Principal Cairns (*Unbelief in the Eighteenth
Century*, 1881, p. 158) as appealing to government " to promote luxury, and,
through luxury, public good, by abolishing all those laws that cherish a
false modesty and restrain libertinage ". Helvétius simply pressed the
consequences of the existing theory of luxury, which for his own part he
disclaimed. *De l'Esprit*, Disc. ii, ch. 15. Dr. Pünjer (i, 462) falls so far
below his usual standard as to speak of Helvétius in a similar fashion.

system, undue straining after popularity, some hasty generalisation, and a greater concern for paradox than for persuasion; but it abounds in acuteness and critical wisdom, and it definitely and seriously founds public ethics on utility.[1] Its most serious error, the assumption that all men are born with equal faculties, and that education is the sole differentiating force, was repeated in our own age by John Stuart Mill; and in Helvétius the error is balanced by the thoroughly sound and profoundly important thesis that the general superiorities of *nations* are the result of their culture-conditions and politics.[2] The over-balance of his stress on self-interest[3] is an error easily soluble. On the other hand, we have the memorable testimony of BECCARIA that it was the work of Helvétius that inspired him to his great effort for the humanising of penal laws and policy.[4] It may be doubted whether any such fruits can be claimed for the teachings of the whole of the orthodox moralists of the age.

14. Over all these men, and even over Voltaire, DIDEROT stands pre-eminent, on retrospect, for variety of power and depth and subtlety of thought; though for these very reasons, as well as because some of his most masterly works were never printed in his lifetime, he was less of a recognised popular force than many of his friends. In his own mental history he reproduces the course of the French thought of his time. Beginning as a Deist, he assailed the contemporary materialists; in the end, with whatever of inconsistency, he was substantially an atheist and a materialist.[5] His early *Philosophic Thoughts*

---

[1] As Mr. Morley notes, Bentham acknowledged Helvétius as his teacher and inspirer. *Diderot*, ed. 1884, p. 329.

[2] *De l'Esprit*, Disc. iii, ch. 30.

[3] Cp. Mr. Morley's criticism, *Diderot*, pp. 331-2.

[4] Beccaria's Letter to Morellet, cited in ch. i of Mr. J. A. Farrer's ed. of the *Crimes and Punishments*, p. 6. It is noteworthy that the partial reform effected earlier in England by Oglethorpe, on behalf of imprisoned debtors (1730-2), belongs to the time of propagandist Deism there.

[5] Cp. Soury's contention (p. 577) that we shall never make an atheist and a materialist out of "this enthusiastic artist, this poet-pantheist" (citing Rosenkranz in support) with his own admissions, pp. 589-590, and with Mr. Morley's remarks, pp. 33, 401, 418. See also Lange, ii, 32, 256.

(1746), which were duly condemned to be burnt by the hangman, show him a keen freethinker at the age of 33, but a satisfied Deist. Like Voltaire and so many other Frenchmen of his century, he read English and was much influenced by the English thinkers and writers of the previous and of his own generation ; but ere long he passed above their plane of thought. It is his peculiar excellence to be an original and innovating thinker not only in philosophy but in psychology, in æsthetics, in ethics, in dramatic art ; and his endless and miscellaneous labors in the *Encyclopédie*, of which he was the most loyal and devoted producer, represent an extraordinary range of interests. He suffered from his position as a hack writer and as a forced dissembler in his articles on religious matters, and there is probably a very real connection between his compulsory insincerities in the *Encyclopédie*—to say nothing of the official prosecution of that and of others of his works— and his misdeeds in the way of indecent fiction. When organised society is made to figure as the heartless enemy of thinking men, it is no great wonder if they are careless at times about the effect of their writings on society. But it stands to his lasting honor that his sufferings at the hands of priests, printers, and parliaments, never soured his natural goodness of heart. He was, in his way, as beneficent as Voltaire, without Voltaire's faults of private malice ; and his life's work was a great ministry of light. It was Goethe who said of him in the next generation that " whoever holds him or his doings cheaply is a Philistine ". His large humanity reaches from the plane of expert thought to that of popular feeling ; and while by his *Letter on the Blind* (1749) he could advance speculative psychology and pure philosophy, he could by his tale *The Nun* (*La*]*Religeuse*, written about 1760, published 1796) enlist the sympathies of the people against the rule of the Church.

15. With Diderot were specially associated, in different ways, D'ALEMBERT, the mathematician, for some years

his special colleague on the *Encyclopédie*, and Baron d'HOLBACH. The former counted for practical Freethought by his miscellaneous articles, his little book on the Jesuits (1765) his *Pensées Philosophiques*, his physics, and the general rationalism of his Preliminary Discourse to the *Encyclopédie*. D'HOLBACH, a naturalised German of large fortune, was on the other hand one of the most strenuous propagandists of Freethought in his age. Imitating the tactic of Voltaire, he produced, with some assistance from Diderot, NAIGEON, and others, a whole series of anti-Christian treatises under a variety of pseudonyms[1]; and his principal work, the famous *System of Nature* (1770), was put out under the name of Mirabaud, an actual person, then dead. Summing up as it does with stringent force the whole anti-theological propaganda of the age, it has been described as a "thundering engine of revolt and destruction".[2] It was the first atheistic[3] treatise of a systematic kind; and it significantly marks the era of modern Freethought by its stern impeachment of the sins of monarchy. Rather a practical argument than a dispassionate philosophic research, its polemic against human folly laid it open to the retort that on its own necessarian principles no such polemic was admissible. If, however, it be termed "shallow"[4] on the score of its censorious treatment of the past, the term will have to be applied to the Hebrew books, to the Gospel Jesus, to Pascal, Milton, Carlyle, Ruskin, and a

---

[1] See a full list of his works, compiled by JULIAN HIBBERT, prefixed to Watson's ed. (1834 and later) of the English translation of the *System of Nature*. The principal freethinking books apart from that work, ascribed in whole or in part to d'Holbach, are :—*Le Christianisme Dévoilé*, 1756, and later ; *La Contagion Sacrée*, 1768, and later ; *Théologie Portative*, 1768, and later ; *Histoire critique de Jésus Christ*, about 1770 ; *Essai sur les préjugés*, 1770 ; *Le Bons Sens*, 1772, and later ; *La politique naturelle*, 1774 ; *Système Social*, 1774 ; *La morale universelle*, 1776 ; *Ethocratie*, 1776.

[2] Morley, *Diderot*, p. 341. The chapter gives a good account of the book. Cp. Lange, ii, 26, ff , as to its materialism.

[3] It is to be noted that the English translation (3 vols., 1820) deliberately tampers with the language of the original to the extent of making it deistic. This perversion has been by oversight preserved in all the reprints.

[4] So Mr. Morley, p. 347. It does not occur to Mr. Morley, and to the Comtists who take a similar tone, that in thus disparaging past thinkers they are doing exactly the thing they blame.

good many other prophets, ancient and modern. The synthesis of the book is really emotional rather than philosophic, and hortatory rather than scientific.

16. The death of d'Holbach (1789) brings us to the French Revolution. By that time all the great free-thinking propagandists and non-combatant Deists of the Voltairean group were gone, save CONDORCET. Voltaire and Rousseau had died in 1778, Helvétius in 1771, Turgot in 1781, D'Alembert in 1783, Diderot in 1784. After all their labors, only the educated minority, broadly speaking, had been made freethinkers; and of these, despite the vogue of the *System of Nature*, only a minority were atheists. Deism prevailed, as we have seen, among the foremost revolutionists; but atheism was rare; and after 1789 the new freethinking works run to critical and ethical attack on the Christian system rather than on theism. VOLNEY combined both lines of attack in his famous *Ruins of Empires* (1791); and the learned DUPUIS in his voluminous *Origin of all Cults* (1795) took an important step, not yet fully reckoned with by later mythologists, towards the mythological analysis of the Gospel narrative. After these vigorous performances, the popular progress of French freethought was for long practically suspended[1] by the tumult of the Revolution and the reaction which followed it, though LAPLACE went on his way with his epoch-making theory of the origin of the solar system, for which, as he told Napoleon, he had "no need of the hypothesis" of a God. The admirable CONDORCET had died, perhaps by his own hand, in 1794, when in hiding from the Terrorists, leaving behind him his *Esquisse d'un Tableau historique des Progrès de l'Esprit humain*, in which the most sanguine convictions of the rationalistic school are reformulated without a trace of bitterness or of despair.

17. No part of the history of Freethought has been more distorted than that at which it is embroiled in the

---

[1] Yet in 1797 we have Maréchal's *Code d'une Société d'hommes sans Dieu*, and in 1798 his *Pensées libres sur les prêtres*.

French Revolution.   The conventional view in England
still is that the Revolution was the work of Deists and
Atheists, but chiefly of the latter; that they suppressed
Christianity and set up a worship of a Goddess of
Reason, represented by a woman of the town; and
that the bloodshed of the Terror represented the
application of their principles to government, or at
least the political result of the withdrawal of religious
checks.[1]   Those who remember in the briefest summary
the records of massacre connected with the affirmation of religious beliefs—the furious strifes of Christian
sects under the Roman Empire; the story of the
Crusades, in which nine millions of human beings are
estimated to have been destroyed; the generation of
wholesale murder of the heretics of Languedoc by the
Papacy; the savageries of the Hussite War; the early
slaughter of Protestant heretics in France; the massacres
of German peasants and Anabaptists; the reciprocal
persecutions in England; the ferocious wars of the French
Huguenots and the League; the long-drawn agony of
the war of thirty years in Germany—those who recal
these things need spend no time over the proposition that
rationalism stands for a removal of restraints on bloodshed.   But it is necessary to put concisely the facts as
against the legend in the case of the French Revolution.

(*a.*) That many of the leading men among the revolutionists were Deists is true; and the fact goes to prove that
it was chiefly the men of ability in France who rejected
Christianity.   But the majority of the Constituent
Assembly was never even deistic; it professed itself cor-
dially Catholic;[2] and the Atheists there might be counted

---

[1] Thus Dr. Cairns (*Unbelief in the Eighteenth Century*, p. 165) gravely
argues that the French Revolution proves the inefficacy of theism without
a Trinity to control conduct.

[2] Cp. Aulard, *Le Culte de la Raison et le Culte de l'Etre Suprême*, 1892,
pp. 17-19.   M. Gazier (*Etudes sur l'histoire religieuse de la révolution française*,
1877, pp. 48, 173, 189, ff.) speaks somewhat loosely of a prevailing anti-
Christian feeling when actually citing only isolated instances, and giving
proofs of a general orthodoxy.   He points out the complete misconception
of Thiers on the subject (p. 202).

on the fingers of one hand.[1] Nor were there lacking vigorous representatives of orthodoxy: the powerful Abbé Grégoire, in particular, was a convinced Jansenist Christian, and at the same time an ardent democrat and anti-royalist.[2] He saw the immense importance to the Church of a good understanding with the Revolution, and he accepted the constitution of 1790. Many of the clergy, however, being refractory, the Assembly pressed its point, and the breach widened. It was solely through this *political* hostility on the part of the Church to the new constitution that any civic interference with public worship ever took place. Grégoire was extremely popular with the advanced types,[3] though his piety was conspicuous[4]; and there were not a few priests of his type.[5] On the flight of the king, he and they went with the democracy; and it was the obstinate refusal of the others to accept the constitution that provoked the new Legislative Assembly to coerce them. Though the new body was more anti-clerical than the old, however, it was simply doing what successive Protestant monarchs had done in England and Ireland; and probably no Government in the world would then have acted otherwise in a similar case.[6] Patience might perhaps have won the day; but the Revolution was fighting for its life; and the conservative Church, as all men knew, was eager to strangle it. Had the clergy left politics alone, or simply accepted the constitutional action of the State, there would have been no religious question. To speak of such a body of priests, who had at all times been eager to put men to death for heresy, as vindicating " liberty of conscience " when they refused fealty to the constitution,[7] is somewhat to strain

---

[1] The Abbé Bergier, in answering d'Holbach (*Examen du Matérialisme,* ii, ch. i, § 1) denies that there has been any wide spread of atheistic opinion.

[2] Gazier, *Etudes sur l'hist. relig. de la révol.*, pp. 2, 4, 12, 19-21, 71, etc.

[3] Gazier, L. ii, ch. 1.   [4] *Id.*, p. 67.   [5] *Id.*, p. 69.

[6] The authority of Turgot himself could be cited for the demand that the State clergy should accept the constitution of the State. Cp. Aulard, *Le Culte de la Raison et le Culte de l'Etre Suprême*, p. 12; Tissot, *Etude sur Turgot*, 1878, p. 160.

[7] Gazier, p. 113.

the terms. The expulsion of the Jesuits under the Old
Régime had been a more coercive measure than the
demand of the Assembly on the allegiance of the State
clergy. And all the while the reactionary priesthood was
known to be in active conspiracy with the royalists abroad.
It was only when, in 1793, the clergy were seen to be the
great obstacle to the levy of an army of defence, that the
more radical spirits began to think of interfering with
their functions.[1]

(*b*) For the rest, the legend falsifies what took place.
The facts are now established by exact documentary
research.[2] The Government never substituted any species
of religion for the Catholic.[3] The Festival of Reason at
Nôtre Dame was not an act of the Convention, but of the
Commune of Paris and the Department; the Convention
had no part in promoting it; half the members stayed
away when invited to attend; and there was no Goddess
of Reason in the ceremony, but only a Goddess of Liberty,
represented by an actress who cannot even be identified.[4]
Throughout, the devoutly theistic Rousseau was the chief
literary hero of the movement. The two executive Com-
mittees in no way countenanced the dechristianisation
of the churches, but on the contrary imprisoned persons
who removed Church properties; and these in turn protested that they had no thought of abolishing religion.
The acts of irresponsible violence did not amount to a
tithe of the " sacrilege" wrought in Protestant countries
at the Reformation, and does not compare with the acts
charged on Cromwell's troopers. The policy of inviting
priests and bishops to abdicate their functions was strictly
political; and the Archbishop Gobel did *not* abjure
Catholicism, but only surrendered his office. That a
number of priests did gratuitously abjure their religion is

[1] Aulard, pp. 19-20.
[2] See the whole details in the definitive work of M. Aulard.
[3] The grave misstatement of Michelet on this head is exposed by M.
Aulard, p. 60.
[4] Yet it is customary among Christians to speak of this lady in the most
opprobrious terms.

only a proof of what was well known—that many priests
were simple Deists. In the provinces, where the movement went on with various degrees of activity, it had the
same general character. " Reason " itself was often
identified with deity, or declared to be an emanation
thereof. Hébert, commonly described as an Atheist for
his share in the movement, expressly denied the charge,
and claimed to have exhorted the people to read the
Gospels and obey Christ.[1] Even Chaumette was not an
Atheist ;[2] and the Prussian Clootz, who probably was,
had certainly no doctrinary influence ; while the two or
three other professed Atheists of the Assembly had no
part in the public action.

(c.) Finally, Robespierre was all along thoroughly
hostile to the movement: in his character of Rousseauist
and Deist he argued that Atheism was " aristocratic " ; he
put to death the leaders ; and he set up the Worship of the
Supreme Being as a counter-move. Thus the bloodshed
of the Reign of Terror, if it is to be charged on any species
of philosophic doctrine rather than on the unscrupulous
policy of the enemies of the Revolution in and out of
France, stands to the credit of the belief in a God, the
creed of Frederick, Turgot, Pitt, and Washington. The
one convinced and reasoning Atheist among the publicists
of the time, the journalist SALAVILLE,[3] opposed the Cult of
Reason with sound and serious and persuasive argument,
and strongly blamed all forcible interference with worship,
while at the same time calmly maintaining Atheism as
against Theism. The age of Atheism had not come; any
more than the triumph of Reason.

§ II.   Germany.

1. After the spontaneous growth of irreligion following
on the Thirty Years of religious war had culminated in the
popular movement of Matthias Knutzen, the clerical class

---

[1] See the speech in Aulard, p. 240 ; and cp. pp. 79-85.
[2] Id., pp. 81-82.
[3] Concerning whom see Aulard, pp. 86-96.

were able so far to take matters in hand as to drive rationalism once more below the surface. The existing culture
was divided among them and the other professional classes,
who naturally made common cause with them; besides,
there was now germinating a philosophic unbelief[1] under
the influence of Spinoza. Nowhere were there more
prompt and numerous answers to Spinoza than in
Germany,[2] whence it may be inferred that within the
educated class he soon had a good many adherents.
Professor Rappolt of Leipzig attacked him as an atheist,
in an *Oratio contra naturalistas* in 1670; Musæus assailed
him in 1674; and the Chancellor Kortholt grouped
him with Herbert and Hobbes as *The Three Great
Impostors* in 1680.[3] After the appearance of the *Ethica*
the replies multipled. On the other hand Cuffelaer
vindicated Spinoza in 1684; and in 1691 F. W. Stosch
published a stringent attack on revelationism, entitled
Concordia rationis et fidei, partly on Spinozistic lines,
which created much commotion and was forcibly
suppressed.[4]

2. For a community in which the reading class was
mainly clerical and scholastic, the seeds of rationalism
were thus already in part sown; but the ground was not
yet propitious. Leibnitz (1646—1716), the chief thinker
produced by Germany before Kant, lived in a state of
singular intellectual isolation[5]; and showed his sense of it
by writing his philosophic treatises chiefly in French.
One of the most widely learned men of his age, he was
wont from his boyhood to grapple critically with every
system of thought that came in his way; and while
claiming to be always eager to learn,[6] he was as a rule
strongly concerned to affirm his own powerful bias.

---

[1] Even Knutzen seems to have been influenced by Spinoza. Pünjer,
Christ. Philos. of Religion, p. 437. Dr. Pünjer, however, seems to have
exaggerated the connection.

[2] Cp. Lange, ii, 35.

[3] Pünjer, *Christ. Philos. of Religion*, Eng. tr. i, 434-6.

[4] Pünjer, p. 439; Lange, ii, 35.

[5] Cp. *Buckle aud his Critics*, pp. 171-2; Pünjer, i, 515.

[6] Letter cited by Dr. Latta, *Leibniz*, 1898, p 2, *note*.

Against Spinoza he reacted instantly and violently, pronouncing the first *Tractatus* an "unbearably bold (*licentiosum*) book", and resenting the Hobbesian criticism which it "dared to apply to sacred Scripture". To the last he called Spinoza a mere developer of Descartes,[1] whom he also resisted. This was not hopeful; and Leibnitz, with all his power and originality, really wrought little for the direct rationalisation of religious thought.[2] His philosophy, with all its ingenuity, has the common stamp of the determination of the theist to find reasons for the God in whom he believed beforehand; and his principle that all is for the best is the fatal rounding of his argumentative circle. Nominally he adhered to the entire Christian system; and he always discussed the Bible as a believer; yet he rarely went to church[3]; and the Low German nickname *Lövenix* (=*Glaubet nichts*, "believes nothing") expressed his local reputation. No clergyman attended his funeral; but indeed no one else went, save his secretary.[4]

3. It is indeed difficult to doubt that his indirect influence not only in Germany but elsewhere had been for Atheism.[5] He and Newton were the most distinguished mathematicians and theists of the age; and Leibnitz busied himself to show that the philosophy of Newton[6] tended to atheism, and that that of their theistic predecessor Descartes would not stand criticism.[7] Spinoza being, according to him, in still worse case, and Locke

---

[1] Latta, p. 24; Martineau, *Study of Spinoza*, p. 75; *Philos. Schriften von Leibnitz*, ed. Gerhardt, i, 34; ii, 563. Cp. *Refutation of Spinoza by Leibnitz*, ed. by Foucher de Careil, Eng. tr. 1855.

[2] His notable surmise as to gradation of species (see Latta, pp. 38-39) was taken up among the French materialists, but did not then modify current science.

[3] Cp. Pünjer, i, 509, as to his attitude on ritual.

[4] Latta, as cited, p. 16; *Vie de Leibnitz*, par De Jaucourt, in ed. 1747 of the *Essais de Théodicée*, i, 235-9.

[5] As to his virtual Deism, see Pünjer, i, 513-5.

[6] *Lettres entre Leibnitz et Clarke*,

[7] *Discours de la conformité de la foi avec la raison*, §§ 68-70; *Essais sur la bonté de Dieu*, etc., §§ 50, 61, 164, 180, 292-3.

hardly any sounder,[1] there remains for theists only his cosmology of monads and his ethic of optimism—all for the best in the best of all possible worlds—which seems at least as well fitted as any other theism to make thoughtful men give up the principle. Other culture-conditions concurred to set up a spirit of rationalism in Germany. After the Thirty Years' War there arose a religious movement, called *Pietism* by its theological opponents, which aimed at an emotional inwardness of religious life as against what its adherents held to be an irreligious orthodoxy around them.[2] Though its first leaders grew embittered with their unsuccess and the attacks of their religious enemies,[3] their impulse went far, and greatly influenced the clergy through the university of Halle, which turned out 6,000 clergymen in one generation.[4] Against the Pietists were furiously arrayed the Lutherans of the old school, who even contrived in many places to suppress their schools.[5] Religion was thus represented by a school of extremely unattractive and frequently absurd formalists on the one hand, and on the other by a school tending alternately to fanaticism and cant.[6] Thus "the rationalist tendencies of the age were promoted by this treble exhibition of the aberrations of belief ".[7]

4. The thin end of the new wedge was the adaptation of the Leibnitzian system made by Wolff, who first came into prominence by a rectorial address at Halle (1722) in which he warmly praised the ethics of Confucius. This was naturally held to imply disparagement of Christianity ; and as a result of the pietist outcry Wolff was condemned

---

[1] The *Nouveaux Essais sur l'Entendement humain*, refuting Locke, appeared posthumously in 1765. Locke in his turn had treated his theistic critic with contempt. (Latta, p. 13.)

[2] Amand Saintes, *Hist. crit. du Rationalisme en Allemagne*, 1841, ch. vi.

[3] Hagenbach, *German Rationalism*, Eng. tr. 1865, p. 9.

[4] *Id.*, p. 39; Pusey, *Histor. Enquiry into the causes of German Rationalism*, 1828, pp. 88, 97.

[5] Pusey, pp. 86, 87, 98.

[6] Cp. Pusey, pp. 37-38, 45, 48, 49, 53-4, 79, 101-9; Saintes, pp. 28, 79-80; Hagenbach, pp. 41, 72, 105;

[7] Pusey, p. 110. Cp. Saintes, ch. vi.

by the king to exile from Prussia, under penalty of death,[1] all "atheistical" writings being at the same time forbidden. Wolff's system, however, prevailed, though he refused to return on any invitation till the accession (1740) of Frederick the Great; and his teaching, which for the first time popularised philosophy in the German language,[2] in turn helped to promote the rationalistic temper,[3] though orthodox enough from the modern point of view. Under the new reign, however, pietism and Wolfism alike lost prestige,[4] and the age of anti-Christian and Christian rationalism began.

5. The initiative force[5] was the literature of English Deism, which began to be translated after 1740,[6] and was widely circulated till, in the last third of the century, it was superseded by the French. The English answers to the Deists were frequently translated likewise, and notoriously helped to promote Deism[7]—another proof that it was not their influence that had changed the balance of activity in England. Under a freethinking king, even clergymen began guardedly to accept the Deistic methods; and the optimism of Shaftesbury began to overlay the optimism of Leibnitz;[8] while a French scientific

---

[1] Hagenbach, pp. 35-36; Saintes, p. 61.

[2] Christian Thomasius (1655-1728) had first delivered German lectures.

[3] Cairns, *Unbelief in the Eighteenth Century*, 1881, p. 173; Pusey, pp. 115-119; Pünjer, p. 529; Lechler, S. 448-9.

[4] Hagenbach, pp. 37-39.

[5] Conrad Dippel (1643—1747), "the Christian Democritus," partly prepared the way by his mystic theism, which set the inner light above Scripture, and scouted theology. Noack, *Die Freidenker in der Religion*, Th. iii, Kap. 1.

[6] Lechler, *Gesch. des englischen Deismus*, S. 447-452. The translations began with that of Tindal (1741), which made a great sensation.

[7] Pusey, pp. 125, 127, citing Twesten. Thorschmid's *Freidenker Bibliothek*, issued in 1765-67, collected both translations and refutations. Lechler, S. 451.

[8] Lange, *Hist. of Materialism*, ii, 146-7. Mr. Morley pronounces (*Voltaire*, 4th ed., p. 123) that French Deism "never made any impression on Germany", and that "the teaching of Leibnitz and Wolff stood like a fortified wall against the French invasion". This is contradicted by much German testimony. Hagenbach shows great ignorance of English Deism, but he must have known something of German; and he writes (p. 57) that "the imported deism soon swept through the rifts of the church, and gained supreme control of literature". Cp. pp. 67-8.

influence began with La Mettrie,[1] Maupertuis, and
Robinet. Even the Leibnitzian school, proceeding on
the principle of immortal monads, developed a doctrine of
the immortality of the souls of animals[2]—a position not
helpful to orthodoxy. On the other hand, it is interesting
to note, the mathematician Euler published a defence of
the faith in *Letters to a German Princess* (1769) of which
the argument curiously coincides with part of that of
Berkeley against the freethinking mathematicians ; while
Von Haller the naturalist likewise wrote *Letters on the principal truths of Revelation* (1772) and other apologetic works.
All alike failed to turn the tide of opinion, now socially
favored by the known deism of the king.

6. Frederick, though a Voltairean freethinker from his
youth, showed himself at first disposed to act on the old
maxim that freethought is bad for the common people.
In 1743 he caused to be suppressed two German books
by one Gebhardi, attacking the Biblical miracles; and in
1748 he sent a young man named Rüdiger to Spandau for
six months' confinement for a similar offence.[3]   But as he
grew more confident in his own methods he extended to
men of his own way of thinking the toleration he allowed
to all religionists ; and he himself, chiefly by way of
French verses, added to the literature of Deism.   Bayle
was his favorite study ; and as the then crude German
literature had no attraction for him, he drew to his court
many distinguished Frenchmen, including La Mettrie,
Maupertuis, D'Alembert, D'Argens, and above all Voltaire,
between whom and him there was an incurable incompatibility of temper and character, which left them
admiring without respecting each other, and unable to
abstain from mutual vituperation.   Under Frederick's
vigorous rule all speech was free save such as he considered personally offensive — as Voltaire's attack on
Maupertuis—and after a stormy reign he could say, when
asked by Prince William of Brunswick whether he did not

---

[1] Lange, ii, 76, 137.   [2] *Id*. ii, 134-5.   [3] Hagenbach, p. 66.

think religion one of the best supports of a king's authority, "I find order and the laws sufficient. . . . Depend upon it, countries have been admirably governed when your religion had no existence."[1]

As the first modern freethinking king, Frederick is something of a test case. Son of a man of narrow mind and odious character, he was himself no admirable type, being neither benevolent nor considerate, neither truthful nor generous; and n international politics he played the old game of unscrupulous aggression. Yet he was not only the most competent, but as regards home administration, the most conscientious king of his time. To find a rival, we must go back to the pagan Antonines and Julian, or at least to St. Louis of France, who, however, was rather worsened than bettered by his creed (Cp. the argument of Faure, *Hist. de Saint Louis*, 1866, i, 242-3; ii, 597). The effect of Frederick's training is seen in his final attitude to the advanced criticism of the school of d'Holbach, which assailed governments and creeds with the same unsparing severity of logic and moral reprobation. Stung by the uncompromising attack, Frederick retorts by attacking the rashness which would plunge nations into civil strife because kings miscarry where no human wisdom could avoid miscarriage. He who had wantonly plunged all Germany into a hell of war for his sole ambition, bringing myriads to misery, thousands to violent death, and hundreds of his own soldiers to suicide, could be virtuously indignant at the irresponsible audacity of writers who indicted the whole existing system for its imbecility and injustice. But he did reason on the criticism; he did ponder it; he did feel bound to meet argument with argument; and he gave his arguments to the world. The advance on previous regal practice is enormous: the whole problem of politics is at once brought to the test of judgment and persuasion. Beside the Christian Georges and the Louis' of his century, and beside his Christian father, his superiority in judgment and even in character is signal. Such was the great Deist king of the Deist age; a Deist of the least religious temper, and of no very fine moral material to begin with. The one contemporary monarch who in any way compares with him in enlightenment, Joseph II of Austria, belonged to the same school. The main charge against Frederick as a ruler is that he did not act up to

[1] Thiébault, *Mes Souvenirs de Vingt Ans de Séjour à Berlin*, 1804, i, 77-79. See ii, 78-80, as to the baselessness of the stories (*e.g.* Pusey, *Histor. Enquiry into German Rationalism*, p. 123) as to Frederick having changed his views in old age.

the ideals of the school of Voltaire. In reply to the rhetorical
demand of d'Holbach for an abolition of all superstitious teaching, he observed that among the 16,000,000 inhabitants of
France at most 200,000 were capable of philosophic views, and
that the remaining 15,800,000 were held to their opinions by
"insurmountable obstacles". Such an answer meant that he
had no idea of so spreading instruction that all men should
have a chance of reaching rational beliefs. (*Examen de l'Essai
sur les préjujés*, 1769. See the passage in Lévy-Bruhl,
L'Allemagne depuis Leibniz, p. 89.) This attitude was his inheritance from the past. Yet it was under him that Germany
began to figure as a first-rate culture-force in Europe.

7. The most systematic propaganda of the new ideas
was that carried on in the periodical published by F.
NICOLAI under the title of "The General German
Library" (founded 1765), which began with fifty contributors, and at the height of its power had a hundred and thirty,
among them being Lessing, Eberhardt, and Moses
Mendelssohn. Its many translations from the English
and French freethinkers, older and newer, concurred
with native work to spread rationalism, now known as
Aufklärung, or enlightenment, through the whole middle
class of Germany.[1] Native writers in independent works
added to the propaganda. ANDREAS RIEM, a Berlin
preacher, wrote vehemently against priestcraft; and
GEORG SCHADE, in a work on Natural Religion (1760)
on the lines of Tindal, was no less pronounced in his
hostility to revelationism.[2] EDELMANN (1698—1767) sought
in his *Divinity of Reason* (? 1742) to fuse Christianity in
pantheism [3]; the Deist C. F. BAHRDT, an erratic scholar,
professor, translator of the New Testament, and D.D., of
wandering and bohemian[4] life (1741—1792), put not a little

---

[1] Hagenbach, pp. 103-4; Cairns, p. 177 ;
[2] Pünjer, i, 545-6.
[3] Noack, *Die Freidenker in der Religion,* Th. iii, Kap. 2 ; Saintes, pp. 85-6.
[4] "The wretched Bahrdt" is Dr. Pusey's Christian view of him.
Hagenbach, with characteristic judgment, calls him "the Theodore Parker
of Germany ". Bahrdt was a great admirer of the Gospel Jesus ; so
Cairns (p. 178) takes a lenient view of his life. On that and his doctrine
cp. Hagenbach, pp. 107-110 ; Pünjer, i, 546-550 ; Noack, Th. iii, Kap. 5.
Goethe satirised him in a youthful *Prolog,* but speaks of him not unkindly
in the *Dichtung und Wahrheit.*

wayward genius in his *System of Moral Religion for the final tranquillising of doubters and thinkers* (1787), a scheme of rational utilitarianism.[1] More socially successful was BASEDOW (1723—1790), who as a vigorous reformer of education was stimulated by the influence of Rousseau, and as a Deist by the French and English rationalistic schools.[2] EBERHARDT, author of a *New Apology of Sokrates; or, the final Salvation of the Heathen* (1772), a vigorous Deist, completed the conversion of Bahrdt.[3] Substantially of the same school was the less pronouncedly deistic cleric STEINBART,[4] author of a utilitarian *System of Pure Philosophy or Christian doctrine of Happiness*, now forgotten, who had been variously influenced by Locke and Voltaire.[5] Among other cautiously freethinking clergymen are named the two Tellers, and Spalding.[6]

8. Alongside of these propagators of popular rationalism stood a group of Deists usually considered apart — LESSING, HERMANN SAMUEL REIMARUS, and MOSES MENDELSSOHN. The last was chiefly active as a constructive theist; the first, rather nervously rejecting alike the popular freethought[7], represented by his friend Mylius, and the attempts of the rationalising clergy to put religion on a common-sense basis, framed (or perhaps adapted[8]) a theory of the *Education of the Human Race* (1780) which has served the rationalising clergy of our own day in good stead; and adapted Rousseau's doctrine that the true test of religion lies in feeling and not in argument.[9] Neither doctrine has a whit more philosophical value than the other "popular philosophy" of the time; and neither was

---

[1] Cp. Saintes, pp. 86-89, as to his other works; and p. 90 as to his disciple Venturini, a young freethinking clergyman.

[2] Hagenbach, pp. 100-3; Saintes, pp. 91-92; Pünjer, p. 536; Noack, Th. iii, Kap. 7.

[3] Hagenbach, p. 109.   [4] Noack, Th. iii. Kap. 8.

[5] Saintes, pp. 92-3; Pusey, p. 148.

[6] Saintes, pp. 93-4; Pusey, pp. 150-1, *note*.

[7] See his rather crude comedy, *Der Freigeist*, and Sime's *Life*, i, 41-2.

[8] As to the authorship, see Saintes, pp. 101-2; and Sime's *Life of Lessing*, i, 261-2, where the counter-claim is rejected

[9] Pusey, p. 51, *n*.

fitted to have much immediate influence; but both
pointed a way to the more philosophic apologists of
religion, while baulking the orthodox.[1] It was by him, too,
that there were published the "Anonymous Fragments"
known as the "Wolfenbüttel Fragments" (1774—
1778), wherein the methods of the English and French
Deists are applied with a new severity to both the Old
and the New Testament narratives. They appear, though
the point is still in some doubt, to be the work of
Reimarus,[2] who had in 1755 published a defence of
"Natural Religion", that is of the theory of a Providence,
against La Mettrie, Maupertuis, and older materialists.
The *Fragments* appeared only after his death, and constituted the most serious attack yet made in Germany on
the current creed, though its theory of the true manner of
the Gospel history of course smacks of the pre-scientific
period.[3] Though Lessing professed to combat the
positions of the *Fragments*, he was led into a fierce controversy over them, and the series was finally stopped by
authority. Thereafter, as a final check to his opponents,
he produced his famous drama *Nathan the Wise*, which
embodies Boccaccio's story of *The Three Rings*, and has
ever since served as a popular lesson of tolerance in
Germany.[4] In the end, he seems to have become a
pantheist[5]; but he never expounded any coherent and
comprehensive set of opinions, preferring, as he put it in
an oft-quoted sentence, the state of search for truth to any
consciousness of possessing it.

9. The spirit of rationalism was now so prevalent that
it began to dominate the work of the more intelligent

---

[1] Compare the regrets of Pusey (pp. 51, 155), Cairns (p. 195), Hagenbach
(pp. 89-97), and Saintes (p. 100).

[2] Lessing said the report to this effect was a lie; but this appears to
have been by way of fulfilling his promise of secrecy to the Reimarus
family. Cairns, pp. 203, 209. Cp. Farrar, *Crit. Hist. of Freethought*, Note 29.

[3] See the sketch in Cairns, p. 197, ff., which indicates the portions produced later by Strauss. Cp. Pünjer i, 550-7; Noack, Th. iii, Kap. 4.

[4] Cp. Introd. to Willis's trans. of *Nathan*.

[5] See Cairns, *Appendix*, Note I, and Willis, *Spinoza*, pp. 149-162, giving
the testimony of Jacobi. Cp. Pünjer, i, 564-585.

theologians, to whose consequent attempts to strain out by the most dubious means the supernatural elements from the Bible narratives [1] the name of "rationalism" came to be specially applied, that being the kind of criticism naturally most discussed among the clergy. Taking rise broadly in the work of Semler[2] (1725-91), Professor at Halle, the method led stage by stage to the scientific performance of Strauss, Baur, and the recent "higher criticism" of the Old Testament. Noteworthy at its outset as exhibiting the tendency of official believers to make men, in the words of Lessing, irrational philosophers by way of making them rational Christians,[3] this order of "rationalism" in its intermediate stages belongs rather to the history of Biblical scholarship than to that of Freethought, since more radical work was being done by unprofessional writers outside, and deeper problems were raised by the new systems of philosophy. In Germany, however, the whole development of opinion after the French Revolution remained largely in the hands of the official university class. In Prussia, the brother of Frederick, who succeeded in 1786, declared himself the champion of religion and the enemy of free-thinking.[4] As late as 1787 there appeared a strongly anti-Christian and anti-clerical work, *The only true system of the Christian religion*, attributed to MAUVILLON[5]; but the new regimen, aided by the reaction against the Revolution, seems for a time to have prevented any such open propaganda, leaving the leaven of anti-supernaturalism and critical philosophy to work all the more effectively among the increasing university-going population.

10. Meanwhile the effect of the age of *Aufklärung* was apparent in the practically freethinking attitude of the two foremost men of letters in the new Germany—

---

[1] The method was at least as old as the *Evangelium medici* of Connor. See above, p. 307.

[2] On whom see Farrar, *Crit. Hist. of Freethought*, pp. 311-316; Saintes, liv. ii, ch. 3; Hagenbach, pp. 77-81.

[3] Cited by Cairns, p. 205.   [4] Hagenbach, p. 125.

[5] Noack, Th. iii, Kap. 9.

GOETHE and SCHILLER. Of the former, despite the bluster of Carlyle, and despite the æsthetic favor shown to Christianity in *Wilhelm Meister,* no religious ingenuity can make more than a pantheist,[1] who, in so far as he touched on Biblical questions, copied the half-grown rationalism of the school of Semler.[2] He has told how, when Lavater insisted that he must choose between orthodox Christianity and Atheism, he answered that if he were not free to be a Christian in his own way *(wie ich es bisher gehegt hätte),* he would as soon turn Atheist as Christian, the more so as he saw that nobody knew very well what either signified.[3] Nor did he ever yield to the Christian creed more than a Platonic amity.

One passage in Goethe's essay on the Pentateuch, appended to the *West-Oestlicher Divan,* is worth noting here as illustrating the ability of genius to cherish and propagate historical fallacies. It runs: "The peculiar, unique, and deepest theme of the history of the world and man, to which all others are subordinate, is always the conflict of belief and unbelief. All epochs in which belief rules, under whatever form, are illustrious, inspiring and fruitful for that time and the future. All epochs on the other hand in which unbelief, in whatever form, secures a miserable victory, even though for a moment they may flaunt it proudly, disappear for posterity, because no man willingly troubles himself with knowledge of the unfruitful" (First ed., S. 424-5). Goethe goes on to speak of the four latter books of Moses as occupied with the theme of unbelief, and of the first as occupied with belief. Thus his formula was based, to begin with, on purely fabulous history, into the nature of which his poetic faculty gave him no true insight whatever. Applied to real history, his formula has no validity save on a definition which implies either an equivoque or an argument in a circle. If it refer, in the natural sense, to epochs in which any given religion is widely rejected and assailed, it is palpably

---

[1] The chief sample passages in his works are the poem *Das Göttliche* and the speech of Faust in reply to Gretchen in the garden scene. It was the surmised pantheism of Goethe's poem *Prometheus* that, according to Jacobi, drew from Lessing *his* avowal of a pantheistic leaning. The poem has even an atheistic ring; but we have Goethe's own account of the influence of Spinoza on him from his youth onwards (*Dichtung und Wahrheit,* Th. III, B. xiv; Th. IV, B. xvi).

[2] See the *Alt-Testamentliches* Appendix to the *West-Oestlicher Divan.*

[3] *Dichtung und Wahrheit,* Th. III, B. xiv, par. 20.

false. The Renaissance and Goethe's own century were ages of such unbelief; and they remain much more deeply interesting than the Ages of Faith. St. Peter's at Rome is the work of a reputedly unbelieving Pope. If on the other hand his formula is meant to apply to belief in the sense of energy and enthusiasm, it is still fallacious. The crusades were manifestations of energy and enthusiasm; but they were profoundly "unfruitful", and they are not deeply interesting. The only sense in which Goethe's formula could stand would be one in which it is recognised that all vigorous intellectual life stands for "belief"—that is to say, that Lucretius and Voltaire, Paine and d'Holbach, stand for "belief" when confidently attacking beliefs. The formula is thus true only in a strained and non-natural sense; whereas it is sure to be read and to be believed, by thoughtless admirers, in its natural and false sense, though the whole history of Byzantium and modern Islam is a history of stagnant and unfruitful belief, and that of modern Europe a history of fruitful doubt, disbelief, and denial, involving new affirmations. Goethe's own mind on the subject was in a state of verbalising confusion, the result or expression of his aversion to clear analytical thought and his habit of poetic allegory and apriorism. Where he himself doubted and denied current creeds, as in his work in natural science, he was most fruitful (though he was not always right—*e.g.*, his polemic against Newton's theory of light); and the permanently interesting part of his *Faust* is precisely that which artistically utters the doubt through which he passed to a pantheistic Naturalism.

11. No less certain is the unbelief of Schiller (1759—1805), whom Hagenbach even takes as "the representative of the rationalism of his age". In his juvenile *Robbers*, indeed, he makes his worst villains freethinkers; and in the preface he stoutly champions religion against all assailants; but hardly ever after that piece does he give a favorable portrait of a priest.[1] He himself soon joined the *Aufklärung;* and all his aesthetic appreciation of Christianity never carried him beyond the positions that it virtually had the tendency *(Anlage)* to the highest and noblest, though that was in general tastelessly and repulsively represented by Christians; and further that in a certain sense it is the only aesthetic religion, whence it

[1] Remarked by Hagenbach, p. 238.

is that it gives such pleasure to the feminine nature, and
that only among women is it to be met with in a tolerable
form.[1]   Like Goethe, he sought to reduce the Biblical
supernatural to the plane of possibility,[2] in the manner of
the liberal theologians of the period ; and like him he often
writes like a Deist,[3] though professedly for a time a
Kantist.   On the other hand, he does not hesitate to say
that a healthy nature (which Goethe had said needed no
Morality, no *Natur-recht*,[4] and no political metaphysic),
needed neither Deity nor Immortality to sustain it.[5]

12. The critical philosophy of KANT may be said to
represent most comprehensively the outcome in German
intelligence of the higher Freethought of the age.   In its
most truly critical part, the analytic treatment of previous
theistic systems in the *Critique of Pure Reason* (1781), he is
definitely anti-religious[6] ; and the rest of his treatment of
religion is an almost avowedly unscientific attempt to
restore the reign of theism on a basis of a mere emotional
and ethical necessity assumed to exist in human nature—
a necessity which he never even attempts to demonstrate.
It is tolerably clear that Kant's motive at this stage was
mere unphilosophic fear that Naturalism would work
moral harm[7]—a fear shared by him with the mass of the
average minds of his age.

> In the preface to the second edition of the *Critique of Pure
> Reason* (1787) he writes that "only through criticism can the
> roots be cut of Materialism, Fatalism, Atheism, freethinking
> unbelief (*freigeisterischen Unglauben*), Fanaticism and Super-
> stition, which may become universally injurious; also of

---

[1] Letter to Goethe, 17 Aug., 1795 (*Briefwechsel*, No. 87).   The passage is
given in Carlyle's essay on Schiller.

[2] In *Die Sendung Moses*.

[3] See the *Philosophische Briefe*.

[4] Carlyle translates, "No Rights of Man," which was probably the
implication.

[5] Letter to Goethe, 9 July, 1796 (*Briefwechsel*, No. 188).

[6] For an able argument vindicating the unity of Kant's system, however,
see Prof. Adamson, *The Philosophy of Kant*, 1879, p. 21 ff., as against Lange.
With the verdict in the text compare that of Heine, *Zur Gesch. der Relig. u.
Philos. in Deutschland*, B. iii (*Werke*, Ausg. in 12 Bn., iii, 81-82).

[7] Cp. Hagenbach, p. 223.

Idealism and Scepticism, which are dangerous rather to the Schools, and can hardly reach the general public". (Meiklejohn mistranslates: " which *are* universally injurious "— Bohn ed. p. xxxvii.) This passage virtually puts the popular religion and all philosophies save Kant's own on one level of moral dubiety. It is however distinctly uncandid as regards the "freethinking unbelief", for Kant himself was certainly an unbeliever in Christian miracles and dogmas. His want of philosophic candor, or at least his readiness to make an appeal to prejudice, again appears when he asks, " Whence does the Freethinker derive his knowledge that there is, for instance, no Supreme Being ? " (*Kritik der reinen Vernunft, Transc. Methodenlehre,* 1 H. 2 Absch., ed. Kirchmann, 1879, S. 587; Bohn tr. p. 458.) He had just before professed to be dealing with denial of the " existence of God "—a proposition of no significance whatever unless " God " be defined. He now without warning substitutes the undefined expression " Supreme Being " for " God ", thus imputing a proposition probably never sustained by any human being. Either, then, Kant's own proposition was the entirely vacuous one that nobody can demonstrate the impossibility of an alleged *undefined* existence, or he was virtually asserting that no one can disprove *any* alleged supernatural existence—witch, demon, Moloch, Krishna, Bel, Siva, Aphrodite, or Isis and Osiris. In the latter case he would be absolutely stultifying his own claim to cut the roots of " Superstition " and " Fanaticism " as well as of freethinking and materialism; for if the Freethinker cannot disprove Jehovah, neither can the Kantist disprove Allah and Satan. From this dilemma Kant's argument cannot be delivered. And as he finally introduces Deity as a psychologically and morally necessary regulative idea, howbeit indemonstrable, he leaves every species of superstition exactly where it stood before— every superstition being practically held, as against "free-thinking unbelief", on just such a tenure. It should be not ed that Kant's doctrine of theism as a need of the emotional and moral nature was popularly put before him by Lessing, and had been put in circulation by Rousseau. Cp. Haym's *Herder nach seinem Leben* . . . *dargestellt,* 1877, i, 33, 48.

For the rest, Kant's attempt to adapt the Christian system to the needs of reason is avowedly an extension of tactics already in vogue, and ethically amounts to saying that truth is to be grafted on falsity because the common people must have, in Middleton's phrase, " some religion or other "—this while he repudiates Christian ethics as immoral, and elsewhere protests against telling a falsehood even to a would-be murderer.

(Compare his *Religion innerhalb der Grenzen der Blossen Vernunft*
(1793) B. iii, Apotome i, Sect. 6 ; B. iv, Apot. ii, preamble and
Sect. i, 3, and 4 ; with the essay in reply to Constant in App.
to Rosenkranz's ed. of *Werke*, vii, 295—given by T. K. Abbott
in his trans. of the *Critique of Judgment*.

The Kantian philosophy had thus the effect of an
assurance to the religious world that though all previous
arguments for theism were philosophically worthless,
theism was safe on the fluid basis of feeling. Naturally
the deeper Theists of his day—as Fichte and Schelling—
when they realised his position, reacted against it, and
sought to restore their faith to a basis of demonstrative
argument. The general result seems to have been the
production of nearly equal quantities of reassurance and
scepticism ; and at the universities the effect of Kant's
system was notably to discredit Christian orthodoxy.[1]
Stäudlin begins the preface to his *History and Spirit of
Scepticism* (1794) with the remark that " Scepticism begins
to be a disease of the age " ; and Kant closes his list of
sceptics. Thus, though the French Revolution intensified
the official hostility to Freethought in Germany[2] there
seems to have been at bottom less religious reaction there
than in either England or France, the anti-supernaturalist
handling of the Scriptures going on continuously, and the
educated class remaining remarkably "emancipated". In
Austria, probably, French ideas were only less freely
current than in Prussia ; but there is thus far no Austrian
name in freethought literature that can stand beside that
of BEETHOVEN,[3] the supreme musician of his age.

§ III.—*The remaining European States.*

1. Traces of new rationalistic life are to be seen in
Scandinàvia at least as early as the time of Descartes.

---

[1] Stuckenberg, *Life of Kant*, 1882, p. 386. Fichte, who was falsely
accused of Atheism, was one of the anti-Christian enthusiasts. Cp.
Hagenbach, pp. 228-9 as to the results noted by Herder.

[2] Kant himself was restricted by the censorship in 1792, and afterwards.
At first he was indignant, but he soon submitted to the king's commands, and
undertook to write no more on religious matters. Stuckenberg, pp. 360-4.

[3] As to whose freethinking see art. on him by Macfarren in *Dict. of
Univ. Biog.*, and Grove's art. in *Dict. of Music and Musicians.*

There, as elsewhere, the Reformation had been substantially a fiscal or economic revolution, proceeding on
various lines. In Denmark the movement began among
the people ; the nobility rapidly following, to their own
great profit[1]; in Sweden the king took the initiative,
having sore need of funds, and a thoroughly anti-ecclesiastical temper.[2]   Towards the middle of the seventeenth
century there are increasing traces of rationalism at the
court of the famous Christina, who already in her youth
is found much interested in the objections of " Jews,
heathens, and philosophers, against Christian doctrine ";[3]
and her invitation of Descartes to her court (1649)
suggests that Sweden had been not a little affected by
the revulsion of popular thought which followed on the
Thirty Years' War in Germany. In the course of a few
years, the new spirit had gone so far as to make church-
going matter for open scoffing at the Swedish court[4];
and the Queen's adoption of Romanism soon after her
abdication appears to have been by way of revulsion
from a state of mind approaching atheism, to which she
had been led by her freethinking French physician,
Bourdelot, after Descartes's death.[5] No literary results,
however, could follow in the then state of Swedish
culture, when the studies at even the new colleges were
mainly confined to Latin and theology[6] ; and Scandinavia
in general, though affected like Russia by the French
freethinking influence in the eighteenth century, has
only in our own age begun to contribute weightily to the
serious thought of Europe.

2. In Poland, where Socinianism had flourished from
the first, positive Atheism is heard of in 1688-9, when
COUNT LISZINSKI, among whose papers, it was said, had
been found the written statement that man had made God
out of nothing, was denounced by the bishops of Wilna

[1] Otté, *Scandinavian History*, 1874, pp. 222-4.
[2] *Id.*, pp. 232-6.
[3] Geijer, *History of the Swedes*, Eng. tr., i, 324.
[4] *Id.*, p. 343.   [5] *Id.*, p. 342.   [6] *Id., ib.*

and Posnovia, tried, beheaded, and burnt, his ashes being
scattered from a cannon.[1] But even had a less murderous
treatment been meted out to such heresy, anarchic Poland
was in no state to develop a rationalistic literature. In
Russia, again, literature and culture, as distinguished
from folklore and monastic writing, only begin in the
sixteenth century ; when we find the usual symptom of
criticism of the lives of the monks.[2] But the culture was
almost wholly ecclesiastical, and in the seventeenth century
the effort of the Patriarch Nicon to correct the sacred
texts was furiously resisted.[3] Gradually there arose
a new secular fiction, under western influence ; and
Peter the Great, who promoted printing and literature
as he did every other new activity, took the singular step
of actually withdrawing writing materials from the monks,
whose influence he held to be wholly reactionary. Now
began the era of translations from the French ; and in
the day of the great Catherine the ideas of the *philosophes*
were the ruling ones at her court,[4] till the outbreak of the
Revolution put the whole school in disgrace with her.
This did not alter the tone of thought of the educated
classes ; but in Russia as in Scandinavia it was not till the
nineteenth century that original serious literature began.

3. Returning to Italy, no longer the leader of European
thought, but still full of veiled freethinking, we find in the
seventeenth century the proof that no amount of such
predisposition can countervail thoroughly bad political
conditions. Ground down by the matchless misrule of
Spain, from which the conspiracy of the monk Campanella
vainly sought to free her, and by the kindred tyranny of
the Papacy, Italy could produce in its educated class only

---

[1] He claimed that certain remarks penned by him in an atheistic work,
challenging its argument, represented not unbelief but the demand for a
better proof, which he undertook to produce.   Art. in *Biographie Universelle*.

[2] L. Sichler, *Hist. de la litt. Russe*, 1887, pp. 88-89, 139.   Cp. Rambaud,
History of Russia, Eng. tr. 1879, i, 309, 321, 328.

[3] Rambaud, i, 414-417,   The struggle (1654) elicited old forms of heresy,
going back to Manicheism and Gnosticism.

[4] She bought the library of Diderot when he was in need, constituted
him its salaried keeper, and actually had him for a time at her court.

triflers, whose unbelief was of a piece with their cynicism.
While Naples and the south decayed, mental energy had
for a time flourished in Tuscany, where, under the grand
dukes from Ferdinando I onwards, industry and commerce
had revived; and even after a time of retrogression,
Ferdinando II encouraged science, now made newly
glorious by the names of Galileo and Torricelli. But
again there was a relapse; and at the end of the century,
under a bigoted duke, Florence was priest-ridden and, at
least in outward seeming, gloomily superstitious; while
the rest of Italy was cynically corrupt and intellectually
superficial.[1] Yet it only needed the breathing time and
the improved conditions under the Bourbon rule in the
eighteenth century to set up a wonderful intellectual
revival. Then came the great work of VICO, the *Principles
of a New Science* (1722), whereof the originality and the
depth, qualities in which it on the whole excels Montesquieu's *Spirit of Laws*, place him among the great freethinkers in philosophy. It was significant of much that
Vico's book, without professing any hostility to faith,
grappled with the science of human development in an
essentially secular and scientific spirit. This is the note
of the whole eighteenth century in Italy. Vico posits
Deity and Providence, but proceeds nevertheless to study
the laws of civilisation inductively from its phenomena.
In the same age Muratori and Giannone amassed their
unequalled historical learning; and a whole series of
Italian writers broke new ground on the field of social
science, Italy having led the way in this as formerly in
philosophy and physics.[2]

4. Between 1737 and 1798 may be counted twenty-
eight Italian writers on political economy; and among
them was one, CESARE BECCARIA, who on another theme
produced perhaps the most practically influential single

---

[1] Zeller, *Hist. d'Italie*, pp. 426-432, 450; Procter, *Hist. of Italy*, 2nd ed.,
pp. 240, 268.
[2] See the *Storia della economia pubblica in Italia* of G. Pecchio, 1829,
p. 61, ff., as to the claim of Antonio Serra (*Breve trattato*, etc., 1613) to be
the pioneer of modern political economy.

book of the eighteenth century,[1] the treatise on *Crimes and Punishments* (1764), which affected penal methods for the better throughout the whole of Europe. Even were he not known to be a Deist, his strictly secular and rationalist method would have brought upon him priestly suspicion; and he had in fact to defend himself against pertinacious and unscrupulous attacks,[2] though he had sought in his book to guard himself by occasionally "veiling the truth in clouds".[3] As we have seen, Beccaria owed his intellectual awakening first to Montesquieu and above all to Helvétius—another testimony to the reformative virtue of all freethought.

5. Of the aforesaid eight-and-twenty writers on economics, probably the majority were freethinkers. Among them, at all events, were ALGAROTTI, the distinguished æsthetician, one of the group round Frederick at Berlin; FILANGIERI, whose work on legislation (put on the *Index* by the Papacy) won the high praise of Franklin; GALIANI, one of the brightest and soundest wits in the circle of the French *philosophes;* GENOVESI, the "redeemer of the Italian mind",[4] and the chief establisher of economic science for modern Italy. To these names may be added those of ALFIERI, one of the strongest anticlericalists of his age; BETTINELLI, the correspondent of Voltaire and author of *The Resurrection of Italy* (1775); Count DANDOLO, author of a French work on *The New Men* (1799); and the learned GIANNONE, author of the great anti-papal *History of the Kingdom of Naples* (1723), who, after more than one narrow escape, was thrown in prison by the King of Sardinia, and died there (1748) after twelve years' confinement. Italy had done her full share, considering her heritage of

---

[1] The *Dei delitti e delle pene* was translated into twenty-two languages. Pecchio, p. 144.

[2] See in the 6th ed. of the *Dei Delitti* (Harlem, 1766) the appended *Risposta ad uno Scritto*, etc., *Parte prima, Accuse d'empietà.*

[3] See his letter to the Abbé Morellet, cited by Mr. Farrer in ch. i of his ed. of *Crimes and Punishments*, 1880, p. 5. It describes the Milanese as deeply sunk in prejudices.

[4] Pecchio, p. 123.

burdens and hindrances, in the intellectual work of
the century; and in the names of Galvani and Volta
stands the record of one more of her great contribu-
tions to human enlightenment. Under Duke Leopold
of Tuscany, the Papacy was so far defied that books put
on the *Index* were produced for him under the imprint of
London;[1] and the Papacy itself at length gave way to
the spirit of reform, Clement XIV consenting among
other things to abolish the Order of Jesuits (1773), after
his predecessor had died of grief over his proved impotence
to resist the secular policy of the States around him.[2]
Such was the dawn of the new Italian day that has since
slowly but steadily broadened, albeit under many a cloud.

6. For the rest of Europe during the eighteenth
century, we have to note only traces of receptive thought.
Spain under Bourbon rule, as already noted, experienced
an administrative renascence. Such men as Count Aranda
(1718-99) and Aszo y del Rio (1742—1814) wrought to cut
the claws of the Inquisition and to put down the Jesuits;
but not yet, after the long work of destruction accomplished
by the Church in the past, could Spain produce a fresh
literature of any far-reaching power. Switzerland, which
owed much of new intellectual life to the influx of French
Protestants at the revocation of the Edict of Nantes,
contributed to the European movement some names, of
which by far the most famous is Rousseau; and the potent
presence of Voltaire cannot have failed to affect Swiss
culture. The chief native service to intellectual progress
thus far, however, was rendered in the field of the natural
sciences, Swiss religious opinion being only passively
liberalised, mainly in a Unitarian direction.

---

[1] Zeller, p. 473.   [2] *Id.*, pp. 478-9.

CHAPTER XV.

EARLY FREETHOUGHT IN THE UNITED STATES.

1. PERHAPS the most signal of all the proofs of the change wrought in the opinion of the civilised world in the eighteenth century is the fact that at the time of the War of Independence the leading statesmen of the American colonies were Deists. Such were BENJAMIN FRANKLIN, the diplomatist of the Revolution; THOMAS PAINE, its prophet and inspirer: WASHINGTON, its commander; and JEFFERSON, its typical legislator. But for these four men, the American Revolution certainly could not have been accomplished in that age; and they thus represent in a peculiar degree the power of new ideas, in fit conditions, to transform societies, at least politically. On the other hand, the fashion in which their relation to the creeds of their time has been garbled, alike in American and English histories, proves how completely they were in advance of the average thought of their day: and also how effectively the mere institutional influence of creeds can arrest a nation's mental development. It is still one of the stock doctrines of religious sociology in England and America that Deism, miscalled Atheism, wrought the Reign of Terror in the French Revolution; when as a matter of fact the same Deism was at the head of affairs in the American.

2. The rise of rationalism in the colonies must be traced in the main to the imported English literature of the eighteenth century; for the first Puritan settlements had contained at most only a fraction of Freethought; and the conditions, so deadly for all manner even of devout heresy,[1] made avowed unbelief impossible. The

[1] See Mr. Brooks Adams's *Emancipation of Massachusetts* (1887) for a vivid account of the clerical tyranny.

superstitions and cruelties of the Puritan clergy, however, must have bred a silent reaction which prepared a soil for deism of the next age. " The perusal of Shaftesbury and Collins," writes Franklin with reference to his early youth, " had made me a sceptic," after being " previously so as to many doctrines of Christianity ".[1] This was in his seventeenth or eighteenth year, about 1720, so that the importation of deism had been prompt.[2] Throughout life he held to the same opinion, conforming sufficiently to keep on fair terms with his neighbours,[3] and avoiding anything like critical propaganda; though on challenge, in the last year of his life, he avowed his negatively deistic position.[4]

3. Similarly prudent was JEFFERSON, who, like Franklin and Paine, extolled the Gospel Jesus and his teachings, but rejected the notion of supernatural revelation.[5] In a letter written so late as 1822 to a Unitarian correspondent, while refusing to publish another of similar tone, on the score that he was too old for strife, he declared that he " should as soon undertake to bring the crazy skulls of Bedlam to sound understanding as to inculcate reason into that of an Athanasian ".[6] His experience of the New England clergy is expressed in allusions to Connecticut as having been " the last retreat of monkish darkness, bigotry, and abhorrence of those advances of the mind which had carried the other States a century ahead of them "; and in congratulations with John Adams (who had written that " this would be

---

[1] Such is the wording of the passage in the *Autobiography* in the Edinburgh edition of 1803, p. 25, which follows the French translation of the original MS. In the edition of the *Autobiography and Letters* in the Minerva Library, edited by Mr. Bettany (1891, p. 11), which follows Mr. Bigelow's edition of 1879, it runs: " Being then, from reading Shaftesbury and Collins, become a real doubter in many points of our religious doctrine. . . ."

[2] Only in 1784, however, appeared the first anti-Christian work published in America, Ethan Allen's *Reason the only Oracle of Man*. As to its positions, see Conway, *Life of Paine*, ii, 192-3.

[3] *Autobiography*, Bettany's ed. pp. 56, 65, 74, 77, etc.

[4] Letter of 9 March, 1790. *Id.*, p. 636.

[5] Cp. J. T. Morse's *Thomas Jefferson*, in " American Statesmen " series, pp. 339-340.

[6] MS. cited by Dr. Conway, *Life of Paine*, ii, 310-311.

the best of all possible worlds if there were no religion in it "), when "this den of the priesthood is at last broken up ".[1] John Adams, whose letters with their " crowd of scepticisms " kept even Jefferson from sleep,[2] seems to have figured as a member of a Congregationalist church, while in reality a Unitarian.[3] Still more prudent was Washington, who seems to have ranked habitually as a member of the episcopal church ; but concerning whom Jefferson relates that, when the clergy, having noted his constant abstention from any public mention of the Christian religion, so penned an address to him on his withdrawal from the Presidency as almost to force him to some declaration, he answered every part of the address but that, which he entirely ignored. It is further noted that only in his valedictory letter to the governors of the States, on resigning his commission, did he speak of the "benign influence of the Christian religion "[4] — the common tone of the American Deists of that day. It is further established that Washington avoided the Communion in church.[5] For the rest, the broad fact that all mention of Deity was excluded from the Constitution of the United States must be historically taken to signify a profound change in the convictions of the leading minds among the people as compared with the beliefs of their ancestors. At the same time, the fact that they as a rule dissembled their unbelief is a proof that even where legal penalties do not attach to an avowal of serious heresy,

---

[1] *Memoirs of Jefferson*, 1829, iv, 300-1. The date is 1817. These and other passages exhibiting Jefferson's deism are cited in Rayner's *Sketches of the Life*, etc., *of Jefferson*, 1832, pp. 513-517.

[2] *Memoirs of Jefferson*, iv, 331.

[3] Dr. Conway, *Life of Paine*, ii, 310.

[4] Extract from Jefferson's Journal under date Feb. 1, 1800, in the *Memoirs*, iv, 512. Gouverneur Morris, whom Jefferson further cites as to Washington's unbelief, is not a very good witness ; but the main fact cited is significant.

[5] Compare the testimony given by the Rev. Dr. Wilson of Albany, in 1831, as cited by R. D. Owen in his *Discussion on the Authenticity of the Bible* with O. Bacheler (London ed. 1840, p. 231), with the replies on the other side (pp. 233-4). Washington's death-bed attitude was that of a Deist. See all the available data for his supposed orthodoxy in Sparks' *Life of Washington*, 1852, app. iv.

there inheres in the menace of mere social ostracism a power sufficient to coerce the outward life of public and professional men of all grades, in a democratic community where faith maintains and is maintained by a competitive multitude of priests. With this force the freethought of our own age has to reckon, after Inquisitions and blasphemy laws have become obsolete.

4. Nothing in American culture-history more clearly proves the last proposition than the case of THOMAS PAINE, the virtual founder of modern democratic free-thought in Great Britain and the States.[1] It does not appear that Paine openly professed any heresy while he lived in England, or in America before the French Revolution. Yet the first sentence of his *Age of Reason*, of which the first part was written shortly before his imprisonment, under sentence of death from the Robespierre Government, in Paris (1793), shows that he had long held pronounced deistic opinions.[2] They were probably matured in the States, where, as we have seen, such views were often privately held, though there, as Franklin is said to have jesuitically declared in his old age, by way of encouraging immigration : "Atheism is unknown ; infidelity rare and secret, so that persons may live to a great age in this country without having their piety shocked by meeting with either an atheist or an infidel ". Paine did an un-equalled service to the American Revolution by his *Common Sense* and his series of pamphlets headed *The Crisis :* there is in fact little question that but for the intense stimulus thus given by him at critical moments the move-ment might have collapsed at an early stage. Yet he seems to have had no thought there and then of avowing his Deism. It was in part for the express purpose of resisting the ever-strengthening attack of atheism in

---

[1] So far as is known, Paine was the first writer to use the expression " The religion of Humanity ". See Conway's *Life of Paine*, 1892, ii, 206. To Paine's influence, too, appears to be due the founding of the first American Anti-Slavery Society. *Id.*, i, 51-2, 60, 80, etc.

[2] Cp. Dr. Conway's *Life of Paine*, ii, 205-7.

France on Deism itself that he undertook to save it by
repudiating the Judæo-Christian revelation; and it is not
even certain that he would have issued the *Age of Reason*
when it did appear, had he not supposed he was going to
his death when put under arrest, on which score he left
the manuscript for publication.[1]

5. Its immediate effect was much greater in Britain,
where his *Rights of Man* had already won him a vast
popularity in the teeth of the most furious reaction, than
in America.   There, to his profound chagrin, he found
that his honest utterance of his heresy brought on him
hatred, calumny, ostracism, and even personal and
political molestation.   In 1797 he had founded in Paris
the little " Church of Theo-philanthropy ", beginning his
inaugural discourse with the words : " Religion has two
principal enemies, Fanaticism and Infidelity, or that which
is called atheism.   The first requires to be combated by
reason and morality; the other by natural philosophy." [2]
These were his settled convictions; and he lived to find
himself shunned and vilified, in the name of religion, in
the country whose freedom he had so puissantly wrought
to win.[3]   The Quakers, his father's sect, refused him a
burial-place.   He has had sympathy and fair play, as a
rule, only from the atheists whom he distrusted and
opposed, or from thinkers who no longer hold by Deism.
There is reason to think that in his last years the deistic
optimism which survived the deep disappointments of the
French Revolution began   to   give   way   before   deeper

---

[1] A letter of Franklin to some one who had shown him a freethinking
manuscript, advising against its publication (Bettany's ed. p. 620) has been
conjecturally connected with Paine, but was clearly not addressed to him.
Franklin died in 1790, and Paine was out of America from 1787 onwards.
But the letter is in every way inapplicable to the *Age of Reason*.   The
remark : " If men are so wicked *with* religion, what would they be *without*
it," could not be made to a devout Deist like Paine.

[2] Conway, *Life of Paine*, 1892, ii, 254-5.

[3] See Dr. Conway's chapter, " The American Inquisition," vol. ii,
c. 16 ; also pp. 361-2, 374, 379.   The falsity of the ordinary charges against
Paine's character is finally made clear by Dr. Conway, ch. xix, and
pp. 371, 383, 419, 423.   Cp. the author's pamphlet *Thomas Paine : an
Investigation* (Bonner).

reflection on the cosmic problem,[1] if not before the treatment he had undergone at the hands of Unitarians and
Trinitarians alike.   The Butlerian argument, that Nature
is as unsatisfactory as revelation, had been pressed upon
him by Bishop Watson in a reply to the *Age of Reason*;
and though, like most Deists of his age, he regarded it as
a vain defence of orthodoxy, he was not the man to remain
long blind to its force against deistic assumptions.   Like
Franklin, he had energetically absorbed and given out the
new ideals of physical science; his originality in the invention of a tubular iron bridge, and in the application of
steam to navigation,[2] being nearly as notable as that of
Franklin's great discovery concerning electricity.   Had
the two men drawn their philosophy from the France of
the latter part of the century instead of the England of
the first, they had doubtless gone deeper.   As it was,
temperamental optimism had kept both satisfied with the
transitional formula; and in the France of before and after
the Revolution they lived preoccupied with politics.

6. The habit of reticence or dissimulation among
American public men was only too surely confirmed by
the treatment meted out to Paine.   Few stood by him,
and the deistic movement set up in his latter years by
Elihu Palmer soon succumbed to the conditions.[3]   All the
while, such statesmen as Madison and Monroe, the latter
Paine's personal friend, seem to have been of his way of
thinking,[4] though the evidence is scanty.   The essential
evil is that the baseness of partisan politics is at all times
ready to turn a man's heresy to his political ruin; such
being in part the explanation of the gross ingratitude
shown to Paine.   Thus it came about that, save for the
liberal movement of the Hicksite Quakers,[5] the secret

---

[1] Conway, ii, 371.
[2] See the details in Conway's *Life*, ii, 280-1, and *note*.   He had also a
scheme for a gunpowder motor (*Id.* and i, 240), and various other
remarkable plans.
[3] Conway, ii, 362-371.
[4] Testimonies quoted by R. D. Owen, as cited, pp. 231-2.
[5] Conway, ii, 422.

American Deism of Paine's day was decorously transformed into the later Unitarianism, the extremely rapid
advance of which in the next generation is the best proof
of the commonness of private unbelief.

7. In the middle decades of the century the conditions
had been so little changed that after the death of President
LINCOLN, who was certainly a non-Christian Deist, and
an agnostic Deist at that,[1] it was sought to be established
that he was latterly orthodox. In his presidential
campaign of 1860 he escaped attack on his opinions simply
because his opponent, Stephen A. Douglas, was likewise
an unbeliever.[2] The great negro orator, FREDERICK
DOUGLASS, was as heterodox as Lincoln.[3] It is even
alleged that President Grant[4] was of the same cast of
opinion. Such is the general drift of intelligent thought
in the United States, from Washington onwards; and
still the social conditions impose on public men the burden
of concealment, while popular history is garbled for the
same reasons.

---

[1] Cp. Lamon's *Life of Lincoln*, and J. B. Remsburg's *Abraham Lincoln
Was he a Christian?* (New York, 1893.)

[2] Remsburg, pp. 318-19.

[3] Personal information.   [4] Remsburg, p. 324

CHAPTER XVI.

FREETHOUGHT IN THE NINETEENTH CENTURY.

As with the cause of democracy, so with the cause of rationalism, the forward movement which was checked for a generation by the reaction against the French Revolution grew only the deeper and more powerful through the check ; and the nineteenth century closes on a record of freethinking progress which may be said to outbulk that of all the previous centuries of the modern era together. So great has been the activity of the century in point of mere quantity that it becomes impossible, within the scheme of a "Short History", to treat it on even such a reduced scale of narrative as has been applied to the past. A detailed history from the French Revolution onwards will require a separate volume nearly as large as the present. It must here suffice, therefore, to take one or two broad and general views of the century's work, leaving adequate critical and narrative treatment for a separate undertaking. The most helpful method seems to be that of a conspectus of (1) the main movements and forces that have affected in varying degrees the thought of the civilised world, and (2) of the advance made and the point reached in the culture of the nations, separately considered. At the same time, the forces of rationalism may be discriminated into Particular and General. We may then roughly represent the lines of movement, in loose chronological order, as follows :—

I.—*Forces of criticism and corrective thought bearing expressly on religious beliefs.*

  1. In Great Britain and America, the new movements of popular free-thought deriving immediately from Paine, and lasting continuously to the present day.

2. In France and elsewhere, the reverberation of the attack of Voltaire, as against official orthodoxy after 1815.

3. German " Rationalism ", culminating in the work of the schools of Strauss and Baur, and all along affecting studious thought in other countries.

4. In England, the neo-Christianity of the school of Coleridge, a disintegrating force, promoting the " Broad Church " tendency.

5. The utilitarianism of the school of Bentham, carried into moral and social science.

6. Comtism, making little direct impression on the " constructive " lines laid by the founder, but affecting critical thought in all directions.

7. German philosophy, Kantian and post-Kantian, in particular the Hegelian, turned to anti-Christian account by Strauss, Baur, Bruno Bauer, Feuerbach, and Marx.

8. German Atheism and Materialism—represented by Feuerbach and Büchner.

9. Revived English Deism, involving destructive criticism of Christianity, as in Hennell, F. W. Newman, W. R. Greg, and Theodore Parker.

10. American Transcendentalism or Pantheism—the school of Emerson.

11. The later or scientific " higher criticism " of the Old Testament— represented by Kuenen and Wellhausen.

12. Colenso's preliminary attack on the Pentateuch, a systematised return to Voltairean common-sense, rectifying the unscientific course of the " higher criticism ".

13. New historical criticism of Christian origins, in particular the work of Renan and Havet in France.

14. Exhibition of rationalism within the churches, as in Germany, Holland, and Switzerland generally; in England in the *Essays and Reviews*, and later in the documentary criticism of the Old Testament ; in America in popular theology.

15. Association of rationalistic doctrine with the Socialist movements, new and old, from Owen to Marx.

16. Communication of doubt and questioning through poetry and *belles-lettres* — as in Shelley, Byron, Wordsworth, Clough, Tennyson, Arnold, Browning, Swinburne, Heine, Victor Hugo, Leconte de Lisle, Leopardi, and some recent English novelists.

II.—*Modern Science, physical, mental, and moral, sapping the bases of all supernaturalist systems.*

1. Astronomy, newly directed by Laplace.

2. Geology, gradually connected (as in Britain by Chambers) with

3. Biology, made definitely non-deistic by Darwin.

4. The comprehension of all science in the Evolution Theory, as by Spencer, advancing on Comte.

5. Psychology, as regards localisation of brain functions.

6. Comparative mythology, as yet imperfectly applied to Christism.

7. Sociology, as outlined by Comte, Buckle, Spencer, and others, on strictly naturalistic lines.

8. Comparative Hierology : the methodical application of principles insisted on by all the Deists.

On the other hand, we may group somewhat as follows the general forces of retardation of freethought operating throughout the century :—

1. Penal laws, still operative in Germany against popular freethought propaganda.
2. Class interests, involving in the first half of the century a social conspiracy against rationalism in England.
3. Commercial pressure thus set up, and always involved in the influence of churches.
4. In England, identification of orthodox Dissent with political Liberalism —a sedative.
5. Concessions by the clergy, especially in England and the United States—to many, another sedative.
6. Above all, the production of new masses of popular ignorance in the industrial nations, and continued lack of education in the others.
7. On this basis, business-like and in large part secular-minded organisation of the endowed churches, as against a Freethought propaganda hampered by the previously named causes, and in England by laws which veto all endowment of anti-Christian heresy.

It remains to make, with forced brevity, the surveys thus outlined.

PART I.—THE CULTURE FORCES.

§ 1. *Popular Propaganda.*

1. If any one circumstance more than another differentiates the life of to-day from that of older civilisations, or from that of previous centuries of the modern era, it is the diffusion of rationalistic views among the " common people ".   In no other age is to be found the phenomenon of widespread critical scepticism among the laboring masses ; in all previous ages the constant and abject ignorance of the mass of the people has been the sure foothold of superstitious systems.   And this vital change in the distribution of knowledge is largely to be attributed to the written and spoken teaching of a line of men who made popular enlightenment their great aim.   Their leading type is THOMAS PAINE, whom we have seen combining a gospel of democracy with a gospel of critical

reason in the midst of the French Revolution. Never before had rationalism been made popular. The English and French Deists had written for the middle and upper classes. Peter Annet was practically the first who sought to reach the multitude; and his punishment expressed the special resentment aroused in the governing classes by such a policy. Paine was to Annet as a cannon to a musket, and through the democratic ferment of his day he won an audience a hundredfold wider than Annet could dream of reaching. The anger of the governing classes, in a time of anti-democratic panic, was proportional. Paine would have been at least imprisoned for his *Rights of Man* had he not fled from England in time; and the sale of all his books was furiously prohibited and systematically punished. Yet they circulated everywhere, even in Protestant Ireland,[1] hitherto affected only under the surface of upper-class life by Deism. The circulation of Bishop Watson's *Apology* in reply only served to spread the contagion, as it brought the issues before multitudes who would not otherwise have heard of them.[2] As the years went on, the persecution in England grew even fiercer; but it was met with a stubborn hardihood which wore out even the malice of piety. A name not to be forgotten by those who value obscure service to human freedom is that of RICHARD CARLILE, who between 1819 and 1835 underwent nine years' imprisonment in his unyielding struggle for the freedom of the Press, of thought and of speech.[3] On the basis of the propagandist and publishing work done by him, and carried on diversely by such free lances as ROBERT TAYLOR (ex-clergyman, author of the *Diegesis*, 1829, and *The Devil's Pulpit*, 1830), CHARLES SOUTHWELL (1814—1860), and William

[1] See Lecky, *Hist. of Ireland in the Eighteenth Century*, ed. 1892, iii, 382.
[2] Cp. Conway's *Life of Paine*, ii, 252-3.
[3] See Harriet Martineau's *History of the Peace*, ed. 1877, ii, 87, as to the treatment of those who acted as Carlile's shopmen. Women were imprisoned as well as men, *e.g.*, SUSANNA WRIGHT and MATILDA ROALFE, as to whom see Wheeler's *Dictionary*, and last ref. Carlile's wife and sister were likewise imprisoned with him; and over twenty volunteer shopmen in all went to jail.

Hone,[1] who ultimately became an independent preacher
—all three subjected to cruel imprisonments—at length
rose a systematic Secularist propaganda, the name having
relation to the term " Secularism ", invented by Mr.
GEORGE JACOB HOLYOAKE.

2. Mr. Holyoake had been a missionary and martyr in
the movement of Socialism set up by ROBERT OWEN,
whose teaching, essentially scientific on its psychological
or philosophical side, was the first effort to give systematic effect to democratic ideals by organising industry.
Owen was a Freethinker in all things; and his whole
movement was so penetrated by an anti-theological spirit
that the clergy as a rule became its bitter enemies, though
such publicists as Macaulay and John Mill also combined
in scouting it on political and economic grounds.   To a
considerable extent it was furthered by the popular deistic
philosophy of GEORGE and ANDREW COMBE, which then
had a great vogue[2]; and by the implications of phrenology,
then also in its most scientific and progressive stage.
When, for various reasons, Owen's movement dissolved,
the freethinking element seems to have been absorbed in
the Secular party, while the others appear to have gone in
part to build up the movement of Co-operation.   The imprisonment of Mr. Holyoake (1842) for six months on a
trifling charge of blasphemy, is an illustration of the
brutal spirit of public orthodoxy at the time.[3]   Where
bigotry could thus only injure and oppress without
suppressing heresy, it stimulated resistance ; and the
result of the stimulus was the founding of a Secular
Society in 1852.   Six years later there was elected to
the Presidency of the London Society of that name the
young CHARLES BRADLAUGH, one of the greatest orators

---

[1] Hone's most important service to popular culture was his issue of the
Apocryphal New Testament, which gave a fresh scientific basis to the popular
criticism of the Gospel history.

[2] Of George Combe's *Constitution of Man*, a deistic work, over 50,000
copies were sold in Britain within twelve years, and 10,000 in America.
Advt. to 4th ed., 1839.

[3] See the details in his *Last Trial by Jury for Atheism in England*.

of his age, and one of the most powerful personalities
ever associated with a progressive movement. Thence-
forward the working masses in England were in large
part kept in touch with a Freethought which drew on
the results of the scientific and scholarly research of the
time, and wielded a dialectic of which trained opponents
confessed the power.[1] When in the year 1880, on Bradlaugh's election to Parliament as member for Northampton,
the Conservative Opposition began the historic proceedings
over the Oath question, they probably did more to
deepen and diffuse the popular Freethought movement
than Bradlaugh himself had done in the whole of his
previous career. The process was furthered by the policy
of prosecuting and imprisoning Mr. G. W. Foote, editor
of the *Freethinker*, under the Blasphemy Laws—a course
not ventured on as against Bradlaugh. When Bradlaugh
took the oath and his seat in 1885, under a ruling of the
Speaker which stultified the whole action of the Speaker
and majorities of the previous Parliament, and no less
that of the Law Courts, straightforward Freethought
stood fivefold stronger in England than in any previous
generation. Apart from their educative work, the
struggles and sufferings of the Secularist leaders had now
secured for Great Britain the abolition within one generation of the old burden of suretyship on newspapers, and
of the disabilities of non-theistic witnesses[2]; the freedom
of public meeting in the London parks; the right of
avowed Atheists to sit in Parliament (Bradlaugh having
finally secured their title to make affirmation instead of
oath); and the virtual discredit of the Blasphemy Laws
as such. It is probable also that the treatment meted
out to Mrs. BESANT marked the end of another form of
tyrannous outrage, already made historic in the case of
Shelley. Secured the custody of her children under a
marital deed of separation, she was deprived of it at

---

[1] See Professor Flint's tribute to the reasoning power of Bradlaugh
and Mr. Holyoake in his *Anti-Theistic Theories*, 4th ed., pp. 518-519.
[2] See Mrs. Bradlaugh Bonner's *Charles Bradlaugh*, i, 149, 288-9.

law (1879) on her avowal of atheistic opinions, with the
result that her influence as a propagandist was immensely
increased.

3. Only in the United States has the public lecture
platform been made a means of propaganda to anything
like the extent seen in Britain : by far the greatest part
of the work in the States being done, however, by Colonel
INGERSOLL, 'the leading American orator of the present
generation, and the most widely influential platform
propagandist of the century.   No other single man, it is
believed, reaches such an audience by public speech.   In
other countries, popular Freethought has been spread, as
apart from books, mainly by pamphlets and journalism,
and, in the Latin countries, by the organisation of
Freemasonry, which is there normally anti-clerical.   In
France, the movement of FOURIER (1772—1837), may
have counted for something as organising the secular
spirit among the workers in the period of the monarchic
and Catholic reaction ; but at no time were the proletariat
of Paris otherwise than largely Voltairean after the Revolution, of which one of the great services (carried on by
Napoleon) was an improvement in popular education.
The new non-Christian systems of SAINT SIMON[1] (1760—
1823) and AUGUSTE COMTE (1798—1857) never took any
practical hold among them ; but throughout the century
they have been fully the most freethinking working-class
population in the world.   In other countries the course
of popular culture in the first half of the century is somewhat difficult to trace ; but in the latter half, especially
in the last twenty years, freethinking journalism has
counted for much in various parts of Europe.   The
influence of such journals is to be measured not
by their circulation, which is never great, but by
their keeping up a habit of more or less instructed
freethinking among readers, to many of whom the

---

[1] Saint-Simon, who proposed a "new Christianity", expressly guarded
against direct appeals to the people.   See Weil, *Saint Simon et son Œuvre*,
1894, p. 193.

instruction is not otherwise easily accessible. Probably the least ambitious of them is an intellectual force of a higher order than the highest grade of popular religious journalism ; while some of the stronger, as *De Dageraad* of Amsterdam, rank as high-class serious reviews. In the more free and progressive countries, however, freethought affects all periodical literature ; and in France it partly permeates the ordinary newspapers. In England, where a series of monthly or weekly publications of an emphatically freethinking sort has been nearly continuous from about 1840,[1] new ones rising in place of those which succumbed to the commercial difficulties.[2] Such periodicals suffer an economic pinch in that they cannot hope for much income from advertisements, which are the chief sustenance of popular journals and magazines. The same law holds elsewhere ; but in England and America the high-priced reviews have been gradually opened to rationalistic articles, the way being led by the English *Westminster Review* and *Fortnightly Review*, both founded with an eye to freer discussion.

4. It is a significant fact that Freethought propaganda is often most active in countries where the Catholic Church is most powerful. Thus in Belgium there are at least three separate federations, standing for hundreds of freethinking "groups" ; in Spain there are freethought societies in all the large towns, and at least half-a-dozen freethought journals; in Portugal there have been a number

---

[1] Before 1840 the popular freethought propaganda had been partly carried on under cover of Radicalism, as, in Carlile's *Republican* and *Lion*, and in the publications of William Hone. Cp. H. B. Wilson's article " The National Church ", in *Essays and Reviews*, 9th ed. p. 152.

[2] Among the earlier may be noted *The Atheist and Republican*, 1841-2 ; *The Blasphemer*, 1842 ; *The Oracle of Reason* (conducted by Southwell), 1842, etc. ; *The Reasoner and Herald of Progress* (largely conducted by Mr. Holyoake), 1846-1861 ; *Cooper's Journal; or, unfettered Thinker*, etc., 1850, etc. ; *Freethinker's Magazine*, 1850, etc. ; *London Investigator*, 1854, etc. Mr. Bradlaugh's *National Reformer*, begun in 1860, lasted till 1893. Mr. Foote's *Freethinker*, begun in 1881, still subsists. Various freethinking monthlies have risen and fallen since 1880—*e.g.*, *Our Corner*, edited by Mrs. Besant, 1883-88 ; *The Liberal*, and *Progress*, edited by Mr. Foote, 1879-87; the *Free Review*, transformed into the *University Magazine*, 1893-1898. The *Reformer*, edited by Mrs. Bradlaugh Bonner, is the latest monthly venture.

of societies, a weekly journal, *O Seculo*, of Lisbon ; and a
monthly review, *O Livre Exame*.   In France and Italy,
where educated society is in large measure rationalistic,
the Masonic lodges do most of the personal and social
propaganda ; but there are federations of freethought
societies in both countries.   In Germany there is a
Freidenker Bund, with branches in many towns ; besides
a number of " free-religious " societies ; neither form of
organisation, however, representing the main strength of
rationalism in either the working or the more educated
classes.   The German police laws, further, put a rigid
check on all manner of platform and press propaganda
which could be indicted as hurting the feelings of religious
people ; so that a jest at the Holy Coat of Treves can
send a journalist to jail.   Some index to the amount of
popular freethought that normally exists under the
surface in Germany is furnished by the strength of the
German freethought movement in the United States,
where, despite the tendency to the adoption of the
common] speech, there are many German societies, a
German federation of atheists, and a vigorous popular
organ, *Der Freidenker*.   In the South American republics
again, as in Italy and France, the Masonic Lodges are
predominantly freethinking ; and in Peru there is a Freethought League, with a weekly organ.

   5. " Free-religious " societies, such as have been noted
in Germany, may be rated as forms of moderate freethought propaganda, and are to be found in all Protestant
countries, with all shades of development.   A movement
of the kind has existed for a number of years back in
America, in the New England States and elsewhere, and
may be held to represent a theistic or agnostic thought
too advanced to adhere even to the Unitarianism which
during the two middle quarters of the century was
perhaps the predominant creed in new England.   One of
the best types of such a gradual and peaceful evolution is
the South Place Institute (formerly "Chapel") of London,
where, under the famous orator W. J. Fox, nominally

a Unitarian, there was preached between 1824 and 1852, a theism tending to pantheism, perhaps traceable to elements in the doctrine of Priestley, and passed on by Mr. Fox to Robert Browning.[1] In 1864 the charge passed to MONCURE D. CONWAY, under whom the congregation quietly advanced during twenty years from Unitarianism to a non-scriptural rationalism, embracing the shades of philosophic theism, agnosticism, and anti-theism. The Institute is now an open platform for rationalist and anti-theological ethics. Part of such an evolution has taken place among most of the Protestant Churches of France, Switzerland, Hungary and Holland[2]; and the orthodoxy of the chief churches in the latter country is now very doubtful.

§ 2.   *Scholarly and Other Biblical Criticism.*

1. While in France, under the restored monarchy, intellectual activity was mainly headed into historical, philosophical, and sociological study, and in England orthodoxy predominated in theological discussion, the German rationalistic movement went on among the specialists, despite the liberal religious reaction of Schleiermacher.[3] Beginning with the Old Testament, criticism gradually saw more and more of mere myth where of old men had seen miracle, and where the first rationalists saw natural events misconceived. In time the process reached the New Testament, every successive step being resisted in the old fashion ; and after much laborious work, now mostly forgotten, by a whole company of scholars, among whom Paulus, Eichhorn, De Wette,

---

[1] Cp. Priestley, *Essay on the first Principles of Government*, 2nd ed. 1771, pp. 257-261, and Conway's *Centenary History of South Place*, pp. 63, 77, 80.

[2] Cp. *The Progress of Religious Thought as illustrated in the Protestant Church of France*, by Dr. J. R. Beard, 1861 ; Wilson's article in *Essays and Reviews;* Pearson, *Infidelity, its Aspects*, etc., 1853, pp. 560-4, 575-84.

[3] As to the absolute predominance of rationalistic unbelief in educated Germany in the first third of the century, see the *Memoirs of F. Perthes*, Eng. tr., 2nd. ed., ii, 240-5, 255, 266-275. Despite the various reactions asserted by Perthes and others, it is clear that the tables have not since been turned. Cp. Pearson, *Infidelity*, pp. 554-9, 569-574.

G. L. Bauer, Bretschneider, and Gabler were prominent,[1] the train as it were exploded on the world in the great *Life of Jesus* by STRAUSS (1835).   Before this time, " German Rationalism" had become the terror of the English orthodox; and henceforth a scholarly "infidelity" had to be faced throughout the educated world.   On other lines as well as Strauss's, the German critical research proceeded continuously till for the English-speaking world the results were combined in the anonymous work *Supernatural Religion* (1874-77), a performance too solid to be disposed of by the episcopal and other attacks made upon it.   Similar work on a less extensive scale had been done in England, France, and America before and after the middle of the century by such writers as C. C. HENNELL (whose *Inquiry concerning the Origin of Christianity*, 1838, was translated into German by Strauss), THEODORE PARKER, F. W. NEWMAN, W. R. GREG, R. W. MACKAY; P. LARROQUE (*Examen Critique des doctrines de la religion chrétienne*, 1860) ; GUSTAVE D'EICHTHAL (*Les Evangiles*, Ptie. I, 1863) ; ALPHONSE PEYRAT (*Histoire élémentaire et critique de Jésus*, 1864) ; THOMAS SCOTT[2] (*English Life of Jesus*, 1871) ; while in France in particular the rationalistic view had been applied with singular literary charm, if with imperfect consistency, by RENAN in his series of seven volumes on the origins of Christianity, and with more scientific breadth of view by ERNEST HAVET in his *Chistianisme et ses Origines* (1872, etc.).   Renan's *Vie de Jésus* especially has been read throughout the civilised world.

2. Old Testament Criticism, methodically begun by scholars before that of the New Testament, has in the last generation been carried to new lengths, after having long missed some of the first lines of advance.   Starting from the clues given by Hobbes, Spinoza, and Simon,

---

[1] See a good account of the development in Strauss's Introduction.   He notes (§ 11, *end*) that the most extended application of the mythical principle to the Gospels before his time was in an anonymous work on *Religion and Mythology* published in 1799.

[2] Whose pamphlet-propaganda on deistic lines had so wide an influence during many years.

and above all on the suggestion of Astruc (whose work
on the subject had appeared in 1753) as to the twofold
element implied in the God-names Jehovah and Elohim,
it had proceeded, for sheer lack of radical scepticism, on
the assumption that the Pentateuchal history was true.
Little sure progress had thus been made between the
issue of the *Critical Remarks on the Hebrew Scriptures* of
the Scotch Catholic priest Dr. GEDDES in 1800 and the
publication of the first part of the work of Bishop
COLENSO on *The Pentateuch* (1862). This, by the admission of KUENEN, corrected the initial error of the
specialists, by applying to the narrative the common-
sense tests suggested long before by Voltaire. Thence-
forward the " higher criticism " proceeded with such
substantial certainty on the lines of KUENEN and WELL-
HAUSEN that whereas Professor Robertson Smith twenty
years ago had to leave the Free Church of Scotland for
propagating Kuenen's views, Canons of the English
Church are now doing the work with the acquiescence
of perhaps nine clergymen out of ten ; and American
preachers are found projecting an edition of the Bible
which shall exhibit the critical results to the general
reader. Heresy on this score is " become merchandise ".
The analytical treatment of the New Testament on the
same principles naturally lags behind ; though even that
is to some extent popularised for general readers in
England by such a work as that of Mr. J. E. Carpenter
on *The First Three Gospels*—a Unitarian publication.

3. The outcome of this criticism is worth noting, in
connection with the results of Assyrian research. Whereas
the defenders of the faith even a generation ago habitually
stood to the " argument from prophecy ", the conception
of prophecy as prediction has now become meaningless as
regards the so-called Mosaic books ; and the constant
disclosure of interpolations and adaptations in the others
has discredited it as regards the " prophets " themselves.
At the same time, a comparison of Biblical with Assyrian
and Babylonian texts reduces the cosmology and anthro-

pology of Genesis once for all to the level of normal
mythology.   The old argument for the compatibility of
the Genesaic creation story with geology is thus welcome
now only to those who are ignorant of the results of
Assyriology.   That the clerical exponents of the higher
criticism should in the face of their own results continue to
speak of the " inspiration " of their texts will not surprise
the reader who has noted the analogous phenomena in
the history of the religious systems of antiquity.

§ 3. *The Natural Sciences.*

1. The power of intellectual habit and tradition had
preserved among the majority of educated men, to the
end of the eighteenth century, a notion of deity either
slightly removed from that of the ancient Hebrews or
ethically modified without being philosophically transformed, though the astronomy of Copernicus, Galileo, and
Newton had immensely modified the Hebraic conception
of the physical universe.   We have seen that Newton did
not really hold by the Christian scheme—he wrote at
times, in fact, as a pantheist—but some later astronomers
seem to have done so.   When, however, the great
LAPLACE developed the nebular hypothesis, previously
guessed at by Bruno and outlined by Kant, orthodox
psychological habit was rudely shaken as regards the
Biblical account of creation; and like every other previous
advance in physical science this was denounced as
atheistic[1]—which, as we know, it was, Laplace having
declared in reply to Napoleon that he had no need of the
God hypothesis.   Confirmed by all subsequent science,
Laplace's system negates once for all the historic theism
of the Christian era ; and the subsequent concrete developments of astronomy, giving as they do such an
insistent and overwhelming impression of physical infinity,
has made the " Christian hypothesis "[2] fantastic save for

---

[1] See Prof. A. D. White's *History of the Warfare of Science with Theology*,
1896, i, 17, 22.
[2] The phrase is used by a French Protestant pastor. *La vérité chrétienne
et la doute moderne* (Conférences), 1879, pp. 24-25

minds capable of enduring any strain on the sense of consistency. Paine brought the difficulty vividly home to the common intelligence; and though the history of orthodoxy is a history of the success of institutions and majorities in imposing incongruous conformities, the perception of the incongruity on this side must have been a force of disintegration. The freethinking of the French astronomers of the Revolution period marks a decisive change.

2. A more direct effect, however, was probably wrought by the science of geology, which in a stable and tested form belongs to the present century. Of its theoretic founders in the eighteenth century, Werner and Dr. JAMES HUTTON (1726—1797), the latter and more important[1] is known from his *Investigation of the Principles of Knowledge* (1794) to have been consciously a freethinker on more grounds than that of his naturalistic science; and his *Theory of the World* (1795) was duly denounced as atheistic.[2] Whereas the physical infinity of the universe almost forced the orthodox to concede a vast cosmic process of some kind as preceding the shaping of the earth and solar system, the formation of these within six days was one of the plainest assertions in the sacred books; and every system of geology excluded such a conception. As the evidence accumulated, in the hands of men mostly content to deprecate religious opposition,[3] there was duly evolved the quaint compromise of the doctrine that Biblical six "days" meant six ages—a fantasy still cherished in the pulpit. Of all the inductive sciences, geology had been most reta ded by the Christian

---

[1] Cp. Whewell, *Hist. of the Inductive Sciences*, 3rd ed , iii, 505.

[2] White, as cited, i, 222-3, gives a selection of the language in general use among theologians on the subject. One of the most angry and most absurd of the early opponents of geology was the poet Cowper. See his *Task*, B. iii, 150-190, for the prevailing religious tone.

[3] The early policy of the Geological Society of London (1807), which professed to seek for facts and to disclaim theories as premature (cp. Whewell, iii, 428; Buckle, iii, 392), was at least as much socially as scientifically prudential.

canonisation of error.[1] Even the plain fact that what is
dry land had once been sea was obstinately distorted
through centuries, though Ovid[2] had put the observations
of Pythagoras in the way of all scholars; and though
Leonardo da Vinci had insisted on the visible evidence;
nay, deistic habit could keep even Voltaire preposterously
incredulous on the subject.[3] When the scientific truth
began to force its way in the teeth of such authorities as
Cuvier, who stood for the " Mosaic " doctrine, the effect
was proportionately marked; and whether or not the
suicide of the orthodox Hugh Miller (1856) was in any
way due to despair on perception of the collapse of his
reconciliation of geology with Genesis,[4] the scientific
demonstration made an end of revelationism for many.

3. Still more rousing, however, was the effect of the
science of zoology, as placed upon a broad scientific
foundation by CHARLES DARWIN. Here again steps had
been taken in previous generations on the right path,
without any general movement on the part of scientific
and educated men. Darwin's own grandfather, ERASMUS
DARWIN, had in his *Zoonomia* (1794) anticipated many
of the positions of the French LAMARCK, who in 1801
began developing the views he fully elaborated in 1815, as
to the descendance of all existing species from earlier
forms.[5] As early as 1795 GEOFFROY SAINT-HILAIRE had
begun to suspect that all species are variants on a
primordial form of life; and at the same time (1794-5)
GOETHE in Germany had reached similar convictions.[6]
That views thus reached almost simultaneously in Ger-

---

[1] Cp. the details given by Whewell, iii, 406-8, 411-13, 506-7, as to early
theories of a sound order, all of which came to nothing. Steno, a Dane
resident in Italy in the 17th century, had reached non-scriptural and just
views on several points. Cp. White, i, 215.

[2] *Metamorphoses*, lib. xv.

[3] See his essay, *Des Singularités de la Nature*, ch. xii; and his *Dissertation
sur les changements arrivés dans notre globe*.

[4] He had just completed a work on the subject at his death.

[5] See Charles Darwin's *Historical Sketch* prefixed to the *Origin of Species*.

[6] Meding, as cited by Darwin, 6th ed., i, p. xv. Goethe seems to have
had his general impulse from Kielmeyer, who also taught Cuvier. Virchow,
Göthe als Naturforscher, 1861, Beilage x.

many, England, and France, at the time of the French
Revolution, should have to wait for two generations
before even meeting the full stress of battle, must be put
down as one of the results of the general reaction. Saint-
Hilaire, publishing his views in 1828, was officially over-
borne by the Cuvier School in France.[1]

4. Other anticipations of Darwin's doctrine in England
and elsewhere came practically to nothing[2] as regarded
the general opinion, until ROBERT CHAMBERS in 1844
published anonymously his *Vestiges of the Natural History
of Creation*, a work which found a wide audience, incurring
bitter hostility not only from the clergy but from some
specialists who, like Huxley, were later to take the
evolutionist view on Darwin's persuasion. Chambers it
was that brought the issue within general knowledge;
and he improved his position in successive editions. It
was after all this preparation, popular and academic, and
after the theory of transmutation of species had been
definitely pronounced erroneous by the omniscient
Whewell,[3] that Darwin produced (1859) his irresistible
arsenal of arguments and facts, the *Origin of Species*,
expounding systematically the principle of Natural Selection, suggested to him by the economic philosophy of
Malthus, and independently and contemporaneously
arrived at by Dr. Alfred Russel Wallace. The outcry
was enormous; but the battle was practically won within
twenty years. Thus the idea of a specific creation of all
forms of life by an originating Deity—the conception
which virtually united the Deists and Christians of last
century against the atheists—was finally and scientifically
exploded. The principle of personal divine rule or
providential intervention had now been philosophically

---

[1] The prevailing spirit in England about the same time may be gathered
from the account, in the first of Lawrence's *Lectures on Physiology, Zoology,
and the Natural History of Man* (1817), of the attacks made on him and the
French physiologists of the day by the orthodox Abernethy.

[2] See Darwin's *Sketch*, as cited.

[3] *Hist. of the Inductive Sciences*, 3rd ed., iii, 479-483. Whewell is said to
have refused to allow a copy of the *Origin of Species* to be placed in the
Trinity College Library. White, i, 84.

excluded successively (1) from astronomy by the system of Newton; (2) from the science of earth-formation by the system of Laplace and the new geology; (3) from the science of living organisms by the new zoology. It only needed that the deistic conception should be further excluded from the human sciences—from anthropology, from the philosophy of history, and from ethics—to complete, at least in outline, the rationalisation of modern thought. Not that the process was complete even as regarded zoology. Despite the plain implications of the *Origin of Species*, the doctrine of the *Descent of Man* (1871) came on many as a shocking surprise; and evoked a new fury of protest. The lacunæ in Darwin, further, had to be supplemented; and much speculative power has been spent on the task by HAECKEL, without thus far establishing complete agreement. But the Judæo-Christian doctrine of special creation and providential design appears, even in the imperfectly educated and largely ill-placed society of our day, to be already a lost cause.

§ 4.   *Abstract Philosophy and Ethics.*

1. The philosophy of Kant, while giving the theological class a new apparatus of defence as against common-sense freethinking, forced none the less on theistic philosophy a great advance from the orthodox positions. Thus his immediate successors Fichte and Schelling produced systems of which one was loudly denounced as atheistic, while the other is not easily distinguishable from pantheism.[1] Neither seems to have had any influence on concrete religious opinion.[2] Hegel in turn, while adapting his philosophic system to practical exigencies by formulating a philosophic Trinity and hardily defining Christianity as "Absolute Religion" in comparison with the various forms of "Natural

---

[1] Such is Saintes's view of Schelling. *Hist. crit. du rationalisme en Allemagne*, p. 323.

[2] *Id.*, pp. 322-4.

Religion ", counted in a great degree as a disintegrating influence, and was in a very practical way anti-Christian.[1] His abstractions lent themselves equally to all creeds, and some of the most revolutionary of the succeeding movements of German thought—as those of Strauss,[2] Feuerbach, and Marx—professedly founded on him. SCHOPENHAUER and HARTMANN in turn being even less sustaining to orthodoxy, and later orthodox systems failing to impress, there came in due course the cry of "Back to Kant", where at least orthodoxy had some formal semblance of sanction. On the whole, the effect has probably been to make for the general discredit of theistic philosophy, the surviving forms of Hegelianism being little propitious to current religion. And though Schopenhauer and NIETZSCHE can hardly be said to carry on the task of philosophy either in spirit or in effect, yet the rapid intensification of hostility to current religion which their writings in particular manifest[3] must be admitted to stand for a deep revolt against the Kantian compromise.

2. From the collisions of philosophic systems in Germany, there emerged two great practical freethinking forces, the teachings of LUDWIG FEUERBACH (1804-76) and LUDWIG BUECHNER. The former, a professed Hegelian, in his *Essence of Christianity* (1841) and *Essence of Religion* (1851), supplied one of the first adequate modern statements of the positively rationalistic position as against Christianity and Theism, in terms of philosophic as well as historical insight, a statement to which there is no characteristically modern answer save in terms

---

[1] Cp. Hagenbach, *German Rationalism*, pp. 364-9 ; Renan, *Etudes d'histoire religieuse*, 5e édit., p. 406.
[2] BRUNO BAUER at first opposed Strauss and afterwards went even further than he, professing Hegelianism all the while. Cp. Hagenbach, pp. 369 372 ; Farrar, *Crit. Hist. of Freethought*, pp. 387-8.
[3] See Schopenhauer's dialogues on *Religion* and *Immortality*, and his essay on *The Christian System* (Eng. trans. in Schopenhauer Series by T. B. Saunders), and Nietzsche's *Antichrist*. The latter work is discussed by the writer in the *University Magazine*, June, 1897.

of the refined sentimentalism of Renan,[1] fundamentally averse alike to scientific precision and intellectual consistency. On Feuerbach's *Essence of Religion* followed the resounding explosion of Büchner's *Force and Matter* (1855), which in large measure, but with much greater mastery of scientific detail, does for the plain man of this century what d'Holbach in his chief work sought to do for the last. Constantly vilified, even in the name of philosophy, in the exact tone and spirit of animal irritation which marks the religious vituperation of all forms of rationalism in previous ages ; and constantly misrepresented as professing to explain an infinite universe when it does but show the hollowness of all supernaturalist explanations,[2] the book steadily holds its ground as a manual of anti-mysticism.[3] Between them, Feuerbach and Büchner may be said to have framed for their age an atheistic " System of Nature ", concrete and abstract, without falling into the old error of substituting one apriorism for another.

3. In France, the course of thought had been hardly less revolutionary. Philosophy, like everything else, had been affected by the legitimist restoration ; and between Victor Cousin and the other " classic philosophers " of the first third of the century, orthodoxy was nominally reinstated. But the one really energetic and characteristic philosophy produced in the new France was that of AUGUSTE COMTE, which as set forth in the *Cours de Philosophie Positive* (1830-42) practically reaffirmed while it recast and supplemented the essentials of the anti-theological rationalism of the previous age, and in that sense rebuilt French positivism, giving that new name to the naturalistic principle. The later effort of Comte to frame a politico - ecclesiastical system never succeeded

---

[1] See his paper, *M. Feuerbach et la nouvelle école hégélienne*, in *Etudes d'histoire religieuse*.

[2] Büchner expressly rejects the term "materialism" because of its misleading implications or connotations. Cp., in Mrs. Bradlaugh Bonner's *Charles Bradlaugh*, the discussion in Part II, ch. i, § 3 (by J. M. R.).

[3] While the similar works of CARL VOGT and MOLESCHOTT have gone out of print, Büchner's, recast again and again, continues to be republished.

beyond the formation of a politically powerless sect ; but both in France and England his philosophy tinged all the new thought of his time, his leading English adherents in particular being among the most esteemed publicists of the day.   In France, the general effect of the rationalistic movement had been such that when TAINE, under the Third Empire, assailed the whole " classic " school in his *Philosophes Classiques* (1857), his success was at once generally recognised, and a non-Comtist positivism was thenceforth the ruling philosophy.   The same thing has happened in Italy, where quite a number of university professors are explicitly positivist in their philosophic teaching.[1]

4. In Britain, where abstract philosophy after Berkeley had been left to Hume and the Scotch thinkers who opposed him, metaphysics were for a generation practically overridden by the moral and social sciences; Hartley's Christian Materialism making small headway as formulated by him.   The proof of the change wrought in the direction of native thought is seen in the personalities of the men who, in the teeth of the reaction, applied rationalistic method to ethics and psychology.   BENTHAM and JAMES MILL were in their kindred fields among the most convinced and active freethinkers of their day, the former attacking both clericalism and orthodoxy:[2] while the latter, no less pronounced in his private opinions, more cautiously built up a rigorously naturalistic psychology in his *Analysis of the Human Mind* (1839).   Bentham's utilitarianism was so essentially anti-Christian that he could hardly have been more disliked by discerning theists if he had avowed his share in the authorship of the atheistic *Analysis of the Influence of Natural Religion* which, elaborated from his manuscript by no less a thinker than GEORGE GROTE, was published in

---

[1] Cp. Prof. Botta's chapter in Ueberweg's *Hist. of Philos.*, ii, 513-516.
[2] In his *Church of Englandism and its Catechism Examined* (1818) and *Not Paul but Jesus* (1823), " by Gamaliel Smith."

1822 ;[1] but his ostensible restriction of his logic to practical problems of law and morals secured him a wider influence than was wielded by any of the higher publicists of his day.   The whole tendency of his school was intensely rationalistic; and it indirectly affected all thought by its treatment of economics, which from Hume and Smith onwards had been practically divorced from theology.   Even clerical economists, such as Malthus and Chalmers, alike orthodox in religion, furthered naturalism in philosophy in spite of themselves.

5. When English metaphysical philosophy revived with Sir William Hamilton and Dean Mansel, they gave the decisive proof that the orthodox cause had been philosophically lost while being socially won, since their theism emphasised in the strongest way the negative criticism of Kant, leaving Deity void of all cognisable qualities.   Their metaphysic thus served as an open and avowed basis for the naturalistic *First Principles* (1860-62) of HERBERT SPENCER, wherein, with an unfortunate laxity of metaphysic on the author's own part, and a no less unfortunate lack of consistency as regards the criticism of religious and anti-religious positions, the new cosmic conceptions are unified in a masterly conception of evolution as a universal law.   Strictly, the book is a " System of Nature " rather than a philosophy in the sense of a study of the grounds and limitations of knowledge : that is to say, it is on the former ground alone that it is coherent and original.   But its very imperfections on the other side have probably promoted its reception among minds already shaken in theology by the progress of concrete science; while at the same time such imperfections give a hostile foothold to the revived forms of theism.   Even these, however, in particular the neo-Hegelian system associated with the name of the late

[1] Under the pseudonym of Philip Beauchamp. See *The Minor Works of George Grote*, edited by Professor Bain, 1873, p. 18; *Athenæum*, May 31, 1873; J. S. Mill's *Autobiography*, p. 69; and *Three Essays on Religion*, p. 76. This remarkable treatise, which greatly influenced Mill, is the most stringent attack made on theism between d'Holbach and Feuerbach.

Professor T. H. Green, fail to give any shelter to Christian orthodoxy. In England, as on the Continent, the bulk of philosophical activity is now dissociated from the Christian creed.

6. The effect of the ethical pressure of the deistic attack on the intelligence of educated Christians was fully seen even within the Anglican Church before the middle of the century. The unstable Coleridge, who had gone round the whole compass of opinion[1] when he began to wield an influence over the more sensitive of the younger churchmen, was strenuous in a formal affirmation of the doctrine of the Trinity, but no less anxious to modify the doctrine of Atonement on which the conception of the Trinity was historically founded. In the hands of Maurice, the doctrine of sacrifice became one of example to the end of subjective regeneration of the sinner. This view is specially associated with the teaching of Coleridge; but it was quite independently held in England before him by the Anglican Dr. Parr (1747—1825), who appears to have been heterodox upon most points in the orthodox creed,[2] and who, like Coleridge and Hegel, held by a modal as against a "personal" Trinity. Such Unitarian accommodations presumably reconciled many to Christianity and the Church who would otherwise have abandoned it; and the only orthodox rebuttal seems to have been the old and dangerous resort to the Butlerian argument, to the effect that the God of Nature shows no such benign fatherliness as the anti-sacrificial school ascribe to him.[3]

7. The same pressure of moral argument was doubtless potent in the development of "Socinian" or other rationalistic views in the Protestant churches of Germany,

[1] As to his fluctuations, which lasted till his death, cp. the author's *New Essays towards a Critical Method*, 1897, pp. 144-7, 149-154, 168-9.
[2] Field's *Memoirs of Parr*, 1828, ii, 363, 374-9.
[3] See Pearson's *Infidelity, its Aspects, Causes, and Agencies*, 1853, p. 215, ff. The position of Maurice and Parr (associated with other and later names) is there treated as one of the prevailing forms of "infidelity,", and called spiritualism. In Germany, the orthodox made the same dangerous answer to the theistic criticism. See the *Memoirs of F. Perthes*, Eng. tr , 2nd ed., ii, 242-3.

Holland, Hungary, Switzerland, and France in the first half of the century. Such development had gone so far that by the middle of the century the churches in question were, to the eye of an English evangelical champion, predominantly rationalistic, and in that sense "infidel".[1] Reactions have been claimed before and since; but in our own age there is little to show for them. In the United States, again, the ethical element probably predominated in the recoil of EMERSON from Christian orthodoxy even of the Unitarian stamp, as well as in the heresy of THEODORE PARKER, whose aversion to the theistic ethic of Jonathan Edwards was so strong as to make him blind to the reasoning power of that stringent Calvinist. At the same time, all such moral accommodations in Protestant churches, while indirectly countenancing freethought, have served to maintain Christian organisations, with their inevitable accompaniments of social intolerance, as against more open freethinking; and in themselves they represent a perversion of the ethics of the intellectual life.

§ 5. The Sociological Sciences.

1. A rationalistic treatment of human history had been explicit or implicit in the whole literature of Deism; and had been attempted with various degrees of success by Bodin, Vico, Montesquieu, Hume, Voltaire, and Condorcet, as well as by lesser men. So clear had been the lead to naturalistic views of social growth in the Politics of Aristotle, and so strong the influence of the new naturalistic spirit, that it is seen even in the work of Goguet (1769), who sets out as biblically as Bossuet; while in Germany Herder and Kant framed really luminous generalisations; and a whole group of sociological writers rose up in the Scotland of the middle and latter parts of the century. Here again there was reaction; but in France the orthodox Guizot did much to promote broader views than his own; EUSEBE SAL-

[1] Pearson, as cited, pp. 560-2, 568-579, 583-4.

VERTE in his essay *De la Civilisation* (1813) made a highly
intelligent effort towards a general view; and CHARLES
COMTE in his *Traité de Législation* (1826) made a marked
scientific advance on the suggestive work of Herder. At
length, in the great work of AUGUSTE COMTE, scientific
method was applied so effectively and concretely to the
general problem that, despite his serious fallacies, social
science again took rank as a solid study. In England
and America by the works of DRAPER and BUCKLE, in
the sixth and later decades of the century, the conception
of law in human history was at length widely popularised,
to the due indignation of the supernaturalists, who saw
the last great field of natural phenomena passing like
others into the realm of science. Mr. Spencer's *Principles
of Sociology* nevertheless clinched the scientific claim by
taking sociological law for granted; and the new science has
continually progressed in acceptance. In the hands of
all its leading exponents in all countries—Lester Ward,
Giddings, Guyau, Letourneau, Tarde, Ferri, Durkheim,
Gumplowicz, Lilienfeld, Schäffle—it is entirely naturalistic,
though some Catholic professors continue to inject into it
theological assumptions. It cannot be said, however,
that a general doctrine of social evolution is even yet
fully established. The problem is complicated by the
profoundly contentious issues of practical politics ; and in
the resulting diffidence of official teachers there arises
a notable opening for obscurantism, which has been duly
forthcoming.

2. Two lines of scientific study, it would appear, must
be thoroughly followed up before the ground can be
pronounced clear for authoritative conclusions—those of
anthropological archæology (including comparative mythology and comparative hierology) and economic analysis.
On both lines, great progress has been made ; but on
both occurs a resistance of vested interests. Such
students as TYLOR, WAITZ, and SPENCER, have sifted and
classified our knowledge as to primitive social life ; and a
whole line of comparative mythologists, from Dupuis and

Volney to Mannhardt and Frazer, have enlarged and classified our knowledge of primitive religious norms and tendencies.   As regards economics, less work has been done.   Buckle applied the economic principle with force and accuracy to the case of the great primary civilisations, but only in a partial and biassed way to modern history; and the school of Marx incurs reaction by applying it fanatically.   Thus economic interests and clericalism join hands to repel an economic theory of history; and clericalism itself represents a vast economic interest when it wards off the full application of the principle of comparative mythology to Christian lore.   The really great performance of Dupuis was not scientifically improved upon, Strauss failing to profit by it.   In his hands the influence of Pagan myth counts almost for nothing; and Renan practically waived the whole principle.   Thus the "higher criticism" of both the Old and New Testaments remains radically imperfect; and specialists in mythology are found either working all round Gospel myth without once touching it, or unscientifically claiming to put it, as "religion", on a plane above science.   All scientific thought, however, turns in the direction of a complete law of historical evolution; and such a law must necessarily make an end of the supernaturalist conception as regards every aspect of human life, ethical, social, religious, and political.   The struggle lies finally between the scientific or veridical instinct and the sinister interests founded on economic endowments, and buttressed by use and wont.

3. Psychology, considered as a department of anthropology, may perhaps as fitly be classed among the sociological sciences as under philosophy; though it strictly overlaps on that as well as on biology.   However defined, it has counted for much in the dissolution of supernaturalist beliefs, from the tentatives of Diderot to the latest refinements of physiological èxperiment.   It was the perception of this tendency that, two generations ago, secured the abandonment of phrenology to the

disastrous devotion of amateurs, after men like GEORGE and ANDREW COMBE, sincere theists, as were GALL and SPURZHEIM before them, had made it a basis of a great propaganda of social and educational reform. The development of the principle of brain localisation, however, is only a question of time, there being between the procedure of the early scientific phrenologists and those of the later anatomists only a difference of method. All the ethical implications of phrenology belong to the science of brain in any of its developments, being indeed implicit in the most general principles of biological science ; and the abstention of later specialists from all direct application of their knowledge to religious and ethical issues is simply the condition of their economic existence as members of university staffs. But the old principle *ubi tres medici, duo athei,* is truer to-day than ever, being countervailed only by the fact signified just as truly in the other saw, *ubi panis, ibi Deus.* While the priest's bread depends on his creed, the physician's must be similarly implicated.

§ 6.   *Poetry and Fine Letters.*

1. The whole imaginative literature of Europe, in the generation after the French Revolution, reveals directly or indirectly the transmutation that the eighteenth century had worked in religious thought.   In France, the literary reaction is one of the first factors in the orthodox revival.   Its leader and type was Chateaubriand, in whose typical work, the *Génie du Christianisme* (1802), lies the proof that whatever might be the "shallowness" of Voltairism, it was as profundity beside the sentimentalism of the majority who repelled it.   The book is essentially the eloquent expression of a nervous recoil from everything savoring of cool reason and clear thought, a recoil partly initiated by the sheer stress of excitement of the near past ; partly fostered by the belief that freethinking in religion had virtually made the Revolution ; partly enhanced by the tendency of every warlike period to

develop emotional rather than reflective life. What was really masterly in Chateaubriand was the style ; and sentimental pietism had now the prestige of fine writing, so long the specialty of the other side. Yet a generation of monarchism served to wear out the ill-based credit of the literary reaction : and *belles lettres* began to be rationalistic as soon as politics began again to be radical. The prestige of the neo-Christian school was already spent before the revolution of 1848; and the inordinate vanity of Chateaubriand, who died in that year, had undone his special influence still earlier. For the rest, the belief that he had brought back Christianity to a France denuded of worship by atheists, is part of the mythology of the Reformation. Already in February, 1795, on the principle of a separation between Church and State, public worship had been put on a perfectly free footing ; and in 1796 the 36,000 parishes were served by 25,000 curés.[1] Napoleon's arrangement with the Papacy had merely restored the old political connections; and Chateaubriand had created merely a literary mode and sentiment.

2. The literary history of France since his death decides the question, so far as it can be thus decided. From 1848 till our own day it has been predominantly naturalistic and non-religious. After Guizot and the Thierrys, the nearest approach to Christianity in a leading French historian is perhaps in the case of MICHELET, who, however, was a mere heretic in the eyes of the faithful. In poetry and fiction the predominance of one or other shade of freethinking is signal. Even Balzac, who grew up in the age of reaction, makes essentially for rationalism by his intense analysis; and

---

[1] See the details in the *Appendice* to the *Etudes* of M. Gazier, before cited. This writer's account is the more decisive seeing that his bias is clerical, and that, writing before M. Aulard, he had to a considerable extent retained the old illusion as to the "decreeing of atheism" by the Convention (p. 313). See pp. 230-260 as to the readjustment effected by Grégoire, while the conservative clergy were still striving to undo the Revolution.

after him the difficulty is to find a great French novelist
who is not frankly rationalistic.   George Sand will
probably not be claimed by orthodoxy; and BEYLE,
CONSTANT, FLAUBERT, MERIMEE, ZOLA, DAUDET, MAU-
PASSANT, and the DE GONCOURTS, make a list against
which can be set only the names of the distinguished
décadent Huysmans, who has become a Trappist after
a life marked by a philosophy of an extremely different
complexion, and of M. Bourget, an artist of the second
order.

3. In French poetry the case is hardly otherwise.
BERANGER was a Voltairean.   Lamartine goes to the side
of Christianity; but De Musset, the most inspired of
décadents, was no more Christian than Heine, save for
what a critic has called "la banale religiosité de *l'Espoir
en Dieu*";[1] and the pessimist Baudelaire had not even that
to show.   The grandiose theism of VICTOR HUGO, again,
is stamped only with his own image and superscription;
and in his great contemporary LECONTE DE LISLE
we have one of the most convinced and aggressive
freethinkers of the century, a fine scholar and a self-
controlled pessimist, who felt it well worth his while
to write a little *Popular History of Christianity* (1871)
which would have delighted d'Holbach.   It is significant,
on the other hand, that the exquisite religious verse of
Verlaine was the product of an incurable neuropath, like
the latter work of Huysmans, and stands for decadence
pure and simple.   While French *belles lettres* thus in
general made for rationalism, criticism was naturally not
behindhand.   Sainte-Beuve, the most widely appreciative
though not the most scientific of critics, had only a
literary sympathy with the religious types over whom he
spent so much effusive research ; EDMOND SCHERER was
an unbeliever almost against his will ; TAINE, though
reactionary on political grounds in his latter years, was
the typical French rationalist of his time ; and though
M. Brunetière, whose preferences are all for Bossuet, makes

---

[1] Lanson, *Hist. de la litt. française*, p. 951.

"the bankruptcy of science" the text of his somewhat facile philosophy, the most scientific and philosophic head in the whole line of French critics, the late EMILE HENNE-QUIN, was wholly a rationalist; and even the rather reactionary Jules Lemaître has not maintained his early attitude of austerity towards Renan.

4. In England, it was due above all to SHELLEY that the very age of reaction was confronted with unbelief in lyric form. His immature *Queen Mab* was vital enough with conviction to serve as an inspiration to a whole host of unlettered freethinkers not only in its own generation but in the next. Whether he would not in later life, had he survived, have passed to a species of mystic Christianity, reacting like Coleridge, but with a necessary difference, is a question pressingly raised by parts of the *Hellas*. But his work, as done, sufficed to keep for radicalism and rationalism the crown of song as against all the orthodoxy of the elderly Wordsworth and of Southey; and Cole-ridge's (amended) orthodoxy came upon him after his hour of poetic transfiguration was past. On the other side, Scott's honest but unintellectual romanticism, as we know from Newman, certainly favored the Tractarian reaction, to which it was æsthetically though hardly emotionally akin; but the far more potent influence of BYRON, too wayward to hold a clear philosophy, but too intensely alive to realities to be capable of Scott's feudal orthodoxy, must have counted for heresy even in England, and was one of the greatest forces of revolutionary revival for the whole of Europe. Nor has the balance of English poetry ever reverted to the side of faith. Even Tennyson, who more than once struck at rationalism below the belt, is in his own despite the poet of doubt as much as of credence, however he might wilfully attune himself to the key of faith; and the unparalleled optimism of Browning evolved a form of Christianity sufficiently alien to the historic creed.[1] In CLOUGH and MATTHEW ARNOLD,

[1] Cp. Mrs. Sutherland Orr's article on *The Religious Opinions of Robert Browning* in the *Contemporary Review*, Dec., 1891, p. 878.

again, we have the positive record of surrendered faith;
and the whole literary influence of Arnold's later life,
with its curious gospel of church-going and Bible-reading
atheism, was inevitably destructive even of the conformities he preached. Alongside of him, Mr. SWINBURNE
put into his verse the freethinking temper that Leconte de
Lisle reserved for prose; and the ill-starred but finely
gifted JAMES THOMSON ("B.V.") was no less definitely
though despairingly an unbeliever. Among our younger
poets, finally, the balance is pretty much the same; Mr.
Watson declaring in worthily noble diction for a high
agnosticism: and Mr. Davidson defying orthodox ethics
in the name of his very antimonian theology; while on
the side of the regulation religion—since Mr. Yeats is but
a stray Druid — can be cited at best the regimental
psalmody of Mr. Kipling, lyrist of trumpet and drum; the
stained-glass Mariolatries of Mr. Francis Thompson; and
the Godism of Mr. Henley, whereat the prosaic godly
look askance.

5. In English fiction, the beginning of the end of
genuine faith was apparent to the prophetic eyes of
Wilberforce and Robert Hall, of whom the former
lamented the total absence of Christian sentiment from
nearly all the successful fiction even of his day;[1] while
the latter avowed the pain with which he noted that Miss
Edgeworth, whom he admired for her style and art, put
absolutely no religion in her books,[2] while Hannah More,
whose principles were so excellent, had such a vicious
style. With Thackeray and Dickens, indeed, serious
fiction might seem to be on the side of faith; both being
liberally orthodox, though neither ventured on religious

---

[1] *Practical View of the Prevailing Religious System*, 8th ed. p. 368. Wilberforce points with chagrin to the superiority of Mohammedan writers in
these matters.

[2] "In point of tendency I should class her books among the most
irreligious I ever read," [delineating good characters in every aspect]
" and all this without the remotest allusion to Christianity, the only true
religion." Cited in O. Gregory's *Brief Memoir of Robert Hall*, 1833, p. 242.
The context tells how Miss Edgeworth avowed that she had not thought
religion necessary in books meant for the upper classes.

romance ; but with GEORGE ELIOT the balance began to lean the other way; her sympathetic treatment of religious types counting for little as against her known rationalism.   At the present time, almost all of the leading writers of the higher fiction are known to be rationalists; and against the heavy metal of Mr. Meredith, Mr. Hardy, Mr. Moore (whose sympathetic handling of religious motives suggests the influence of Huysmans) and the deistic Mrs. Humphrey Ward, orthodoxy can but claim artists of the third or lower grades.

6. Of the imaginative literature of the United States, the same generalisation broadly holds good.   The incomparable Hawthorne, whatever his psychological sympathy with the Puritan past, wrought inevitably by his art for the loosening of its intellectual hold ; POE, though he did not venture till his days of downfall to write his *Eureka*, thereby proves himself an entirely non-Christian theist; and EMERSON's poetry constantly expresses his pantheism. The economic conditions of American life have till recently been peculiarly unfavorable to the higher literature, as apart from fiction ; but the unique figure of WALT WHITMAN stands for a thoroughly naturalistic view of life ; Mr. HOWELLS appears to be at most a theist; Mr. HENRY JAMES does not even exhibit the bias of his gifted brother to the theism of their no less gifted father; and some of the most esteemed men of letters since the Civil War, as Dr. WENDELL HOLMES and Colonel WENTWORTH HIGGINSON, have been avowedly on the side of rationalism, or, as the term goes in the States, "liberalism".

7. Of the vast modern output of *belles lettres* in continental Europe, finally, a similar account is to be given.   The supreme poet of modern Italy, LEOPARDI, is one of the most definitely rationalistic as well as one of the greatest philosophic poets in literature ; and despite all the claims of the Catholic socialists, there is no modern Catholic literature in Italy of any European value.   In Germany we have seen Goethe and Schiller

distinctly counting for naturalism; and the line is found
to be continued in HEINRICH VON KLEIST, the unhappy
but masterly dramatist of *Der Zerbrochene Krug*, one of
the truest geniuses of his time ; and above all in HEINE,
whose characteristic profession of reconciling himself on
his deathbed with the deity he had imaged as "the Aristophanes of the universe" serves so scantily to console the
orthodox lovers of his matchless song.   His criticism of
Kant is a sufficient clue to his serious convictions.   Since
Heine, German *belles lettres* has hardly been a first rate
influence in Europe: but some of the leading novelists, as
AUERBACH and HEYSE, are well known to have partly
shared in the rational philosophy of their age.

8. But perhaps the most considerable evidence, in
belles lettres, of the predominance of rationalism in modern
Europe is to be found in the literary history of Scandinavia
and Russia.   The Russian development indeed had gone
far ere the modern Scandinavian literature had well
begun.   Already in the first quarter of the century, the
poet Poushkine was an avowed heretic ; and Gogol even
let his art suffer from his preoccupations with the new
humanitarian ideas; while the critic BIELINSKY, classed
by Tourguénief as the Lessing of Russia,[1] was pronouncedly rationalistic, as was his contemporary the
critic Granovsky,[2] reputed the finest Russian stylist of his
day.   At this period, *belles lettres* stood for every form of
intellectual influence in Russia[3]; and all educated thought
was moulded by it.   The most perfect artistic result is
the fiction of TOURGUENIEF, the Sophocles of the modern
novel.   His two great contemporaries, Dostoyevsky and
Tolstoy, count indeed for supernaturalism ; but the truly
wonderful genius of the former is something apart from
his philosophy, which is merely childlike ; and the latter,
the least masterly artist of the three, makes his religious
converts in Russia chiefly among the uneducated.   It

---

[1] Tikhomirov, *La Russie*, 2e édit., p. 343.
[2] Arnaudo, *Le Nihilisme et les Nihilistes*, French trans., p. 30.
[3] Tikhomirov, p. 344.

does not appear that the younger writer, Potapenko, a fine artist, is orthodox, despite his extremely sympathetic presentment of a superior priest. In Scandinavia, again, there are hardly any exceptions to the freethinking tendency among the leading living men of letters. The pre-eminent IBSEN, though his *Brand* was counted to him for righteousness by the churches, has shown himself a profound naturalist in all his later work; BJORNSON is an active freethinker; the eminent Danish critic, GEORG BRANDES, early avowed himself to the same effect; and his brother, the dramatist, EDWARD BRANDES, was elected to the Danish Parliament in 1881 despite his declaration that he believed in neither the Christian nor the Jewish God. Most of the younger *littérateurs* of Norway and Sweden seem to be of the same cast of thought.

PART II.—THE STATE OF THOUGHT IN THE NATIONS.

If it be a sound general principle that freethought is a natural variation which prospers according to the environment, it will follow that where, culture-opportunities being roughly equal, there are differences in the amount of ostensible freethinking, the explanation lies in some of the social conditions. We have seen rationalism, in the sense of a free play of critical reason on traditional creeds, flourish variously in various ages and civilisations according to its opportunities; till in our own day, with a maximum of political freedom, a minimum of priestly power, a maximum of popular culture, and a maximum development of science and special research, there has occurred by far the greatest diffusion and the most thorough cultivation of anti-supernaturalist thought. Yet in some of the most civilised countries countenance is given by the greater part of the newspaper press, and by the machinery of government in general, to the assumption that the doctrine of the Christian churches is still in full possession of the educated intelligence, and that "unbelief" is a noxious weed. This phenomenon is to be explained like any other, after a comparison of the conditions.

§ 1.—*Britain and the United States.*

In this country we have noted the natural collusion of the clerical and propertied classes to put down free-thought, as a dangerously democratic force, after the French Revolution. Between the positive persecution of the popular forms and the social ostracism of the others, it had come about that up to the middle of the century few writers ventured to avow even a guarded hostility to the current creed. Though the stress of the attack was chiefly on the popular propaganda, the spirit of tyranny was so strong, and at the same time so unintelligent, that in 1822 the protection of copyright was refused by the Court of Chancery to Byron's publisher in the case of his *Cain*, on the score that it contained blasphemous matter, and to the *Lectures* of Dr. Lawrence on the score that they discountenanced belief in immortality.[1] Such pro-ceedings had a very practical influence. Eminent authors who are known to have rejected the Christian creed, as Carlyle and John Mill, avoided any open breach, and received much orthodox approbation. Privately they would speak of the need for speaking out without speaking out;[2] and Carlyle was so false to his own doctrine of veracity as even to disparage all who did.[3] The prevailing note is struck in Macaulay's description of Charles Blount as "an infidel, and the head of a small school of infidels who were troubled with a morbid desire to make converts".[4] All the while, Macaulay was himself privately "infidel"; but he cleared his conscience by thus denouncing those who had the courage of their opinions. In this simple fashion some of the sanest writers in history were complacently

[1] Harriet Martineau, *History of the Peace*, ed. 1877, ii, 87. Cp. Lawrence's opening lecture for his views.
[2] See Professor Bain's *J. S. Mill*, p. 86.
[3] Cp. Froude's *London Life of Carlyle*, i, 458.
[4] *History*, ch. xix, Student's ed. ii, 411.

put below the level of the commonplace dissemblers who aspersed them ; and the average educated man saw no baseness in the procedure. It was assumed that a sanhedrim of shufflers could make courage ridiculous by calling themselves " the wise " ; and it became current doctrine that " the wise man " conceals his opinions when they are unpopular.

In this way, honest and narrow-minded believers were trained to regard their views as really triumphant over all attacks,[1] and " infidelity " as a disease of an ill-informed past ; and as the Church had really gained in conventional culture as well as in wealth and prestige in the period of reaction, the power of mere convention to override ideas had become enormous. Above all, social and religious prejudices were aided by the vast leverage of economic interest throughout a thoroughly commercialised community. This holds good alongside of a clear balance of literary power on the side of unbelief. The commercial history of England and America throughout the century has been broadly one of ever-increasing competition in all classes; and to hold an " unpopular " view is in general to stand at a serious disadvantage in business and professional life. Even of the known rationalists among the serious writers of the latter half of the century, many have perforce confined themselves to pure science or scholarly research ; and others have either held safe official posts or enjoyed private means. In one or other of these classes stand such names as those of GROTE, the two MILLS, Professors BAIN, HUXLEY, TYNDALL and CLIFFORD, DARWIN, ARNOLD, F. W. NEWMAN, LEWES, and in a measure SPENCER, who however long felt the pinch of unpopularity severely enough. Detached men of letters like Mr. Morley and Mr. Stephen, while taking up freethinking positions, are perhaps not uninfluenced by

---

[1] In 1830, for instance, we find a Scottish episcopal D.D. writing that " Infidelity has had its day ; it, depend upon it, will never be revived—NO MAN OF GENIUS WILL EVER WRITE ANOTHER WORD IN ITS SUPPORT ". Morehead, *Dialogues on Natural and Revealed Religion*, p. 266.

the hostile environment. In any case it is perfectly well known to all freethinkers that there are many of their way of thinking on all hands who dare not declare themselves. And whereas religious sects, if at all numerous, can in large measure indemnify themselves against others by holding together, rationalists are under the difficulty that their special opinions do not call for institution-making save of the most disinterested kind. Every religionist is under some religious compulsion from his own creed to worship; and every priest preaches for the institutions by which he lives. We have seen how impossible it is to set up freethinking *institutions* in a primitive society. The difficulty is still great, though different, in a commercial community, where even among freethinkers the disinterested concern for the diffusion of truth is constantly dulled by the social struggle for existence; while, moreover, the instructed man's dislike of sectarianism is a further dissuasive from action that he thinks might tend to further it. And as regards the main source of most religious endowments, bequest by will, freethought is in this country absolutely interdicted from any save circuitous provision. Various bequests for specifically freethinking purposes have been quashed under the Blasphemy Laws; and all the while ingenuous Christians taunt freethinkers with their lack of sectarian institutions. Thus, educated reason standing aloof or inhibited, while educated self-interest conspires with ignorance, an enormous revenue is annually devoted to the maintenance of beliefs not held by multitudes of the clergy themselves; and the propaganda of free-thought rests wholly with the "quixotic" few. Nearly every freethinking writer is advised by prudent friends to give up such unprofitable work; and the very desire to wield an influence for good, as in politics, makes many rationalists conceal the opinions which they know would restrict their audience. Only great orators, as Bradlaugh and Ingersoll, can make a good income by platform propaganda; and Bradlaugh was prematurely worn out by the atrocious burdens laid upon him in his parliamentary struggle, with the active connivance of many Conservative partisans who believed no more than he.

It would thus appear that until the " social problem " is solved in some fashion which shall make intellectual honesty a much safer thing than at present, the profession of supernaturalism and the vogue of real superstition among the mass of the less intelligent of all classes is likely to continue in many communities alongside of the fullest scientific disproof of the beliefs in question.   Any creed whatever can subsist under the modern system of endowments.   Had a Church of Isis and Osiris by any chance survived with good endowments through the ages of Christian destruction and confiscation of other systems, it could to-day find educated priests and adherents in such a society as ours.   The general faculty for consistent thought is at best not great.   Scientific rationalists, finding excuses for their official conformities to the current creeds, argue privately that all that is needed is non-contentiously to put true doctrines in circulation—that without argument they must needs expel the false.   All modern culture-history proves this to be a fallacy.   Even gifted brains can harbor childish errors on the side on which they are undeveloped.   We need not go back to Faraday to find scientific men clinging to the religion of their nurseries.   An eminent mathematician, entirely unqualified in other fields, pays tribute to Paley ; and the average church-goer straightway claims that " science " is with him.   To say nothing of the habitual employment of the Bible in the churches, the vogue of such a book as the late Mr. Henry Drummond's *Natural Law in the Spiritual World* is a sufficient proof of the general capacity for digesting the grossest inconsistencies in science.   It was possible for multitudes of people to suppose that Darwin, buried as he was in Westminster Abbey, had died a Christian, until it was shown by his letters that he had definitely abandoned theism.   On the other hand, it takes a rare combination

of intellectual power, moral courage, and official freedom,
to permit of such a directly rationalistic propaganda as
was carried on by the late Professor CLIFFORD, or even
such as has been accomplished by President ANDREW
WHITE in America under the comparatively popular
profession of Deism. It was only in his leisured latter
years that Professor HUXLEY carried on a general conflict
with orthodoxy. In middle age, he frequently covered
himself by attacks on professed freethinkers ; and he did
more than any other man of his time to conserve the
Bible as a school manual by his politic panegyric of it in
that aspect at a time when bolder rationalists were
striving to get it excluded from the State schools.[1]

The survival of theism itself, as well as the common
preference in England of such a term as " agnosticism "
to either " naturalism " or " atheism ", is in part a
psychological result of social pressure. Mr. Spencer in
his earlier works used the language of Deism,[2] at a time
when Comte had discarded it ; and he and many other
rationalists have later made a serious stand for their
property in the word " religion ", though the reasons
urged are as applicable to the word " God ", and even in
part to " Christ ". Draper and White in the United
States, again, and Buckle and the author of *Supernatural
Religion* in England, show how some elements of essentially emotional and traditionary supernaturalism, in the
shape of theism, can be long clung to by able men
engaged in rationalistic and even in anti-theological
argument. The opposition still made by English Comtists
to straightforward freethinking propaganda illustrates the
same normal tendency. In the English-speaking countries
the coinage of the term "agnostic ", though objected to
by the Comtists, is largely on all fours with their own

---

[1] I am informed on good authority that in later life Huxley changed
his views on the subject.   He had abundant cause.   As early as 1879 he is
found complaining (pref. to Eng. tr. of Haeckel's *Freedom in Science and
Teaching*, p. xvii) of the mass of " falsities at present foisted upon the young
in the name of the Church ".

[2] *E.g.* the *Education*, small ed., pp. 41, 155.

practice.   In France and Italy, freethinkers do not find it
necessary to refine on the term "atheist" and draw
paralogistic distinctions; the necessity, when felt, is the
psychological product of special social conditions.

From these there emerges the general result that in
the British Islands and the United States the avowal
of unbelief and the disinterested effort to enlighten
others are relatively more common among the workers,
whose incomes are not as a rule affected thereby, than
among the middle classes, where the economic motive is
strong, and the upper, where the social motive specially
operates.   Wealthy Conservatives never publicly avow
unbelief; yet it is well known that many disbelieve.   In
the House of Commons and the American Congress there
are probably scores of such on both sides.   It is easy to
blame them ; as it is easy to blame the many clergymen
who hold office without conviction.   But such insincerities,
in which laymen so abundantly share, are strictly on the
same ethical footing as the endless immoralities of
ordinary commerce ; the clergy being under economic
pressure like other men.   Of recent years, attempts have
been made in England and America by the societies for
" Ethical Culture " to carry on a non-theological teaching
that generally guards against being anti-theological.   Such
a policy escapes a number of the ordinary social and
economic obstacles, while incurring the special difficulties
involved in the application of ethics to the social problem.
It does not operate, however, as a dissolvent of theology
save in so far as theology is incidentally criticised; at least,
the fact that the same view of ethics was proclaimed
nearly three hundred years ago by Charron, and nearly
two hundred years ago in some of the British churches,
makes it seem unlikely that its simple affirmation can
undermine the economic bases of supernaturalism.

In sum, other things being equal, open freethought is
least common where commercialism is most stringent,
and in communities where social pressure is most easily
felt.   In Scotland, where the culture-movement of last

century was succeeded in this by a pietistic reaction and
a new ecclesiastical ferment and schism, the intellectual
life is less free than in England. It was so when the
clergy proposed to sit in judgment on Hume in 1756 ; it
was emphatically so when Buckle summed up Scotch life
forty years ago ; it is so to-day, when the economic conditions send to England and the colonies most of the
innovating elements, leaving the rival churches in undisturbed possession, with their numerous rationalistic
clergy afraid to declare themselves against the conservative mass. In the United States, sheer preoccupation
with business, and lack of leisure, counteract in a measure
the relative advantage of social freedom ; and while
culture is much more widely diffused than in England, it
remains on the whole less radical in the " educated "
classes so-called. So far as it is possible to make a
quantitative estimate, it may be said that in the more
densely populated parts of the States there is less of
studious freethinking because there is less leisure than in
England ; but that in the Western States there is a
relative superiority, class for class, because of the special
freedom of the conditions and the independent character
of many of the immigrants who constitute the new populations.[1]

In the Australasian colonies, again, there is some such
relative superiority in freedom as is seen in the American
West, and for similar reasons. In New Zealand, prominent statesmen, as Sir ROBERT BALLANCE and Mr.
JOHN STOUT, have held office despite their avowed freethinking ; and in Australia a popular freethought journal
has subsisted for over fifteen years. But there too the
commercial environment and the ecclesiastical basis of
endowment tell adversely.

From the fact that in New England the supremacy
appears to be passing from Unitarianism to Episco-

---

[1] This view is not inconsistent with the fact that popular forms of
credulity are also found specially flourishing in the West. Cp. Bryce,
The American Commonwealth, 3rd ed., ii, 832-3.

palianism, it may be inferred that the more religiously biassed types in the former sect tend to gravitate to the more emotional worship, and the more rationalistic to withdraw; though the economic interest of the Unitarian clergy conserves their institutions.   In England is seen the analogous phenomenon of the advance of Romanist ritualism in the Church of England.   While the more emotional and unintellectual believers thus zealously promote what may be termed the most religious form of religion, there is a prospect that the many semi-rational conformists will be in part driven to a more rationalist attitude; since, save for the certainly great power of the purse—seen in the outward collapse of the Tractarian movement on Newman's conversion—Anglican modera- tion is as powerless against ritualism as is modern Protestantism against Catholicism in general.   For the rest, all the forces of religious conservatism in commercial communities are backed by the economic interest of the general newspaper press, wherein multitudes of unbelieving journalists perforce treat orthodoxy as being what it claims to be, and at best describe their own opinions as "peculiar" when openly avowed by public men.   The determining force is revenue, which depends on advertisements, which depend on circulation.   For lack of these bases free- thinking journals, even when aiming at comparative popularity, must be relatively expensive.   In the United States, the habitual freedom of the newspapers allows of more fairplay to avowed freethought; but the main economic forces are similar.   Thus on every ground the organised forms of freethought are restricted and appa- rently uninfluential in comparison with the known amount of rationalism, which nevertheless quietly increases from decade to decade; so that within a generation the in- tellectual balance has shifted till the "sensations" of serious literature are no longer produced by attacks on the popular creed, but by the few noteworthy attempts to justify it.

This last phenomenon seems decisively significant as

to the real state of opinion among educated people, under all the conformities of the commercial system. The works of Mr. Drummond, Mr. Benjamin Kidd, and Mr. A. J. Balfour, are the most prominent pleas for Christianity put forth in England in the past twenty years. The first was recognised even by many theologians as a tissue of fallacy; the second is a suicidal formula of professed Irrationalism; and the third is a more skilful revival of the old resort to scepticism, so often and so vainly employed by apologists in the past. Meanwhile the few remaining Churchmen of high literary standing, as Bishop Stubbs and Bishop Creighton, rank as simple historians, not as thinkers; and the apologetic labors of the churches in general range between respectable reiterations of Paley and a popular traffic in " Christian Evidences " that is beneath criticism. On the other hand, under all the social stress set up by orthodoxy, women are found in ever-increasing numbers giving up the faith, and even doing effective rationalist propaganda. Thus HARRIET MARTINEAU and GEORGE ELIOT (Marian Evans) are specially significant names in the history of modern English Freethought. The popularisation of the Positive Philosophy by the former, and the translations of Strauss and Feuerbach by the latter, were services as workmanlike as any done by their male contemporaries; and though the reversion of Mrs. BESANT to mysticism in the form of Theosophy was a chagrin to many, it could not undo the work she had done as a rationalist teacher.[1] Even in the time of persecution, in the first half of the century, women did unflinching service to the ostracised cause. The second wife of Richard Carlile was his worthy helpmate; and FRANCES WRIGHT (Madame D'Arusmont) was in the front of

---

[1] The argument, sometimes heard, that such a reversion, and such recurrences of religious emotion as may be noted in the latter years of George Eliot, point to a special and permanent unfitness for the rationalist life among women, is worth notice only for the sake of pointing to the quite contrary conclusion deducible from the case of Miss Martineau.

all the rational and ethical[1] propaganda of her time (1795 —1852).

§ 2.—*The Catholic Countries.*

As already noted, there prevails in the Catholic countries a more general and a more direct division between faith and rationalism than usually exists under Protestantism, where the possibilities of gradation and adjustment, as well as the admission of the laity to a share in Church administration, moderate matters. In these countries, too, commercialism has come later on the scene and is much less developed than in England and America; so that social pressure tells only partially on the side of the Church. The result is that as a rule in France and Italy, and to a large extent also in Spain, educated men are unbelievers ; and atheism is no bar to political influence. For many years the Paris Municipal Council has been a predominantly freethinking body. After a period in which such teachers as Michelet and Renan could suffer suspension, university teaching in all there countries is substantially open, and professors can freely indicate their opinions. On the other hand, the higher life of all Catholic countries suffers from the common assumption that a religion of prayer and penance is a necessity for women. Women there are accordingly found as a rule on the side of faith and churchgoing : and it results that in all social and domestic matters in which they are intimately concerned, the Church has still a strong footing. Baptisms, marriages, and funerals are in the great majority of cases religious functions, the men shrugging their shoulders and making no general effort to enlighten their wives and daughters.[2] In this state of things there is as constant an element of loss to progress as takes place in our own society through the organised

---

[1] " She bought 2,000 acres in Tennessee, and peopled them with slave families she purchased and redeemed " (Wheeler, *Biog. Dict*).

[2] The case of M. Littré, whose family pressed him to recant on his deathbed and destroyed his papers after his death, is a painful illustration of the frequent outcome of such a policy.

activity of the churches; a continual reproduction of artificial ignorance, so to speak, going on in both cases. A reform in the education and status of women is therefore as peculiarly necessary to the advance of Freethought in the Catholic countries as is a correction of commercialist conditions in ours. English and American experience goes to show that women under fair conditions can live the rationalist life as well as men, their relapses to mysticism being no more frequent than those of men, and much less frequent than their abandonment of supernaturalist beliefs. Indeed there have been cases enough of freethinking educated women in France and Italy to show the error of the conventional assumption among the other sex. It is so far satisfactory that the Socialist movement, which gains ground among all the " Latin " peoples, makes substantially for the more equal culture of the sexes, as against the contrary policy of the Church.

§ 3.—*Germany.*

Alongside of the inveterate rationalism of modern Germany, a no less inveterate bureaucratism preserves a certain official conformity to religion. University freedom does not extend to open criticism of the orthodox creed.[1] Feuerbach was deprived of his chair at Erlangen for his *Thoughts upon Death and Immortality* (1830) ; Büchner lost his chair of chemistry at Tübingen on publishing *Force and Matter;* and Bruno Bauer's brother Edgar was imprisoned four years for his work on *The Strife of Criticism in Church and State.* On the other hand, the applause won by Virchow in 1877 on his declaration against the doctrine of evolution ; and the tactic resorted to by him in putting upon that doctrine the responsibility of Socialist violence, are instances of the normal operation of the lower motives against freedom in scientific teaching.[2] The pressure

---

[1] It is recorded by the friends of UEBERWEG, author of the fairest of modern histories of philosophy, that he was an atheist and materialist. But this could only here and there be divined from his writing.

[2] See Haeckel's *Freedom in Science and Teaching,* Eng. tr., with pref. by Huxley, 1879, pp. xix, xxv, xxvii, 89-90.

operates in other spheres in Germany, especially under such a regimen as the present. Men who never go to church save on official occasions, and who have absolutely no belief in the church's doctrine, nevertheless remain nominally its adherents ;[1] and the Press laws make it peculiarly difficult to reach the common people with freethinking literature, save through Socialist channels. Thus the Catholic Church is perhaps nowhere—save in Ireland and the United States — more practically influential than in nominally "Protestant" Germany, where it wields a compact vote of a hundred in the Reichstag, and can generally count on well-filled churches as beside the half-empty temples of Protestantism.

Another circumstance partly favorable to reaction is the simple maintenance of all the old theological chairs in the universities. As the field of scientific work widens, and increasing commerce raises the social standard of comfort, men of original intellectual power grow less apt to devote themselves to theological pursuits even under the comparatively free conditions which so long kept German Biblical scholarship far above that of other countries. It can hardly be said that men of the mental calibre of Strauss, Baur, Volkmar, and Wellhausen continue to arise among the specialists in their studies. Harnack, the most prominent German Biblical scholar of our day, despite his great learning, creates no such impression of originality and insight, and exhibits often a very uncritical orthodoxy. Thus it is *a priori* possible enough that the orthodox reactions so often claimed have actually occurred, in the sense that the experts have reverted to a prior type. A scientifically minded " theologian " in Germany has now little official scope for his faculty save in the analysis of the Hebrew Sacred Books ; and this has there been on the whole very well done ; but there is a limit to the attraction of such studies for minds

---

[1] Professor Büchner, for straightforwardly renouncing his connection with the State Church, was blamed by many who held his philosophic opinions.

of a modern cast. Thus there is always a chance that chairs will be filled by men of another type.[1]

At the same time, a religious Government can do, and has done, much to hamper the natural evolution. The statistics of the theological faculties in the universities show a series of ups and downs of a very significant kind. Thus the numbers of Protestant and Catholic theological students in all Germany have varied as follows:— *Protestant :* 1831, 4,147 ; 1851, 1,631; 1860, 2,520; 1876, 1,539; 1882-3, 3,168. *Catholic :* 1831, 1,801 ; 1840, 866; 1850, 1,393 ; 1860, 1,209; 1880, 619.[2] Still, the main movement is clear. In an increasing proportion, the theological students come from the rural districts (69.4 in 1861-70), the towns furnishing ever fewer;[3] so that the conservative measures do but outwardly and formally affect the course of thought ; the clergy themselves showing less and less inclination to make clergymen of their sons.[4] Even among the Catholic population, though that has increased from ten millions in 1830 to sixteen millions in 1880, the number of theological students has fallen from 11 to 4 per 100,000 inhabitants.[5] Thus, after many " reactions " and much Bismarckism, the *Zeit-Geist* in Germany was still pronouncedly sceptical in all classes in 1881,[6] when the church accommodation in Berlin provided for only 2 per cent. of the population, and even that provision outwent the demand.[7] And though there have been yet other alleged reactions since, and the imperial influence is zealously used for orthodoxy, the mass of the intelligent workers remain socialistic and freethinking ; and the mass of the educated classes remain unorthodox

---

[1] Cp. Zeller's pref. to his work on *The Acts of the Apostles*, Eng. tr., 1875, i, 89, as to the tendency of German Protestantism to stagnate in " Byzantine conditions ".

[2] Conrad, *The German Universities for the last Fifty Years*, Eng. tr., 1885, p. 74. See p. 100 as to the financial measures taken ; and p. 105 as to the essentially financial nature of the " reaction ".

[3] *Id.*, p. 103.   [4] *Id.*, p. 104.

[5] *Id.*, p. 112.   See pp. 118-119 as to Austria.

[6] *Id.*, pp. 97-98.

[7] Prof. A. D. White, as above cited, i, 239.

in the teeth of the Socialist menace.   Reactionary professors can at most make an academic fashion : the great body of instructed men remains tacitly naturalistic.[1]

§ 4.   *Russia and Scandinavia.*

Under the widely different political conditions in Russia and the Scandinavian States, it is the more significant that in all alike rationalism is in the ascendant among the educated classes.   In Scandinavia, especially in Norway, the latter perhaps include more working people than can be so classed even in Germany; and rationalism there is proportionally strong; though social freedom is still far from perfect.   In 1820 the eminent Swedish historian GEIJER was subjected to a prosecution for an impeachment of the orthodox creed in his book entitled *Thorild ;* but the jury acquitted him ; and not till a freethinking journalist, V. E. LENNSTRAND, was prosecuted, fined, and imprisoned for denial of the Christian religion in 1888, did the old temper again strongly assert itself in Sweden.   It is the old story of toleration for a dangerously well-placed freethought, and intolerance for that which reaches the common people.   The Scandinavian churches, however, though backward and bigoted, have no such relative wealth and power as the English, or even the American ; and the intellectual balance, as already noted, is distinctly on the freethought side.   It would be well if the rationalist temper could so far assert itself as to check the unhappy racial jealousies of the three Scandinavian peoples, and discredit their irrationalist belief in fundamental differences of " national character " among them.   But that problem, like those of industry and social structure, is still to solve.

In Russia, rationalism has before it the still harder task of transmuting a system of tyranny into one of self-

[1] As against reactionary views of Christian origins, the German laity has recently been supplied with an excellent conspectus of the Gospel problem in the *Vergleichende Uebersicht der vier Evangelien,* by S. G. Verus (Leipzig : Van Dyk, 1897), a work of the most laborious kind, issued at a low price.

government. In no European country, perhaps, is rationalism more general among the educated classes; and in none is there a greater mass of popular ignorance. The popular icon-worship in Moscow can hardly be paralleled outside of Asia. On the other hand, the aristocracy became Voltairean last century, and has remained incredulous since; while the democratic movement, in its various phases of socialism, constitutionalism, and Nihilism, has been markedly anti-religious since the second quarter of the century.[1] This state of things subsists despite the readiness of the government to suppress the slightest sign of official heterodoxy in the universities.[2] The struggle is thus substantially between the spirit of freedom and that of despotism; and the fortunes of freethought will go with the former. Were Russia an isolated community, both alike might be strangled by the superior brute force of the autocracy, resting on the loyalty of the ignorant mass; but the unavoidable contact of surrounding civilisations seems to make such suppression impossible.

§ 5.   *The Oriental Civilisations.*

We have already seen, in discussing the culture histories of India, China, and Moslem Persia, how ancient elements of rationalism continue to germinate more or less obscurely in the unpropitious soils of Asiatic life. Ignorance is too immensely preponderant to permit of any other species of survival. But sociology, while recognising the vast obstacles to the higher life presented by conditions which with a fatal facility multiply the lower, can set no limit to the possibilities of upward evolution. The case of Japan is a sufficient rebuke to the thoughtless iterators of the formula of the " unprogressiveness of the East ". While superstitious religion is there still normal among the mass, the transformation of the political ideals

<hr />

[1] Cp. E. Lavigne, *Introduction à l'histoire du nihilisme russe*, 1880, pp. 149, 161, 224; Arnaudo, *Le Nihilisme*, French tr., pp. 37, 58, 61, 63, 77, 86, etc.
[2] Tikhomirov, *La Russie*, pp. 325-6, 338-9.

and practice of the nation under the influence of European
example is so great as to be unparalleled in human
history; and it has inevitably involved the substitution
of rationalism for supernaturalism among the great
majority of the educated younger generation. That they
should revert to Christian orthodoxy is as impossible as
such an evolution is seen to be in educated Hindostan,
where the higher orders of intelligence are certainly not
relatively more common than among the Japanese. The
final question, there as everywhere, is one of social
reconstruction and organisation; and in the enormous
population of China, the problem, though very different
in degree, is the same in kind. Perhaps the most hopeful
consideration of all is that of the ever-increasing inter-
communication which makes European and American
progress tend in every succeeding generation to tell more
and more on Asiatic life.

As to Japan, Professor B. H. Chamberlain, a writer with
irrationalist leanings, pronounces that the Japanese "now bow
down before the shrine of Herbert Spencer" (*Things Japanese*,
3rd ed., 1898, p. 321. Cp. *Religious Systems of the World*, 3rd
ed., p. 103), proceeding in another connection (p. 352) to describe them as *essentially* an undevotional people. Such a
judgment somewhat shakes trust. The Japanese people in
the past have exhibited the amount of superstition normal in
their culture stage (cp. the *Voyages de C. P. Thunberg au Japon*,
French trans., 1796, iii, 206); and in our own day they differ
from Western peoples on this side merely in respect of their
greater general serenity of temperament. Professor Chamberlain appears to construe "devotional" in the light of his
personal conception of true devotion. Yet a Christian observer
testifies, of the revivalist sect of Nichirenites, "the Ranters of
Buddhism", that "the wildest excesses that seek the mantle
of religion in other lands are by them equalled if not excelled"
(Griffis, *The Mikado's Empire*, 1876, p. 163); and Professor
Chamberlain admits that "the religion of the family binds
them [the Japanese in general, including the "most materi
alistic"] down in truly sacred bonds"; while another writer,
who thinks Christianity desirable for Japan, though he
apparently ranks Japanese morals above Christian, declares
that in his travels he was much reassured by the superstition

of the innkeepers, feeling thankful that his hosts were "not Agnostics or Secularists", but devout believers in future punishments (Tracy, *Rambles through Japan without a Guide*, 1892, pp. 131, 276, etc.). A third authority with Japanese experience, Professor W. G. Dixon, while noting that "among certain classes in Japan not only religious earnestness but fanaticism and superstition still prevail", decides that ' at the same time it remains true that the Japanese are not in the main a very religious people, and that at the present day religion is in lower repute than probably it has ever been in the country's history. Religious indifference is one of the prominent features of new Japan" (*The Land of the Morning*, 1882, p. 517). The reconciliation of these estimates lies in the recognition of the fact that the Japanese populace is religious in very much the same way as those of Italy and England, while the more educated classes are rationalistic, not because of any "essential" incapacity for "devotion", but because of enlightenment, and lack of countervailing social pressure. To the eye of the devotional Protestant, the Catholics of Italy, with their devotion to externals, seem "essentially" irreligious; and *vice versa*. Buddhism triumphed over Shintôism in Japan both in ancient and modern times precisely because its lore and ritual make so much more appeal to the "devotional" sense. (Cp. Chamberlain, pp. 358-362 ; Dixon, ch. x ; *Religious Systems of the World*, pp. 103, 111 ; Griffis, p. 166.)

So universal is sociological like other law, that we find in Japan, among some freethinkers, the same disposition as among some in Europe to decide that religion is necessary for the people. Professor Chamberlain (p. 352) cites Mr. Fukuzawa, "Japan's most representative thinker and educationist", as openly declaring that " It goes without saying that the maintenance of peace and security in society requires a religion. For this purpose any religion will do. I lack a religious nature, and have never believed in any religion. I am thus open to the charge that I am advising others to be religious while I am not so. Yet my conscience does not permit me to clothe myself with religion when I have it not at heart. . . . Of religions, there are several kinds—Buddhism, Christianity, and what not. From my standpoint there is no more difference between those than between green tea and black. . . . See that the stock is well-selected and the prices cheap. . . . " (*Japan Herald*, 9th Sept., 1897). Further reflection, marked by equal candor, may lead Mr. Fukuzawa to see that nations cannot be led to adore any form of "tea" by the mere assurance of its indispensableness from leaders who confess they never take any. His view is doubtless shared by those priests concerning whom "it may be questioned whether in their fundamental beliefs the more scholarly of the Shinshiû priests differ very widely from the materialistic agnostics of Europe" (Dixon, p. 516). In this state of things the Christian thinks he sees his special opportunity. Professor Dixon writes (p. 518), in the manner of the missionary, that " decaying shrines and broken gods are to be seen everywhere. Not only is there indifference, but there is a rapidly growing scepticism. . . . . The masses too are becoming affected by it. . . . . Shintôism and . . . . Buddhism are doomed. What is to take their place ? . . . . It must be either Christianity or Atheism. We have the brightest hopes that the former will triumph in the near future. . . ." As against the assumption that the black "tea" must needs replace the green, it seems rather more probable that all forms of the psychological stimulant may in future be found unnecessary.

And the same principle would appear to hold good even in the case of Turkey. The notion that Turkish civilisation in Europe is unimprovable, though partly countenanced by despondent thinkers even among the enlightened Turks,[1] has no justification in social science ; and though Turkish freethinking has not in general passed the theistic stage,[2] and its spread is grievously hindered by the national religiosity,[3] which the age-long hostility of the Christian States so much tends to intensify, a gradual improvement in the educational and political conditions would suffice to evolve it, according to the observed laws of all civilisation. It may be that a result of the rationalistic evolution in the other European States will be to make them intelligently friendly to such a process, where at present they are either piously malevolent towards the rival creed or merely self-seeking as against each other's influence on Turkish destinies.

[1] See article on "The Future of Turkey" in the *Contemporary Review*, April, 1899, by "A Turkish Official".

[2] Yet, as early as the date of the Crimean War, it was noted by an observer that " young Turkey makes profession of atheism". Ubicini, *La Turquie actuelle*, 1855, p. 361.

[3] Ubicini (p. 344), with most other observers, pronounces the Turks the most religious people in Europe.

The general conclusion, then, is that the spirit of Freethought, which has survived and modified the long malaria of primeval superstition, the systematically destructive aggression of the medieval Christian Church, and even the forces of decivilisation in most of the more backward communities, will be able to survive the economic pressure which in some of the leading States is now its most formidable obstacle. Perhaps a new danger now lies in the tendency of many who recognise this side of the case to concentrate their whole effort on the problem of social justice and leave the cause of disinterested truth to the future; which is as if, in indignation at the ill-distribution of the heritage of art among the multitude, one should propose to suspend all artistry till a new society be established. But it seems incredible that those who are concerned to solve the greatest of all human problems should ever be led in mass to suppose that the solution can be hastened by dropping from their hands one of the main instruments of intellectual discipline and moral enlightenment.

INDEX.